A Very Fine Regiment

The 47th Foot during the American War of Independence, 1773–1783

Paul Knight

Helion & Company

Helion & Company Limited
Unit 8 Amherst Business Centre
Budbrooke Road
Warwick
CV34 5WE
England
Tel. 01926 499619
Email: info@helion.co.uk
Website: www.helion.co.uk
Twitter: @helionbooks
Visit our blog at http://blog.helion.co.uk/

Published by Helion & Company 2022
Designed and typeset by Mach 3 Solutions Ltd (www.mach3solutions.co.uk)
Cover designed by Paul Hewitt, Battlefield Design (www.battlefield-design.co.uk)

Text © Paul Knight 2022
Cover: Private of the 47th Foot, by Giorgio Albertini © Helion & Company 2022
Illustrations © as individually credited
Maps by George Anderson © Helion & Company 2022

Every reasonable effort has been made to trace copyright holders and to obtain their permission for the use of copyright material. The author and publisher apologise for any errors or omissions in this work, and would be grateful if notified of any corrections that should be incorporated in future reprints or editions of this book.

ISBN 978-1-914059-86-5

British Library Cataloguing-in-Publication Data.
A catalogue record for this book is available from the British Library.

All rights reserved. No part of this publication may be reproduced, stored in a retrieval system, or transmitted, in any form, or by any means, electronic, mechanical, photocopying, recording or otherwise, without the express written consent of Helion & Company Limited.

For details of other military history titles published by Helion & Company Limited, contact the above address, or visit our website: http://www.helion.co.uk

We always welcome receiving book proposals from prospective authors.

Contents

Foreword iv

1. Introduction 7
2. The First 20 Years 15
3. Who Were the 47th Foot? 31
4. Tactical Evolution 61
5. New Jersey, New York, New England 96
6. With Carleton in Canada 118
7. With Burgoyne to Albany 143
8. The Convention Army 177
9. With Aubrey and Gamble on the Great Lakes 200
10. Conclusion 214

Appendices
I   Townshend's 'Rules and Orders for the Discipline of the Light Infantry Companies in His Majesty's Army in Ireland' 217
II Light Infantry Movements before his Majesty at Richmond Park 3rd October 1774 221
III Articles of Convention Between Lieutenant General Burgoyne and Major General Gates 223

Bibliography 226

Foreword

Some 250 years ago in 1772 my ancestor, General Sir Guy Carleton was appointed Colonel of the 47th Regiment of Foot. Departing shortly thereafter to resume his duties as Governor of Quebec it is unlikely that he saw his regiment again until 1776 when it arrived to relieve him and his garrison, lifting the Siege of Quebec and defeating the American insurgents. Carleton subsequently drove the American Rebels out of Quebec Province and down to New York securing Canada's independence from what would become the United States of America. As the last Commander-in-Chief of the British Army of North America he finally withdrew his Army in 1783 handing New York to George Washington, ending the war before returning to Canada as the country's first Governor-General. Throughout, the 47th Foot were in the vanguard of the campaign.

So, it is a great privilege to be invited to contribute a foreword to this fascinating and meticulously researched account of the experiences of a single British regiment during the American War of Independence. This enthralling regimental history of the 47th Foot follows their fortunes through the monumental tide of events that culminated in the humiliation of the global superpower at the hands of the victorious Americans and the loss of the British Colonies of North America. It is a compelling tale of ordinary men and women facing up to extraordinary circumstances thousands of miles from home, confronting a tenacious adversary, extremes of climate and geography, hardship and deprivation. But it is also a reminder of the astonishing resilience of the British soldier, and the importance of leadership, morale, discipline and flexibility as the Regiment adapted to the very distinct tactical challenges of fighting a conventional urban enemy in Boston at Bunker Hill and a later rural insurgency in the woods and valleys around Saratoga. Soldiering has always been about evolution, never more so than on campaign and Paul Knight expertly narrates this human tale of transformation revealing the enduring lessons that in combination result in tactical success.

General Sir Mark Carleton-Smith KCB CBE ADC Gen
Chief of the General Staff

Acknowledgements

Writing a book like this starts a great many years before pen is put to paper. The inspiration and initial research owes a great deal to the historical reenactors of the 47th Foot during the American War of Independence, past and present, in the UK, France, Germany and the USA. My particular thanks go to Nigel Hardacre.

In the UK, a great many conversations have contributed to the ideas behind this book, including David Babington-Smith (descendent of Lieutenant John Rotten), Alan Ball, Andrew Ball, Dr David Blackmore, Dr Juliette Desplat, Francis Kerner, Sean Phillips, James Tanner, Dr Thomas Whitfield, Edward and Alister Wilson, Marty Young, and John Downham and all the staff at the Lancashire Infantry Museum. Also, the staff of the National Portrait Gallery, National Museum of Wales, and The National Archives.

The National Monuments Service in Ireland provided the images of Charles Fort. I was unable to visit due to COVID travel restrictions but am grateful for the staff at the fort and Michael Hayes for their support. In Germany, Walter Ernst proved invaluable in navigating the German archives which led to the von Germann watercolours in the Brunswick State Archives. The Library and Archives of Canada proved to be a fascinating source of images. In the United States, Steven M. Baule, Frank Cecela, Marcio da Cunha, Vivian Davies, Don Hagist, Jim Hollister, Paul Pace, Greg Shipley, Scott Tomlinson, Tommy Tringale, Don Troiani, John van Vliet, Matthew Zembo and Matthew Keagle, Kevin D. Mahr, the staff at Fort Ticonderoga, the staff at the New York Public Library, Lake Champlain Maritime Museum, and the Huntingdon Library have all been very helpful.

Finally, thanks must go to Dr Andrew Bamford, Rob Griffith, Giorgio Albertini and George Anderson at Helion who turned my ideas into a published book.

1

Introduction

'A Very Fine Regiment and Fit for Service.'[1] Thus Major General Charles, the Earl of Drogheda reported on the 47th Regiment of Foot on its final inspection report before departing from the British Isles for North America. Over the next few years, the regiment would be engaged in a phase of warfare which the British Army has always struggled with, the transition from peacetime to wartime soldiering. Houlding's opening chapter in *Fit for Service* addressed 'The Friction of Peace' whereby other tasks detract from the army's core function, which is training for winning wars. Whatever training was undertaken was for 'a war', that is against a generic future foe: predicting future conflict is notoriously difficult. Readers will be familiar with the concept of the 'fog of war', the uncertainty faced by commanders during operations in 'the war', that is the war which you are now faced with is highly unlikely to be the war that you trained for.[2] More recently, the British Army's Major General (Retd) Dr Andrew Sharpe summarised this situation thus:

> Professional armies need to practice if they are to be capable armies. Time to train and free of other commitments, therefore, will always be a measure of actual or potential military capability, whether considering an army in 'normal times' or an army that is required to expand its capacity to deal with an increased threat.[3]

In between is the transition phase between peacetime training for 'a war' with all of its incumbent friction, and adopting practices and procedures for 'the war'. Part of this process is identifying what the threat is in order to formulate how to operate within 'the war'.

---

1   'This Regiment performed all their Exercise, and Manoeuvres, with the greatest Exactness & Attention And is a Very Fine Regiment and Fit for Service.' The National Archives (TNA): WO 27/26: Inspection Reports, Irish, 1772, 47th Foot.
2   J.A. Houlding, *Fit for Service: the Training of the British Army, 1715-1795* (Oxford: Oxford University Press, 1981), pp.1–98.
3   A. Sharpe, 'What Are the Enduring Lessons?', in M. Strohn (ed.), *How Armies Grow: the expansion of military forces in the age of total war, 1789-1945* (Oxford: Casemate, 2019), p.171.

This work aims to address that transitional phase in the American War of Independence through the lens of one regiment, the 47th Regiment of Foot. The 47th was a standard British Army regiment of foot of the time. The regiment deployed to North America in the years of increasing political tension before the outbreak of open rebellion. They were then transferred to Boston and were involved in the transitional phase as the rebellion spread. Later, they were part of the armies of General Sir Guy Carleton and Lieutenant General John Burgoyne which drove the rebels out of Quebec as far as Saratoga during 1776 and 1777. Tactically and operationally, those years were extraordinarily successful; the current author will show an army evolving to address the conditions of 'the war'. Despite these successes at the tactical and operational levels, at the strategic level the British Army had yet to adapt to the realities of 'the war'. The 1777 strategy was for General the Honourable Sir William Howe to advance from New York northwards along the Hudson River to Albany where he would join with his two subordinates, Lieutenant General John Burgoyne advancing southwards along the Lake Champlain route and Lieutenant Colonel Barry St Leger advancing westwards from the Great Lakes. This move was intended to split the rebel forces leading to their defeat. In the event, Howe's decision to embark on his Philadelphia expedition undermined the grand strategy of 1777; it neither supported Burgoyne and St Leger, nor did it defeat Washington.

The majority of the 47th Foot became part of the 'Convention Army' which laid down its arms at Saratoga. Burgoyne's surrender at Saratoga was a result not of tactical and operational failure to adjust to the realities of 'the war', but of a failure at the higher levels to adopt strategy to the realities of 'the war'.

For the younger members of the 47th, it must have been a humiliating end to an adventure which had seen them cross the Atlantic and travel through the rivers and forests of Canada. For the more senior members who had fought in Canada during the French and Indian War, the humiliation and perhaps relief at the ending of an increasingly difficult and desperate campaign would have been tinged with anger at the perfidy of the colonial rebels who they had previously fought to protect.

Who were the officers and men of the 47th Foot? Where did they come from and how did they fight? What were their attitudes to the regiment, the army and the rebels? These are the questions which this work aims to address. Delving into the life, training and performance of one regiment helps us to analyse the war which these soldiers knew. There has been an increase in research into the British Army in recent years, primarily led by American scholars. This addresses a relative lack of research into the British Army in the American War of Independence relative to the (ultimately) more successful French and Indian War which proceeded it, and the French Revolutionary and Napoleonic Wars which followed.

Brendan Simms titled his 2008 study of Britain in the eighteenth century *Three Victories and a Defeat*, referring to the War of the Spanish Succession, the War of the Austrian Succession, and the Seven Years War (which included the French and Indian War), with the American War of Independence being the defeat. The independence of the Thirteen Colonies

INTRODUCTION

and the restoration of East and West Florida to Spain was undoubtedly a major blow to British prestige. Rick Atkinson devotes most of the prologue of *The British Are Coming: the War for America 1775–1777* to describing an outwardly confident and happy Britain blessed by a devoted monarch as it commemorated the tenth anniversary of the 1763 Treaty of Paris. This was the era when George, 1st Earl Macartney, coined the phrase 'a vast Empire on which the sun never sets.' As a diplomat to Russia and colonial administrator in the West Indies, Grenada, Madras and China, he witnessed the expansion of Britain's global reach.[4]

However, Atkinson also recognises that all was not well within the British state. Victory had come at immense financial cost. Defeated enemies were only defeated temporarily and would return to the international stage chastened and vengeful. Many of the wartime-constructed 'wooden walls' which had secured victory were coming to the end of their service life prematurely due to demand for seasoned oak exceeding supply; replacement or repair would be costly and time consuming. During the Falkland Islands Crisis of 1770–1771, plans to mobilise the fleet were hampered by the state of ships which had been laid up for years.[5] There were also the complexities and contradictions of governing a far-flung empire which stretched the abilities of the late-eighteenth century administrators. British subjects in the American colonies (and also, it has to be said, in Great Britain) objected to the Government's solutions to several vexatious questions. The Proclamation Line (1763) aimed to prevent American colonial expansion westwards. Expansion antagonised Native Americans which resulting in conflicts which the regular British Army would have to resolve. The Quebec Act (1774) established the principle that a conquered territory should be governed by its own rules until replaced by British legislation. The prospect of the British government supporting absolutist French laws and culture, including the Roman Catholic church, was too much for the Puritans of New England. In contrast, when Spain took over control of Louisiana and attempted to introduce Spanish language and law, the French settlers there rebelled and were bloodily suppressed. The Québécois, as we shall see, were lukewarm through to hostile towards the rebels, even if they were equally lukewarm about supporting the war beyond their borders. Financial mismanagement of the East India Company required the first bail-out of a corporate entity 'too big to fail' on a scale not experienced again until the banking crisis of 2007. Tax reductions on tea alienated smugglers by undermining their profit while a monopoly on its sale alienated those who saw it as evidence of the growth of absolutist government. The question of slavery came before the English courts in 1772. Lord Mansfield's ruling on the Somerset Case (on whether a slave could be forcibly removed from England) contained his finding that '[Slavery] is so odious, that nothing can be suffered to support

---

4 B. Simms, *Three Victories and a Defeat: The Rise and Fall of the First British Empire, 1714-1783* (London: Penguin, 2007); Atkinson, *The British Are Coming*, pp.1–31, the Macartney quote is on p.6.

5 G.W. Rice, 'British Foreign Policy and the Falkland Islands Crisis of 1770-1771', *International History Review*, 32, No. 2 (June, 2010), pp.289–291.

it, but positive law.' As there was no law permitting slavery in England, he continued 'I cannot say this case is allowed or approved by the law of England; and therefore the black must be discharged.'[6] It has been argued that this limited step in England towards abolition encouraged those slave-owners in the Thirteen Colonies who wanted to maintain slavery towards independence, including signatories of the Declaration of Independence.

European foreign affairs naturally preoccupied the British government's attention, especially the Corsican Crisis of 1769 with France, the Falklands Crisis of 1770 with Spain, and the coronation of Louis XVI of France in 1774. The latter was expected to herald a more vigorous and aggressive French foreign policy. It also saw the first of three Polish partitions. In the first case, Britain failed to act to defend the Corsican Republic (recently ceded by Genoa to France) against a French invasion, which undermined Britain's supposed position as guarantor of European liberties. With regards to the Falklands Islands, a negotiated settlement was reached with Spain once France made it clear that it would not support Spain in a conflict with Britain. War with Spain would have allowed a westwards expansion for the British colonies in North America but that war would, like the French and Indian War, have been bankrolled by Britain and would have increased the already significant imperial burdens upon which London was struggling. In response to this negotiated settlement, the Massachusetts House of Representatives chided London: 'Such an act of hostility [by Spain] could not but be followed with the most spirited resolution on the part of the British administration, to obtain a satisfaction fully adequate to the insult offered to His Majesty, and the injuries his subjects have sustained.' Fine words, which we should remember for just a few years later.[7]

Then there is the matter of taxation.

Boston, Massachusetts would become the focus of opposition to London's policies. Richard Archer traces this from 1761. It could arguably be placed seven years earlier when Lieutenant Colonel George Washington of the Virginia Militia massacred a French parlay party at Jumonville Glen on 23 May 1754. Far more than at Lexington Green, this was a shot heard around the world because it sparked what Winston Churchill would call the 'first world war'. The ensuing conflict, the Seven Years War, was truly global. After initial setbacks (Monongahela in 1755, Menorca, 1756, Fort William Henry in 1757, Convention of Kloster Zeven in 1757), British arms were ultimately successful in India (Plassey 1757, Buxar 1764), in Africa (Senegal 1758), in Europe (Minden 1759, Warburg 1760), in the Caribbean (Guadeloupe 1759, Martinque 1762, Havana 1762), in East and West Florida, in New France (Louisbourg in 1758 and Quebec in 1759) and Manila in the Philippines in 1762. At sea, the Royal Navy, after its own initial failings for which Admiral the Honourable John Byng paid with his life, 'in order to encourage the

---

6   S. Usherwood, 'The Black Must Be Discharged', *History Today*, vol.31, Issue 3 (March, 1981), pp.40–45.
7   D.H. Robinson, 'Britain Between Continents', *History Today*, vol.71, Issue 3 (March 2021), pp.50–57 esp. p.54; see also Rice 'Falkland Islands Crisis of 1770-1771', pp.273–305; Simms, *Three Victories and a Defeat*, pp.555–575.

others,'[8] but 'the others' were encouraged at battles like Quiberon Bay (1759), Lagos (1759) and Cape Finisterre (1761), and relieving the siege of Quebec in the spring of 1760 (as they would do in 1776). It was not without reason that Frank McLynn's *1759* is subtitled *The Year Britain became Master of the World*. Or so it seemed.

War is expensive. The Seven Years War cost about £100 million. The British national debt approached £250 million, although Heale puts the figure at £130 million and Archer at £150 million. Servicing this debt absorbed about 50 percent of the British Treasury's £12 million annual receipts. It has been estimated that the tax revenue raised in Great Britain was 25 shillings per person per annum (£1.25 in modern money), whereas that in the Thirteen Colonies was just 6d (2 ½ pence in modern money), a difference of a factor of 50.[9] There was a feeling, not without justification, that the American colonies were the main beneficiaries of the war, while shirking their share of the financial responsibility. Prime Minister William Pitt estimated that 50,000 troops were required to subdue Quebec, and, not unreasonably given all the other theatres the British Army was operating in, that half of these should be provided from Britain and half from the Thirteen Colonies, with each colony providing in proportion to its wealth and population. The colonies prevaricated. The British government provided the weapons, so all the colonies needed to do was provide the pay and clothing, but still they quibbled. Even the provision of £200,000 against costs resulted in not one colony fulfilling its obligations. At the 1758 Siege of Louisbourg, for example, of 12,301 officers and men, only about 500 were colonial troops; Britain also supplied the 40 warships with over 14,000 crewmen for the operation. The following year Quebec was an overwhelmingly European battle with British regulars taking the brunt of the fighting. The removal of Paris' influence from North America (Quebec passed to the British and Louisiana to the Spanish) removed that threat to the Thirteen Colonies. Post-1763, the government believed there was a requirement to maintain more British regiments in North America, at a cost of between £200,000 and £400,000 per annum. Their role was to protect the colonists from the Native Americans (and vice versa) with Pontiac's Rebellion being a case in point. They were also to deter European designs in North America. French and Spanish defeat in 1763 would only bring temporary respite to Great Britain; a war of revenge (*revanche*) was anticipated once the French and Spanish fleets had been rebuilt. Spain remained a power in North America and, as we have seen, there was nearly war in 1770. The British Army in North America amounted to some 10,000 troops, about three times the pre-war level. Opposition focused on well-established concerns over a standing army in peacetime. There was also a cost to the colonies for housing these troops. According to Archer, 10,000 troops was far more than would be needed for security but as events would

---

8   R. Cavendish, 'The Execution of Admiral Byng', *History Today*, vol.57, Issue 3, (March, 2007), pp.60–61.
9   Atkinson, *The British are Coming*, p.8; R. Archer, *As If an Enemy's Country: the British Occupation of Boston and the Origins of Revolution* (Oxford: Oxford University Press, 2010), pp.3–4; M.J. Heale, *The American Revolution* (London: Meuthen, 1986), pp.5–7.

show after 1775 shows, 10,000 troops were woefully inadequate. In 1777, Burgoyne and St Leger departed Quebec with about 10,000 troops and that was clearly inadequate. Experience from the French and Indian War showed that the Royal Navy's control of the North Atlantic could not be guaranteed and there would be delays between the call for regular soldiers to defend the colonies and their safe arrival. There would be a further delay while those soldiers from the British Isles becoming adept to campaigning in North America. The French navy had intercepted British convoys in the 1750s; this happened again after 1775 with supplies captured at sea being turned against their former owners.[10]

From the early-twenty-first century perspective, three of these four issues are indicative of Britain moving in a relatively liberal direction: protection of Native American rights from colonial expansion, the right of the Québécois to live under their own laws and religion, the emancipation of slaves. Whether or not governments should bail out failing corporate entities remains as controversial today as in the 1770s. What is apparent is that there was a divergence of global outlook in the British world on both side of the Atlantic.

The 1783 Treaty of Paris granted independence to the United States of America. Great Britain had been humbled. This had been France's main war aim. However, beyond the loss of the Thirteen Colonies and the two Floridas, was Britain defeated? On land, Britain still held the major east coast port cities of New York, Charleston and Savannah while to the north Detroit, Niagara and Michilimackinac were amongst the forts where the Union Flag flew (and would do for some years after the treaty was signed). Although General Charles, Earl Cornwallis' army now joined Burgoyne's in captivity, there were still significant British forces at each of those ports and forts.

At sea, the Royal Navy had regained dominance. After their failures which had permitted French *Vice Amiral* François, Comte de Grasse to blockade Cornwallis at Yorktown in 1781, Rear Admiral Sir George Rodney defeated de Grasse at the Battle of the Saintes in April 1782. In the space of a year, Rodney would capture one French, one Dutch and two Spanish admirals. The Royal Navy's supremacy cut the American rebels from their French backers.

In terms of the Britain's colonial possessions, Quebec had refused to send representatives to the Continental Congress and had fought against the rebels to remain British. Loyalists were re-settled in what would become Ontario and their descendants would defeat the United States' attempt to capture Canada during the War of 1812. Britain retained Gibraltar despite The Great Siege (1779–1783) although Spain regained possession of Minorca and Florida.[11]

---

10   G.M. Wrong, *Canada and the American Revolution* (New York: Cooper Square, 1935), p.139; R. Chartrand, *Louisbourg 1758: Wolfe's first siege* (Oxford: Osprey, 2000), pp.39–40; S. Reid, *Quebec 1759: the battle that won Canada* (Oxford: Osprey, 2003), pp.66–67; Archer, *As If an Enemy's Country*, pp.3–4; A.R. Cain, *I See Nothing but the Horrors of a Civil War* (Independently published, 2019), p.26; Rice 'Falkland Islands Crisis of 1770–1771', pp.274, 278.

11   R. Chartrand, *Gibraltar 1779–83: the Great Siege* (Oxford: Osprey, 2006), pp.88–91.

INTRODUCTION

Looking across the whole of George III's reign, 1783 was undoubtedly a low point of humiliation and shame. Brendan Simms' *Three Victories and a Defeat* has been mentioned previously but there is also Peter Brown's *The Army of George II 1727–1760* which is subtitled *The Soldiers who Forged an Empire*. The army of George III would later wage war against, and defeat, Revolutionary and Napoleonic France.[12] 1783 was an anomaly.

This was the world in which the 47th Regiment of Foot existed.

How and why did the 47th fight? National pride? As we shall see, 45 percent of the 47th were Irish, who, we are led to believe, had no love for the British monarchy. Regimental pride? The regiment was less than 40 years old and its first action, Preston Pans in 1745, was a humiliating rout. The regiment's performance during the French and Indian War had been significantly more impressive, but by 1775 only 20 percent of the regiment had sufficient length of service to have participated. Even then, it was 15 years previously. Professional pride? Most of the regiment had less than three years' service, which is not long to establish such an ethos. These were hardly the veterans of popular mythology. Personal pride? Soldiers were expected to perform their duty, but in North America, 3,000 miles from home, who would know if you avoided your duty? Maybe it was the right thing to do. Maybe, when you find yourself in an impossible situation from which you cannot escape, the best you can do is to fight through and hope you come out unscathed at the opposite side. Such thoughts are those of the private individual and usually not recorded, although the work of Don Hagist has explored the mindset of the common soldiers, such as the records permit. In an older work, Richard Sampson in his *Escape in America* shows British soldiers held in captivity after Saratoga would escape captivity, undertake the perilous journey to British lines and resume the fight, usually in a different regiment. This is hardly the image of a soldier who served under duress and had to be driven into action by brutal NCOs.[13]

How did the 47th fight? Throughout the American War of Independence as a whole, the British Army was invariably successful on the field of battle. The present author would suggest that the three most significant British defeats – Boston, Saratoga and Yorktown – arose because the British Army had manoeuvred itself into a geographical position from which it could not extricate itself. The 47th was one of those regiments caught off balance in the transition from peacetime soldiering but evolved into a highly effective fighting force, as Mark Urban subtitled his book *Fusiliers*, '*How the British Army lost America but Learned to Fight*'. I would argue that for the 47th, having shown it could fight highly effectively from Cape Breton to Montreal in the previous decade, it was not learning, but re-learning after 1775.

---

12 P. Brown, *The Army of George II, 1727-1760: the Soldiers who Forged an Empire* (Warwick: Helion, 2020).
13 D. Hagist, *British Soldiers, American War: voices of the American Revolution* (Yardley, PA: Westhome Publishing, 2012) and *Noble Volunteers: the British Soldiers who fought the American Revolution* (Yardley, PA: Westhome Publishing, 2020); R. Sampson, *Escape in America: the British Convention Prisoners, 1777–1783* (Chippenham: Picton, 1995).

This study of the 47th Foot is, therefore, an analysis of the men, commissioned and enlisted, thrown into the maelstrom of some of the most dramatic events in history. Who were they, where were they from, how did they respond to these events, and how did they fight and survive?

During the First World War centenary there was a proliferation of battalion studies. These sought to identify the 'personality' of a battalion.[14] This historiography becomes more difficult as the historian delves further back because the records required for such a study do not exist on the same scale. Drs David Blackmore and Andrew Bamford have been successful for the British Army in the Napoleonic Wars.[15] For the American War of Independence, Mark Urban's *Fusilier* and Steven Baule's *Protecting the Empire's Frontier* have successfully studied the 23rd and 18th Foot respectively.[16]

Fusiliers is fortunate that the 23rd served throughout the whole war, generating a wealth of material for Urban's study. He is wrong, albeit only slightly, to say that the 23rd were the only regiment to serve throughout the war. The 47th was part of the Convention Army following Saratoga. However, two of the companies, Aubrey's and Gamble's, had been detached previously. These escaped the fate of the majority of the regiment and continued to fight throughout the remainder of the war.

This was the world in which the officers and men of the 47th Foot lived. This is their story.

---

14 See, for example, the work of John Hartley on 6th Manchesters; Kevin Shannon on 4th and 5th King's Own, and 6th King's; Keith Mitchinson on 6th Londons; Adrian Gregson on 7th King's; John Sheenan and Andrew Kirk on 5th, 7th and 8th West Yorkshires, amongst others.

15 For example, A. Bamford, *Discipline and Gallantry: the 12th Light Dragoons at War with Wellington* (Pen & Sword: Barnsley, 2014); D. Blackmore, *So Bloody a Day: the 16th Light Dragoons in the Waterloo Campaign* (Helion: Warwick, 2019).

16 M. Urban, *Fusiliers: how the British Army lost America but learned to fight* (London: Faber and Faber, 2007); S.M. Baule, *Protecting the Empire's Frontier: officers of the 18th (Royal Irish) Regiment of Foot during its North American Service, 1767–1776* (Athens, OH: Ohio University Press, 2014).

2

The First 20 Years

The Regiment[1]

On 3 January 1741, Colonel Sir John Mordaunt (1697–1780) was authorised to raise what became the 47th Regiment of Foot in Scotland. Mordaunt was of good military and political pedigree. His father was Lieutenant General Harry Mordaunt (1663–1720). The younger Mordaunt was commissioned in 1721, rising to become lieutenant colonel in the 3rd Foot Guards in 1741 and Colonel of the 18th (Royal Irish) Foot the following year. During the 1745 Jacobite Rebellion, Mordaunt commanded a brigade at the Battle of Falkirk and at the Battle of Culloden he commanded the reserve, which was used to pursue the retreating Jacobites in the aftermath of their defeat.[2] For his service, Cumberland presented him with Charles Stuart's coach. With the Jacobite threat to Britain neutralised, Cumberland returned to the Continent and Mordaunt, now promoted to major general, commanded a brigade of infantry at the Battle of Lauffeld in 1747.

The outbreak of the Seven Years War in 1756 brought an opportunity for further advancement. The following year, Mordaunt was chosen to command a raid on Rochefort. He was aided by Major General Henry Conway and Colonel Edward Cornwallis, uncle of the Cornwallis of American War of Independence fame. The Quartermaster General was James Wolfe, who had also fought at Culloden and Lauffeld. The expedition captured Ile d'Aix but found the water too shallow for the fleet to get closer in than 1½ miles from the shore. Colonel Wolfe conducted a reconnaissance against Rochefort and concluded that it was lightly garrisoned. He argued that with 500 men he could take the town. A council of war resulted in no action, and following a second with even more inactivity, Admiral Sir Edward Hawke declared that

---

1 For convenience, the regiment will be referred to as the 47th throughout although until the 1748 Treaty of Aix-la-Chapelle it was 58th in order of seniority. It was not until 1751 that numbers were brought in as the official title. Until then the regiment was officially named after the colonel, so Mordaunt's, Lascelle's and then Carleton's. Although names and numbers were used interchangeably. County and other titles were not adopted until 1783.

2 H.C. Wylly, *The Loyal North Lancashire Regiment*, (London: Royal United Services Institution, 1933), vol.I, pp.15–17; S. Reid, *Culloden Moor 1746: the death of the Jacobite cause* (Osprey: Oxford, 2002), pp.27, 51, 60.

unless the army was prepared to act, the fleet would sail for Great Britain. There were other demands on his ships, and he could not wait.

Prime Minister William Pitt was furious at the great expense which the expedition had incurred for no results. Mordaunt was court martialled. Although he was acquitted on a technicality, he never held military office again. The careers of both Conway and Cornwallis suffered too. George II refused to employ Conway again and Cornwallis became Governor of Nova Scotia (1749–1752), spending the last 15 years of his life as Governor of Gibraltar (1761–1776). Wolfe was the only one to come out unscathed and the affair brought him to Pitt's attention. Pitt believed that the best gains could be achieved in North America, where France was weak, rather than on the Continent. Wolfe was appointed brigadier general and sent to Major General Jeffrey Amherst who was preparing to capture Louisbourg on the St Lawrence River.

Back in Scotland, the colonelcy of the regiment passed to Lieutenant General Peregrine Lascelles on 13 March 1742. He served in that capacity until his death on 26 March 1772. Commissioned into Lovelace's Regiment in 1706 for service during the War of the Spanish Succession, he transferred to Lepell's Regiment two years later when Lovelace was appointed Governor of New York and New Jersey. He fought in Spain at the Battles of Almanara, Zaragossa and Villaviciosa but the regiment was disbanded at the end of the war. On half-pay, Lascelles joined Grant's Regiment which was raised in response to the 1715 Jacobite Rebellion. Grant's Regiment was disbanded in 1718, but Lascelles was made an honorary Burgess of Glasgow for his service. During the 1720s he served as a captain in Churchill's Dragoons and then captain lieutenant in the 1st Foot Guards. He was an extremely experienced officer.[3]

When Lascelles became colonel of the regiment, it was employed building the new military road between Dumbarton and Inveraray. This was completed just two months before the 1745 Jacobite Rebellion began. Two companies of the 47th were detached to join the garrison of Edinburgh Castle while the remainder joined Lieutenant General Sir John Cope's army. Cope's government army and Charles Stuart's Jacobite army clashed at Prestonpans on 21 September 1745. In 15 minutes, the government army was destroyed and scattered. Lascelles escaped but much of the regiment was captured. Cope, his deputy Brigadier General Thomas Fowke (who had also served in Lapell's Regiment) and Lascelles were all court-martialled. Although exonerated, Cope would never command again.[4]

Shortly afterward, the regiment would depart on its first tour in North America. Far from conforming to some pre-determined *roulemont*, the *Derby Mercury* of 27 April 1750 reported the selection criteria: 'Yesterday, pursuant to an order issued out for the purpose, dice were thrown on a drum head between the Regiments commanded by General Otway, Colonel

---

3   Wylly, *Loyal North Lancashire*, vol.I, p.17.
4   Wylly, *Loyal North Lancashire*, vol.I, pp.17–26; Reid, *Culloden Moor*, pp.9, 14.

Thomas Murray and Colonel Lascelles to determine which of them should embark for Nova Scotia, when the chance fell on Colonel Lascelles.'[5]

The Treaty of Aix-le-Chapelle (1748) ended the War of the Austrian Succession and ceded all of Arcadia to Britain, when it was renamed Nova Scotia. Arcadia was a separate colony from New France (Quebec). The 47th arrived there in 1750 and were plunged straight into a guerrilla campaign known as Father Le Lourtre's War. From the early 1600s, the French had settled in the area of Maritime Canada into Quebec and south to modern-day Maine. They settled alongside, and intermarried with, the indigenous Mi'kmaq to produce a unique culture. But almost immediately there was conflict with the New England colonies. Port Royale was settled in 1604 and became the capital of Arcadia, but would be captured or destroyed on several occasion by forces from Great Britain and New England. Port Royale was captured for the final time in 1710 and renamed Annapolis Royal. The establishment of Halifax in Nova Scotia in 1749 by Cornwallis breached the treaties which had ended Father Rale's War; its foundation provoked Father Le Loutre's War.[6]

When the French and Indian War commenced in 1755, the 47th was already stationed in North America and well positioned for operations against France's Atlantic colonies. This transpired to be their good fortune as they avoided participating in the early British defeats at Monongahela, Fort William Henry and Fort Carillon (Fort Ticonderoga). The 47th's first objective was Louisbourg, the French fortress city founded in 1720 to protect the entrance to the St Lawrence River and Quebec. It also operated as a naval base for French operations against New England and the Royal Navy. Louisbourg was situated between the two British colonies of Nova Scotia and Newfoundland. The French concentrated a fleet there in 1757 which forced the postponement of British operations. In June of the following year, Admiral Frances Boscawen arrived with a fleet of 40 ships and 14,600 men escorting 127 transports crewed by 6,000 men and transporting some 13,000 soldiers. The 47th was one of 14 regiments to participate in the siege. Louisbourg surrendered on 26 July 1758. At the far end of the St Lawrence, Lieutenant Colonel John Bradstreet captured Fort Frontenac (modern day Kingston, Ontario) where the river enters Lake Ontario. Slowly, the tide was turning against New France.[7]

1759 saw Major General James Wolfe's famous advance up the St Lawrence River. The 47th was there again, landing on the Isle d'Orléans off Quebec City in June of that year. The regiment suffered during an unsuccessful battle at the Montmorency Falls at the end of July, just a few days after Fort Carillon fell to the British. Major General Wolfe's inspirational, and desperate, landing at the Anse-au-Foulon (Wolfe's Cove) followed by the Battle of the Plains of Abraham on 13 September resulted in the deaths of both the British and French commanders, Wolfe and Montcalm. Wolfe had been standing

---

[5] I am indebted to John Downham for this source, which is taken from his forthcoming history of the Duke of Lancaster's Regiment.
[6] Wylly, *Loyal North Lancashire*, vol.I, pp.26–30.
[7] Wylly, *Loyal North Lancashire*, vol.I, pp.30–35; see also Chartrand, *Louisbourg 1758*.

beside the 47th when mortally wounded. The 47th appears to have gained the moniker 'Wolfe's Own' around this time. It also appears to have changed the regimental lace to include two black lines in mourning for Wolfe's death. Also wounded was Lieutenant Colonel Guy Carleton, serving as Quartermaster General, and future Colonel of the 47th. The city surrendered on 18 September. Quebec had been severely bombarded during the siege which resulted in many damaged buildings. As the besiegers now became besieged in a Canadian winter, they suffered greatly in the war-damaged city. The St Lawrence froze which cut them off from Britain, but not from French troops still operating out of Montreal.[8]

The Battle of St Foy was fought the following spring on the same ground as the Plains of Abraham but with the opposing forces having exchanged positions. The weakened British Army was defeated and withdrew back into the city walls. Both armies, besieged and besiegers, now awaited the breaking up of the river ice to await relief from Europe. On 9 May, a sail was spotted. HMS *Lowestoffe* saved the British garrison and Quebec for Britain, although it would be another six days and the arrival of two more Royal Navy ships, *Vanguard* and *Diana*, before the siege was abandoned. This allowed Brigadier General James Murray, with the 47th, to advance along the St Lawrence as part of a three-pronged attack on Montreal. Starting in July, Major General Jeffery Amherst advanced from Lake Ontario and Brigadier General William Haviland from Crown Point. Montreal surrendered on 9 September 1760.[9] The 47th remained in Canada until 1763 when they sailed for Ireland.

The Generals

Two generals played a key role in the regiment's experiences when it returned to North America in 1773, through to Saratoga four years later: Guy Carleton and John Burgoyne. It is worth analysing their lives and careers to gain an understanding of these men as their decisions directly impacted on the lives and careers of the 47th.

Guy Carleton's biographer, Paul Reynolds, wrote of his subject in glowing terms in his introduction: 'Only a handful of men in the eighteenth century can have any claim to have changed history. Surely Sir Guy Carleton must be numbered among those few.'[10] Born in Strabane near Londonderry in County Tyrone on 3 September 1724, Carleton was the third son in a family of six. His father died when he was 14 and his mother remarried to an Anglican clergyman with a parish in County Down. This aided Carleton's education, but it was through the assistance of a wealthy friend of his father that, aged 18, he was able to purchase an ensigncy in the 25th Foot. Peacetime promotion for a man without means was slow but Carleton was fortunate to make the friendship of James Wolfe, a man with more connections and wealth, to aid his promotion. In 1752, Wolfe did Carleton a great favour. The Duke of

---

8 Wylly, *Loyal North Lancashire*, vol.I, pp.35–44; Reid, *Quebec 1759*, pp.69–92.
9 Wylly, *Loyal North Lancashire*, vol.I, pp.46–49; Reid, *Quebec 1759*, pp.84–92.
10 P. Reynolds, *Guy Carleton: a biography* (New York: William Morrow, 1980), p.xiii.

Richmond purchased a captaincy for his son and heir in Wolfe's 20th Foot. Richmond asked Wolfe to recommend a military tutor. Wolfe recommended Carleton. The future duke and Carleton undertook a six-week tour of the fortifications of the Low Counties and the latter established a powerful contact at the heart of government. This connection would pay dividends in the future when in 1773, William Pitt 'the Elder', former Prime Minister and by then Earl of Chatham, chose the 47th for his eldest son, John. John later resigned his commission rather than fight the rebels, although he did rejoin the army in response to France's entry into the war.[11]

Wolfe failed to have Carleton appointed to his staff when sent to Nova Scotia in preparation for the attack on Louisbourg but was more successful when, as commander of the Quebec expedition, Carleton was appointed his Quartermaster General. However, Carleton appears to have made disparaging remarks about the performance of Hanoverian troops which reached the ears of George II and turned the king against him.[12]

Outside of Quebec an incident occurred which showed a humane side to Carleton, one which would follow him throughout his career. A group of Québécois refugees made homeless by the bombardment of the city were living in a shanty village next to the river. There they were constantly being pestered by First Nation warriors in search of rum and other items, of which the refugees had none. Carleton arranged for their evacuation and relocation shortly before their village was ransacked.[13] Carleton's career was often marked by his humanity, as will be explored below with regards to the Quebec Act (1774), his treatment of rebel prisoners in 1775 and 1776, and *The Book of Negroes,* which listed runaway slaves evacuated by the British in 1783. After being wounded during the Battle of the Plains of Abraham, during which his friend Wolfe was killed, Carleton returned to England. He participated in operations at Belle-Isle in 1761 and Havana in 1762.[14]

In 1766, the then Brigadier General Carleton accepted the post of acting Governor of Quebec. The military and then civil governor had been Brigadier General James Murray, one of Wolfe's brigadiers from 1759. He was recalled to London to answer charges made against him by certain sections of Québécois society. While this is not the place to explore British policy towards Quebec, the problems can be summarised as two issues. Firstly, conflicts between the traditional Québécois community and a growing 'Anglo' community of merchants and traders from Britain and New England. Secondly, there was the nature of British rule, law and administration of an alien culture. As acting governor (and governor from 1768), Carleton attempted to place the colony's administration on a more balanced footing. In 1770 he returned to England to sponsor the Quebec Act (1774). This

---

11 Reynolds, *Carleton*, pp.1–2; B. Ruppert, 'Those Who Could Not Serve', *Journal of the American Revolution* (20 January, 2017), <https://allthingsliberty.com/2017/01/those-who-could-not-serve/> accessed 20 September 2021; S.M. Baule and S. Gilbert, *British Army Officers who Served in the American Revolution, 1775–1783* (Westminster, MD: Heritage Books, 2008), p.145.
12 Reynolds, *Carleton*, pp.2–3.
13 Reynolds, *Carleton*, p.5.
14 Reynolds, *Carleton*, p.8.

A VERY FINE REGIMENT

At the memorial to General Lascelles. Lieutenant General Peregrine Lascelles was born in Whitby, and was buried in St Mary's Whitby 86 years later. He was Colonel of the 47th Foot from 1743 for almost 30 years, until his death in 1772. (Catherine Maginn-Roberts)

was a ground-breaking piece of legislation which confirmed the rights and religion, laws and language until changed by positive legislation – George III, who was also the head of the Anglican Church, was guaranteeing the existence of Roman Catholicism and the rights of the Frenchmen in one of his realms. It was highly controversial. In September 1774, the Suffolk Resolves were passed as a list of 19 grievances by the inhabitants of Suffolk County, Massachusetts. The tenth resolve objected to the Quebec Act as it was 'dangerous in an extreme Degree to the Protestant Religion, and to the civil Rights and Liberties of all America.'[15]

Following the death of Lieutenant General Lascelles on 26 March 1772, Carleton became colonel of the 47th Foot.[16] The following year he married Lady Maria Howard with whom he had 12 children.[17] He was also promoted to major general. Returning to Canada with Maria in May 1774, he was undoubtedly aware of the deteriorating political situation in the American colonies. Shortly after his arrival in July 1774, he despatched two of his four regiments (the 10th and the 52nd) to support Lieutenant General Thomas Gage in Boston, leaving just two for the defence of Quebec (the 7th and the 26th). A fifth regiment, the 8th, was garrisoning the western frontier.

In 1776, the Boston garrison was evacuated and landed in Halifax, Nova Scotia. The majority of the regiments followed General William Howe to New York. The 47th was the exception. They left Howe's army to join Carleton at Quebec City. Their selection was no doubt because Carleton was the 47th's Colonel. Never a man of great personal wealth, Carleton did not lavish money on his regiment. His time in Canada also mitigated against any attention he might have bestowed on them until this point.

During the period 1775 to 1777, Carleton was Commander-in-Chief, Quebec with Major General Burgoyne acting as his deputy during 1776 and then taking command of forces once they crossed into New York. Carelton was promoted to the local rank of general and Burgoyne to the local rank of lieutenant general in March 1776.[18] Despite his inspirational defence of Quebec, the ejection of rebel forces out of the province and their destruction as far as Fort Ticonderoga, his failure to recapture the fort and avenge the ignominy of 1775 was unacceptable to Lord George Germain, Secretary of State for the American Department. Germain and Carleton had a strained relationship which probably arose from the cashiering of the 'Coward of Minden'. During the Battle of Minden (1759), Germain had commanded a joint British-Hanoverian cavalry force. When ordered to advance, Germain first moved in the wrong direction being unable to see his target, and then clarified his orders. By the time he was prepared to move, the moment had been lost. Accused of refusing to advance, Germain was court martialled, found guilty as 'unfit to serve His Majesty in any military Capacity whatever',

---

15 'At a Meeting of the Delegates of every Town and District in the County of Suffolk ...', MHS Collections Online, <http://www.masshist.org/database/viewer.php?item_id=696>, accessed 6 March 2021.
16 Wylly, *Loyal North Lancashire*, vol.I, p.17.
17 J. Kelly, *Valcour: the 1776 Campaign that Saved the Cause of Liberty* (New York: St Martin's Press, 2021), p.115.
18 *The Gazette*, 23 March 1776, issue 11651, p.2.

and cashiered.[19] But in 1777, Germain was Carleton's political senior. Carleton was replaced as governor in 1778 by Frederick Haldimand. It is also likely that Germain fell out with the Howe brothers at the planning of the St Malo operation in 1758.[20]

After a period of well-deserved rest and stability at home, Carleton's services were called upon following Cornwallis' surrender at Yorktown in 1781. Carleton replaced General Henry Clinton as Commander-in-Chief. Initially despatched to conclude a peace treaty (a not unreasonable assignment given his reputation from Quebec) together with Admiral Robert Digby with a peace commission; it was soon clear that the British government would agree to complete independence. In these closing years of the war, there was no fighting between the British Army and the regular American forces. There was, however, an ongoing fratricidal civil war between loyalists and rebels. Excesses, often in revenge for previous outrages, continued.

Carleton oversaw the smooth and efficient evacuation of the British Army, all of the supporting structures, loyalists and freed slaves. Many runaway slaves were claimed as lawfully belonging to Americans. To placate them and in promise of future compensation from the British government, should their claims be validated, Carleton had the details recorded in the *Book of Negroes*. This detailed 3,000 freed slaves. The British government did not pay compensation for any of the former slaves. The loyalists and freed slaves were resettled in Nova Scotia and what became Ontario. Thousands of people, dispossessed of all they owed by the rebels (unless they were former slaves, in which case that was nothing to start with) and leaving New York with just what they could carry, required government aid for years to come while they rebuilt new lives elsewhere.

Carleton returned to Canada in 1786 as Governor General of British North America. This post was intended to oversee the several governors of what would become Canada. It was a move which preceded confederation, but in Carleton's lifetime had very little authority. He died at his home, Stubbings House, near Maidenhead as 1st Baron Dorchester in 1808. Carleton was described by his friend Wolfe as 'grave Carleton' and the Duke of Richmond as 'distant and reserved in manner', and by his successor as Governor of Quebec, Frederick Haldimand, that one 'should not be repelled by his cold manners that he was a perfect gentleman and one of the best officers in the service.'[21] He appears to have epitomised the aloof aristocrat, while also to have been well regarded in Quebec, efficient in his eviction of the rebels in 1776 once he had adequate troops for the role, and industrious in driving the war into New York. He was diligent in supporting Burgoyne's expedition, despite an understandable disappointment at not being chosen to lead it. He was, however, cautious. Ensuring he had sufficient vessels to

---

19 O'Shaughnessy, *The Men who Lost America* (London: One World, 2013), p.169.
20 K.J. Weddle, *The Complete Victory: Saratoga and the American Revolution* (Oxford: Oxford University Press, 2021), p.29; for a recent assessment of Germain at Minden, see E. Carmichael, *Like a Brazen Wall: the Battle of Minden, 1759, and its Place in the Seven Years War* (Warwick: Helion, 2021), pp.159–170, 202–203.
21 Reynolds, *Carleton*, p.11.

dominate Lake Champlain in 1776 took time, and the summer drew to a close. His reluctance to invest Fort Ticonderoga was militarily correct. Carleton realised that the limited forces available to him were all that kept Canada British and had to be preserved; he could not afford to lose them on ambitious adventures. Politically, Carleton's failure to revenge Ticonderoga's surprise capture by Ethen Allen and Benedict Arnold on 10 May 1775 set him at odds with the Secretary of State for the American Department, Lord George Germain.

John Burgoyne is usually introduced as a playwright, as if to have a hobby outside of his military career was a detriment. In contrast, biographies of rebel generals emphasise their non-military, pre-rebellion careers as if it made them a better, well rounded candidate for command.[22] Compared with Carleton, Burgoyne was a more outgoing and gregarious individual who was free and easy with his money, earning him the nickname 'Gentleman Johnny'. David McCoy noted that this nickname does not appear until George Bernard Shaw's 1897 play *The Devil's Discipline*; Edward de Fonblanque's 1875 biography of Burgoyne does not use the expression. However, Andrew O'Shaughnessy states that it was a contemporary sobriquet from his soldiers during the Seven Years War for the care and attention he treated them with. Burgoyne was not without his critics in his day, and although today he is the exemplar of British Army aristocratic incompetence, he was the least aristocratic of the senior British commanders.[23]

Burgoyne's first commission in the Horse Guards was sold in 1741, allegedly to settle his gambling debts. He obtained a free commission as an ensign in the 1st Royal Dragoons for the War of the Austrian Succession, rising to captain by the war's end. Marriage to Lady Charlotte Stanley, daughter of Lord Derby who was one of the leading politicians and landowners in the country, should have secured Burgoyne financially. However, her father's permission was refused and he cut them off without a dowry or other means of support. Burgoyne sold his commission for £2,600 and the pair lived off that money until Charlotte gave birth to a daughter, Charlotte Elizabeth, in 1754. This softened Lord Derby's attitude to the couple.[24]

The outbreak of the Seven Years War saw Burgoyne back in uniform, first in the 11th Dragoons and later in the Coldstream Guards. He participated in the raids on the French coast while also being instrumental in the development of light cavalry in the British Army. His new ideas were used to great effect in Portugal from 1762. Extracts of his 'Code' are transcribed in McCoy's biography, including the progressive observations that: 'Admitting then that English soldiers are to be treated as thinking beings, the reason will immediately appear of getting insight into the character of each particular

---

22 D. McCoy, *General John Burgoyne: Soldier, Statesman, Playwright* (Massillon, OH: Spare Change Press, 2020), pp.3–4.
23 McCoy, *Burgoyne*, p.75; O'Shaughnessy, *The Men who Lost America*, pp.124, 128.
24 O'Shaughnessy, *The Men who Lost America*, p.125.

man, and proportionally accordingly the degrees of punishment and encouragement.'[25]

From 1768, Burgoyne was MP for Preston. He voted against the peace treaty with Spain following the Falklands Crisis. He also voted against the Carib War of 1772–1773 on St Vincent, where British settlers wanted to take over the lands of the indigenous Caribs, and then devoted much of his political energy to attacking Lord Clive (of India) and demanding an investigation of the management of the East India Company. It was also during this period that he devoted time to the theatre, with *The Maid of the Oaks* being produced by David Garrick in 1775.[26]

Burgoyne's early role in the American War of Independence during the Siege of Boston was frustrating as he was a general without a command. He left Boston for England before the end of the siege. His next post was to Quebec as Carleton's deputy. While the pair appear to have worked well together, his reports to the king and government on Carleton's performance in 1776 may have undermined Carleton, while promoting Burgoyne and his own scheme for operations in New York. The caution which marked Carleton's advance from Quebec City to Fort Ticonderoga was also a feature of Burgoyne's advance to Saratoga. Despite Carleton's understandable disappointment at not commanding the New York expedition, he supported Burgoyne as well as he could, given the limited resources available to him. Following Saratoga, Burgoyne returned to Britain to defend himself. His political and military fortunes were temporarily restored in 1782 and 1783 under the Rockingham government, but with Rockingham's fall, he adopted a more private life. This was his most productive period as a playwright. Following the death of his wife in 1776, he had four children by Susan Caulfield. One of his grandchildren, Hugh, was awarded the Victoria Cross in 1855. John Burgoyne died peacefully in 1792.

Burgoyne's 'Gentleman Johnny' moniker reflected his dissolute youth with allegations of gambling debts, eloping with the daughter of a senior peer, his interest in the theatre and a reputation for fine living on campaign. His military performance during the War of the Austrian Succession and the Seven Years War was competent and professional. While his performance at Saratoga has been highly criticised, his was only one of three concurrent campaigns. The defeat of St Leger's Expedition was not critical to Burgoyne's failure. General Sir William Howe was the senior commander in North America with the largest army and the most secure base (New York). Both Burgoyne and St Leger were campaigning through the North American wilderness to meet their theatre commander. It was Howe's failure to make that junction with Burgoyne and St Leger at Albany which undermined the 1777 strategy. Above Howe, the only person capable of coordinating that was Lord George Germain as Secretary of State for the American Department.

---

25 McCoy, *Burgoyne*, pp.23–27; O'Shaughnessy, *The Men who Lost America*, pp.125–127.
26 O'Shaughnessy, *The Men who Lost America*, pp.128–134.

The Army

The 47th Foot existed within the institution of the British Army. Although we talk of the 'British Army', there were in fact two establishments which were different in command, structure, and purpose. The 1707 Act of Union combined the English and Scottish Armies, resulting in a British and an Irish Establishment, as Ireland was still a separate kingdom. The former was the smaller and temporary in nature, being subject to annual Parliamentary approval. The Irish Establishment was fixed at 12,000 men in 1699 until 1769 when it was raised to 15,000.[27] This increase in manpower was a result of more soldiers per regiment, rather than more regiments. For the period under study, the 47th Foot was part of the Irish Establishment.

The two establishments had their own Commanders-in-Chief and staffs. For the Irish Establishment, the Lord Lieutenant was the commander and his staff operated from Dublin Castle. He was not subordinate to the Commander-in-Chief of the British Establishment and could, and indeed, did, ignore instructions. One example of this was that of the reestablishment of infantry battalions' light companies. Battalions consisted of eight centre (sometimes referred to as 'hat' or 'battalion') companies and one grenadier company. The former formed the core of the battalion while the grenadiers were the battalion's elite or shock troops. On campaign, it was not uncommon for the grenadier companies to be detached to form composite grenadier battalions. During the French and Indian War, a tenth, light company was added as skirmishers to protect the battalion on the march, or its vulnerable flanks and rear in battle. At the end of the French and Indian War, light companies were disbanded as part of the general movement to reduce the size of the army.

The reestablishment (or establishment for those regiments who had never created then in the first place) of light companies in the different establishments were authorised on different dates and by different instructions. While the British Commander-in-Chief's writ ran to distant garrisons like Gibraltar, Minorca and Nova Scotia, it did not stretch to Ireland. The Irish Establishment was the larger; Houlding calculated it had an average of 25 battalions in Ireland in the 1760s and early 1770s. When the light companies were authorised in September 1771 there were 27 battalions. In contrast, the British Establishment averaged 13 battalions.[28] The Irish Establishment had one significant advantage over the British, in that it was permanently established and was accommodated in purpose-built barracks, for example Charlesfort near Cork where the 47th was based. The British Establishment, being only temporary in nature, needed fewer barracks.[29]

Regiments of Foot were also termed 'Marching Regiments', which reflected their transitory nature, primarily around Britain. Barracks existed in Britain

---

27　Brown, *Army of George II*, p.9; Houlding, *Fit for Service*, pp.45, 51.
28　Houlding, *Fit for Service*, pp.46-47, 158, 197; R.H.R. Smythies, *Historical Records of the 40th Regiment* (Devonport: A.W. Swiss, 1894), pp.547–548.
29　Brown, *Army of George II*, pp.31, 33; Houlding, *Fit for Service*, pp.52–57; Carmichael, *Like a Brazen Wall*, p.53.

in a few major garrisons, around ports and in the Highlands of Scotland. The Guards in London were also provided with barracks because their purpose was to guard the monarch; they were not 'Marching Regiments'. Limited accommodation across the country meant that 'Marching Regiments' were invariably well dispersed. Houlding estimated that for up to two thirds of the year, regiments could be well dispersed or on the march. Furthermore, whole regions of the British Isles rarely saw the army because it was either inaccessible due to poor roads, or lacked the agricultural infrastructure to sustain the soldiers. This included most of Wales, the Pennines, parts of Devon and Cornwall and the Highlands of Scotland.[30]

Operating in dispersed garrisons limited the quality and quantity of collective training. When soldiers were brought together, it took time to correct differences in drill practice. This limited the time available for regimental training, let alone brigade training. The commanding officers of three regiments concentrated in Dublin in the spring of 1777 required four to six weeks to bring their regiments to the required standard. This seems an exceptionally long period of time to bring their regiments up to scratch during wartime. In contrast, the 45th Foot was a regiment worn out after 20 years of North American service. In 1767, the inspection returns described the 45th as under-strength and full of recruits. The following year, it was up to strength, but half of its ranks were recruits so it was still unfit for service. In 1769, it was much improved and was predicted to be at the required standard the following year, which it was. It took over three years to re-build the regiment in the quiet of Ireland. The 47th returned from North America in 1763 after 13 years overseas. The inspection returns from that period have not survived, but it is likely that they experienced a similar process. The military effectiveness of a regiment fluctuated greatly depending on the tasks to which they were assigned.[31]

Regiments moved between the establishments as required. With the exception of Highland regiments, it would be wrong to apply any national characteristics to regiments at this time. As we will see in the following chapter, although the 47th was part of the Irish Establishment in the early 1770s less than half of its soldiers were Irish.

Until 1770, a regiment on the Irish Establishment had a strength of 297, while one on the British Establishment had a strength of 497. In 1770, they were equalised at 442. Houlding calculated that it took two years for the Irish Establishment to recruit up to the new strength.[32] Before 1770, a company on the Irish Establishment was composed of three officers, two sergeants, two corporals, one drummer and 28 privates. Although an Irish Establishment regiment had a third fewer private soldiers than one on the British Establishment, the number of NCOs were the same. This provided a regimental structure ideal for training recruits and for expansion in wartime.

---

30   Houlding, *Fit for Service*, pp.1–2, 8, 28, 41.
31   Houlding, *Fit for Service*, pp.290, 294–295.
32   Houlding, *Fit for Service*, pp.128–129, n.60, 270, 419, 421.

In September 1771, the re-establishment of the light companies increased the establishment of all regiments to 477.[33]

This meant that before 1770, any regiment moving from one establishment to the other had to recruit, or discharge, significant numbers of soldiers. Clearly this was inefficient. It also meant that an Irish Establishment regiment had to recruit significantly before it was at full strength to deploy overseas. The most extreme example of this was probably in the mid-1730s when, in response to a Franco-Spanish declaration of war against Austria, eight battalions moved from Ireland to reinforce British defences, which necessitated recruiting 6,680 additional soldiers, all of whom were discharged when the international situation settled down and the regiments returned to Ireland.[34]

There were three means of bringing an understrength regiment up to or close to full strength: recruiting, drafting and additional companies. Recruiting 'by beat of drum' was the normal means of attracting new soldiers. The downside was that recruits needed training when time would be at a premium for a regiment warned off for an operational deployment. The proficiency of recruits was always going to be below that of pre-war soldiers. Drafting was an established practice for bringing under strength regiments up to full strength, but at the expense of rendering some regiments *hors de combat* for several years. It did at least provide the receiving regiment with trained soldiers. Peter Brown gives an extreme example of the 93rd Foot which lost 515 men in three drafts during 1760 and 1761, so it could only muster 188 rank and file, of which 45 were sick. The 93rd was operationally non-effective while the morale of any remaining officers and senior NCOs would have been greatly reduced. The process of drafting was regulated, as shown in by an order of 3 December 1775, where the privates of the 18th and 59th Foot were drafted into the other regiments of the Boston garrison. The receiving regiments paid £5 per man to the old regiment for the expense of replacing the soldier and also settled the man's accounts for rations etc. The draftees were to receive a uniform of the receiving regiment and 1½ Guineas. The 54th Foot was reviewed at Cork and found not 'fitt [sic] for service' having drafted many men to the Boston Garrison, including the 47th.[35] At the end of the war, survivors of the 47th in Canada were drafted into the 8th Foot. Similarly, the 44th Foot returned from Canada in 1787 having drafted half of its strength to regiments remaining there, receiving indifferent men in exchange, and so was also unfit for service.[36] The additional companies method was a wartime expedient for recruiting for a regiment serving overseas. Two additional companies were authorised per regiment in 1775. Details of the augmentation were issued in Boston on 20 November 1775, but would have been promulgated earlier for regiments in Britain and Ireland.

---

33   Smythies, *40th Regiment*, pp.547–548.
34   Brown, *Army of George II*, p.81; Houlding, *Fit for Service*, pp.49, 51.
35   Houlding, *Fit for Service*, p.14.
36   Brown, *Army of George II*, p.25; Houlding, *Fit for Service*, pp.121, 125, 273–274; E.E. Hale, B.F. Stevens, and W.H. Howe (eds), *General Sir William Howe's Orderly Book* (London: Benjamin Franklin Stevens, 1890), p.159, 3 December 1775.

The new establishment of 12 companies included a third sergeant and second drummer per company and a total strength of 855. Commanding officers of regiments in the Boston garrison were to consider which officers and NCOs were to raise the additional companies, but were not to consider officers in the grenadier or light companies. Additional companies could be combined for battalion level training, but were not intended to be operational sub-units. They recruited, trained, and sent soldiers to join the regiment; Lieutenant Thomas Anburey (29th Foot) escorted a party of 47th recruits to Quebec City in late 1776. In 1777, both of the 33rd's additional companies were sent to Quebec City. They had expected to join the remainder of the regiment there but the 33rd had moved to New York, so the additional companies were employed supporting Burgoyne's artillery. Burgoyne's freedom of movement was severely curtailed by logistical difficulties arising from poor roads worsened by the actions of retreating rebels forces, such as felling trees over roads or diverting waterways to flood them, and a lack of wagons and horses from the outset. However, two companies of recruits under military discipline would ease the logistical challenges faced by Burgoyne's artillery, in contrast with unreliable civilian contractors.[37]

During peacetime, and also during wartime, the major occupation for the British Army in the British Isles was support to the civil authorities, which today would be called Military Assistance to the Civil Authorities (MACA). The army undertook duties which today would be the responsibility of the police or similar agencies, principally civil disorder, and anti-smuggling. Civil disorder generally arose from two impetus, economic change (either from economic downturn or changing practices), and food (hunger) riots. 1766 was a particularly bad year for hunger riots, with 131 being recorded following a poor harvest. Some turned violent, as at the Nottingham Cheese Fair.[38] Support to excise officers in anti-smuggling operations occupied many troops for long periods in isolated detachments operating against well-armed and well-motivated smuggling gangs with detailed local knowledge and support.[39] Political riots occurred regularly. The Massacre of St George's Field occurred in London in May 1768 following the imprisonment of radical member of parliament, John Wilkes, resulting in six or seven killed. The most serious and notorious in this period was the 1780 anti-Catholic Gordon Riots during which the government lost control of London for 10 days. Thousands of troops were deployed into London when they could have been better employed on anti-invasion duties. Riots also occurred in opposition to taxation, for example on cider in 1763 which was met which such opposition that it was repealed in 1766. So, while Boston in particular, and to a lesser extent, New York, are held up as exemplars of riot in protection of English liberties, relative to their cousins in Britain and Ireland, the colonies were

---

37 Houlding, *Fit for Service*, pp.118-119; T. Anburey, *Travels through the Interior Parts of America* (London: William Lane, 1789), vol.I, p.5, Letter II, 11 Sept 1776; Hale, Stevens & Howe (eds), *Orderly Book*, pp.145–146, 20 November 1775.
38 Brown, *Army of George II*, pp.42–43; J. Bohstedt, *The Politics of Provisions: Food Riots, Moral Economy and Market Transition in England, c. 1550–1850* (Farnham: Routledge, 2010), p.122; Houlding, *Fit for Service*, pp.60, 66–74.
39 Brown, *Army of George II*, pp.43–45; Houlding, *Fit for Service*, pp.75–90.

surprisingly pacific and quiet.[40] This reflected the light hand of parliament on the colonies until after 1763.

Between the end of the Williamite Wars in 1691 and the 1798 Irish Rebellion, Ireland was relatively quiet; Houlding described it as 'one of the most quiet' periods in Irish history. There were riots and other tasks to assist the civil authorities, but the same as occurred in England, Wales and Lowland Scotland. The lower establishment of regiments in Ireland does not suggest the need for a heavy-handed military. Houlding sees the Irish Establishment not as an army of occupation, but as an strategic reserve.[41] The increase to regimental strength for the Irish Establishment and its equalisation with its British counterparts occurred during a period of quiet in between two global wars. It was a sensible reform to ease the movement of regiments around the British Isles and overseas; it was not a reaction to any Irish instability. In 1769, the 5th, 38th and 47th Regiments were reviewed together in Limerick. Six years later, they would serve together at Bunker Hill. Houlding has identified that of the 27 regiments to undertake reviews and mock battles at Phoenix Park, Dublin, between 1768–1777, all served overseas in the American War of Independence. Similarly, 17 of Howe's 27 regiments which fought on Long Island in 1776 had previously exercised on Phoenix Park.[42] This all strengthens the idea of the Irish Establishment as preparing regiments for overseas operational deployments.

It is also interesting to note a difference between the inspection regimes of the British and Irish Establishments. These reports did highlight deficiencies where they were found, as has been shown above. Reports for both establishments are approximately A2 (ANSI C) sized printed forms with additional information recorded in immaculate copperplate script. The information recorded about the 47th Foot is discussed in further detail in Chapter 3. Four of the 47th's inspection returns for the years 1768, 1769, 1771 and 1772 have been examined. The pages concerning the inspecting officer's observations are full of the description of their appearance and, more importantly, the 'Movements, Evolutions, Firings & Manoeuvres'. The other inspection returns examined follow this pattern: 5th, 38th and 47th Foot at Dublin in 1768; the 5th and 47th Foot at Limerick in 1769; and six regiments at Dublin in 1771. In contrast, those of the British Establishment were noticeably less detailed in their information: the 20th Foot at Exeter, 29th Foot at Dover and the 33rd Foot at Plymouth, all in 1774.[43] There is a noticeable distinction which further suggests that the regiments on the Irish Establishment were held at a higher readiness state than those on the British Establishment.

---

40   Houlding, *Fit for Service*, pp.62, 64–65.
41   Houlding, *Fit for Service*, p.48; M. Zembo, 'Counter insurgency: Ireland and America', *The Lion and the Dragon* (forthcoming, Spring 2022).
42   Houlding, *Fit for Service*, pp.309–310; TNA: WO 27/17: Inspection Returns, Irish, 1769.
43   TNA: WO 27/15: Inspection Returns, Irish, 1768; WO 27/17: Inspection Returns, Irish, 1769; WO 27/23: Inspection Returns, Irish, 1771; WO 27/26: Inspection Returns, Irish, 1772; WO 27/30: Inspection Returns, British, 1774. The author was only able to conduct a limited survey due to the restrictions existing in 2020, but this topic would benefit from a more extensive survey.

The British Army in the decade of peace of the early-1760s and the mid-1770s operated in a duality of separate establishments. Their main tasks were support to the civil authorities, and marching to and occupying various dispersed garrison locations. All of this detracted from their training requirements although the Irish Establishment was fortunate with a much more comprehensive network of barracks than existed elsewhere in the British Isles. At the beginning of this period, the strength of a regiment on the Irish Establishment was significantly less than that of a regiment on the British Establishment. This produced a pool of trained and experience officers and NCOs upon which a future expansion of the army could be based. The process of raising new regiments was expensive, and it took time to gain the level of experience required at all ranks. In 1770, the equalising of the regimental strengths was a sensible rationalisation which made the Irish Establishment regiments more readily deployable. The annual inspection reports did not simply rubberstamp a regiment's appearance and performance. They could and did report harshly on those regiments which needed to improve. The Irish Establishment reports appear to have been more detailed, which might suggest that they were held at a higher state of readiness for operations. When you combine the increase in the regimental strength, the more detailed observations in the inspection returns and Houlding's observation on the large number of the Irish Establishment to serve overseas during the American War of Independence, this all points towards the Irish Establishment being a force developed for expeditionary warfare in defence of the growing empire. Once regiments left the Irish Establishment for an overseas posting, they were replaced by another from the British Establishment which would provide them with the opportunity for their state of readiness to be raised. This was not an army of occupation, but an army for imperial defence.

3

Who Were the 47th Foot?

The Sources

This chapter will analyse the officers and soldiers of the 47th Foot, their appearance and characteristics, and will be predominantly based on three inspection returns for 1768, 1769, 1771 and 1772. The report for 1770 is unfortunately missing. These returns are held at The National Archives as parts of WO24/14, WO 27/17, WO 27/23 and WO 27/26 respectively. There are no surviving returns from the regiment's time in North America. In addition, quarterly muster rolls have been used for the following periods:

- Quebec, October 1760 to August 1763
- Ireland, January 1772 to May 1773
- Various locations in North America, January 1774 to July 1778 (incomplete)
- England, February 1782 and August 1783.

Muster rolls listed the officers, NCOs, drummers and fifers, and private soldiers by company on a specific date. They also specified the company's location and provided a descriptor for those who were not present, for example 'sick', 'furlough' or 'deserted'. The muster rolls are also held at The National Archives as WO 12/5871.

The 1772 inspection return provided the most current information on the regiment before it sailed for North America. When read in conjunction with earlier inspection returns, they provide an opportunity for analysis of the regiment's changing characteristics over time.

The Regimental Structure

The 47th was conventionally structured in nine companies, one grenadier and eight centre companies. The formation of a light company was ordered on 18 September 1771 and together with the grenadier company were collectively referred to as the flank companies as when the battalion was in

Field return 47th Foot, 1772. This shows a strength of 313 of an 'allowance' of 360 around the time when the 47th sailed for North America. (The National Archives)

Return of arms, 1772. The 47th had been receiving new arms and accoutrements over the previous two or three years. (The National Archives)

The ensigns of the 47th, 1772. Thomas Handfield had 13 years' service as an ensign. He was commissioned when the regiment fought in the St Lawrence Campaign in 1759 and may have been commissioned from the ranks. He was evidently without the connections or financial resources to advance. In contrast, his fellow ensigns were all recently commissioned with less than three years' service. (The National Archives)

WHO WERE THE 47TH FOOT?

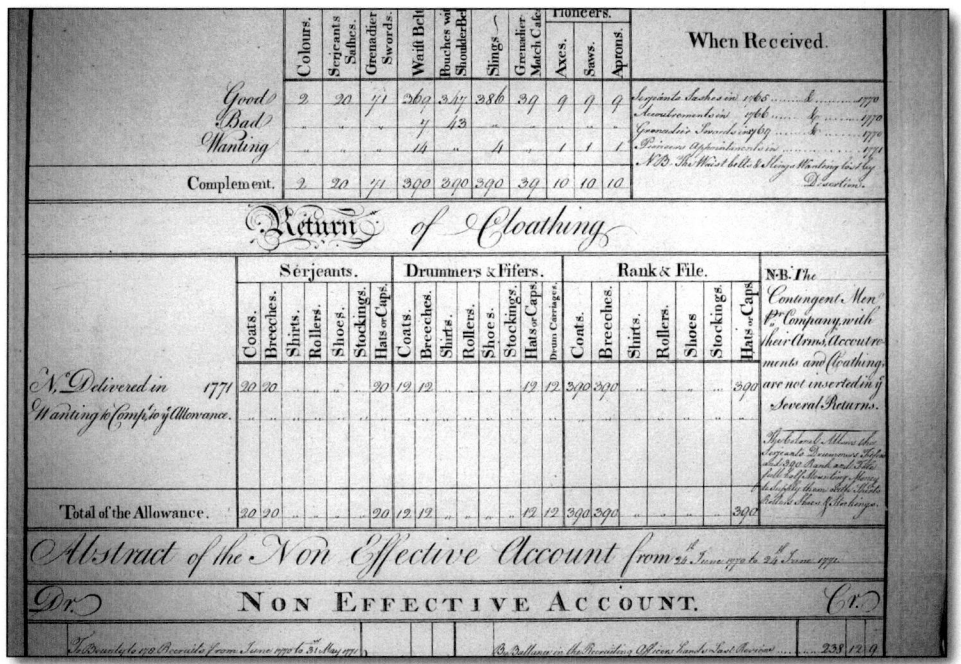

Ages by companies, 1772. Most of the 47th were young men in their twenties. (The National Archives)

Nationality by Company, 1772. There were almost the same number of English (including Welsh) and Irish soldiers in the 47th, but relatively few Scottish. The 'Foreign' men present were born in the British territories outside of the British Isles. (The National Archives)

Return of clothing, 1772. In 1771, the 47th received enough clothing for two serjeants, one Drummer and 39 corporals and privates for each of the 10 companies; two fifers for the grenadier company accounts for the extra 'Drummers and Fifers'. (The National Archives)

Length of service by company, 1772. There were a number of old hands with over 10 years' service which would have provided them with operational experience from the French and Indian War. This experience would be vital when the regiment returned to Quebec in 1776. This contrasts with over half the regiment having one or two years' service. This was hardly a veteran formation. (The National Archives)

Size by company, 1772. Most men were around five feet seven inches tall, but there were a number around six feet or more who must have towered over their fellows. (The National Archives)

line the grenadiers formed on the right and the light company on the left.[1] The company naming convention was by the captain's name, including for the flank companies. After 1770, the standard company consisted of one captain, one lieutenant, one ensign, two sergeants, three corporals, a drummer and 38 private soldiers. The flank companies can be identified in the muster rolls by their different establishment; the officers were a captain and two lieutenants. This reflected the traditional detached nature of these companies which required more experienced officers. The grenadier company also had two fifers in addition to the standard single drummer.

Three of the company captains were not actually captains. The colonel, the lieutenant colonel and the major were also captains and their companies were described as '[senior rank] and Captain'. The colonel was Major General Carleton and he was styled 'Major General and Colonel and Captain'. To recognise the reality that colonels did not serve with their regiments, his lieutenant held the rank of captain lieutenant. For the lieutenant colonel's and major's companies, their companies were commanded by their lieutenant. These companies were usually referred to as the colonel's or

---

1 Smythies, *40th Regiment*, pp.547–548.

general's, lieutenant colonel's, or major's companies. Although a regiment was established for 30 regimental officers (three per company), three did not serve with their companies which reduced the company officer strength at company level by 10 percent.

The company commanders in April 1773 are listed below:

Major General Guy Carleton
Lieutenant Colonel William Nesbitt
Major Hugh Carncross
Captain John Alcock
Captain Thomas Aubrey
Captain James Craig
Captain Richard England
Captain Aemelius Irving
Captain William Sherriff (light)
Captain Thomas Smelt (grenadier)

The Regiment, its Appearance, Weapons and Equipment

Arms

The appearance of the 47th Foot was regulated by the Royal Clothing Warrant of 1768. The annual inspection return would confirm the regiment's adherence to policy and noted any variations from it. At Limerick in 1769, Major General the Earl of Drogheda, confirmed that the officers 'All Conform to His Majesty's Last Regulations', being 'Well Dressed' with coats 'Scarlet with White Cape, lappells & Cuffs, lined with white' and 'White Waistcoat & Breeches'. The presence of the white 'cape' (collar), waistcoat and breeches conformed to the new 1768 Clothing Warrant. The red waistcoats and breeches, and coat without a 'cape' of the old uniform were gone. The officer's wore silver epaulettes and, unusually, 'Silver Scolloped Laced Hatts', but the section ends with a very strange statement that 'Officer's Swords & Gorgets bespoke but not yet come to the Regiment'. As it is unlikely that officers would be without swords or gorgets, this comment implies that items which varied from the standard patterns had been ordered. The sergeants, drummers, and rank and file were 'Clean and Well Dressed', although it went on to describe the clothing as 'Old but Clean Well fitted And agreeable to the Patterns approve of by the Board of General Officers'. The one item of clothing which stands out is 'Black Gaiters with Stiff Tops & Black Garters'.

Two years later, at Phoenix Park, Dublin in front of Lieutenant General Michael Dilkes, they were described as wearing 'Black Gaytors' and in 1772 at Charlesfort near Cork in front of the Earl of Drogheda again, they were wearing 'Spatterdashes according to Order'. Over the four years covered by the three inspections, the 47th had moved from knee length gaiters with leather knee pads, to a shorter style reaching just to the lower calf. The only negative comment in 1772 referred to the accoutrements, some of which were found wanting.

A VERY FINE REGIMENT

In 1769, under 'Return of the Arms', the regiment held 261 muskets which were described as 122 'Good', 129 'Bad', and 10 'Wanting', that is not possessed by the regiment for example due to deserters taking a musket with them. Later, the inspecting general's 'Observations of the Arms' recorded: 'Bright But very Bad'. Two years later there were 387 'Fuzils' and 'Firelocks' which had been received in 1769 and 1770. Unsurprisingly, 355 of these muskets were 'Good', with only 20 'Bad' and 10 'Wanting'; the inspecting general described the arms as: 'Bright and in good Order'. The following year, there were 390 muskets with 287 'Good', 88 'Bad' and 15 'Wanting' ('lost by Desertion'), and described as 'Clean and in good Order'. Clearly, there was a marked improvement in the quality of the muskets carried after 1771 compared with 1769, which is supported by statements that they were received in 1769 and 1770. It likely that these new muskets received in 1769 and 1770 were the 1769 Short Land Pattern. As the 47th were based in Ireland, it is likely that they were the Irish rather than the British pattern. Goldstein and Mowbray speak of 20 regiments receiving the Irish Pattern 1769 before departing to the Americas after the outbreak of hostilities. The 47th was not on that list of 20, having sailed to the Americas in 1773.[2]

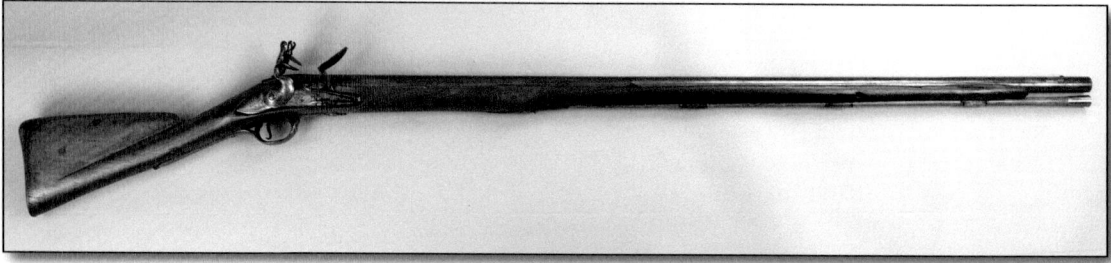

1742 Long Land Pattern Musket with wooden ramrod once belonging to the 47th Foot (Fort Ticonderoga)

---

2   E. Goldstein, & S. Mowbray, *The Brown Bess: an identification guide and illustrated study of Britain's most famous musket* (Woonsocket, WI: Mowbray, 2010), pp.102–111.

The question of the musket carried by the regiment is confused by the existence of a 1742 Long Land Service Musket in the collection of the Fort Ticonderoga Museum engraved with '47 REGT FT' on the barrel. It is also stamped 4/79. Initially, this would suggest a company number and 'butt number', but there were fewer than 79 soldiers in a company. In 1773 this averaged 43, and even at the end of the French and Indian War, when company strengths were significantly larger, they were not that large.[3] This could represent a regimental 'butt number'.

Where does this place the Fort Ticonderoga Long Land Pattern? It is believed that this was brought to North America during the American War of Independence by a recruit joining the regiment, possibly by one of those escorted by Thomas Auburey in 1776.[4]

Colours, Sashes and Other Accoutrements
Regiments carried two colours, the King's Colour based on the Union Flag, and the Colonel's Colour based on the regiment's facing colour, white, which also included the red Cross of Saint George. Two new colours had been received in 1760, which seems curious given that they were fighting in and around Quebec and Montreal with a style of warfare where the carrying of colours was inappropriate. These were presumably the colours taken to America in 1773 and whose fate following the Saratoga campaign remains a mystery.

In 1771, there were supposed to be 387 sets of accoutrements, although as some items were missing there were only 360 complete sets; a year later this was nominally 390 sets. The additional sets were new that year. There were also nine sets of equipment for pioneers (axes, saws and aprons) which were all inspected with new 'Appointments' that year. The pioneer's roles included route clearance and bridge building for the regiment on the march, and also destruction of obstacles. It is assumed that they were distributed one per company but as none of the soldiers are ever identified as pioneers, who they were and how they were organised regimentally remains a mystery.

Amongst the uniform items which distinguished the grenadiers were the sword (or hanger) which were no longer worn by the other soldiers in the regiment, and the matchcase. This was a brass item worn on the cartridge pouch strap which originally contained the lit match for igniting the grenades but by the 1770s was no longer used for that purpose. In 1771, there were 71 grenadier's swords, bought in 1769 and 1770 but only 39 matchcases. The extra swords are accounted for if the sergeants, drummers and fifers are included, implying that wore the same style of grenadier's sword.

Sergeants were identified by their halberd, sash and coat. In 1768, there were 18 sergeant's sashes, two for each of the nine companies, and they were new in 1764, shortly after the regiment returned from North America. Were

---

3   Captain Thomas Smelt's company at Charlesburg in August 1763 only had 54 privates, three corporals, three sergeants and four officers, making 64 who could require a musket; TNA: WO 12/5871: Muster Rolls, 47th Foot August 1763.
4   Private communication with Don Troiani 10 January 2020; Anburey, *Travels*, vol.I, pp.4–7, Letter II, 11 Sept 1776.

these amongst the niceties of European warfare which had been discarded in the face of the realities of forest warfare in North America? The sergeant's sashes were also new in 1769 and 1770. There were 27, representing three sergeants for each of nine companies. There were also 27 sergeant's coats and breeches. By 1772 there were just 20 sets of halberds, sergeant's sashes, coats, breeches and hats or caps. This represented two sergeants for each of the 10 companies including the two sergeants of the new light company. Waistcoats are not mentioned.

Grenadiers, drummers and fifers wore a bearskin cap with a lacquered plate at the front. In 1769 they were described as newly delivered the previous year. There were 18 caps for the sergeants (two per company) and nine caps for the drummers (one per company), but this left the two fifers of the grenadier company without a cap. Similarly, the number of 'Hats or Caps' for the enlisted men (261) matched the number of coats and sets of accoutrements. Benedict Cuthbertson recommended wearing a hat for everyday duties to preserve the bearskin cap for best, but there is no evidence of that practice in the 47th[5]. By 1772, there were 12 drummer's hats, coats and breeches (again, waistcoats are not mentioned), drums and drum carriages. That would be one drummer for each of 10 companies and an additional two fifers for the grenadier company. The fifers were clearly classed as drummers for the purposes of clothing and accoutrements, but were listed separately on the muster roll.

The Manual Exercise

Having been inspected, the regiment (sometimes in concert with other regiments) performed first the manual exercise and, secondly, movements, evolutions, firing and manoeuvres. The former was a set drills with the musket and bayonet including facing (turning) to the left, right and about (through 180 degrees). On all four occasions they were performed to satisfaction:

> 1768 – Well performed and aggregable to His Majesty's Last Regulations.
> 1769 – Exceedingly Well Performed and Exactly according to HM's Regulations.
> 1771 – Well performed and according to His Majesty's last Regulations.
> 1772 – Performed very well, and Exactly to His Majesty's Regulations.

The movements, evolutions, firing and manoeuvres were considerably more complicated and could only be practiced during a regimental concentration. When this practice occurred is unclear because, as will be shown below, the regiment was normally divided into several garrison locations. Nevertheless, these movements were performed to the inspecting general's satisfaction. Using the 1772 inspection as an example, having received the general (saluted him) and performed the manual exercise, the regiment fired by subdivisions (companies), from right to left. They then advanced by grand

---

5   B. Cuthbertson, *A System for the Complete Interior Management and Œconomy of a Battalion of Infantry* (London: J. Millan, 1779), p.58.

divisions (pairs of companies), then by wings (the four companies either side of the colours) and finally the whole battalion. The battalion then retreated by grand divisions in an Indian (single) file and the light company covered the retreat. Once the battalion had formed, the light company took up positions on the flank. The battalion then advanced and retreated in column, formed battalion (line) and fired by subdivisions (companies). Each wing then formed a column to the right by grand division, that is a column with a frontage of two companies, advanced, retreated and fired in column. Then they formed battalion and fired by grand divisions. The next manoeuvre was to form square, then they marched to the front, advanced, retreated, fired twice, and charged. The battalion then re-formed and fired once by subdivision.

They next formed a solid column from the centre during which the grenadier company covered the head and the light company the rear. They then fired from the different facings and charged from the centre divisions. Next, they formed a reserve of colours, formed battalion, and fired by grand divisions. The next manoeuvre was arguably more relevant to the trials that they would face in North America. In order to cross a river by a bridge, the light company lined the banks to fire, and then rushed the bridge. Presumably the remainder of the battalion followed across as they formed the battalion again and fired by subdivisions. They then repassed the bridge, fired by grand divisions and broke down into subdivisions, then reformed the battalion to fire by subdivisions. Next, they wheeled by wings from the centre to protect their flanks, then fired twice by subdivisions from the centre of each wing. The battalion was reformed and fired once by wings. They then formed an 'oblong square'[6] in which formation it marched and retreated.

Once again, they formed battalion, advanced by wings, formed battalion once more and changed 'Front to the Right and Fired by Sub Divisions'. They then retreated by the left by grand divisions and by subdivisions, forming the battalion by the left. They then wheeled to the right by the centre and fired by subdivisions. Next, they retreated from the right by subdivisions by files and formed the battalion by the right. They formed the oblong square again, formed the 'Battalion on the Long March', formed the square, formed the battalion on the march, formed the battalion on its 'First Front', fired and retreated by subdivisions alternatively twice, formed the battalion on the right, formed the battalion on its 'First Front', fired a volley and charged. All of this was performed at the double-quick time, 180 paces per minute. All the proceeding drill must have been exhausting at that pace with so many constant manoeuvres to perform. It does show that the regiment was capable of conducting a wide range of manoeuvres, at speed, with obstacle

---

6   The square was formed by two centre companies forming each side of a square. A platoon (half company) of the grenadier and light companies each reinforced a corner. The 'Oblong Square' was formed from a column of companies in line. The grenadier and light companies formed the front and rear respectively. The eight centre companies then wheeled outwards a platoon (half company) to fill the gap between the front and rear. The front and rear had a frontage of one company, but the length had the frontage of the equivalent of four companies. See T. Simes, *The Military Guide for Young Officers* (Philadelphia, PA: Humphreys, Bell and Aitken, 1776), vol.II, Frontspiece.

crossings, to counter any threat that they were likely to encounter. Major General Drogheda was satisfied, reporting: 'This Regiment Performed all their Exercise, and Manoeuvres, with the greatest Exactness & Attention And is a Very Fine Regiment and Fit for Service.'[7]

Garrison Distribution

Between deployments to North America, the 47th was stationed in Ireland, including Dublin, Athlone, Carrick-on-Shannon and Limerick. During the early 1770s, the regiment was normally distributed in several garrisons around Cork.[8] In January and April 1772, the regiment was concentrated at Charlesfort (sometimes written Charles Fort) located on the north side of Kinsale Harbour, 17 miles north of the city of Cork. The fort was built in 1682 by Charles II as a bastion fort with a section of the curtain wall built in the star style. It remained as a British Army barracks until the Anglo-Irish Treaty of 1921; the following year it was burned by retreating anti-treaty Irish forces.

While at Charlesfort in 1772, the inspection return described the buildings, utensils and 'firing' as good although, 'The greatest part of the bedding totally unfit for use.'[9] The previous year at Dublin Castle their accommodation was: 'in General in good Order. The Rooms Gallerys and Stair Cases want to be White Washed. The Bedsteads, Tables & Fourms in very Bad Repair.'[10] While two years previously in the Castle Barracks of Limerick it was 'in Good Order & repair' and the 'Firing' and Candles were all in accordance with the Government allowances.[11]

From Cork, the outlying garrisons radiated out in all directions to about 30 miles. Inchigeelagh was some 34 miles to the west and Clonakilty a similar distance to the southwest. Bandon is 27 miles southwest of Cork. Youghal lies 32 miles to the east. Monks Town is nine miles to the southeast and Cove (Cobh) is 14 miles east of Cork. From early 1772, the regiment was dispersed in five locations with between one and three companies in each. Cork or Cork Harbour had three companies (Irving's, Smelt's and Sherriff's) until May 1773 when they were joined by England's company immediately before departing for New York. Bandon was garrisoned by Lieutenant Colonel Nesbitt's company and from October 1772 by Craig's company. Youghal was garrisoned by Aubrey's and England's companies. Clonakilty was the home of Alcock's and Craig's companies until the latter moved to Bandon in October 1772. At Inchigeelagh were Colonel Carleton's and Captain Carncross's companies. By May 1773 there was a significant re-deployment of the companies. In addition to a fourth company moving to Cork, one (Aubrey's) moved to Cove and the remainder to Monks Town. This concentration was very likely in preparation for the regiment's deployment to North America.

---

7   TNA: WO 27/26: Inspection Return, Irish, 1772 47th Foot.
8   Wylly, *Loyal North Lancashire*, vol.I, p.50.
9   TNA: WO 27/23: Inspection Returns, Irish, 1772, 47th Foot.
10 TNA: WO 27/31: Inspection Return, Irish, 1771, 24th Foot.
11 TNA: WO 27/17: Inspection Returns, Irish, 1769, 47th Foot.

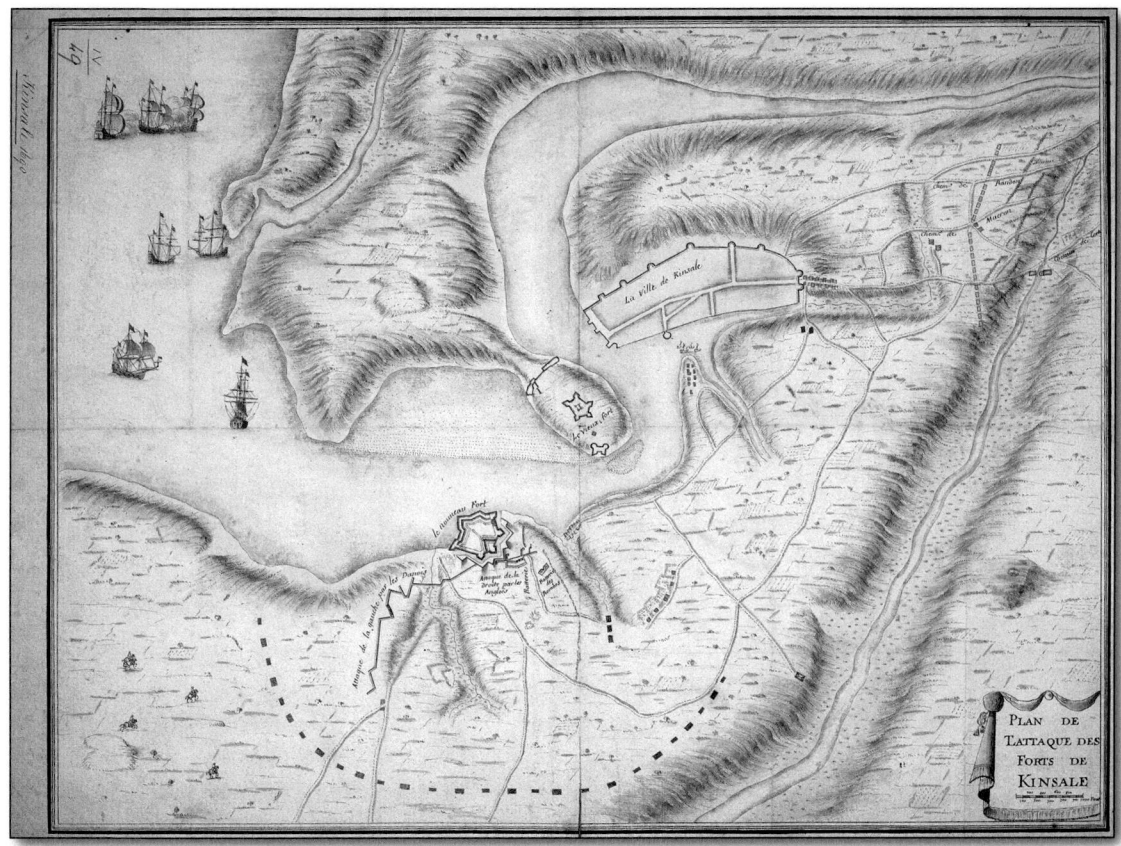

Charles Fort and the smaller James Fort positioned to protect Kinsale from the sea. (Royal Collection Trust / © Her Majesty Queen Elizabeth II 2021 RCIN 724049)

Regimental Strength

Over the 18 months of 1772 and early 1773, the six quarterly muster rolls show an average of 43 officers and men per company, although this dipped to a low of just under 40 per company in October 1772. Recruiting fluctuated, with an average of 11 per quarter, peaking in April 1773 with 34 recruits, or over half the total for the period. The nationality (English (including Welsh), Scottish, Irish or Foreign) of those recruits is not recorded. Seven men died in service, or just over one per quarter. No causes of death were given. Thirteen men or just over two per quarter, were discharged. Again, no further details were provided.

Desertion is an issue used to highlight the (stereotypically) harsh, brutal life of a soldier, even in peacetime. Over the period, eight men deserted (just over one per quarter) but also four men returned. The names of the four returnees are not the same as any of those listed as deserting. It is assumed that they deserted before January 1772 and the details would be recorded in muster rolls which have not been examined. Dr Ilya Berkovich has observed that British Army muster rolls do not indicate whether a deserter returned voluntarily or forcibly. The 47th's muster rolls follow this pattern.[12]

12　I. Berkovich, *Motivation in War: the experiences of common soldiers in Old-Regime Europe* (Cambridge: Cambridge University Press, 2017), p.68.

In 1772, each company could be expected to have three private soldiers on furlough in any one quarter, or about 10 percent of the company strength. By 1773, however, this tailed off quickly with less than two per company in January of that year, and by April, only four across the whole regiment, or about one percent. With their embarkation date drawing closer, furlough was curtailed.

The 1772 inspection return shows that the 47th had a regimental strength of around 360 men, although analysis of the muster rolls for April 1773 show a lower figure of 338. The regiment was established for the following when it sailed to America:

Regimental Officers – 30
Staff – 5
Sergeants – 20
Corporals – 30
Drummers – 10
Fifers – 2
Other Ranks – 380

So, the regiment was recruited to 95 percent of its authorised strength.[13] This was much smaller than the seven infantry regiments studied by Pippin (see Table 3.4 below), by about 175 men but, as has been shown in the previous chapter, once hostilities commenced regimental strengths were increased. Pippin's larger, later war regiments represent the expanded wartime-establishment from three officers, two sergeants, 38 corporals and private men, and one drummer per company to three officers, three sergeants, two drummers, and 56 corporals and private soldiers per company.[14]

The Regimental Officers

Table 3.1 shows the biographical details from the return of officers in 1772, consisting of the rank, name, nationality, age and length of service, and the date at which they had attained their respective ranks. Of the 27 officers listed, the majority (17, or 63 percent) were Irish. There were only six English officers (which included Welsh), and one of those was Colonel Lascelles who appears never to have been present with the regiment in this period. Lascelles would be replaced by Irish-born Carleton on 4 April 1772 which further increased the Irishness of the regiment. Three officers were Scottish and one 'Foreigner' – Ensign John Webb. Unfortunately, Webb's nationality is not recorded. He was commissioned, aged about 21, in 1759 so it is likely that he was born in one of Britain's North American colonies. Steven Baule's study of the 18th Foot, the Royal Irish, found that it was often 'more Irish in name than in fact', with English (and Welsh) providing about 40 percent of the officers.[15] The 47th's officers were more Irish than those of the Royal Irish.

---

13 Smythies, *40th Regiment*, pp.547–548.
14 Hale, Stevens & Howe (eds), *Orderly Book*, p.132, 10 November 1775.
15 Baule, *Protecting the Empire's Frontier*, p.39, Table 1.3, Table 1.4.

WHO WERE THE 47TH FOOT?

Table 3.1: Return of Officers from TNA: WO 21/23: Irish Inspection Return 1771 for the 47th Foot

Rank	Name		English	Scotch	Irish	Foreigners	Age	Service	Ensign	Lt	Capt Lt	Capt	Major	Lt Col	Col
Colonel	Peregrine	Lascelles[16]	1				87	65	12 Apr 06						13 Mar 42
Lt Col	William	Nesbitt			1		41	20	20 Apr 51	15 Oct 54		2 Sept 56	4 Feb 60	24 Nov 62	
Major	Hugh	Carncross			1		32	11	3 Mar 60	26 Jan 62		21 Mar 65	29 Sept 70		
Capt	Thomas	Smelt	1				40	25	9 Apr 46	1 Jun 50	18 Dec 56	20 Mar 58			
Capt	Henry	Goddard			1		43	26	4 Nov 45	23 Jun 53	28 May 60	15 Feb 61			
Capt	Nicholas	Evans			1		30	12	25 Aug 59	21 May 65		18 Jun 66			
Capt	Paulus	Irving			1		22	9	28 Sept 61	15 Jun 64		29 Oct 68			
Capt	Richard	England			1		24	6	24 Nov 65	6 Nov 69		29 Sept 70			
Capt	Thomas	Craig	1									14 Mar 71			
Capt Lt	Richard	L'Estrange			1		26	6	13 Jun 65	1 Jun 69	6 Nov 69				
Lt	George	Mountain	1				40	16	26 Jun 55	9 Dec 55					
Lt	Henry	Marr		1			35	16	3 Jul 55	20 Mar 58					
Lt	Richard	Gold	1				32	15	30 Jun 56	23 Aug 58					
Lt	John	McKinnon		1			30	9	24 Feb 62	15 Jun 65					
Lt	Michael	Hudson			1		26	7	15 Jun 64	29 Oct 68					
Lt	John	Alcock			1		23	4	13 Mar 67	6 Nov 69					
Lt	Christopher	Hilliard			1		23	3	28 May 68	10 Feb 70					
Lt	Thomas	Storey			1		16	8	N/K	20 Apr 63					
Lt	John	Gabbett			1		21	2	1 Jun 69	29 Sept 70					
Ensign	John	Webb				1	33	12	15 Apr 59						
Ensign	Robert	Dupont	1				31	12	25 Sept 59						
Ensign	Donald	McLoed		1			34	11	4 May 60						
Ensign	Benjamin	Sprout			1		23	3	29 Oct 68						
Ensign	Pool	England			1		22	2	6 Nov 69						
Ensign	Gerrard	Irvine			1		22	2	6 Nov 69						
Ensign	James	Poe			1		20	1	10 Feb 70						
Ensign	James	Parnier			1		20	1	29 Sept 70						

---

16   Replaced by Guy Carleton on 4 April 1772.

Table 3.2: Average Age and Length of Service by Rank in 1771

Rank	Average Age	Average Service	Average Age at Commissioning
Colonel	87	65	22
Lieutenant Colonel	41	20	21
Major	32	11	21
Captain	31.8	15.6	16.2
Captain Lieutenant	26	6	20
Lieutenant	27.3	8.9	18.4
Ensign	25.6	5.5	20.1

Table 3.2 shows the average age at commissioning, by rank. This was around 20. The youngest at commissioning in the 47th were Lieutenant Thomas Storey, aged 16 but already with eight years' service so commissioned aged eight, and 22 year old Captain Paulus Irving with nine year's service so commissioned around 13. Baule's study of the 18th Foot gives an average age of 18, but with examples as young as 10 or 11.[17] Amongst the captains we see a significantly reduced age at commissioning of around 16. Thomas Smelt and Henry Goddard had been commissioned at the time of the 1745 Jacobite Rebellion at the age of 15 and 17 respectively.

Returning to Table 3.1, at the other extreme were several senior lieutenants and even ensigns with over a decade's service. Their dates for appointment were all during the French and Indian War. Wartime vacancies could be filled by commissioning from the ranks or promotion at the lieutenant colonel's discretion. Ensigns John Webb, Robert Duport and Donald McLoed all had 11 or 12 years of service having been commissioned in 1759 or 1760. Despite numerous opportunities for promotion to lieutenant, they did not receive one. Similarly, Lieutenants George Mountain, Henry Marr and Richard Gold all had 15 or 16 years service, received wartime commissions (in 1755 or 1756) and wartime promotions to lieutenant in 1755 or 1758), but had subsequently progressed no further.

Two of the officers were listed in the inspection return of 1771 (dated 22 May) but were not mentioned the following year; Ensigns Webb and Sprout. Sprout was 23 and commissioned when aged 20. He does not appear on the 1772 Army List so probably resigned his commission. Webb transferred to the 28th Foot on 5 June 1771, after the 47th's inspection return of that year, on promotion to lieutenant to create a vacancy for John Pitt, whose career in the 47th will be discussed in detail later on.[18] It is possible that some of these long-serving junior officers were commissioned from the ranks but lacked the financial resources or social connections to obtain promotion. Houlding examined the commissioning of NCOs in the British Army during the

---

17   Baule, *Protecting the Empire's Frontier*, p.53.
18   Baule, *Protecting the Empire's Frontier*, p.44 identified 11-year-old Ensign James Taylor Trevor who was considered too young to travel with the 18th Foot to the frontier. He transferred to another regiment, the 55th, which had returned from North America a few years previously and so were unlikely to go back for the foreseeable future. They did participate in operations around New York from 1776. Webb and Sprout do not appear to fall into the same category. TNA: WO 27/23: 47th Inspection Return 1771; TNA: WO 65/22: Army List 1772, 47th Foot, pp.82, 156, 159.

eighteenth century. He confirmed that commissioning from the ranks was a wartime phenomenon, and this accounted for 85 percent of his examples. He did identify a handful of NCOs who reached senior commissioned ranks, although this was clearly the exception rather than the rule.[19]

Table 3.3 Changes Amongst the Officers, 1771–1772

Inspection Return	Name		Country				Service		Date	
			English	Scotch	Irish	Foreigners	Age	Years		
1771	John	Webb				1	33	12	15 Apr 59	Not there
	Robert	Dupont	1				31	12	25 Sept 59	Lt 1 Sept 71
	Donald	McLoed		1			34	11	4 May 60	Lt 16 Dec 71
	Benjamin	Sprout			1		23	3	29 Oct 68	Not there
	Pool	England			1		22	2	6 Nov 69	
	Gerrard	Irvine			1		22	2	6 Nov 69	Lt 30 Apr 71
	James	Poe			1		20	1	10 Feb 70	10 Feb 69
	James	Parnier			1		20	1	29 Sept 70	John Paumier in 1772
1772	Thomas	Handfield				1	30	12	22 May 59	
	Henry	Baldwin			1		22	1	30 Apr 71	
	William	Carter			1		25	1	5 Jun 71	
	Arthur	French			1		18	1	16 Dec 71	
	James	Purfoy			1		25	1	16 Dec 71	

Table 3.3 shows variations amongst the officers between the 1771 and 1772 inspection returns. An officer newly arrived in the regiment, Thomas Handfield, was also a 1759-commissioned officer who evidently did want to travel to (or return to?) North America. He was also described as 'Foreign'. The muster roll for Craig's company in October 1772 lists him as absent without leave, and by January 1773 his post was filled by William McDermot. The remaining four new ensigns were all Irish with an average age of 22½, slightly older than the 1771 average of 20. Of the captains, Goddard and Evans had left the regiment by 1772. The former being commissioned during the 1745 Jacobite Rebellion and the latter at the time of the Battle of Quebec. Age and prior experience in North America may have persuaded them that this was a journey which they did not want to undertake again. They were replaced by three captains (the third being due to the reestablishment of the light company), all of which were new to the regiment.

Sherriff was the most experienced captain and the longest serving officer of the regiment, commissioned in 1750 and a captain for 10 years. The 1772 inspection return states that he was absent and serving as a 'Quarter Master General in America'. His appointment to the 47th coincided with the appointment of Guy Carleton as Colonel of the 47th on 2 April 1772. The following May, Carleton was promoted to Major General. He employed several officers from his regiment in North America which seems to be his main example of regimental patronage. In the October 1760 muster roll, Sheriff is listed as a lieutenant in Major John Hussey's company, Adjutant in the Colonel's company, and a prisoner. The following month his is described

---

19   J.A. Houlding, 'Commissioning of Non-Commissioned Officers, 1725-1792', *Journal of the Society for Army Historical Research*, vol.98, No. 395 (Winter, 2020), pp.348–361.

as 'Absent Continent' (Colonel's company) and 'Absent' (Malone's company). By May the following year he was back in the regiment and promoted to captain lieutenant in the Colonel's company, and in July is both captain lieutenant and adjutant, a situation which remained until 28 September 1762 when he was promoted to captain, replacing Captain Peter D'Arcy, who resigned.

The Staff

In addition to the regimental officers, there were a number of staff positions, namely the adjutant, quartermaster, chaplain, surgeon and surgeon's mate. The adjutant was responsible for the administration of the regiment for the commanding officer. The quartermaster was responsible for the regiment's equipment, stores, accoutrements, clothing and weapons. He was also responsible for the accommodation of the regiment, whether in barracks, inns on the march, or in the field when on campaign. On campaign he was assisted by the pioneers who would go forward to prepare the regiment's camp ground for their arrival and 'Camp Collourmen [sic]' each with a small regimental flag to mark out the camp.[20] A chaplain was appointed to oversee the spiritual well-being of the regiment. The surgeon and surgeon's mate were responsible for the physical well-being of the regiment. Both in barracks and on campaign, they were assisted by wives as nurses. Cuthbertson also recommends a sergeant or corporal as a clerk while Simes calculated that in the first year of service, four shillings and four pence should be a 'Deduction for Surgeon, &c'.[21]

The post of adjutant could be held in addition to a regimental duty. From May 1768, the adjutant was Ensign Thomas Turner, apparently without any other responsibilities. By August 1774 he was described as 'Sick Port Amboy' and again 'Sick in Boston' in September 1775, although in between (January 1775) was reported as well. By January 1776, he was 'Promoted' (although 'posted' may be the best word as he was still an ensign) to the Colonel's company. The new adjutant, Lieutenant James Poe was appointed on 12 July 1775 and also served as a lieutenant in Irving's company. He would still be the adjutant in February 1782.[22]

The quartermaster was Henry John Philpott. In the 1771 inspection return, he was described as being 23 years old with one year's service having been appointed on 15 January 1770. That year saw the establishment of the quartermaster's post on the Irish Establishment, one of the changes aligning British and Irish Regiments. This was a relatively young officer which is in contrast with traditional image of the quartermaster being an experienced

---

20 E.B. O'Callaghan (ed.), *Orderly Book of Lieutenant General John Burgoyne from his entry into the State of New York until his Surrender at Saratoga, 16th October, 1777* (Albany, NY: J. Munsell, 1860), p.25, 3 July 1777 and p.62, 1 August 1777; Cuthbertson, *Complete Interior Management*, pp.115–116.

21 Cuthbertson, *Complete Interior Management*, pp.31–40; T. Simes, *The Military Medley*, (Dublin: S. Powell, 1767), pp.201–202; see also, for example, Hale, Stevens & Howe (eds), *Orderly Book*, p.10, 20 June 1775 and O'Callaghan (ed.), *Orderly Book*, p.45, 18 July 1777 for two women per 'Corps' or battalion to be sent to the general hospital.

22 Hale, Stevens & Howe (eds), *Orderly Book*, p.41, 12 July 1775.

soldier commissioned from the ranks. According to the muster rolls, he was 'Sick in New York' when the remainder of the regiment was in Boston in January 1775 but subsequently re-joined them.[23]

The surgeon was Leonard Dobbin and his mate was Medlicote Burrows. In the 1771 inspection return, Dobbin was 26 years old and in his first year's service having been appointed on 28 January of that year. Burrows (or Burroughs) was 22 and had one year's service, having been appointed in March 1770 (the 1772 inspection return states 6 March 1772 but this is clearly an error). In the muster rolls, Burrows also appears in the ranks as a private soldier in the Colonel's company (where the staff were administered) from at least August 1772 until August 1774. By January 1775, Burrows was no longer in the ranks, but was still being listed as the surgeon's mate. Burrows was not unlike Corporal Roger Lamb (9th Foot) who served in both the ranks and as a surgeon's mate.[24] On 22 November 1775, Burrows was commissioned as an ensign in Douglass' company. Burrows may have been occupying the position usually ascribed to volunteers, young gentlemen lacking the means to purchase a commission but serving in the ranks until they were noticed, and a suitable vacancy appeared, although in this case, Burrows also served as surgeon's mate.

The chaplain, Edward Whitty, was appointed on 20 May 1767 according to the 1771 inspection return but in the muster rolls was described as absent from 23 May 1771 and throughout the war. He was described on 26 January 1775 and 20 September 1775 as 'Officiating by Deputy'; the deputy was never recorded. The inspection return for 1769 also says that he was absent, but in this case The Reverend Mr Ingram officiated. General Howe recorded Whitty's retirement on 9 September 1776, to be replaced by the Reverend Irwin Whitty. Irwin does not appear to have joined the regiment either.[25]

Lieutenant Thomas Anburey (29th Foot) described two incidents with the 47th's (unfortunately unnamed) chaplain during the Saratoga Campaign. On 5 July 1777 at Fort Ticonderoga, a 'very singular circumstance' occurred when the 'centinal' saw a man in the woods reading a book, whom he challenged. The man declared that he was the chaplain of the 47th, but was not believed and so detained until the guard was relieved. The guard commander took the chaplain to Brigadier General Simon Fraser who was suspicious as he thought he knew all of the chaplains and because the camp of the 47th was a couple of miles away. The commanding officer of the 47th was summoned and confirmed that the chaplain had arrived with a letter from General Sir Guy Carleton but had only joined the regiment the previous evening. The dilemma resolved, yet as Anburey noted, 'The studious gentleman little foresaw to what dangers he had exposed himself by his morning ramble, till he was stopped by the centinal.' On the 17th, while at Skenesboro (now

---

23 Houlding, 'Commissioning Non-Commissioned Officers', p.352 and n.9.
24 D. Hagist, *A British Soldier's Story: Roger Lamb's Narrative of the American Revolution* (Baraboo, WI: Ballindalloch Press, 2004), p.21.
25 Hale, Stevens & Howe (eds), *Orderly Book*, p.250, 10 April 1776; TNA: WO 65/22: Army List 1772, 47th Foot, p.101; WO 65/25: Army List 1775, 47th Foot, p.93, states he was appointed 9 September 1775.

Whitehall, New York, 26 miles south of Fort Ticonderoga), the clergyman preached a sermon 'and an exceeding good one it was, for a parish church, but not in the least applicable for the occasion.'[26]

As it is clear that Whitty never joined the regiment in this period, this anonymous clergyman may have been a deputy. There was no chaplain or deputy with the 47th when they surrendered at Saratoga; there were no chaplains in the whole army, just one deputy, a Reverend Brudenell.[27] In 1771, only the chaplain and adjutant were listed as English while the remaining three staff were all Irish. This supports the notion of an Irish-dominated officer corps.

Detached Officers

At full strength, there were three officers per company plus the staff of five making 35 in total. In practice, however, one of the officers was usually absent from most companies, starting with Carleton who was Governor of Quebec. As Colonel, he was not expected to serve with the regiment. In the early 1770s, the muster rolls show that some officers were on leave, like Captain Paulus Irving, and Ensigns Arthur French, William McDermot, James Poe and Poole England. Captain William Sherriff and Ensign William Buckannon were on leave in America. Ensign Milbourne West was on leave throughout 1772 but absent without leave throughout 1773. His absence may be in relation to his transfer to the 29th Foot on 14 March 1774.[28] Lieutenant William Shaw had 'Not Joined'. The reason for their delayed return or arrival is not recorded but it could simply have been due to travel or communications difficulties rather than deserting their posts. Captain Richard England and Lieutenant Garrett Irvine were away recruiting. Only Lieutenant Colonel William Nesbitt's and Captain Thomas Smelt's companies had their full complement of officers with them.

Most of this leave was probably 'Pre-Embarkation Leave', to use the modern term. By April 1773, eight were still on leave, although two of those were Carleton and Chaplain Whitty, who were never present with the regiment. Those on leave who would normally be expected to parade with the regiment were Surgeon Dobbin, Captain Irving and Ensigns French, McDermot, England and Poe. Also not present were, Ensign Shaw, described as 'Not joined', and Ensign Milbourne who was 'Still absent without leave'.

The Enlisted Men

The muster rolls and inspection returns provide a wealth of information on the sergeants, drummers and fifers, and rank and file of the 47th. These sources provide different information when compared with that of the officers. The 1772 inspection return provided the most current description prior to their departure to the Americas. This data has been compared with D.J. Pippin's study of seven regiments, plus the Royal Artillery, in Canada in

---

26 Anburey, *Travels*, vol.I, pp.315–317, Letter XXX, 5 July 1777; p.360, Letter XXXIV 17 July 1777.
27 Baule, *Protecting the Empire's Frontier*, p.43.
28 TNA: WO 65/24: Army List 1774, 29th Foot, p.83.

1782 and 1783 (with the proviso that allowances need to be made for the late war characteristics of Pippin's cohort) and 10 regiments immediately prior to deployment overseas examined by Dr Matthew Spring.[29]

Major General the Earl of Drogheda considered the men to be 'Of a Good Size… Well made…' while the recruits were 'Young and Well made, and of a Good Size' when he reviewed the regiment at Charlesfort on 13 June 1772. This contrasted with Drogheda's inspection of the 35th Foot at Dublin two years later. He considered that the regiment 'mostly being young' was not fit for service. Youthful soldiers did not necessarily make a regiment serviceable, but the 47th's recruits were clearly not a problem.[30]

Table 3.4: Pippin's research into the nationality of British soldiers in Canada in 1782 and 1783, 47th Foot added.[31]

Regt	Year	English	Scotch	Irish	Foreign	American	Total
1/84th	1782	93	126	177	124		520
1/KRRNY[32]	1782	36	102	80	41	344	603
8th	1783	429	93	131	42		695
29th	1782	252	43	132	58		485
31st	1782	271	120	97	21		509
44th	1782	226	72	211	10	6	525
47th	1772	177	16	168	14		375
53rd	1782	248	95	110	108		561
RA	1782	105	79	63	1		248

Nationality

This data on the 47th and Pippin's research are shown in Table 3.4. The 1772 inspection return provided the origin of 375 enlisted men in the 47th. The majority of which were either English (including Welsh) (177 or 47.2 percent) or Irish (168 or 44.8 percent).[33] The remaining 30 men were either 'Scotch' (16 or 4.2 percent) or 'Foreign' (14 or 3.7 percent). Unfortunately, the muster rolls do not contain any 'Foreign' surnames which might indicate a country of origin. As with the single 'Foreign' officer, the term is taken to indicate a British subject born outside of the British Isles.

In Pippin's sample, 40 percent were English which is only slightly below the 47th's 47 percent. These figures are skewed downwards by the 1/84th (a Highland regiment) at 17.8 percent and the loyalist King's Royal Regiment of New York (KRRNY) at below 6 percent; on the other hand, the 8th Foot at 61 percent had clearly been very active recruiting in England despite having been garrisoning Quebec since before the outbreak of hostilities. The 'Scotch'

---

29 D.J. Pippin, *For Want of Provisions: an archaeological and historical investigation of the British soldier at Fort Haldimand (1778–1784)* (MA, Syracuse, 2010), Tables 26, 27; M. Spring, *With Zeal and With Bayonets Only: the British Army on Campaign in North America, 1775–1783* (Norman, OK: University of Oklahoma Press, 2010), p.106.
30 TNA: WO 27/26: Inspection Returns, Irish, 1772, 47th Foot; WO 27/32: Inspection Returns, Irish, 1774, 35th Foot.
31 Pippin, *For Want of Provisions*, Tables 26 and 27.
32 King's Royal Regiment of New York
33 Baule, *Protecting the Empire's Frontier*, p.38, noted that the Royal Irish was predominantly English with only between a quarter and a third being Irish.

contingents in Pippin's regiments were four times greater than in the 47th, but still less than one in five; the supposedly Highland 1/84th was only a quarter Scottish. Irish were far more prevalent in the 47th than in Pippin's regiments with only the 44th (40 percent) approaching the 47th's levels. In Pippin's data, 'Foreign' was distinct from American. Foreign was three times as prevalent as in the 47th, although predominately in the 53rd and the (supposedly Highland) 1/84th. By removing those two regiments, the percentage of foreign soldiers is below 1 percent, far lower than the 47th's 1772 figure. Finally, the presence of Americans was higher, but almost entirely, as would be expected, within KRRNY. As will be shown later, the 47th were able to recruit in New York and New Jersey before the commencement of hostilities. One of these men would petition for exchange with a regiment staying in North America on the grounds that he had no family or connections in Britain. Drafts of German troops into British regiments may account for some of the foreign soldiers; the 47th was due to receive a draft while in Canada, but they were detained in New York by General Howe and never arrived.[34]

Height

The heights of 375 men were recorded in the 1772 inspection return. Table 3.5 shows the heights of soldiers by company. The vast majority of the enlisted men fell within a height range slightly smaller than, but not too dissimilar to modern British males. 264 (70.4 percent) were between five feet six inches and five feet 10 inches. However, almost a quarter (89 or 23.7 percent) were below five feet six inches tall. Only five percent were taller than five feet 10 inches (22 men). With the exception of two men in the Colonel's company, the remaining 20 were, unsurprisingly, in Captain Smelt's grenadier company. Those 20 men ranged between five feet 10½ inches and six foot two inches, with five measuring five feet 11½ inches. Cuthbertson's recommendation was that soldiers should be between five feet six and half inches and six feet.[35] The 47th had seven men above that range, and 67 below, or 20 percent. This means that 80 percent of the 47th were within Cuthbertson's recommended height range.

These figures have a close corollary with those in Pippin for 1782 and 1783. Pippin's Table 28 charts 3,449 men in seven regiments in 1782 while Table 29 describes 2,834 men in five regiments the following year. Pippin found about a quarter were five feet six inches or below (22 percent in 1782 and 25 percent in 1783). At the upper range, six percent were five feet 10 inches or taller. In the range of five feet six inches to five feet 10 inches were again around 70 percent of the men (70 percent in 1782, 68 percent in 1783). So, the height range identified in the 47th was consistent with the height range in Pippin's larger sample.[36]

---

34   TNA: WO 4/94: Secretary-at-War, Out Letters, General Letters, 3 August 1776; WO 4/100: Secretary-at-War, Out Letters, General Letters, 18 July 1777.
35   Cuthbertson, *Complete Interior Management*, p.42.
36   Pippin, *For Want of Provisions*, Tables 28 and 29; see also Hagist, *Noble Volunteers*, p.19.

WHO WERE THE 47TH FOOT?

Table 3.5: Soldiers' Heights by company from TNA: WO 21/26: Irish Inspection Return 1772 for the 47th Foot

Height	Carleton	Nesbit	Carncross	Smelt	Sherriff	Irving	England	Craig	Aubrey	Alcock	Total
6'2				1							1
6'1 ½											
6'1				2							2
6'0 ½				2							2
6'0				2							2
5'11 ½	1			5							6
5'11	1			4							5
5'10 ½				4							4
5'10		2		3			2	1		1	9
5'9 ½	2	1	3	14		2				1	23
5'9	1		2	4		1	2	6		1	17
5'8 ½	3	2				5	2	2		4	18
5'8	5	4	3			2	8	2	9	3	36
5'7 ½	6	8	7		2	2	9	7	3	8	32
5'7	3	4	6	1	7	6	2	2	2	7	40
5'6 ½	2	2	6		3	8	6	3	9	2	41
5'6	2	1	1		7	3		7	3	4	28
<5'6	10	11	10	2	22	8	4	7	10	5	39
Total	36	35	38	44	41	37	35	37	36	36	375

Table 3.6: Soldiers' Age by company from TNA: WO 21/26: Irish Inspection Return 1772 for the 47th Foot

Age	Carleton	Nesbit	Carncross	Smelt	Sherriff	Irving	England	Craig	Aubrey	Alcock	Total
55											
50	1	1							1	1	4
45		1	2					1	1	2	7
40		3		6		2	2	1	1	1	16
35	4	3	2	1	1	2	2	3	3	5	26
30	4	4	6	6	3	4	3	7	2	5	44
25	10	8	18	20	10	15	13	9	11	14	128
20	14	10	6	9	27	12	12	11	11	7	119
18	3	5	4	2		2	3	4	6	2	31
Total	36	35	38	44	41	37	35	37	36	36	375

Age

Table 3.6 shows that two thirds (247) of the 47th were in their twenties, with only 31 being described as 18 years of age or younger. A quarter (97) were listed as being 30 years old or older. Cuthbertson recommended recruits being between 17 and 25 years of age, as they made the 'most tractable Soldiers'. It is not possible to cross reference the length of service against age to determine an age at enlistments, but given the large number of soldiers with two years' service and the large number aged in their twenties, Cuthbertson's recommendations seem to match the 47th's experience.[37]

---

37 Cuthbertson, *Complete Interior Management*, p.42; see also Hagist, *Noble Volunteers*, pp.19–20, 22.

A VERY FINE REGIMENT

Table 3.7: Soldiers' Length of Service by company from TNA: WO 21/26: Irish Inspection Return 1772, 47th Foot

Years' Service	Carleton	Nesbit	Carncross	Smelt	Sherriff	Irving	England	Craig	Aubrey	Alcock	Total
35											
30		1	1	1			1	1	1	2	8
25		2	1	2		1		2	1		9
20	2	3		1	1	2	2	1	2	1	15
15	4	4	3	4	1	1	4	3	3	5	32
10	1	2	1	2	2	1	3			1	13
8	6	2	8	8	3	3	4	2	2	4	42
7		3	1	3		3	1	4	1		16
6	1	3	2	5		1				1	13
5			2	1	1	2	1	1		3	19
4		3		7	5	3	3	2	3	2	28
3			2	1	1	2	1	1		3	11
2	12	8	11	6	26	9	7	8	14	10	111
1	7	3	4	2	2	11	5	12	6	6	58
Total	36	35	38	44	41	37	35	37	36	36	375

Length of Service

The British Army in 1775 is generally characterised with the adjectives 'professional' or 'veteran'. Professional simply means that you are paid full-time to perform a task; veteran implies service from a previous war. Table 3.7 shows that the 47th Foot had clearly been conducting a recruiting drive in the two years before deploying to North America, with 169 or 45 percent of the enlisted men having less than two years' service. There was a second, smaller spike at the eight-year point (42 or 11.2 percent), which would have occurred around 1764, when the regiment returned to Britain from North America. This does mean that 77 Enlisted Men, or 20 percent, had sufficient length of service that they could have had operational experience from North America during the French and Indian Wars. This also means that 80 percent had never heard a shot fired in anger. The 47th could hardly be described as a 'veteran' unit.

How do these figures compare with the wider Army? Pippin examined regiments in 1782 and 1783 which reflect wartime recruiting practises and so are not comparable with the 47th's peacetime figures. Matthew Spring analysed 10 regiments before they deployed overseas. These figures will more closely reflect peacetime recruiting and retention practices of the 47th. The regimental figures compiled from Table 3.7 have been added to Spring's data to create Table 3.8.

WHO WERE THE 47TH FOOT?

Table 3.8 Soldiers' Length of Service in Eleven Regiments of Foot[38]

Regiment (Date of Review)	Years of Service								Total Enlisted Men
	1 or Less	2	3	4	5 – 9	10 – 14	15 – 19	20+	
4th Foot 7 April 1774	66 15.6%	32 7.6%	36 8.5%	30 7.1%	129 30.6%	75 17.8%	36 8.5%	18 4.3%	422
63rd Foot 14 May 1774	40 10.5%	20 5.3%	56 14.7%	47 12.4%	107 28.2%	13 3.4%	81 21.3%	16 4.2%	380
49th Foot 25 July 1774	57 14.0%	19 4.7%	17 4.2%	81 20.0%	102 25.1%	24 5.9%	53 13.1%	53 13.1%	406
55th Foot May 1775	31 7.8%	25 6.3%	28 7.0%	12 3.0%	183 45.8	51 12.8%	22 5.5%	48 12.0%	400
46th Foot 15 May 1775	39 9.9	45 11.5%	27 6.9%	26 6.6%	208 52.9%	8 2.0%	17 4.3%	23 5.9%	393
42nd Foot 30 May 1775	23 6.1%	44 11.6%	19 5.0%	33 8.7%	160 42.3%	39 10.3%	41 10.8%	19 5.0%	378
27th Foot 7 June 1775	51 13.6%	24 6.4%	37 9.9%	35 9.4%	160 42.8%	11 2.9%	8 2.1%	48 12.8%	374
17th Foot 9 June 1775	54 13.5%	24 6.0%	26 6.5%	40 10.0%	210 52.5%	7 1.8%	14 3.5%	25 6.3%	400
9th Foot 17 July 1775	70 18.0%	59 15.2%	36 9.3%	77 19.8%	81 20.8%	7 1.8%	23 5.9%	36 9.3%	389
33rd Foot 17 July 1775	44 11.6%	23 6.1%	50 13.2%	26 6.8%	147 38.7%	17 4.5%	65 17.1%	8 2.1%	380
47th Foot 13 June 1772	58 15.5%	111 29.6%	11 2.9%	25 6.6%	90 24.0%	13 3.5%	32 8.5%	32 8.5%	375
By Age Range	533 12.0%	426 9.9%	343 7.9%	432 10.0%	1577 36.7%	265 6.1%	392 9.1%	326 7.5%	4,297
Five Year Average	40.3%				36.7%	6.1%	9.1%	7.5%	

In comparison with the other 10 regiments, the 47th's strength sits towards the lower end, with 375 enlisted men: just below the 33rd (380) and only the 27th had fewer enlisted men (374). The average strength was 390 so the 47th was only slightly below the average. By age, the five-year average of one to four and five to nine years' service are not dissimilar with 40.3 percent and 36.7 percent respectively, then markedly falling off for more than 10 years' service. This coincided with the ending of hostilities in 1763 and demobilisation. In all 11 regiments, 3,311 Enlisted Men, or 77 percent, had insufficient length of service to have had previous operational experience in wartime.

There is one anomaly in the 47th's figures. There is a marked increase in those with up to two years' service, 111 Enlisted Men or 29.6 percent. The remaining 10 regiments vary between 4.7 and 15.2 percent. The explanation for this anomaly may be that the 47th's inspection return was two or three years before that of Spring's regiments. By adding two- or three-years' service to them, that anomaly is moved to the four, or five to nine, years' service category. While the 47th also shows a spike in the five to nine years' service, it is the second smallest of the 11 regiments being only slightly greater than that of the 9th Foot.

Desertion
The populist narrative expects desertion to have been a common feature of the eighteenth century army, with soldiers enduring poor pay, the wrath of their officers and kept in line only by the threat of violence,

---

38 Spring, *With Zeal and With Bayonets Only*, Table 2, p.106.

especially punishments of the lash measured in the hundreds. Enlistment in peacetime was for life, or until 'worn out'. In the insecure working environment of the time, service for life provided a degree of security which few other professions could offer. Don Hagist has shown how young men ran away to the sanctuary and excitement of the army from the routine and boredom of civilian life. Equally, he has also explored the reasons for desertion to escape army life, including dissatisfaction with his career prospects, to drinking and being carried off by rebels, or serving as an officer's servant and being beaten.[39] Ilya Berkovich has studied the experiences of the private soldiers to replace the commonly held belief that they were 'motivated primarily by coercion' with 'a broader examination of the motivation of the rank and file serving in the armies of old-regime Europe.'[40] He examines a range of studies into desertion during the eighteenth and nineteenth centuries and identified desertion rates ranging between one and 15 percent. Another study of British Army units based in Great Britain shows 3.4 percent and 3.9 percent for 1758 and 1759 respectively while 1769 Irish-based units experienced eight percent desertion, increasing during the 1780s and 1790s. The First Foot Guards in the late eighteenth century experienced eight percent desertion, but with an average of a third returning, the actual 'irrecoverable losses' was 4.4 percent.[41] The 47th while engaged on routine garrison duties in Ireland could expect a desertion rate of around three to four percent.

Table 3.9 shows the deserters (and returning deserters) from the 47th between 1772 and 1776 based on the muster rolls. This period starts with a normal year in Ireland (1772). 1773 is a split year with the first half preparing to sail and the second half at sea, for which there are no muster rolls. 1774 was spent in New Jersey and New York, before the regiment arrived in Boston. There are clear differences between the desertion rates over the different phases. The muster rolls were compiled four times per year for the previous quarter. This section uses the dates at which the muster rolls were compiled as the basis of the annual reports, referred to here as the muster roll year.

Desertion Ireland, 1772

1772 is indicative of a normal year for the regiment. It was dispersed in several garrisons around Cork and the notable activities appear to have been recruiting and the annual inspection. During this muster roll year, there were six desertions. A seventh report was a duplicate entry. Only two of the desertions occurred on the same day and from the same company, that of Robert Green and Joseph Hunter, both in Alcock's company on 7 December 1771 while based in Charlesfort. That year also saw two soldiers return to the regiment from desertion: James Hendley returned to Major Carncross' company at Inchigeelagh on 9 April 1772 and on 24 May 1772 Daniel Martin returned to Captain Irving's company at Cork Harbour. The date of their

---

39 Hagist, *British Soldiers, American War*, Ch. 1 for enlisting to avoid 'roguery' esp. pp.14–15; Ch. 2 for enlisting for adventure and p.75 for the drudgery of being a tailor; for desertion, pp.1, 220–221, 244.
40 Berkovich, *Motivation in War*, pp.5.
41 Berkovich, *Motivation in War*, pp.58–59, 74, 91, 92.

WHO WERE THE 47TH FOOT?

Table 3.9: Desertions, 1772 – 1776 from TNA: WO 12/5871 Muster Rolls, 47th Foot, various dates

Country	Garrison	Muster Roll	Date of Desertion	Date of Return	Rank	First Name	Surname	Company	Comments
Ireland	Charlesfort	Jan-72	07-Dec-71		Pvt	Robert	Green	Alcocks	Same Event?
	Charlesfort	Jan-72	07-Dec-71		Pvt	Joseph	Hunter	Alcocks	Same Event?
	Charlesfort	Jan-72	21-Nov-71		Pvt	Thomas	Boyland	Irvings	
	Charlesfort	Apr-72	20-Mar-72		Pvt	Henry	Connor	Irvings	
	Inchigeelagh	Aug-72		09-Apr-72	Pvt	James	Hendley	Carncross	
	Cork Harbour	Aug-72	15-Apr-72		Pvt	Henry	Connor	Irvings	Listed twice with different dates
	Cork Harbour	Aug-72		24-May-72	Pvt	Daniel	Martin	Irvings	
	Inchigeelagh	Oct-72	29-Sep-72		Pvt	Ross	McIlroy	Colonels	
	Cork Harbour	Oct-72	10-Aug-72		Pvt	George	Darby	Sherriffs	
	Inchigeelagh	Jan-73	31-Oct-72		Pvt	James	McAlister	Colonels	
	Cork Harbour	Apr-73	25-Jul-73		Pvt	George	Ekin	Sherriffs	
	Inchigeelagh	Apr-73	13-Feb-73		Pvt	Richard	Ashton	Carncross	
	Inchigeelagh	Apr-73	13-Feb-73		Pvt	Philip	Morrison	Carncross	
	Cork Harbour	Apr-73	25-Feb-73		Pvt	William	Johnson	Irvings	
	Monks Town	May-73	12-Apr-73		Pvt	Charles	Crowly	Carncross	
	Monks Town	May-73	ND		Pvt	William	King	Alcocks	
	Cove	May-73	14-May-73		Pvt	Robert	Murray	Aubreys	
	Cove	May-73	18-Apr-73		Pvt	Patrick	Clancy	Aubreys	
	Cove	May-73	15-May-73		Pvt	Joseph	Cunningham	Aubreys	
	Monks Town	May-73	12-May-73		Pvt	Micheal	Hinds	Craigs	Same Event?
	Monks Town	May-73	12-May-73		Pvt	James	Kelly	Craigs	Same Event?
	Monks Town	May-73	17-May-73		Pvt	Micheal	McKinney	Craigs	
	Cork Harbour	May-73	10-Apr-73		Pvt	Francis	Syna	Irvings	
	Cork Harbour	May-73	16-Apr-73		Pvt	Charles	Hussey	Smelts	Grenadier
NJ	Brunswick	Jan-74	ND		Pvt	George	Clifford	Nesbitt	
	Brunswick	Jan-74	30-Aug-73		Pvt	John	Kelly	Alcocks	
	Brunswick	Jan-74	30-Oct-73		Pvt	Jas.	Hodgson	Alcocks	Same Event?
	Brunswick	Jan-74	30-Oct-73		Pvt	John	Bell	Alcocks	Same Event?
	Elizabeth Town	Jan-74	24-Oct-73		Pvt	Edward	Hartley Jnr	Aubreys	Same Event?
	Elizabeth Town	Jan-74	24-Oct-73		Pvt	George	Barnstrong	Aubreys	
	Elizabeth Town	Jan-74	30-Oct-73		Pvt	Robert	Wardel	Aubreys	
	Elizabeth Town	Jan-74	19-Nov-73		Pvt	William	Bucket	Aubreys	
	Port Amboy	Jan-74	20-Nov-73		Pvt	Richard	Callahan	Craigs	
NY	New York	Aug-74	01-May-74		Cpl	Joseph	Miles	Colonels	
	New York	Aug-74	20-May-74		Pvt	Alexander	McLean	Colonels	
	New York	Aug-74	15-Mar-74		Pvt	Jeffrey	Robinson	Aubreys	
	New York	Aug-74	01-May-74		Pvt	James	Thompso	Aubreys	
	New York	Aug-74	29-Apr-74		Pvt	John	Hilden	Craigs	
	New York	Jan-74	24-Jul-74		Pvt	David	Richards	Irvings	
MA	Boston	Jan-75	09-Oct-74		Pvt	John	Connery Jnr	Englands	Same Event?
	Boston	Jan-75	09-Oct-74		Pvt	Thomas	Swindells	Englands	Same Event?
	Charleston	Sep-75		26-Dec-74	Pvt	Thomas	Swindells	Englands	
	Boston	Jan-75	09-Aug-74		Pvt	John	McLean	Colonels	
	Boston	Jan-75	01-Oct-74		Pvt	Thomas	Carney	Colonels	
	Boston	Jan-75	22-Sep-74		Pvt	John	Grimes	Nesbitt	
	Boston	Jan-75	27-Sep-74		Pvt	John	Greening	Nesbitt	

Country	Garrison	Muster Roll	Date of Desertion	Date of Return	Rank	First Name	Surname	Company	Comments
	Boston	Jan-75	29-Sep-74		Pvt	John Kennig	Nesbitt		
	Boston	Jan-75	22-Aug-74		Pvt	William	Alsop	Smelts	Same Event?
	Boston	Jan-75	22-Aug-74		Pvt	Edward	Burk	Smelts	Same Event?
	Boston	Jan-75	03-Oct-74		Pvt	William	Stewart	Smelts	
	Boston	Jan-75	07-Oct-74		Pvt	Timoth	O'Harra	Smelts	
	Boston	Jan-75	19-Sep-74		Pvt	George	Moore	Alcocks	
	Boston	Jan-75	20-Sep-74		Pvt	Benjamin	Cooper	Aubreys	
	Boston	Jan-75	01-Oct-74		Pvt	Barry	May	Aubreys	
	Boston	Jan-75	07-Oct-74		Pvt	Jacon	Lazarus	Aubreys	
	Boston	Jan-75	26-Jul-74		Pvt	James	Hardwick	Irvings	
	Boston	Jan-75	04-Sep-74		Pvt	John	Kyte	Irvings	
	Boston	Jan-75	02-Oct-74		Pvt	James	Morris	Irvings	Entered
	Boston	Jan-75	03-Dec-74		Pvt	Thomas	Leakey	Irvings	Entered
	Boston	Jan-75	11-Dec-74		Pvt	James	Brown	Irvings	Entered
	Boston	Jan-75	25-Sep-74		Pvt	John	Lowe	Sherriffs	
	Boston	Jan-76	22-Nov-75		Pvt	John	Smyth	Alcocks	Same Event?
	Boston	Jan-76	22-Nov-75		Pvt	Edward	Smyth	Gambles	Same Event?

desertion is not recorded. This amounted to a net loss through desertion of four, or about 1 percent of regimental strength. This places the regiment well below the desertion rates established for British and Irish-based units. Berkovich concludes his chapter on desertion with an observation which should call into question all the pre-conceived ideas on motivation in Old Regime European soldiers like those of the 47th in the early 1770s: given that desertion provided a relatively easy and risk-free means of escaping service, 'it is puzzling why *more* men did not desert.'[42]

Desertion Ireland, early 1773

For the first half of this year, the regiment continued in distributed garrisons while slowly concentrating in Cork in preparation for sailing to America in the latter part of the year. During the first half of the year, it would have become common knowledge that the regiment was due to deploy overseas. Corporal Roger Lamb (9th Foot) serving in Ireland wrote how the expectation that his regiment would sail for America made marriage to soldiers all the more attractive, and that an officer had to authorise the union.[43] The 47th's data does not including any information on marriages. The regiment experienced 15 desertions and none returning from desertion in six months. This represents a 500 percent increase on the previous year. If the officers who left the regiment at this time are included, then the regiment was clearly going through an extremely disruptive phase.

Fifteen desertions accounts for over six percent of the regimental strength, well above the three to four percent desertion rate established above. The prospect of an overseas posting answers Berkovich's conundrum about why more men did not desert. When faced with a clearly unpopular posting,

---

42 Berkovich, *Motivation in War*, p.93.
43 Hagist, *British Soldier's Story*, p.14.

there was an increased risk that they would desert. So, it was not service in the Army *per se* which was the problem, but the specifics of a posting. Two of the desertions appear to have occurred together, Michael Hinds and James Kelly both from Captain Craig's company based at Monk's Town on 12 May 1773. A further indicator of the disruption is that another deserter, Charles Hussey, was from Captain Smelt's grenadier company. These were supposed to be the elite of the regiment and most reliable.

The prospect of a posting to the Americas seems to have had an adverse effect on the moral of the regiment. These postings could last over decade. The last time the regiment had been posted to North America, in 1750, their tour lasted 13 years and including a rebellion followed by the French and Indian Wars. As maybe one in five of the regiment had sufficient length of service to remember the French and Indian Wars, then there was clearly an institutional memory, and that memory was not a good one.

Desertion New York and New Jersey, 1774

The 47th Foot arrived in New Jersey in late-1773. In January 1774 the companies were distributed between three garrisons:

> Perth Amboy: Colonel's, Craig's, Sherriff's, and Smelt's companies.
> Elizabeth Town: Carncross', Aubrey's, and England's companies.
> New Brunswick: Lieutenant Colonel's, Alcock's, and Irving's companies.

The regiment experienced further desertions. Nine men deserted from four companies (Nesbitt's, Alcock's, Aubrey's and Craig's) distributed between the three garrison locations: one from Perth Amboy and four from the other two. The date of desertion is recorded for eight of the nine examples. Five of the deserters from Alcock's company in New Brunswick and Aubrey's company in Elizabeth Town occurred on 24 or 30 October 1773. The inference is that several deserters did so in coalition at the earliest opportunity and that the planning would have taken place during the sea voyage. In an era when the only way for poor people to cross the Atlantic was seven years of indentured service for their sponsor, a paid crossing at His Majesty's expense followed by desertion was clearly worth considering.

Private George Clifford's date of desertion is unrecorded. He was enlisted into the Lieutenant Colonel's company in Morris Town, Ireland, on 2 May 1773, and was the only member of that company to desert. Did he enlist knowing that the regiment was bound for America and see it simply as a means of a free passage? Similarly, Private John Bell deserted Captain Alcock's company in New Brunswick on 30 October 1773, having enlisted at Monk's Town, Ireland, on 5 May of that year. With him went James Hodgeson. Was this another example of conspiracy on the crossing? John Kelly from the same company had already deserted on 30 August, two months earlier. The most unexpected deserter was Edward Hartley, junior, from Captain Aubrey's company in Elizabeth Town on 24 October 1773. George Barnstrong from the same company also deserted on the same day, presumably together. Neither were new recruits. Barnstrong had served from at least January 1772 while Hartley was most likely the son of Corporal Edward Hartley, senior, also in Aubrey's company. Maybe the son did not want to follow in the father's footsteps.

Of the nine deserters, it would appear that most likely Clifford and Bell and possibly also Kelly and Hartley, junior may have been serving to get free passage across the Atlantic. Hodgeson and Barnstrong, in contrast, had several years' service before choosing to desert. The speed of which most of the desertions occurred after arriving in America suggests pre-meditation, probably planned while at sea. Deserting in pairs is unique to this period which further suggests pre-meditation.

By August 1774, most of the regiment had been concentrated in New York city, leaving just Captain Sherriff's in Perth Amboy and Captain Irving's in New Brunswick. Six more desertions occurred, half of which were recent recruits. David Richards of Irving's company had been enlisted on 2 March 1773 and deserted on 24 July 1774. Alexander McLean of the Colonel's company enlisted on 16 November 1772 and deserted on 30 May 1774. Richard Holden deserted from Craig's company on 29 April 1774 and had enlisted into Irving's company on 5 April 1773. Each desertion occurred on a different day starting in the spring of 1774 which suggests a more opportunistic approach to desertion rather than a planned scheme with accomplices. The two deserters from Aubrey's company (although on different dates, de-linking any co-operation), Jeffrey Robinson and James Thompson, were serving from at least 15 January 1772 at Charlesfort. Finally, the most-high ranking of all the deserters was Joseph Miles. In May 1773 he was a corporal in the Colonel's company. The question of anti-government agitation encouraging desertion to undermine crown forces must be considered. The speed of several desertions after disembarkation must preclude the opportunity for sedition to take effect. Furthermore, while there was anti-crown sentiment in New Jersey, the 47th Foot's short stay there appears to have been without incident.

Desertion Boston, 1775

The 47th landed in Boston, Massachusetts on 23 October 1774.[44] There were 23 desertions while the regiment was based in Boston or Charleston, with one of those later returned to the regiment. The vast majority (21) of those desertions occurred in late-1774 and were recorded in the January 1775 muster roll, with two occurring in November 1775 and being recorded in the January 1776 muster roll. This surge in desertions replicates that of early 1773, possibly provoked by a transatlantic posting; now it was the prospect of a politically charged posting.

One of the deserters, Thomas Swindells, returned on 26 December 1774. He had deserted on 9 October 1774 from Captain England's company in Boston. How this could have occurred when the regiment was transiting from New York to Boston at his time is unclear, unless he handed himself into the army in New York and joined the regiment on a later voyage John Connor junior also deserted from the same company on the same day. As we

---

44 Wylly, *Loyal North Lancashire*, vol.I, p.51.

saw with the Hartleys, above, Connor senior served in England's company, but this father and son relationship failed to retain the son. Another pair of privates, William Alsop and Edward Burk, deserted from Captain Smelt's company on 22 August 1774.

The greatest concentration of desertions occurred in Captain Irving's company between October and December 1774. What distinguished James Morris, Thomas Leakey and James Brown from the other desertions was that all three had been enlisted in July to September 1774. Their enlistment and desertion dates are all different which suggests that there was no coordination. The enlistment dates all suggest that the three soldiers were Americans recruited in New Jersey and New York. Where these content to serve in the 47th while it was garrisoning in the region from where they had been recruited, but not over 200 miles to the north? Or did they fraudulently enlist simply to gain the recruitment bounty? Unfortunately, the evidence for this is not available.

Don Hagist has analysed the desertion patterns in the Boston garrison. For the 10 months June 1774 to March 1775, there were 11 court martials for desertion while there were 13 returning deserters out of a garrison of some 6,000.[45] Although the court martials do not include successful desertions, they only represent 0.2 percent of the garrison strength. A similar number returned to the army. This implies a fluid environment, not one of mass desertions by soldiers serving against their will.

Desertion Boston, 1776

John and Edward Smyth were the only two to desert in 1775, on 22 November. They served in different companies, Alcock's and Gamble's companies respectively. John Smyth had been recently drafted from the 37th Foot on 3 April 1775. There is a marked distinction between the desertion rates recorded in the 1775 and 1776 muster rolls. The desertions recorded in the January 1775 muster roll all occurred in late 1774. The January 1776 muster roll recorded two desertions in November 1775, a year after those recorded in the January 1775. Boston evidently did not provide the opportunity to desert in the atmosphere of heightened political, and later, military tensions.

Conclusion

The five desertions in 1772 are taken as the base line for desertions during routine peacetime soldiering. By comparing the 47th with the desertion rates identified by Berkovich, the 47th had a low desertion rate which can be indicative of a content and well managed unit. As Berkovich commented, if military service was based around coercion, why did not more soldiers desert? Over the next four years we see fluctuating desertion rates which may reflect two features, a positive reason to desert for better opportunities, or a desire not to follow the regiment to the new positing. The prospect of a transatlantic journey to a posting 3,000 miles from home lasting a decade or more may have put some soldiers off going to America. We see a similar

---

45   Hagist, *Noble Volunteers*, pp.4–7.

spike in desertions correlating to a posting from a relatively benign New York and New Jersey to a politically charged Boston. For some, however, the prospect of enlisting for free passage across the Atlantic could have been a motive for enlisting.

The opportunity to desert for the prospect of a better life was available in New Jersey and New York. Once in Boston, however, this was simply not available and the two desertions for the 1775 were less than half of the 1772 desertion rate. Increased security as the military situation deteriorated would have made desertion more difficult and increased the punishments if apprehended, but this would have been offset by a concerted effort by rebels to undermine the British Army through desertion, presumably by offering the quality of life unavailable to them in the British Isles. Despite their best efforts, Boston was the least attractive location for desertion.

Who were the 47th Foot?

In 1773, the average officer in the 47th was most likely to be Irish and commissioned around the age of 20. Wartime conditions during the 1745 Rebellion and the French and Indian War encouraged younger ages of commissioning, and also saw the commissioning of worthy individuals without the financial means or social contacts to advance. The assumption that the purchase system and patronage placed unsuitable candidates in positions of authority will be assessed in later when the regiment's operational performance is discussed. In 1773, the average enlisted man in the 47th was likely to be in his twenties with two years' service, between five feet six inches and five feet 10 inches tall, and either English or Irish. He was unlikely to have had previous wartime service, with only 20 percent having had sufficient length of service for that. He was a professional, in that he was paid full time for his soldiering, but with limited service, he was still relatively new to his craft; he certainly was not a veteran. He was extremely unlikely to desert in normal routine garrison life which indicates that soldiering was probably not bad career choice, when compared with the options outside. However, like any human, he could look upon upheaval with both dread, and as an opportunity. Some may not have wanted a transatlantic posting lasting a decade or more, while others may have seen it as an opportunity for a passage they could never afford themselves. By focusing on the relatively small numbers who deserted during times of stress, we risk losing sight of those who did not. The 15 desertions in early 1773 should not detract from the approximately 360 who remained with the colours and sailed to New Jersey. It is these men, not the deserters, who would fight over the next decade.

The concluding lines of the 1772 inspection show that the extensive manoeuvres had been 'performed in Double Quick time' which were performed with the 'greatest Exactness & Attention' so that the inspecting general concluded 'And is a Very Fine Regiment and Fit for Service.' (The National Archives)

4

Tactical Evolution

The British Army of the American War of Independence has suffered in the popular imagination, like most failed armies, and has been castigated for incompetence, arrogance, obsolete tactics and equipment, and failure to adequately understand the terrain and opponents. The rebel armies have a popular reputation disproportionate to their decidedly unimpressive tactical and operational performance over eight years of fighting. The British Army under George III, in contrast, built upon the successes of his grandfather and conducted itself with great credit during the Seven Years War, and the French Revolutionary and Napoleonic Wars, and the War of 1812. Four book titles, or sub-titles, summarised this era: Frank McLynn's *1759: The Year Britain Became Master of the World*; Brendan Simms' *Three Victories and a Defeat: The Rise and Fall of the First British Empire,* David Blackmore's *Destructive and Formidable,* and Peter Brown's 2020 book *The Soldiers who Forged an Empire*.[1] Defeat in the American War of Independence was, therefore, the exception rather than the rule.

The British Army did not rely on obsolete weapons, tactics and equipment during the war. There was a new drill manual introduced in 1764, new uniform in 1768 and the new Short Land Pattern Musket in 1769. Light companies on the Irish Establishment (which included the 47th Foot) were re-established on 18 September 1771, in response to a potential war with Spain.[2] There were two new light infantry manuals published by Lieutenant General George Townshend (1772) and Major General William Howe (1774).[3] Institutional memory preserved the experiences from North America before 1763, not that there was any intention of fighting there except on the frontiers. The

---

1   McLynn, F., *1759: The Year Britain Became Master of the World* (London: Jonathan Cape, 2004); Simms, *Three Victories and a Defeat;* D. Blackmore, *Destructive and Formidable: British Infantry Firepower 1642-1765* (Barnsley: Pen & Sword, 2014); Brown, *Army of George II.*
2   B.E. Hubner, *The Formation of the British Light Infantry Companies and their Employment in the Saratoga Campaign of 1777* (MA thesis, Saskatchewan, 1986), p.1.
3   Smythies, *40th Regiment*, pp.549-52, 'Rules and Orders for the Discipline for the Light Infantry companies in His Majesty's Army in Ireland', Townshend, 15 May 1772; NAM: 6807-157-6: *Discipline Established by Major General Howe for Light Infantry in Battalion* (Sarum, 1774).

47th's inspection returns shows a light company exercising in a rural, rather than a wilderness, environment which would have been applicable in a developed agricultural environment as found would be found in Western Europe, or around Boston and New York.[4]

This does not mean that the British Army's reforms were right for the next war – armies always prepare to fight the last war, so the saying goes – nor does it mean that the British Army's failures were as a result of these reforms. Sometimes, no amount of superior moral, technology or doctrinal advantage can overcome the operational challenges. The war developed into a global one which stretched Britain's capabilities to the limit.

It should not be surprising that the army's performance around Boston in 1775 was lacking. Since 1763, the army had suffered from peacetime malaise and financial cuts.[5] The British Army always commences wars with reversals. Examples abound: Prestonpans proceeded Culloden; Dettingen came after 26 years of peace and the performance reflected this, but the army recovered for Fontenoy over the next few years; Monongahela, Fort William Henry and Fort Carillon proceeded Quebec; the Convention of Klosterzeven before Minden; Boston before New York. Even the 1914 and 1940 British Expeditionary Forces started with significant withdrawals. The common theme is the transition from peacetime soldiering to wartime soldiering.

The British Army in 1775 is often described as 'professional' or 'veteran', as if to raise expected performance from them and, by inference, increasing the achievements of the amateur minutemen, militia and early Continental line regiments.[6] Professional simply means that you are paid full time to do something, but does come with the expectation that you are good at it. Although the minutemen and militia are lionised for their performance around Boston in 1775, Congress increasingly relied on the professional Continental line regiments and wished to emulate the professional British Army. Furthermore, Houlding identified multiple reprints of the 1764 manual in North America, James Tanner shows how the rebels emulated British Army drummers and fifers, and Bell describes how Boston artillerymen had been trained by the Royal Artillery. Hardly indicative of an army relying on obsolete concepts.[7] In the previous chapter, we have seen that 20 percent of the 47th had sufficient length of service to have served in the French and Indian War. But that was 12 years before. Veterans grow old and soft in a comfortable garrison, loose their edge away from the forests, and their war stories grow more fanciful to the new recruits.

---

4 TNA: WO 27/26: Inspection Returns, Irish, 1772, 47th Foot.
5 Houlding, *Fit for Service*, Chapter 1.
6 Most recently, Jack Kelly described Brigadier General Patrick Gordon's brigade in Quebec in July 1776 as 'crack unit', *Valcour*, p.65. It consisted of the 21st, 29th and 62nd Foot. These regiments landed in Quebec City a few months earlier and had limited opportunity to achieve 'crack' status. The brigade, and Gordon's appointment as its brigadier general, had only been ordered in June 1776, J.M. Hadden, *Hadden's Journal and Orderly Book: A Journal Kept in Canada and Upon Burgoyne's Campaign in 1776 and 1777* (Albany: Joel Munsell's Sons, 1884), pp.175-176, 10 June 1776.
7 J.L. Bell, *The Road to Concord: how four stolen cannon ignited the Revolutionary War* (Yardley, PA: Westholme Publishing, 2016); pp.48–49; Houlding, *Fit for Service*, pp.208–225 especially p.215; J. Tanner, *Instruments of Battle: the fighting drummers and buglers of the British Army from the late 17th century to the present day* (Oxford: Casement, 2017), pp.96–98, 100.

If the British Army's performance in the American War of Independence was not up to the standards of the earlier and later wars, then why was that? The first question has to be, was the performance any less than in the other wars? David Blackmore's *Destructive and Formidable* charts the tactical evolution of the British Army in the early-eighteenth century. He commences with the thoroughly un-militaristic English society at the outbreak of the War of the Three Kingdoms, through to the end of the Seven Years War, with 1759 being the *annus mirabilis*. One difference between the American War of Independence and the other conflicts is that the British Army operated as part of a coalition, and usually as a junior partner in the land component, although able to bring to bear far greater resources in fields like maritime and fiscal. During the American War of Independence, Britain fought a global conflict without European allies except for those German states which hired out auxiliaries, commonly referred to as 'Hessians'.

As the eighteenth century progressed, the British Army was increasingly deployed around the world in growing numbers, often in multiple theatres at great distances from any home base. One could also add the activities of the East India Company army. Although it was funded, raised and equipped separately to the crown's forces, the recruitment of European officers and men came from the same sources.[8] This growth in responsibilities added significant challenges in terms of logistics, naval escorts, reinforcements and new opponents.

Fire in Conventional Conflict

Blackmore has identified that shortly after the inconclusive opening of the English Civil War at Edgehill (1642), there was a rapid and significant change in how fire was delivered: reserving fire until the enemy were in the range of a pike (five to 10 yards) before delivering a volley of three ranks firing together.[9] This was effectively the same as delivered at Waterloo, 173 years later, although with increased musketry ranges and two ranks rather than three. The line between Edgehill and Waterloo was one of evolution not revolution, of constant refinement brought about by changes in equipment, contemporary theories from Europe, personal preferences and changing foes. The enemy always influenced this process.

It is possible to track the characteristics and developments of the British Army under the late-Stuart and Hanoverian monarchs. These can be characterised as short-range firing; a weight of fire to achieve effect; rate of fire; stability under pressure and closing in rapidly to engage in hand-to-hand combat. In the 1660s, Charles II provided military support to Portugal in its struggle for independence from Spain. Colonel James Apsley wrote about the 1663 Battle of Ameixal: 'The English marched on shouting as if victorious, but discharged no shot till they came within push of pike of the enemy, and then they poured their shot so thick upon them that made them quit their ground

---

8   W. Dalrymple, *The Anarchy: The Relentless Rise of the East India Company* (London: Bloomsbury, 2019), pp.316–317.
9   Blackmore, *Destructive and Formidable*, pp.13-16, 18.

and fly…'. While the Portuguese generals were concerned: 'having not been accustomed to see so close an approach before firing, did give up the English for lost and did believe they all had intended to joined with the Castillians, but when they saw their thick firing and the good success the English obtained thereupon, they called us comrades and good Christians.' While the King of Portugal recognised their contribution 'though not much considerable in numbers', 'did perform the toughest part of the service, and first shewd them the way of using the Rests of the Musquet to knock down the Enemy; which made the French-men cry out, *Faisont comme les anglois,* Let's do as the English.'[10]

It was generally recognised that the first volley would have the greatest effect, having been loaded prior to the engagement commencing. Some 80 years later, at Fontenoy in 1745, the French opened fire at 80 yards. Their re-loading became panicked and less efficient. Meanwhile the British advanced, ignoring the French ineffectual fire until close enough to deliver a single devastating volley.[11]

The ongoing problem faced by the infantry was the length of time it took to load the musket. The unloaded infantryman was vulnerable to attack despite the presence of pikemen. In the mid-seventeenth century, this had required, in theory at least, up to 10 ranks of muskets with the front-rank firing, peeling off to the rear to reload, while the second rank stepped forward to fire. By the time the original firers returned to the firing line, they should have reloaded. Fire could be delivered continuously, and the re-loading musketeers were protected, but only a small proportion of the musketeers could fire at any one time. Sir William Turner in his 1683 *Pallas Armatas* advocated six ranks, but that still limited the number of musketeers who could fire at any one time. *The Swedes Way* advocated three ranks, which would become the standard for much of the eighteenth century.[12]

Technological innovations allowed quicker re-loading which reduced the number of unloaded muskets at any one time. James II ordered the army re-equipped with flintlocks in 1685, although it would be the reign of Queen Anne before the last of the matchlocks were replaced. The introduction of the plug, and later socket, bayonet enabled the pike to be withdrawn from service and all soldiers equipped with muskets. This process, as Mark Shearwood has shown, was neither straight forward nor easy to track. An aborted scheme to equip all English soldiers with plug bayonets by Charles II seems to have been replaced by a more limited scheme to just grenadiers and dragoons, two troop types which operated without the protection of the pike.[13] By the mid-eighteenth century metal ramrods were introduced, as was the paper cartridge when the powder horn was phased out. In the

---

10 Blackmore, *Destructive and Formidable*, pp.27-28, n.70. Blackmore believes the reference to the 'Rests' actually refers to the butt being used as a club in close combat, musket rests having fallen out of service by this time.
11 Blackmore, *Destructive and Formidable*, p.104.
12 Sir J. Turner, *Pallas Armata* (London: Chiswell, 1683) and Anon., *An Abridgement of the English Military Discipline* (London: Bill, Barker, Newcomb & Hills, 1676) quoted in Blackmore, *Destructive and Formidable*, pp.43, 44.
13 M. Shearwood, *The Perfection of Military Discipline: the plug bayonet and the English Army, 1660–1705* (Warwick: Helion, 2020), pp.32–33, 41–42.

1750s, drill manuals increased the space between the ranks which removed the need for a deliberate movement to open the spacings. At the same time, having fired, instead of bringing the musket to the recovery (vertically, with the lock at neck height), it was now brought immediately into position ready for priming.[14] Each incremental evolution saved a few seconds.

In the late-1680s, platoon firing started to appear. This provided a number of 'firings', usually three or four, each composed of a number of platoons, evenly distributed across the battalion to ensure that no section of the line was left vulnerable. This gave rise to complex configurations for firing. Companies could be broken up to achieve the correct number of platoons to deliver the firings for a particular battle, splitting some files from their familiar comrades.[15] Improvements in the rate of re-loading meant that unloaded platoons were less exposed. The reduction of the number of platoons to eight, the same number as the centre companies, meant that the platoon and company became interchangeable. It was beneficial to the moral component if the firing unit (platoon) and the administrative unit (company) were one and the same with the soldier being led by officers he was familiar with and who knew him. This can only have further improved the efficiency and effectiveness of fire discipline. 'Alternate fire' based around company rather than the platoon was being used in the British Army from the end of the War of the Austrian Succession.[16] By the American War of Independence, a platoon was a tactical subdivision of a company.

Despite the uncertain performance at the Battle of Dettingen, *Maréchal de France* Adrien-Maurice de Naoilles, Duc de Naoilles, described the British infantry to Louis XV: 'Their infantry was closed and held themselves brazenly, they conducted a fire so lively and so sustained that the old officers never has seen anything like it, and so superior to ours one could not make any comparison, this resulting from our troops being neither exercised nor discipline as to be suitable.'[17]

The pinnacle of the British Army's performance was described by Captain John Knox of the 43rd Foot at Quebec in 1759:

> The forty-third and forty-seventh regiments, in the centre, being little affected by the oblique fire of the enemy, gave them, with great calmness, as remarkable a close and heavy discharge, as ever I saw performed at a privet field of exercise, insomuch that better troops than we encountered could not possible withstand it: and, indeed, well might the French Officers say, that they never opposed such a shock as they received from the centre of our line, for they believed every ball took place, and such regularity and discipline they had not experienced before; our troops in general, and particularly the central corps, having levelled and fired, – comme une coupe de cannon.[18]

---

14 Blackmore, *Destructive and Formidable*, pp.125, 126.
15 Blackmore, *Destructive and Formidable*, p.48.
16 Brown, *Army of George II*, p.39.
17 Quoted in Blackmore, *Destructive and Formidable*, p.121.
18 Quoted in S. Reid, *North America 1755–63: British Redcoat versus French Fusilier* (Oxford: Osprey, 2016), p.56.

Blackmore has estimated that at battles like Culloden and Fontenoy, a British battalion firing eight companies alternatively at 30 yards, could inflict between 100 and 120 casualties every 20 seconds.[19] The effect of that weight of fire on those attempting to re-load and aim effectively was debilitating, as Naoiles described.

Hand-to-hand combat appears to have died out in 1690s, with Chandler believing that it was left to the cavalry to make the final destructive charge. The infantry now had sufficient firepower to deliver an effect without risking becoming disorganised in the mêlée and therefore vulnerable to a counterattack. This seems at odds with the earlier hand-to-hand combat with the musket butt, and the later bayonet charge. Shearwood noted that drill manuals retained the 'club muskets' alongside the 'bayonet charge'; both these orders were still retained in the *1764 Regulations*. This is part of the evolutionary process: it was not a clearly defined, linear process.[20]

One thing the British infantry generally did not get drawn into was a prolonged firefight. Blackmore identified Laffeld in 1747 as one example when they did, and were successful. Monongehela was another example, where the fighting lasted three hours before the ammunition ran out. However, both were ultimately British defeats.[21] One final observation on these evolutions. Unlike with Continental armies, in Britain there was no debate about the appropriateness of these tactics; debate was focused on refining them. Conversely, despite their evident utility in the British Army, they were never adopted by their Continental foes or allies.

Non-Conventional Challenges – the Highland Charge

Not all of these evolutions proved successful in all combat scenarios: the Highland charge and the skirmishing of the Native Americans proved the most challenging to overcome. In both cases, British commanders recognised that they were facing a different challenge and adopted their tactics accordingly. Whether those adoptions were sufficient is another matter, what is important is that they identified, learned, and eventually overcame the threat.

The fundamental challenge presented by the Highland charge was the speed at which it was delivered, thus severely limiting the weight of fire which could be delivered to halt it. Before Killiekrankie in 1689, for example, platoon firing was practiced to deliver a continuous fire in an attempt to discourage the Highland charge. This was unsuccessful. Weight of fire alone was similarly unsuccessful at Prestonpans and Culloden. Before Culloden, there was time to introduce and practice a new bayonet drill which prevented

---

19 Blackmore, *Destructive and Formidable*, p.136.
20 D. Chandler, *The Art of Warfare in the Age of Marlborough* (London: Spellmount, 1990), p.111; Blackmore, *Destructive and Formidable*, pp.66–67; Shearwood, *Perfection of Military Discipline*, p.73, although the use of the bayonet indicates it was for cavalry whereas the clubbed musket was for infantry.
21 Blackmore, *Destructive and Formidable*, pp.3, 6, 104, 116, 119, 146–149; R. Chartrand, *Monongahela 1754–55: Washington's Defeat, Braddock's Disaster* (Oxford: Osprey, 2004), pp.61–84.

a repetition of the collapse and route as experienced at Killiekrankie and Prestonpans. At Killiekrankie, the musketeers were equipped with plug bayonets which prevented firing, but were defended by pikes, at about 25 percent of the strength. At both Prestonpans and Culloden there were no pikes and socket bayonets had been issued. These increased the volume of fire which could be delivered for the same number of soldiers.[22]

More important than tactics is confidence in those tactics. The 47th was one of those regiments who broke and fled at Prestonpans. Yet their performance at Quebec 14 years later as described by Knox, above, is in marked contrast. Prestonpans was the 47th's first exposure to combat, and it showed. Two years earlier at Dettingen (1743), the British infantry's performance had also been a cause for concern. It was their first major action for a generation, since Malplaquet (1709). Of the 15 battalions which fought at Culloden, five had fought at Dettingen (3rd, 4th, 13th, 20th and 21st Foot), eight fought at Fontenoy (1st, 3rd, 8th, 13th, 20th, 21st, 25th and 34th Foot) and four at both (3rd, 13th, 20th and 21st Foot).[23] They had confidence in the tactic of holding fire until the last moment. While apparently the most dangerous option, it delivered the greatest effect and therefore was the safest.

Non-Conventional Challenges – Native Americans

It was in North America that the British Army faced its more prolonged non-conventional threat, while also retaining the ability to fight a conventional battle when needed. So successful were the British Army that it has been suggested that their opponents were forced to change their own tactics. The French and Indian War started disastrously for the British at Monongahela. Major General Edward Braddock is discredited as entirely out of touch with the reality of frontier warfare (and the myths of George Washington and Ethan Allen created), but Braddock had recognised the nature of the threat facing him and had issued instructions to address that threat. Although these tactics failed to win the battle, they did hold off the French and Native Americans for three hours. It was only when the British infantry ran out of ammunition that they broke. As discussed above, the British did not often engage in protracted firefights. Their achievement for maintaining the fight in woodland against foes firing individually from cover was, actually, impressive.[24]

The doctrinal lessons from Monongahela led to the formation of the light infantry. Ranging companies were raised, of which Roger's Rangers remains the most famous. Regular units like Lieutenant Colonels George Howe's 55th Foot and Thomas Gage's 80th Foot became 'light'. Gage had commanded Braddock's vanguard at Monongahela. Battalion light companies were raised. The later were established under an order from Lord Amherst of 14 April

---

22 Blackmore, *Destructive and Formidable*, p.48; Shearwood, *Perfection of Military Discipline*, pp.75, 81.
23 Reid, *Culloden Moor 1746*, p.27; Blackmore, *Destrucive and Formidable*, p.119.
24 Blackmore, *Destructive and Formidable*, pp.146–149; Chartrand, *Monongahela*, pp.61–84.

1759 and consisted of a new company of one captain, one lieutenant, one ensign and 70 other ranks.[25] Innovations included shorter, lighter muskets with browned barrels to prevent them reflecting sunlight. Powder horns full of finer powder for priming were issued, as were buckshot and spare balls for double loading. Bayonets were withdrawn, replaced with tomahawks, and then re-issued, depending on the commander's preferences. Light tactics were introduced. This was a period of evolution, but the success is shown in one memoir from the siege of Quebec when the Native Americans were reluctant to face the British but would ambush them from the shelter of woods.[26] The light companies could be combined into light battalions, as was established practice with the grenadier companies.

Major General James Wolfe had raised a light company for the 20th Foot in 1755 while stationed in England on anti-invasion duties. Later, in North America, on 28 June 1758 he instructed that: 'When the light infantry of the line are formed into one corps, they are to receive their orders from Colonel [William] Howe (58th Foot), who has Major [John] Hussey (47th Foot) to assist him.'[27]

Colonel William Howe was George Howe's brother. He was also, as Major General Howe, to take command of the Boston Garrison in 1775 and decisively defeated George Washington around New York in 1776. The appointment of Major John Hussey as his deputy placed the 47th central to the evolution of light tactics on the St Lawrence River. It was Howe's light infantry which led Wolfe's army during its famous landing at the Anse de Foulon on the night of 12/13 September 1759. During the subsequent battle on the Plains of Abraham, the light infantry provided rear and flank protection. This successful evolution of light tactics paralleled George Howe's 55th Foot and Thomas Gage's 80th 'light armed foot' which were operated in the Hudson valley. George Howe's untimely death on 8 July 1758 as part of Major General James Abercromby's failed operations against Fort Carillon (Ticonderoga) deprived the British Army of this innovative commander but Gage's military career would continue in North America.[28] Unfortunately, Hussey is recorded as having 'dyed since 24th April', according to the muster roll of 4 October 1760.[29] The 47th's light company continued to serve under Howe so their experience did not end with Hussey's death.

It is worthwhile noting that that despite these New World innovations, the critical battles of the campaign, Louisburg (1758) and Quebec (1759 and 1760) were conventionally fought as if on the fields of Europe. The British Army was able to perform both roles concurrently. We see both innovation and adaptation to the new environment, plus retention of core soldiering skills to deliver a battle winning effect. With the end of the Seven Years War, the British Government naturally looked for defence savings. The light

---

25 Reid, *Quebec 1759*, p.16.
26 Blackmore, *Destructive and Formidable*, pp.149–155, 159–160.
27 Quoted in Reid, *Quebec 1759*, p.16.
28 R. Chartrand, *Ticonderoga 1758: Montcalm's victory against all odds* (Oxford: Osprey, 2000), pp.29, 38–39, 42–43.
29 TNA: WO 12/5871: Muster Rolls, 47th Foot, November 1760.

companies were one of the victims of the peace. This is usually taken to imply that the British Army lost its skirmishing capability.

1763 And Beyond

The 1764 Regulations[30]

The *1764 Regulations* abolished platoon firing. It would now be conducted by companies or paired companies (grand divisions) firing alternatively, from the centre out, the flanks in or from left to right. Minor modifications, like simplifying the procedure for returning the ramrod, while not significant, continued to speed up reloading. The grenadier company continued to act in its traditional flanking role. The light companies were re-established in 1771 or 1772. For the remaining eight companies, the *1764 Regulations* laid down the distribution of the companies. The field officers (lieutenant colonel and major) were to command the battalion with support from the adjutant. The senior captain took command of the colour guard in the centre of the battalion. The second and third senior captains were next when extending from the centre to command a wing each; the second, third, fourth and fifth captains were then positioned to command the four grand divisions, each of two companies. The sixth company commander was the captain lieutenant. Each company commander could command their own company, but should it be necessary to divide each company into its two platoons, junior subalterns would be called forward.[31]

A regiment should have paraded 30 regimental officers, that is three per company. The regime described in the *1764 Regulations* assumes a full complement of officers but this was rarely achieved. The January 1775 muster roll shows that the 47th was already short by three officers (two serving in Quebec and one vacant).[32] During campaigns, this situation would only deteriorate. When on campaign, the commanding officer would distribute his companies as equitably as possible. The 47th's orderly book covers the Saratoga Campaign and describes the distribution of six companies:

Captain John Alcock's, the right
General's, the left
Lieutenant Colonel's, left of Captain Alcock
Captain Richard L'Estrange, right of the General's
Captain William Sherriff's, right of the centre
Major's, left of the centre[33]

---

30   *New Manual and Platoon Exercise: with an Explanation. Published by Authority* (Dublin, 1764) and *The Manual Exercise, as Ordered by His Majesty in 1764* both underwent multiple reprints on both sides of the Atlantic, especially in mid-1770s America which Houlding considered 'the sincerity of emulation can hardly have seemed flattering'. Collectively these manuals are referred to as the *1764 Regulations*. Houlding, *Fit For Service*, pp.209–15, 427.
31   Spring, *With Zeal and With Bayonets Only*, pp.77–79.
32   TNA: WO 12/5871: Muster Rolls, 47th Foot, January 1775.
33   Collection of the Fort Ticonderoga Museum: *Orderly Book of the 47th Regiment of Foot*, 9 September 1777; Spring, *With Zeal and With Bayonets Only*, p.79. The flank companies had

Without a colour guard in the centre, the 47th would have paraded thus:

General   L'Estrange   Major   Sherriff   Lieutenant Colonel   Alcock

The general's (colonel's) company was commanded by Captain Lieutenant Henry Marr, who had been promoted and appointed on 25 August 1775 (muster rolls) or 12 February 1776 (army list). The difference in dates are likely to be the between the earlier date when he took up the post, and the later date when his appointment was authorised by the army. He was the junior company commander. Captain Richard L'Estrange had been the captain lieutenant in the general's company until promoted and gaining his own company on 25 August 1775 (muster rolls) or 25 May 1772 (army list), with the difference in date being similar to that experienced by Marr. Although L'Estrange was the junior captain, he had commanded the general's company prior to that date.

Major and Captain Paulus Irving took command of the major's company 31 March 1775 having previously commanded a company as a captain. Captain William Sherriff was an established company commander, having been appointed to that position on 25 December 1765. The lieutenant colonel's company was commanded by Lieutenant Robert Duport.

Captain John Alcock was, like Sherriff, an established company commander, having been in that post since 1771.[34]

In accordance with the *1764 Regulations,* two of the most senior company commanders were in the centre of the regiment which positioned them to command the respective wings. The two most junior company commanders commanded the general's and lieutenant colonel's companies. If the regiment was divided into grand divisions of paired companies, this would place junior company commanders on the left of an established company commander.

Tactical Innovations after 1764

Despite the disbandment of the light companies, this capability was not lost to the British Army. In October 1767, the 18th Foot was newly arrived in Philadelphia en route to garrisons in Illinois. Major General Thomas Gage reviewed the 18th 'representing a Bush Fight, which gave great Satisfaction to some Thousands of spectators.' Baule goes on to show that the 18th would need those tactics in Illinois. Hubner has shown there was an unofficial retention of light companies in a number of regiments.[35] The light companies were reinstated in 1771–1772; on 21 December 1770, Thomas Thynne, Viscount Weymouth, the Secretary of State for the Southern Department, asked George III for an augmentation of the army in response to the growing tension with Spain over the Falkland Islands. Spanish Louisiana posed a

---

been detached to light and grenadier battalions and two other companies had been detached.
34   TNA: WO 65/27: Army List 1777, 47th Foot, p.101; WO 12/5871: Muster Rolls, 47th Foot, January 1776.
35   Baule, *Protecting the Empire's Frontier*, p.14; Hubner, *British Light Infantry Companies*, pp.31–33.

particular threat in North America.[36] Following the re-establishment of the light companies, two doctrines were published: Lieutenant General Lord George Townshend, the Lord Lieutenant of Ireland, issued his *Rules and Orders for the Discipline of the Light Infantry Companies in His Majesty's Army in Ireland* in 1772 (abbreviated here to Townshend's *Instructions*, see also Appendix I), while Major General William Howe's manuscript booklet *Discipline Established by Major General Howe for Light Infantry in Battalion* was published in Salisbury in 1774.[37] As Spring observed, there was no army-wide training for the light infantry until Major General David Dundas's *Rules and Regulations for the Formations, Field-Exercise, and Movements, of His Majesty's Forces* (1792).[38]

Dundas was critical of the 'American scramble' open order because of the problem of 'never relinquishing the touch of his neighbour' which he elaborates:

> Each man is necessarily employed to preserve a required distance from his neighbour; he is obliged to turn his head for that purpose, this distorts his body, a constant opening and closing takes place, the whole move loose and unconnected. If this must necessarily happen in the regulating battalion, its influence on a line may be easily imagined, and also the condition in which it will arrive near an enemy.[39]

The looseness of the lighter tactics employed meant that the soldiers were not locked into their 'proper' place by close order drill which in turn reduced the effectiveness of the battalion to deliver the effect on the enemy.

Dundas has been criticised for being overly-rigid but, as James Tanner has argued, that was certainly not the intention. In both previous wars, drill manuals had been successfully adapted. That Dundas' regulations remained largely extant throughout the titanic struggle against Revolutionary and Napoleonic France shows that his ideas were fundamentally right. He had the unenviable task of rebuilding the exhausted British Army following the American War of Independence in preparation for its next challenge. In this, his task was not dissimilar to that in 1763 although at least on the earlier occasion the army had the moral comfort of having won a war. Philip Haythornthwaithe's observation that 'tactics suitable for North American conditions were not necessarily ideal for European warfare' could also apply to 1763 and 1783. On both occasions, there was about a decade to prepare for war. Fundamentally, in rebuilding the army, Dundas had to re-establish old principles of close order drill and volley fire to deliver the maximum effect. This had more in common with Culloden Moor, Dettingen and Quebec (1759) than the American War of Independence. War against Revolutionary

---

36   Hubner, *British Light Infantry Companies*, pp.26–30; Rice 'Falkland Islands Crisis of 1770-1771', p.286; Robinson, 'Britain Between Continents', p.52.
37   Smythies, *40th Regiment*, Appendix IV, pp.549–552, *Rules and Orders for the Discipline for the Light Infantry companies in His Majesty's Army in Ireland*, Townshend, 15 May 1772; NAM: 6807-157-6: *Discipline Established by Major General Howe for Light Infantry in Battalion*, (Sarum, 1774).
38   Spring, *With Zeal and With Bayonets Only*, pp.245–247.
39   D. Dundas, *Principles of Military Movements* (London: Cadell, 1788) p.52.

A VERY FINE REGIMENT

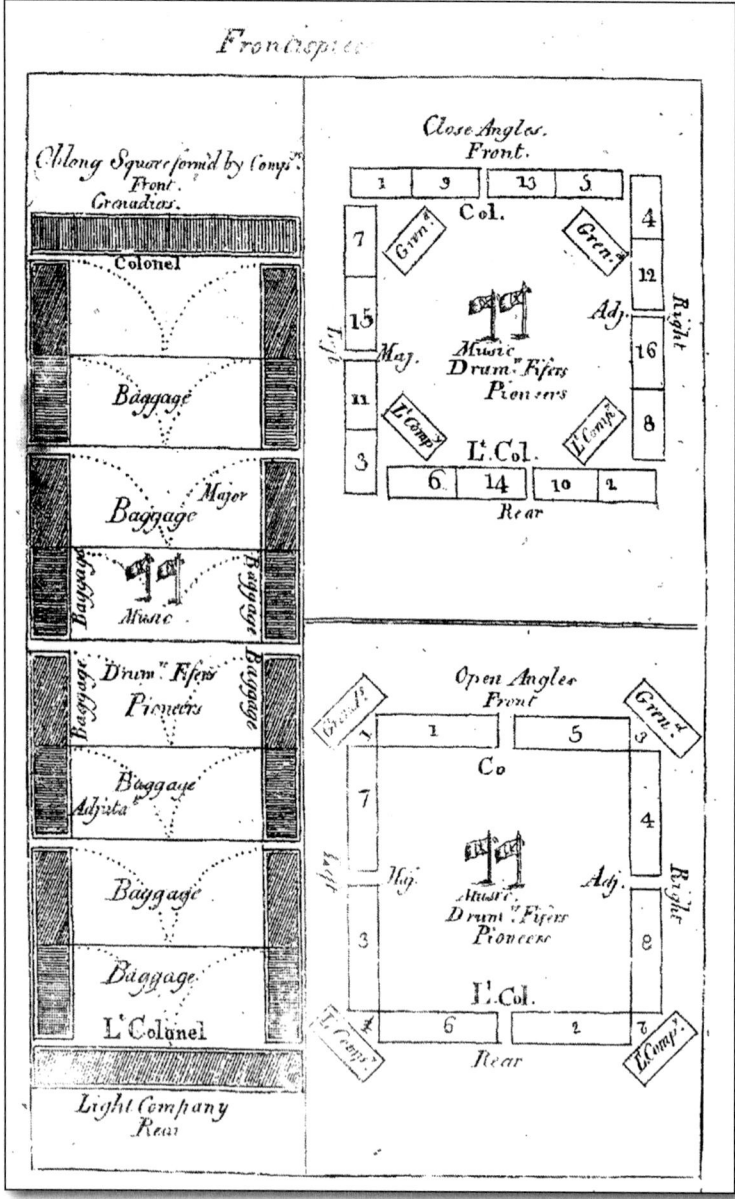

From the Frontispiece of Thomas Simes' *The Military Guide for Young Officers*. These formations are routinely recorded in the inspection returns. The lack of cavalry in the American War of Independence meant that these formations were not used in North America. They were important formations in European warfare and at the time that the 47th Foot was practicing them, a conventional European war was more likely than a colonial revolt.

France proved to be different from expected, as always, with the deployment of large numbers of *tirailleurs* and *voltigeurs* which forced the British Army to reconsider its policy on light troops but, unlike during the American War of Independence, the army did not move entirely away from the close order volley which we see at Waterloo. It is worth considering that the anticipated threat that Dundas faced was the same threat that was faced in the late-1760s and early-1770s.[40]

Townshend and Howe were veterans of the French and Indian War, as were Carleton and Gage who were in command in Quebec and Boston respectively at the outbreak of hostilities. The army possessed sufficient institutional memory to retain the earlier lessons. At the regimental level, with 20 percent of the 47th having sufficient length of service to have experienced fighting in Quebec there was a foundation to reconstitute the light company. To this can be added men like Major Paulus Aemilius Irving whose namesake father commanded the 15th Foot at the 1759 Battle of Quebec and would have had relevant experiences to pass on to Irving junior.[41] Townshend's *Instructions* were quite different from Howe's *Discipline* with the former being in the style of guidance for officers raising the new light companies. Howe's was a set of orders for how to deploy a composite light battalion, which contrasts with the manoeuvres used during regimental inspections where the light company provided direct

---

40 Tanner, *Instruments of Battle*, pp.113, 114, 118, 125; P. Haythornthwaite, *British Napoleonic Infantry Tactics, 1792-1815* (Oxford: Osprey, 2004), p.5 quoted on Tanner, *Instruments of Battle*, p.114.

41 Reid, *Quebec 1759*, p.68; O'Callaghan (ed.), *Orderly Book*, pp.165–166.

support to the regiment. Both Howe's and Townshend's ideas came from the same experience; they occupied the same conceptual space. If read together rather than in isolation, they present a coherent whole.

Townshend was Lord Lieutenant of Ireland and the commander in chief of the Irish Establishment of some 27 infantry regiments with its own staff in Dublin.[42] This represented the largest concentration of British infantry regiments. Townshend's views should have had the widest currency but as it was Howe who became commander in chief in America, it was his views on the deployment of light companies which had the greatest impact. Nevertheless, Townshend's views should not be ignored. Townshend specified deploying in two ranks, whereas Howe implies two ranks but does not specify it. So, in 1774 the inspecting officer objected to the 44th Foot's light company being formed up in three ranks. The previous year, the 53rd's light company had also not paraded according to the orders. Townshend's *Instructions* were being interpreted, at least by the inspecting officer, as orders. On the other hand, Townshend only has one size of open order, being one pace, or two feet, apart. The manual exercise is not discussed except that when in woodland or some secret activity, the musket should be lowered in two rather than three motions. Volley firing is not mentioned, but the light company should keep up a continuous fire which was achieved by only one rank firing at a time, and simply exchanging position with their file partner. Firing from behind a tree was also recommended. Woodland was the natural environment of the light infantryman, but was also a double-edged sword; it could provide protection from cavalry but also be a place of ambush – they must be 'silent and attentive.'[43]

What is not described are any details of how to manoeuvre the light companies. Townshend as much as admits this when he wrote 'And officers commanding Regiments may employ the Light Infantry in the manner which shall appear to them most proper for the safety and protection of the Battalion whether upon a March or in The Field.' This implies that the light companies would be employed to protect the battalion, as was exercised during an inspection, rather than as a composite light battalion, as had been practiced in the French and Indian War, as would be described by Howe, and as would be used in the American War of Independence. In another 20 years, General Sir David Dundas, as Commander-in-Chief of a unified British Army (rather than two separate establishments) saw this as a weakness. Although he complimented the light infantry for their service during the war, he noted in the 1792 regulations that the light companies had not supported their parent battalions.[44] In contrast, Howe's *Discipline* was a drill manual for the deployment of a composite light battalion. It was taught to the seven Salisbury regiments (3rd, 11th, 21st, 29th, 32nd 36th and 70th Foot) during a camp

---

42   Hubner, *British Light Infantry Companies*, p.48 lists these as these as the 5th, 9th, 24th, 27th, 28th, 34th, 38th, 40th, 42nd, 44th, 45th, 46th, 47th, 48th, 49th, 50th, 53rd, 55th, 57th 62nd and 63rd Foot. This list includes the 9th in which Roger Lamb served and the 47th which sailed to America in mid-1773.
43   Smythies, *40th Regiment*, Appendix IV, pp.549–552.
44   Spring, *With Zeal and With Bayonets Only*, pp.139, 246–247; Hubner, *British Light Infantry Companies*, pp.47–50, 141–142.

there between 6 August and 22 September 1774 before giving a demonstration to the King on 3 October. The demonstration was apparently a great success. The light companies then rejoined their parent battalions.[45]

The *Discipline* commences by describing the spacings between the files and the speed at which the companies were to operate at. There were three 'orders': at order was two feet interval between files, open order was four foot intervals and extended order was 10 foot intervals. The 'march' was slow time (75 paces per minute), 'march march' (120 paces per minute) was quick time, and the advance was at a run. Howe mentions 'run' on several occasions which indicates the speed at which he expected these manoeuvres to be executed. The standard formation throughout was the file which is a column two men wide. This was the most convenient and speedy mode for traversing through tracks and close country. However, to bring the full firepower to effect, the column needs to transition into line so that all of the muskets can be brough to bear on the enemy. The battalion had to 'Front Form' if the enemy was to their front, or to the right, left or about, depending on where the enemy were. To effect this change, the lead company would front form on the lead files by the left, right or centre (left and right simultaneously) with the subsequent companies forming on the first company to the left, right or centre (left and right simultaneously). The route taken should be 'the shortest line' with companies marching obliquely to reach their required station. There were then variations on the theme, reversing the front (simply executed by turning about and walking past your file partner), retiring and reforming the column to resume the march.

A loading drill followed the *1764 Regulations*, but without individual orders, simply 'Prime and Load'. The process is reduced to 15 motions with some clearly combined for speed, for example, motion 13: 'Drive the Rammer home bringing up the Piece with the Left Hand to the Shoulder seizing it with the Right hand under the back, keeping the Left Hand act at the swell turning the Body Square to the Front, and reducing the Right Foot' which merges the act of returning the ramrod and bringing the musket to the shoulder.[46]

The Salisbury regiments' demonstration before the King at Richmond Park on 3 October 1774 illustrated how a composite light battalion could be utilised. These manoeuvres are summarised in Appendix II. What Howe showed the King was a scheme of manoeuvre which was designed not only to exhibit their complexity, but also a scenario which reflected the reality of a battlefield. As well as the routine manoeuvring in the open parkland, the light companies moved into woodland. They moved in, though and out of, the woods, including firing; taking a tree and firing by files was exactly as had been practiced in North America during the last war and would be required there again in a few short years. The enemy occupied a house which was assaulted, taken and then abandoned when threatened by encirclement. This was more than just going through the motions, but exposed young soldiers and young officers to the sort of scenarios they might face in warfare; the

---

45   Hubner, *British Light Infantry Companies*, pp.49–50.
46   NAM: 6807-157-6: Howe, *Discipline*, pp.15–17.

complexities of control in woodland or participation in a successful attack only to be faced by the wrath of the enemy in the form of a counterattack.[47]

The 47th Foot's 1772 inspection return recorded the motions undertaken by light company, including covering the battalion's retreat. Later the battalion formed a column of grand divisions (two companies) which was covered by the light company on the flanks. When the battalion formed a column from the centre, the grenadier company covered the advance while the lights covered the rear. Finally, in order to cross a river, the light company formed up along the bank, fired, and then rushed the bridge. This is closer to the employment which Townshend and Dundas had in mind, rather than Howe, where the light company protected the remainder of the regiment.

The 47th would have received a copy of Townshend's *Instructions* but was already in North America when Howe was instructing his *Discipline* to the Salisbury regiments in 1774. It would be interesting to speculate about the intellectual environment in which the 47th existed before their departure overseas. The 47th had served in Townshend's brigade at Quebec in 1759 and Howe had commanded a composite light battalion with the 47th's Major Hussey as his deputy. Howe followed the 47th to Boston and it would have been inconceivable if they were not exposed to his *Discipline* there. The regiment was known to both of these generals.

How were these ideas distributed across an army without a central training directorate and with two establishments operating independently? Corporal Roger Lamb (9th Foot) claimed that Howe's *Discipline* was an 'excellent mode of discipline for light troops' well suited for North America. The 9th Foot was on the Irish Establishment and not one of the Salisbury regiments. He was also in a centre company, not the light company. Lamb's statement needs to be treated with some caution. He had only been serving for 18 months and he had joined a regiment which was not fit for service. After six years garrisoning Florida, the inspection reports were particularly scathing. In 1772 the inspecting officer commented, 'This Regiment is realy [sic] a Very Bad One. Nothwithstanding they Performed the Firings Well and Marched Well. By the Plan laid down by the Colonel must Certainly improve' and by the following year the report included 'much Mended Since the Last Review, and Doubt not but it will be better against the Next, as most of the Old Men are Discharged. All the Movements & with Briskness.' By 1774, they were described as a 'pretty good Body of Men, Pretty well dressed, Wants a great many men to Complete' but the 9th were still not fit for service when they were deployed to Quebec.[48] As Lamb enlisted in August 1773, he would not have participated in that year's inspection, which had taken place on 18th May, although he may well have seen it at Phoenix Park. The 1774 inspection took place at Waterford where it was in a single-battalion cantonment which greatly limited the scope of their exercise compared with the previous two years where the 9th had participated in divisional-level exercises. Coincidentally, Lamb never served under Howe. His exposure to

---

47 Spring, *With Zeal and With Bayonets Only*, p.139.
48 TNA: WO 27/26, WO 27/29, WO 27/32: Inspection Returns, Irish, 9th Foot for 1772, 1773 and 1774. The 9th Foot did particpate in a divisional-sized exercise in Dublin in 1775.

operational tactics (rather than training) and to the style of light infantry warfare both occurred under Carleton and then Burgoyne in Quebec and upper New York.[49]

Lamb does not specify what he was taught. He states that it was Howe's *Discipline* and calls it a 'new exercise'; if read in isolation, Lamb's account suggests that these light tactics were being introduced into the Irish Establishment for the first time.[50] Phoenix Park, Dublin was the British Army's largest peacetime exercise ground where they routinely conducted divisional level exercises, that is up to six battalions in three brigades with artillery support and troops to play 'enemy'. There was also a three-battalion exercise at Cork in 1773. This contrasts with the British Establishment where a single battalion exercise was the norm, one of the few multi-battalion reviews was the 7th and 23rd Fusiliers at Chatham in 1771.[51] A review of the 9th Foot's 1773 exercise shows a complexity exceeding that described by Howe's *Discipline* the following year. There were three brigades composed of the 9th and 28th, 27th and 46th, and 45th and 17th Foot, each brigade being supported by three field pieces. A squadron of cavalry provided an enemy. A summary of the exercise has the line entering a wood, four of the light companies detached to take possession of some marshy ground on the right while two further companies took possession of a house and hedges on the right. Later the left brigade would advance, form battalions and link up with the light companies on the marsh. Columns of infantry retired with the 'head of the Column' firing and then retiring under the cover of the smoke. Two companies of grenadiers were detached to block a ride through the woods and it was probably these who retired while keeping up a constant fire by platoons. The light companies skirmished to protect the flanks of brigade columns. The light companies also occupied a wood. The left brigade simulated breaking and reforming to the rear behind the grenadiers which had formed a 'Corps De Reserve'. The left brigade formed to their left to defend their flank six deep, with the front three ranks remaining kneeling until the rear three ranks had fired over their heads. The whole exercise concluded with a volley and bayonet charge.[52]

These Phoenix Park exercises were conducted twice a year. They exercised not just the tactical skills of the private solider and the junior officer, but provided senior officers with the opportunity to gain experience at the operational (not 'combat') level. Battles are not the activity of individual battalions, but of brigades and divisions. Burgoyne in 1777 commanded two divisions (usually referred to as 'wings', one British and one German) each of three brigades plus artillery, while Howe at Long Island commanded three divisions (two British and one German) each of three or four brigades. Within these Phoenix Park exercises are elements not dissimilar to those conducted by Howe, including

---

49   Hubner, *British Light Infantry Companies*, p.50; Hagist, *British Soldier's Story*, pp.7, 15; Houlding, *Fit For Service*, p.296.
50   Hagist, *British Soldier's Story*, p.15.
51   TNA: WO 27/29: Inspection Returns, Irish, 1773, 34th, 35th and 48th Foot; WO 27/21: Inspection Returns, British, 1771, 7th and 23rd Foot.
52   Houlding, *Fit For Service*, p.55; TNA: WO 27/29: Inspection Returns, Irish, 1773, 9th, 17th, 27th, 28th, 45th and 46th Foot.

TACTICAL EVOLUTION

detaching several companies (not necessarily light companies) to secure flank positions, operating in woodland, advancing and retiring while giving fire, or skirmishing. Other manoeuvres being practiced in Ireland where the training estate permitted, included the 27th Foot in 1772 operating in Indian (single) file, two and three 'deep', covering a bridge crossing and forming square against cavalry. The same year, the 47th Foot also formed square and covered a bridge crossing with 'The whole performed in Double Quick Time.'[53] Townshend's *Instructions* would have probably been applied at Phoenix Park. If the Irish Establishment was already practising these movements, why was Lamb being taught Howe's *Discipline* by the 33rd Foot? Afterall, Lamb would spend far more time being instructed in light tactics under Carleton and Burgoyne, and later Clinton and Cornwallis. Lamb's instructors would have been trained in Howe's *Discipline*. Was 'Howe' a shorthand for these light tactics? It is, however, clear that the Irish Establishment inspection returns expected, and recorded, a high level of efficiency, which conforms to Houlding's idea that Ireland provided a strategic reserve.[54]

Hubner has tracked the distribution of Howe's *Discipline* throughout the wider army. The 33rd Foot taught the *Discipline* to the 20th Foot while both regiments were in Plymouth preparing to sail to Ireland. This was in April 1774, four months before it was taught to the Salisbury regiments. How and when the 33rd had learnt the *Discipline* is unclear but considering the attention which the 33rd's colonel, Lord Cornwallis, bestowed upon his regiment, it would be unsurprising if an early copy of the *Discipline* had not been acquired by him. Hubner estimated there was an average of 13 infantry regiments in Britain. If Howe wanted to trial his *Discipline* on a regiment before training the seven Salisbury regiments which culminated with a Royal review, it only leaves about six regiments from which to select one to test his *Discipline* on. His own regiment, the 46th, was stationed in Ireland and so unavailable. The 33rd Foot's 1774 inspection return was conducted by Howe at Plymouth on 31 March. Their manoeuvres resembled that of Howe's Richmond Park manoeuvres later in the year, including an enemy with cannon to exercise against. The 20th Foot would be reviewed by Howe a few days later in Exeter, on 2 April. Their inspection return is a much simpler report without reference to the nature of the ground or the presence of an enemy. It does report that the flank companies operated as four platoons and the light company 'dispersed & fired irregularly'.[55] What it does show, however, was that the 20th Foot's flank companies were developing their own doctrine in an unusual and innovative manner to provide the commanding officer with four, rather than two, flank manoeuvre units. Once in Ireland, on 18 May 1774, the 20th and 33rd conducted a tactical exercises as part of their inspection at Charlesfort, until recently the home of the 47th Foot. The exercise is interesting in that it consisted of manoeuvres by the 'Garrison' against an 'Enemy', at both the company and battalion levels. This differed from standard British inspections where regiments were usually inspected

---

53 TNA: WO 27/26: Inspection Returns, Irish, 1772, 47th Foot.
54 Houlding, *Fit For Service*, p.48.
55 TNA: WO 27/32: Inspection Returns, Irish, 1774, 20th Foot.

individually, or the Irish 1773 inspections where on each of two occasions, six regiments manoeuvred in three brigades. The 33rd plus the 20th's flank companies landed on a beach in Kinsale Bay, attempted to take the fort and were eventually driven back by the eight centre companies of the 20th.[56] Howe's *Discipline* was designed for the deployment of a composite light battalion, not just a light company. Was the *Discipline* being used by all 10 companies of each battalion? There is nothing in the language of the 1774 inspection return that either the 20th or 33rd performed the exercise as a light infantry battalion in accordance with Howe's *Discipline*.

Corporal Roger Lamb (9th Foot) says that he was taught Howe's *Discipline* by the 33rd Foot during a camp in the Spring of 1775 in Dublin, although they only taught him a part of the *Discipline*. The colonel of the 9th had sent Lamb 'among several other non-commissioned officers to be instructed in the new exercise which shortly before had been introduced by Major General Howe. It consisted of a set of manoeuvres to be practiced in the different regiments.' The Dublin Garrison at this time consisted of the 15th, 34th, 37th and 46th Foot as well as the 9th and 33rd. The 24th, 53rd and 62nd Foot were also on the Irish Establishment at this time and would later serve in Canada and New York. Howe was Colonel of the 46th and it would be unusual if his

Charles Fort near Kinsale was the impressive home of the 47th Foot in the years before they sailed to New York. (Photographic Archive, National Monuments Service, Government of Ireland)

---

56 Hubner, *British Light Infantry Companies*, p.73; TNA: WO 27/32: Inspection Returns, Irish, 1774, 20th and 33rd Foot; for the Phoenix Park exercises the previous year, see WO 27/29: Inspection Returns, Irish, 1773, 5th, 9th, 17th, 27th, 28th, 42nd, 45th, 46th, 54th, 55th, 62nd and 63rd Foot.

TACTICAL EVOLUTION

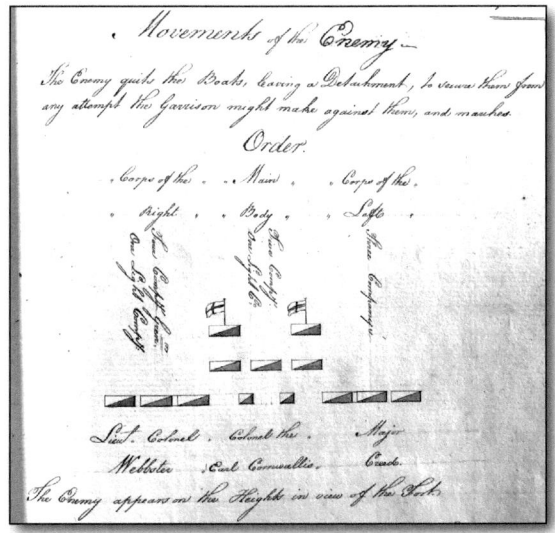

These instructions for the 'Enemy' – the 33rd Foot – for the two-battalion exercise conducted on 18 May 1774 near Kinsale. The details of this exercise included in the inspection return of the 20th Foot (WO 32/32) are unique amongst the returns examined for this book. (The National Archives)

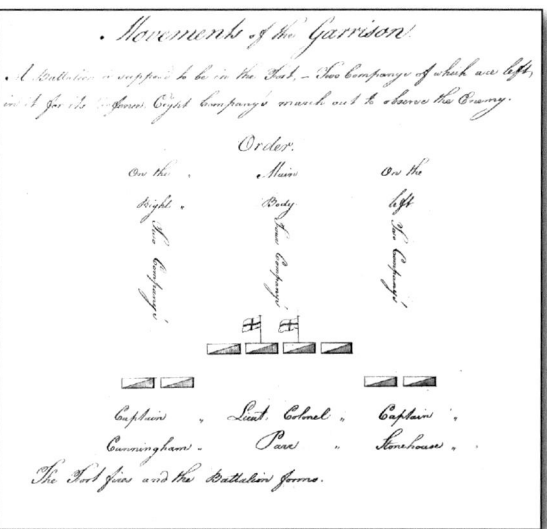

The 'Garrison' – the 20th Foot – which defended a fort and opposed the 'Enemy' 33rd Foot. (The National Archives)

own regiment had not received a copy of the *Discipline* with instructions to implement it. Lamb was taught some of the *Discipline* despite not being from the light company. Were Howe's ideas being distributed around all companies to make the army more flexible? The light infantry concept did not die out after 1763 and regiments were innovating in their own light tactics. In the next couple of years, all companies in Canada at least would adopt light tactics. This would suggest that Howe's *Discipline* was being disseminated throughout the British Army in general and not just the light companies, as had been practiced at Salisbury.[57]

Ten British regiments would serve under Carleton and Burgoyne in Canada and New York in 1776 and 1777. Seven of these would be the whole regiment (9th, 20th, 21st, 24th, 47th, 53rd and 62nd Foot) while three would contribute just their flank companies (29th, 31st and 34th Foot) to Burgoyne's 'Canada Army' in 1777. Of these, the 21st and 29th were Salisbury regiments which trained on Howe's *Discipline* in 1774 while five more (9th, 24th, 47th, 53rd and 62nd Foot) would have received Townshend's *Instructions* while part of the Irish Establishment. Only two regiments are not known to have had the opportunity to train on Howe's *Discipline* in the British Isles – the 31st and 47th. The 47th had departed Ireland for North America in mid-1773. In the spring of 1775, when Lamb was being instructed in Dublin, the 47th were already facing the reality of warfare in North America. Howe's arrival in Boston in 1775 could have exposed the garrison to his *Discipline*. The 31st Foot was serving in the West Indies when their light company was raised in Britain. The 31st returned to Britain, 299 strong, in 1771 and then

---

57   Hubner, *British Light Infantry Companies*, pp.72–75; Hagist, *British Soldier's Story*, p.15.

joined its light company. In 1775 the regiment marched to Scotland before sailing for Canada. The 31st does not appear to have had the opportunity to learn Howe's *Discipline*.[58]

Hubner has also identified a link between the Salisbury regiments, the 33rd's camp in Dublin, and Canada in the form of Charles Stanhope, Viscount Petersham and captain in the 29th Foot's light company. Promoted on 26 July 1773, he could be expected to have participated in the Salisbury exercises or received instruction in it from the company's instructors. In 1776, Stanhope travelled to Canada where he was a friend of both Lieutenant General Burgoyne and Brigadier General Simon Fraser who would command Burgoyne's Advance Corps in 1777. The former 'particularly noticed his talents and services' and in 1777 made Stanhope his aide-de-camp. Fraser considered Stanhope 'one of the most promising young officers in the service at that trying time.'; Lieutenant Thomas Anburey served in Petersham's grenadier company of the 29th Foot during the Saratoga Campaign and dedicated his *Travels* to him. Brigadier General Fraser was also a lieutenant colonel with the 24th Foot which was on the Irish Establishment and would have been instructed in both Townshend's *Instructions* and Howe's *Discipline*. Fraser himself had developed an expertise in light infantry tactics both in North America and in Europe during the previous war[59]

Speed

Howe's *Discipline* made it clear that he expected his tactics to be conducted at the trot. The 47th's 1772 inspection return recorded: 'The Whole performed in Double Quick time.'[60] The 47th were ahead in their doctrinal theory. On operations, this speed could be extremely beneficial: in June 1776 while pursuing the rebels out of Canada, three light companies would jog for three miles.[61] Major General William Phillips (RA), who would serve as second in command to Burgoyne in 1777, during the winter of 1776/1777 exercised his troops, much to the horror of the German commanders who were unfamiliar with 'galloping'. *Hauptmann* Pausch of the Hanau Artillery recorded his surprise at these novel innovations, in two entries in his journal:

> Every one was obliged to be at Parade [at 11 am] – the English Artillery as well as my own. The companies formed in line at the barracks and were taken by companies to the Parade Ground. They were obliged to run sometimes for a half, and sometimes for a whole hour.[62]

---

58   Hubner, *British Light Infantry Companies*, p.75.
59   Hubner, *British Light Infantry Companies*, pp.75–76, 81–82; O'Callaghan (ed.), *Orderly Book*, pp.167–168; TNA: WO 65/27: Army List 1777, 29th Foot, p.85.
60   TNA: WO 27/26: Inspection Returns, Irish, 1772, 47th Foot.
61   J.P. Baxter (ed.), *The British Invasion from the North – The Campaigns of Generals Carleton and Burgoyne, from Canada 1776-1777, with the Journal of Lieut. William Digby of the 53rd, or Shropshire Regiment of Foot* (Albany, NY: Joel Munsell's Sons, 1887), p.118; G.F.G. Stanley, *For Want of a Horse* (Sackville, NB: Tribune Press, 1961), p.75, also quoted in Spring, *With Zeal and With Bayonets Only*, p.61.
62   W.L. Stone (ed.), *Journal of Captain Pausch – Chief of the Hanau Artillery during the Burgoyne Campaign* (Albany: Joel Munsell's Sons, 1886), p.100.

Every day, to my disgust, I have to practice the [lately] introduced quick-step, which we do not have, nor do they have it in Prussia – nay not in the world, except in the chase, with fast horses and good dogs! This is a splendid exercise for the men in winter; but in the summer, when the weather is warm, it is detrimental to the health of the men. It has no good result except to make the spectators laugh – for by this manoeuvre no closed ranks could be kept in an attack upon the enemy. In case, therefore, of a retreat, we would not only fare badly, but would be exposed to the well deserved censures of the European and American press.[63]

This was an Army in training for rapid mobility, rather than a slow, pedestrian advance.

Fire Discipline

Spring discusses the fashion for following Prussian 'quick-fire' whereby the enemy could be intimidated or supressed, rather than killed or wounded. Blackmore has shown that the British Army had been steadily improving its rate of fire over the previous century, which was achieved by lessening the time that muskets were unloaded and also vulnerable to counterattack. A few well delivered volleys were, it was believed, more effective than the Prussian approach of up to six rounds per minute.[64] Performing drills quickly and efficiently through practice and confidence was not the same as quick firing. The *1764 Regulations* were 'to be done as quick as possible.'[65] This is, of course, the purpose of drills which are practiced until they become automatic and can be performed automatically when under pressure. Lieutenant General Gage, in 1774, reminded his soldiers in Boston that in conducting the drills they 'cannot be too quick'. During the retreat from Lexington and Concord, one of the officers complained that the young soldiers had 'been taught that everything was to be effected by a quick firing.'[66]

There was a conflict between the rate of fire (the speed of firing) and weight of fire (which is the effect on the battlefield). As discussed above, Blackmore has established the importance placed on the British Army of delivering a controlled volley at short range to have maximum effect. This also required confidence, and that can only be gained from operational exposure. Cuthbertson wrote how the annual entitlement for firing ball rounds was four rounds per annum; blank rounds were called 'squibs'. Peacetime economies limited the opportunities for live firing. The deteriorating security situation in North America resulted in a relaxation of the parsimonious supply of ammunition, but as with all military skills, they take time to develop. In Boston in 1774 and 1775, live firing at marks was a regular occurrence to increase confidence, as will be shown below.[67]

---

63 Pausch, *Journal*, p.108.
64 Spring, *With Zeal and With Bayonets Only*, p.205; Carmichael, *Like a Brazen Wall*, p.46.
65 *1764 Regulations*, p.10 quoted in Spring, *With Zeal and With Bayonets Only*, p.205.
66 MacKenzie quoted in Spring, *With Zeal and With Bayonets Only*, p.205.
67 Cuthbertson, *Complete Interior Management*, p.85.

Volley Firing

The British soldier was not some automaton simply pointing and firing his musket to the front, despite the description given in the *1764 Regulations* as: 'raise up the butt so high upon the right shoulder, that you may not be obliged to stoop so much with the head (the right cheek to be close to the butt, and the left eye shut), and look along the barrel with the right eye from the breech pin to the muzzle.'[68] But this tactic did have value on an open battlefield against a conventional enemy, as was repeatedly shown from the English Civil War to Waterloo.

On 14 August 1774, Gage in Boston ordered troops to adopt three-rank firing with close order unless ordered otherwise.[69] Gage's performance around Boston was lacklustre, but we must still assume that a general officer of his experience in North American warfare made this ruling for a purpose. In the first place, firing in three ranks was still standard practice as shown in the inspection returns.[70] General Howe re-introduced three ranks with 18 inches between files for the grenadier and centre companies on 25 May 1776 while at Halifax, but in preparation to sail for New York.[71] Gage's order was not a retrograde step, but reaffirmed standard practice. If he expected his army to be opposed by a large, but unsteady, local militia then arguably the best tactic in an open battlefield would be break the enemy's moral cohesion through a single, concentrated, devastating volley. His army would lose their advantages if engaged in skirmishing or hand to hand combat against a larger foe who was familiar with the terrain and able to take advantage of defensive features, like walls and fences.

Firing at Marks

It has long been established that live 'firing at marks' was practiced. In Boston, just three days before Bunker Hill, Gage issued an order relating to recruits that '[p]roper marksmen [are] to instruct them in taking aim, and the position in which they ought to stand in firing, and to do this man by man before they are suffered to fire together.' He had previously noted, in November 1774, 'that the men be taught to take good aim, which if they do they will always level well.'[72]

Lieutenant Frederick Mackenzie (23rd Fusiliers) described live firing in Boston in January 1775:

> The regiments are frequently practised at firing with ball at marks. Six rounds per man at each time is usually allotted for this practice. As our regiment is quartered on a wharf which projects into part of the harbour, and there is a very considerable range without any obstructions, we have fixed figures of men as large as life, made

---

68 Quoted in Spring, *With Zeal and With Bayonets Only*, p.207.
69 TNA: WO 36/1: North America, Entry Books, Orders, 14 August 1774.
70 In 1774 several but not all British inspection returns mention firing in two ranks – the 3rd, 11th, 20th and 33rd Foot (WO 27/31) while the 4th Foot's front rank did not kneel when firing in three ranks (WO 27/30) however in Ireland the same year the 44th's light company was formed up in three ranks contrary to orders (WO 27/32).
71 Hale, Stevens & Howe (eds), *Orderly Book*, p.294, 25 May 1776.
72 Quoted in Spring, *With Zeal and With Bayonets Only*, pp.207–208.

of thin boards, on small stages, which are anchored at a proper distance from the end of the wharf, at which the men fire. Objects afloat, which move up and down with the tide, are frequently pointed out for them to fire at, and premiums are sometimes given for the best shots, by which means some of our men have become excellent marksmen.[73]

So, not only were the soldiers practicing, but there was an incentive to encourage good shooting rather than just firing quickly to get the exercise over so that they could get out of the cold of the firing range and back into the warmth of a building. Two months later, a visitor described the Marines and another regiment at a similar exercise:

I saw a regiment and a body of Marines each by itself, firing at marks. A target being set up before each company, the soldiers of the regiment stepped out singly, took aim and fired, and the firing was kept up in this manner by the whole regiment till they had all fired ten rounds. The Marines fired by platoons, by companies, and sometimes by files, and made some general discharges, taking aim all the while at targets the same as the regiment.[74]

Proficiency in live firing was considered essential for providing soldiers with confidence in their weapons. During the Salisbury exercises of September 1774, Howe issued 90 blank and 20 live rounds per man and the year before had been concerned when he realised that the 4th Foot 'wants practice in firing ball.'[75] In January 1776, Howe instructed: 'The Command[in]g Officers of Corps to practice their Recruits and drafts in fireing at marks, and may, when they think it necessary, order the whole out for that purpose.'[76]

The Bayonet

The bayonet supplemented firepower. The British Army tried to avoid becoming engaged in protracted firefights which it felt it would lose, as shown in examples given previously. In the context of a conventional battle, driving the enemy from the battlefield at the point of bayonet would constitute a victory, for example at Quebec in 1759 when a volley was followed by a bayonet charge.

The *1764 Regulations* gave no more instruction on the use of the bayonet other than fixing and charging, that is for the front rank to level the bayonet while the second and any subsequent ranks kept their arms vertical. There was no instruction on how to fight with the bayonet. Cuthbertson, who has a comment on everything, recommended that soldiers became 'more familiar

---

73   A. French (ed.), *A British Fusilier in Revolutionary Boston: being the diary of Lieutenant Frederick Mackenzie Adjutant of the Royal Welch Fusiliers* (Cambridge: Harvard University Press, 1926), pp.28–29, 15 January 1775.
74   Robert Honeyman, *Colonial Panorama*, p.44, for 22 March 1775 quoted in Spring, *With Zeal and With Bayonets Only*, p.208 and D. Saul, *No Contemptible Commander: Sir William Howe and the American War of Independence, 1775-1777* (PhD, Chester, 2013), pp.70–72.
75   Hubner, *British Light Infantry Companies*, pp.51, 55; TNA: WO 27/30: Inspection Returns, British, 1773, 4th Foot.
76   Hale, Stevens & Howe (eds), *Orderly Book*, p.201, 20 January 1776.

with the bayonets than is the custom.'[77] This approach was pursued in North America. In June 1776, Lieutenant James Hadden's *Orderly Book* recorded that 'No Exercise need be practised, except Loading, Levelling, charging with Bayonets, and marching….' and he later added he believed that 'the Bayonet in the hands of the Valiant is irresistible', going on to explain that as the enemy relied on 'Intrenchments', they will have to be stormed.[78] Roger Lamb of the 9th Foot made a similar comment, that '[t]o prime, load, fire and charge with the bayonet expeditiously were the chief points worthy of our attention.'[79] Lieutenant Thomas Anburey (29th Foot) in a letter of 20 May 1777, wrote: 'Our success in any engagement must greatly rest on the bayonet, the great utility of which General Burgoyne pointed out in an order a few days since, strongly recommending the officers in inculcate that idea into the minds of the men.'[80]

Blackmore has shown that a combination of deliberate volley fire followed by a bayonet charge was the most effective means of defeating an enemy in the open. The bayonet had slowly replaced the pike as the anti-cavalry weapon, developing into an anti-personnel weapon during the eighteenth century. The absence of a cavalry threat in North America emphasised the utility of the bayonet's anti-personnel role. The American rebel's propensity, at least initially, to operate from behind defensive positions (walls and fences) which protected them from at least some of the incoming fire and in greater numbers than the British Army could field, meant that breaking their moral cohesion through the shock of a bayonet charge was deemed the most effective means of driving the enemy from the battlefield. Furthermore, in the early years of the war, rebel militias were believed to lack the firmness required to withstand a bayonet charge. They also often lacked bayonets with which to engage in hand-to-hand combat or to deliver their own bayonet charge, although clubbed muskets remained an option. The speed at which the British Army routinely manoeuvred in North America only added to the potency of their bayonets. The disadvantages of the bayonet charge were the exhaustion and disorganisation of the soldiers, which was illustrated most disastrously at Cowpens in 1781, and was also a problem at both Saratoga battles. Blackmore argued that the infantry becoming embroiled in a mêlée had fallen out of favour in the early eighteenth century European campaigns because they risked exhaustion and disorganisation. Those campaigns operated in an environment where there was sufficient cavalry to support the infantry and fulfil the mêlée function, which was notably absent in most of the North American campaigns.

At the Battle of Freeman's Farm (or the First Battle of Saratoga as it was also known) on 19 September 1777, the bayonet simply did not deliver the desired effect. Captain John Money, Deputy Quarter Master General, wrote that 'the 62nd Regiment charged four times…. quitting their position each time…. [T]he rebels fled at every charge deeper still into the woods; but when

---

77 Cuthbertson, *Complete Interior Management*, p.123.
78 Hadden, *Journal*, p.74, 25 June 1776; p.197, 29 June 1776.
79 Hagist, *British Soldier's Story*, p.37.
80 Anburey, *Travels*, vol.I, pp.212–213, Letter XVIII, 20 May 1777.

the British troops returned to their position, they were slowly followed, and those who had been the most forward in the pursuit were the first to fall.'[81] Lieutenant James Hadden (RA), added that the rebels attempted to outflank the 62nd by advancing through the woods.[82] Burgoyne's despair is palpable:

> Few actions have been characterized by more obstinacy in attack or defense. The British bayonet was repeatedly tried ineffectually. Eleven hundred British soldiers, foiled in these trials, bore incessant fire from a succession of fresh troops in superior numbers, for above four hours; and after a loss of above a third of their numbers (and in one of the regiments, above, two thirds), forced the enemy at last. Of a detachment of a captain and forty-eight artillerymen, the captain and thirty-six were killed or wounded.[83]

The expected result of a well delivered bayonet attack was to drive the enemy from the field followed by the cavalry to continue the rout. The relatively small fields surrounded by woodland gave the rebels the opportunity to withdraw into a safe area where they could reform and counterattack the crown forces. Lieutenant William Digby (53rd Foot) perceived of their doctrine: 'it has always been the wish of the Americans to avoid a general engagement, except they have a great superiority, and to surround small parties of ours, and get them into a wood, where the discipline of our troops is not of such force.'[84]

British commanders faced a dilemma. Well before 1775, the British Army was adopting light, loose and fast tactics. Throughout the long eighteenth century, the British Army was a minor player in land operations. These novel tactics would allow the British Army to 'punch above its weight' alongside a larger European ally and in the face of larger European foes. Mathematically, the numerically inferior British would lose a protracted exchange of volleys against a numerically larger foe, which included most foes they were likely to meet. The problem was that the looser formations adopted in North America negated the shock of the bayonet charge. For maximum effect, the bayonet charge had to be delivered by companies in close order of at least two ranks. Howe in Boston adopted three ranks for a short period while Burgoyne even exercised in four ranks, while in Virginia in 1781 his former deputy, Phillips, stipulated that the 'charging order' should be three or four deep.[85] This was the dichotomy of the British Army in North America.

Command and Control

The company was the primary tactical unit following the demise of platoon firing. The company commander's ability to deliver a volley on the

---

81 Money on 62nd quoted in Spring, *With Zeal and With Bayonets Only*, pp.256–257.
82 Hadden, *Journal*, pp.164–166, 19 September 1777.
83 Burgoyne quoted in D. Snow, *1777: Tipping Point at Saratoga* (Oxford: Oxford University Press), p.151.
84 Baxter, *British Invasion*, pp.273–274.
85 Phillips quoted in Hagist, *Noble Volunteers*, p.87.

commanding officer's order was fundamental to British Army doctrine. The looser formations being adopted in North America made command and control increasingly difficult. The even looser formations adopted by the introduction of light tactics on the larger, open battlefields or the woodlands of North America only exasperated this difficulty. The increasing distances over which a company, let alone a battalion, deployed over also made situational awareness increasingly difficult.

Major General William Phillips (RA), served as Burgoyne's deputy in Canada. He addressed this in May 1777 when he explained that although the company was a part of the battalion, and should operate as part of the battalion, yet the company should also be expected to operated individually as required: 'that every company may form a respectable body singly, and though attached to its place in battalion, yet always ready to act separate from it, as the nature of the ground may require, or as the nature of local service they may be sent on make necessary.' And to facilitate command and control, 'the commanding officer of a battalion to put himself at the head of one company, and to manoeuvre that company; while the other companies … follow the evolutions so given by the commanding officer.'[86] In his review of the Battle of Hubbardton, Anburey saw exactly what Phillips had described: 'Both parties engaged in separate detachments unconnected with each other, and the numbers of the enemy empowered them to front flank and rear.'[87]

What Phillips advocated and Anburey described was something akin to the modern 'mission command' whereby a subordinate commander understood their commander's intent and could then make decisions to act in support of that intent without having to seek confirmation first. Confirming the commander's intent could be a time-consuming process. While this was being sought, fleeting tactical advantages could be lost.

The flank companies traditionally operated in isolation or detached from the battalion; for this reason, as Shearwood has shown earlier, the grenadier companies were equipped with bayonets for anti-cavalry protection before the centre companies which benefited from the protection of the pikes. This detached service was the reason why the officer establishment for flank companies, in addition to the captain, contained two lieutenants, rather than a lieutenant and ensign as in the centre companies. Additional experience was necessary for detached service. This idea of detached service continued with the establishment of composite grenadier and light battalions. The remaining centre companies were not normally detached in the same way as the flank companies. They could be detached for what Phillips called local service, and, as we will see, two of the 47th's centre companies were detached to guard Diamond Island in 1777. Like the detached service of the flank companies, local service required responsible officers who could be relied upon to exercise their duties. The centre companies which remained with the regiment were now operating in a looser environment. This made both command and control, and situational awareness for officers and NCOs increasingly challenging.

---

86 Quoted in Spring, *With Zeal and With Bayonets Only*, pp.183–184 n.55, n.56.
87 Anburey, *Travels*, vol.I, p.337, Letter XXXII, 14 July 1777.

Roger Lamb, summed up the difficulties arising from this form of warfare, and how it was not just the commanders who had to change:

> [E]xperienced generals and old soldiers are left at a loss and obliged to encounter unforeseen obstacles and accidents which demand new movements and momentary measures in the execution whereof, every officer ought to be an excellent general, and every company ably disposed for whatever the passing minute of time might bring about. It is therefore plain that the best army, so circumstanced, cannot co-operate or concentrate itself with effect of advantage.[88]

In his article on the commissioning of NCOs, Houlding has argued that:

> [W]e can conclude that NCOs were becoming more highly regarded than we have been led to suppose, and that officers were not, in fact, dumping but rather sharing the burden of administration in their increasing confidence in the Other Rank. This is implicit in [*With Zeal and with Bayonets Only*], in which it is plain that the regimental officers could never have adopted so loose, dynamic, and aggressive a system without having had confidence in their men to carry it out; and it is explicit in [*Motivation in War*'s] analysis of the behaviour, motivation, and military values that developed widely among the eighteenth century soldiery.[89]

In other words, in order for all of these innovations to occur, regimental officers needed confidence that their sergeants and corporals would carry out part of the command and control function, and that the private soldiers would perform their roles too. This could not have happened in an army of automatons motivated by brutality and alcohol.

Command and control is the function of officers and NCOs to deliver the maximum effect. This could be a well-delivered volley to break the enemy's moral cohesion, or a force deployed to dislocate and disrupt the enemy's own command and control functions. An example of this was when Burgoyne positioned artillery to dominate Fort Ticonderoga resulting in a precipitous evacuation. Although this work is not overly concerned with grand strategy, it is not practical to entirely disconnect the impact of higher order strategy from the lower order application of tactics. The established methods of command and control were the drum, voice, probably augmented by a whistle, and personal example. Looser tactical formations, dispersed companies and operating in woodlands, which reduced situational awareness, all made command and control more challenging.

In an Operational Environment, 1775–1777

As has been established previously, confidence was critical to the efficient and successful application of tactics and technology, but that confidence was lacking in the opening phases of a conflict. Time provided the opportunity to

---

88 R. Lamb, *Memoir of his Own Life* (Dublin: J. Jones, 1811), p.200.
89 Houlding, 'Commissioning of Non-Commissioned Officers', p.361.

gain experience which would allow that confidence to develop. Why should 1775 be any different? The British Army in Boston faced the realities, not the theories, of war. Spring would write: 'Surprisingly perhaps, the outbreak of rebellion in America in April 1775 revealed that the redcoats in Boston were unprepared to form, manoeuvre, and fight in any other than conventional fashions'.[90]

For the reasons given above, time and a disjointed command structure worked against this aim. Nevertheless, there were moves afoot to address that shortcoming. Whether or not it was in time to save the crown's authority in North America was another matter. In 1775, the Governor of Massachusetts and Commander-in-Chief of the British Army in North America was Lieutenant General Thomas Gage. He possessed extensive experience in North America which included commanding Braddock's vanguard at Monongahela followed by raising the 80th Light Infantry. In 1767 he watched the 18th Foot going through bush fighting drills. Despite his long service and residence in North America, his performance in 1775 was not as dynamic as was required. His order to form three deep was reversed on 3 June 1775 following Lexington and Concord, but before Bunker Hill: 'The troops will draw up two deep on their regimental parades as well as on the general parade.'[91] And, as mentioned above, Howe reintroduced three ranks just before departing Halifax for New York. Clinton, one of the triumvirate of generals sent to assist Gage in Boston, criticised this two-deep disposition, writing that it 'was one long straggling line two deep'. Flexibility, rather than dogma, was dominant.[92]

Howe arrived in Boston in March 1775 and probably brought his *Discipline* with him. He formed composite grenadier and light battalions on 17 June 1775, which conforms to his ideas from the *Discipline* and established practice from the previous war. On 3 August 1775, the strengths of the grenadier and light companies were to be made up to 35 rank and file which continued the practice of maintaining the flank companies at the expense of the centre companies.[93]

Increasing the space between files further increased the 'long straggling line' which would become derided as the 'American Scramble'. Howe ordered a change to the disposition on 29 February 1776 to open the spacings between files to 18 inches 'which they will take care to practice for the future, being the Order in w[hich] they are to Engage the Enemy.'[94] While this may be a looser formation than normal, it was still a closer order than any of those specified by either Townshend's *Instructions* or Howe's *Discipline* previously recommended. Just before the Battle of Brandywine, *Oberst* Karl Emil von Donop expressed his concern about the British practice of fighting 'with its

---

90   Spring, *With Zeal and With Bayonets Only*, p.139.
91   TNA: WO 36/1: North America, Orders, 14 Aug 1774; 3 June 1775; Hale, Stevens & Howe (eds), *Orderly Book*, p.294, 25 May 1776.
92   Clinton quoted from Spring, *With Zeal and With Bayonets Only*, p.140.
93   Hale, Stevens & Howe (eds), *Orderly Book*, p.1, 17 June 1775; p.59 3 August 1775.
94   Hale, Stevens & Howe (eds), *Orderly Book*, p.222, 29 February 1776.

files four feet apart', and this was not even the fullest extent of open order as envisaged by Howe.[95]

In an operational environment with many, close obstacles, as in the walls experienced around Lexington and Concord or fence lines at Bunker Hill, a shorter, denser line may have been easier to deploy and manoeuvre. At the same time, a concentrated volley or bayonet charge had the best prospect of defeating and dispersing a rebel militia. Conversely, in a wider, open battlefield like the forests of upper New York, the two-deep disposition with greater file spacings would have been more appropriate. This is not a situation where there is a right or wrong tactic, but rather the commanders possessed the ability to utilise a range tactics to the prevailing operational environment.

On the failure of the light companies at Lexington and Concord, Townshend wrote to Lieutenant General Jeffrey Amherst. Although neither were serving in Massachusetts in 1775, the pair knew one another well having served as brigadiers under Wolfe at Quebec in 1759 and were experienced in North American warfare. Townshend wrote: '[A]s to the loss of the flanking parties I do not wonder at it – it is not a short coat or half gaiters that makes a light infantryman, but as you know, Sir, a confidence in his aim, and that stratagem in a personal conflict, which is derived from experience.'[96] By implication, there was more to understanding skirmishing warfare than a uniform and learning the drills. The light companies had drilled on Boston Common in a manner not dissimilar to that described in the 47th's last inspection return in Ireland:

> Every regiment here has a company of light infantry, young active fellows; and they are trained in the regular manner, and likewise in a peculiar discipline of irregular and bush fighting. They run out in parties on the wings of the regiment where they keep up a constant and irregular fire. They secure their retreat and defend their front while they are forming. In one part of the exercise they lie on the backs and charge their pieces and fire lying on their bellies. They have powder horns and no cartouch boxes.[97]

These activities were undertaken as part of the parent regiment, not as part of a composite light battalion which is how they would operate shortly afterward at Lexington and Concord.

During the return march from Lexington and Concord, the soldiers were criticised for a lack of fire control and marksmanship. In the diary of Lieutenant Frederick Mackenzie (adjutant, 23rd Fusiliers) is an anonymous account from one of the flank company officers. He described a lack of 'coolness and steadiness which distinguishes troops who have been inured to service' as '[m]ost of them were young soldiers who had never been in action … A good deal of this unsteady conduct may be attributed to a sudden and unexpected commencement of hostilities, and the too great eagerness of the

---

95 Quoted in Spring, *With Zeal and With Bayonets Only*, p.152.
96 Townshend quoted in Spring, *With Zeal and With Bayonets Only*, pp.251–252.
97 Honeyman, *Colonial Panorama*, quoted in Spring, *With Zeal and With Bayonets Only*, p.250 and Saul, *No Contemptible Commander*, pp.69–70.

soldiers in the first action of a war.' He continued, saying that soldiers 'threw away their fire very inconsiderately, and without being certain of its effect', in other words, firing without aiming, or firing with too much eagerness, so that at first most of it was thrown away.[98]

However, those responsible for controlling the soldiers firing were the officers and they must take some of the blame. Lieutenant John Barker (4th Foot) went further. During the retreat 'our soldiers … although they showed no want of courage, yet were so wild and irregular, that there was no keeping them in any order; [and] by their eagerness and inattention they killed many of our own people.'[99] In the 47th Foot, a fifth of the soldiers had sufficient length of service to have gained operational experience in the previous war but the light companies were to be composed of the youngest, fittest soldiers, which would have precluded the 'old sweats' who had been under fire previously.

It takes time for an army to evolve from peacetime soldiering into an effective wartime organisation, especially in a non-militaristic society like Britain. The British Army had no intention of waging war on its American cousins. The transition from peacekeeping to warfighting operations is complicated enough when there is a clearly defined enemy (for example, a nation state) and a clearly identifiable moment (for example, crossing a border). In Boston in April 1775 there was neither a clearly defined enemy nor a clearly defined Rubicon moment. The 'grey zone' is the term used to describe the period between war and peace when deniable activities take place, usually escalating, but are short of a clearly defined act of war. This term describes the deteriorating security situation around Boston over the decade before 1775; an example of this was the mob's provocation which led to the Boston Massacre. Any escalation in the army's state of preparedness during this phase would be interpreted by the rebels as an act of aggression and risked an escalation in response by the rebels. In an environment where the crown wanted to de-escalate the political tension, any action which threatened to escalate the political tension was politically undesirable.

This alone does not explain the army's poor performance at Lexington and Concord. The terrain encountered in the vicinity of Boston was urban and developed farmland after over a century of European settlement. This was not an undeveloped wilderness. It was the type of terrain which Howe would have utilised for his Salisbury exercises and envisaged in his *Discipline*, and which the 47th used for their manoeuvres when they were inspected. From the tactical point of view, that is the deployment of companies, composite battalions and regiments, there should have been no reason why they struggled at Lexington and Concord in 1775. This was, after all, the type of terrain they had practiced on.

Following the evacuation of Boston, Howe reassembled his army at Halifax, Nova Scotia. His notional order of battle of 16 May 1776 had the two light battalions in the vanguard, followed by the artillery, while the two

---

98   Mackenzie, *British Fusilier*, pp.65–66, 19 April 1775.

99   E.E. Danna, *John Barker diary – The British in Boston* (Cambridge, MA: Harvard University Press, 1924), p.39, 19 April 1775.

grenadier battalions forming a 'corps de reserve' at the rear. This formation allowed his light battalions to cover the advance while the grenadier battalions acted as a reserve. In contrast, the following year, in 1777 Burgoyne's right wing which was composed of his British units and led by an Advance Corps consisting of his composite grenadier and light battalions, plus the 24th Foot and a company of select marksmen. Howe had a larger army with four composite flank battalions to Burgoyne's two. Burgoyne simply did not have the troop numbers to provide a sufficiently strong vanguard to patrol and protect the main body, plus a reserve to exploit victories of the size necessary to achieve operational success.[100]

By the middle of the 1777 campaign, there is evidence that the troops in Canada were gaining confidence and familiarity in their new operational environment, which is all the more surprising because the wilderness was far more alien to them than the settled farmland of around Boston. We can track this growing self-assurance in combat from Trois-Rivières on 8 June 1776. Corporal Roger Lamb (9th Foot) described his first combat. The young soldier took heed of the more experienced soldiers, and grew in confidence:

> This being the first skirmish I ever was engaged in, it really appeared to me to be a very serious matter, especially when the bullets came whistling by our ears. In order to encourage the young soldiers amongst us, some of the veterans who had been well used to this kind of work, said, 'there is no danger if you hear the sound of a bullet, which is fired against you, you are safe, and after the first charge all your fears will be done away.' These remarks I found to be perfectly true many a time afterwards.[101]

Starting with an operational pause which occurred following Carleton's recovery of St Johns and eviction of the rebels from Canada, he was able to start the re-training of regular soldiers who had gone into combat almost straight off the ship following a trans-Atlantic journey. Unfortunately, the comments were not all positive, showing that the process of gaining confidence and familiarity was an ongoing process. Anburey thought 'the Americans are by much our superiors at wood fighting, being habituated to the wood from their infancy.'[102] This assumes, of course, that the rebels were backwoodsmen. Some would have been, but there were also growing urban areas and rural settlements with the same characteristics as the homes of the British regulars. During operations in Canada and upper New York in 1776 and 1777, it is difficult to see where the British regulars were at a tactical disadvantage *viz* the rebels.

In Quebec, Carleton and then Burgoyne continued to develop the tactical training. Carleton ordered the troops to deploy in two ranks with 18 inches

---

100 Spring, *With Zeal and With Bayonets Only*, p.92; Hale, Stevens & Howe (eds), *Orderly Book*, pp.272–273, 14 May 1776 lists the composition of the four composite battalions; B. Morrissey, *Saratoga 1777: Turning Point of a Revolution* (Oxford: Osprey, 2000), p.14.
101 Hagist, *British Soldier's Story*, p.26.
102 Anburey, *Travels*, vol.I, p.212, Letter XVIII, 20 May 1777.

between files on 29 June 1776.[103] Spring believes this may have followed Howe's order of 29 February 1776 being brought to Quebec by the 47th Foot which had arrived in May 1776 or by one of the regiments arriving direct from Ireland, like the 9th Foot. This was reiterated by Burgoyne the following year, that they were to follow 'the present established rule of open files, and two deep.'[104] That this formation was still in use at the end of the campaign is shown by the description by one rebel officer before the Battle of Bemis Heights, when the British advanced, 'displayed, formed the line, and sat down in double ranks with their arms between their legs.'[105] This is reminiscent of Quebec 18 years before, which is indicative of where this doctrine originated. Major General Phillips, Burgoyne's deputy in 1777, referred to 'the common open order of two deep' in Chesapeake Bay in 1781[106]. So, there was a general and long-term adoption of the two-deep formation from 26 February 1776 for the duration of the war. Deploying in a single rank may have been used once, at Fort Anne by the 9th Foot when Lieutenant Colonel Hill required all 190 muskets in extended order to prevent his flank from being turned: 'at the summit of the hill they formed Indian file, and kept up a well directed fire til all the ammunition was expended.'[107]

The British Army during the war was supported by contract troops, or auxiliaries, from seven German states, with the largest contributing state being Hessen-Kassel. These were not mercenaries, but were provided by contracts agreed between two sovereign states. It was entirely normal and routine in European warfare for states like Britain, who maintained a small peacetime army, to quickly expand their military capability, and indeed the British Army at the Battle of Dettingen (1743) fought as contract troops.[108] There was some resistance in introducing these new tactics to German troops. Those serving in New York retained their close order tactics but discarded their third rank, apparently throughout the war.[109] In Canada, the Germans were still drilling in three ranks in July 1776. The same month, Carleton also wanted them to adopt open order tactics and to use the trees for cover as they advanced so that they could match the enemy. By August 1776, *Generalmajor* Baron Frederick von Riedesel, commanding the Germans in Canada, was training his own regiment to move through woods with skirmishers to the front. The following month, *Oberstleutnant* Heinrich von Breymann's grenadiers drilled in close order before 300 of Riedesel's regiment repeated their light drills in the woodland before the three British generals. The inference that

---

103 Hadden, *Journal*, pp.197–198, 29 June 1776.
104 Spring, *With Zeal and With Bayonets Only*, p.142; Hadden, *Journal*, p.75; O'Callaghan (ed.), *Orderly Book*, p.4, 20 June 1777.
105 Wilkinson, *Memoirs of My Own Times*, p.1:267 quoted in Spring, *With Zeal and With Bayonets Only*, p.142.
106 Phillips quoted in Spring, *With Zeal and With Bayonets Only*, p.143.
107 Hagist, *British Soldier's Story*, p.40. I am indebted to Matthew Zembo for raising this point.
108 D. Krebs, *A Generous and Merciful Enemy: life for German Prisoners of War during the American Revolution* (Norman: University Oklahoma Press, 2013), pp.3, 19–24 esp. Table 1; M., McNally, *Dettingen 1743: Miracle on the Main* (Oxford: Osprey, 2020), p.17.
109 Spring, *With Zeal and With Bayonets Only*, p.143.

all companies, not just the light troops, were trained in light tactics can be taken as indicative that they were adopted by all the British companies too.[110]

As well as training in open order, close order was retained for the bayonet charge, as the Regiment von Riedesel and two companies of Regiment von Rhetz demonstrated when they charged at the Battle of Freeman's Farm, saving the British centre 'with closed ranks.'[111] Early in 1777 while still in Canada, Burgoyne had his army drilling in two, three and even four ranks, the latter being most effective at delivering the bayonet charge. Spring quotes Phillips' instructions following the British defeat at Cowpens, issued in April 1781, in which they also practiced forming in two, three and four deep, and that they 'should be accustomed to charge in all these orders. In the latter orders … the files will … be closer, so as to render a charge of the greatest force.'[112] There was a recognition that for the bayonet charge at least, close order was preferable.

Hadden recorded an instruction for the piquets to be drilled, under the inspection of the Brigadier of the Day 'in marching and charging Bayonets' so that the British and German troops 'may acquire an uniformity of pace and motion when acting together in Line.'[113]

Writing in the middle of 1777 following the Battle of Hubbardton, Lieutenant Thomas Anburey reviewed the reality of combat:

> In this action I found all manual exercise is but an ornament, and the only object of importance it can boast of was that of loading, firing, and charging with bayonets: as to the former, the soldiers should be instructed in the best and most expeditious method. Here I cannot help observing to you whether it proceeded from an idea of self preservation, or natural instinct, but the soldiers greatly improved the mode they were taught in, as to expedition, for as soon as they had primed their pieces, and put the cartridge into the barrel, instead of ramming it down with their rods, they struck the butt end of their piece upon the ground, and bringing it to the *present*, fired it off.[114]

Anburey was describing 'tap loading' which increased the rate of fire. This was at the expense of compression, which was achieved by ramming down the ball, paper and powder with the ramrod. Tap loading reduced the power behind the ball. When talking about the 'effect' of fire as a battle winning tool, as at Quebec in 1759, tap loading reduced the 'effect' of a shot fired. This is usually expressed in terms of a reduced range which could be entirely appropriate in a close environment such as woodland. It also means that the shot was fired with less force and the effect of even a direct hit could be that it did not kill or incapacitate its target. Tap loading also alludes to the pressure which they found themselves under. Corporal Lamb of the 9th described the

---

110 M. von Eelking and W.L. Stone, (eds), *Memoirs, and Letters and Journals of Major General Riedesel during his Residence in America* (Albany, NY: J. Munsell, 1868), vol.I, pp.58, 64.
111 Eelking & Stone, (eds), *Memoirs, and Letters and Journals*, vol.I, p.204.
112 Quoted in Spring, *With Zeal and With Bayonets Only*, pp.142–144, 153.
113 Hadden, *Journal*, p.77. See also O'Callaghan (ed.), *Orderly Book*, p.3, 20 June 1777.
114 Anburey, *Travels*, vol.I, pp.333, Letter XXXI, 12 July 1777.

same procedure. He did not fight at Hubbardton but he did fight with his regiment at Fort Anne the following day. This suggests that this procedure was common throughout the army in Canada.[115]

As late as the Battle of Freeman's Farm in September 1777 and despite the training which had been undertaken prior to the campaign in Canada, Burgoyne instructed:

> [T]he impetuosity and uncertain aim of the British troops in giving their fire, and the mistake they are still under in preferring it to the bayonet, is much to be lamented. The Lieutenant General is persuaded this error will be corrected in the next engagement, upon the conviction of their own reason and reflection, as well as upon that general perception of discipline, never to fire but by order of an officer.[116]

Anburey significantly described one failure of drills at Hubbardton, when a misfired musket was repeatedly reloaded. Had this musket fired in this state, it would probably have blown the breech with potentially fatal results to the firer. The soldier in question was part of the Advance Corps, the élite of the army in Canada, and it indicates the pressure which they were under: 'The confusion of a man's ideas during the time of action, brave as he may be, is undoubtedly great. Several of the men, upon examining their muskets, after all was over, found five or six cartridges which they were positive to the having discharged.'[117]

Invariably, the battles fought by Burgoyne's troops in Canada in 1777 were long, protracted affairs which left them exhausted, especially at Hubbardton, Freeman's Farm and Bemis Heights. As has been established earlier in this chapter, the British Army tried to avoid prolonged and extended exchanges of fire. The exhaustion of these battles precluded an exploitation of the tactical victory which was the decisive factor. Without either the physical stamina or a fresh reserve to exploit a victory, the victory itself becomes meaningless. This is a scenario we see repeated in 1777; there were simply not the numbers available to exploit the successes which the army created in Canada.

Conclusion

Carleton's troops in Canada took the opportunity to apply the most modern military thought with the introduction of both skirmishing tactics and rapid manoeuvre. Firing at marks was encouraged as was the utility of the bayonet. This was introduced to the German troops as well as the British. Carleton was very much aware of how close he had come to loosing Quebec for the crown. This was probably all the more worrying as he had helped to capture the province 16 years before. Reinforcements arrived from Ireland and Germany

---

115 Hagist, *British Soldier's Story*, p.37.
116 O'Callaghan (ed.), *Orderly Book*, p.116, 21 September 1777.
117 Anburey, *Travels*, vol.I, pp.333–334, Letter XXXI, 12 July 1777.

and went straight into combat after their transatlantic voyage. There was also the arrival of Burgoyne and the 47th smarting from defeat at Boston.

Carleton, and subsequently Burgoyne, made good use of these new tactics, even if their practitioners were not always the most conversant with their new operational environment. The effectiveness of these tactics would be tested to the extreme as the crown's forces moved from the relative security of interior lines in Canada to the increasingly insecure exterior lines of upper New York. Nevertheless, there was a clear trend that the British Army in 1776 and 1777 had adjusted to the new operational reality. After the humiliations of 1775, British forces operating in and out of Canada and New York were able to inflict multiple operational defeats on the rebels. These tactics did work. The 24th Foot at Freeman's Farm, for example, 'received orders to file off by the left. They took the wood before them, firing after them own manner from behind tress, and twice repulsed their repeated reinforcements without any assistance.'[118]

The light infantry tactics, with the open files and the individual firing, no matter how accurate, never delivered those decisive volleys we see in the European-style battles described previously, including Quebec, through to Waterloo. The wooded terrain, absence of cavalry and the small size of the crown's forces over extended frontages all encouraged tactics which, from a modern perspective, are forward looking, innovative, even modern. That is, perhaps, why we find them so appealing.

This chapter has shown that British officers were innovative and conscientious of training; from the theorists and peacetime trainers for 'a war' in the British Isles to the operational practitioners in 'the war'. There are multiple examples of field commanders also being theorists, something not generally attributed to the likes of Burgoyne whose interest in the theatre is prominent in biographies of him. In training, new tactics were introduced and practiced; individuals shooting at targets emphasised and fitness regimes introduced. These all gave the British soldier the best advantage possible in the early stages of the war. However, it takes time to perfect these under operational conditions, with not a little good fortune to ensure that battlefield errors do not translate into strategic failure during this transitional phase. Afterall, the British Army frequently begins wars with an uncertain start. This reflects the absence of militarism with British society. Why should 1775 be any different?

---

118 Hadden, *Journal*, p.164.

5

New Jersey, New York, New England

1773 was not the first time the 47th had visited Boston and New Jersey. Following the Siege of Louisbourg in 1758, the regiment sailed first to Boston and then to New Jersey where it wintered. In the spring, they re-joined Wolfe for his advance along the St Lawrence River, which would culminate in the Battle of Quebec.[1]

Military histories usually stay clear of political history, as if the two operate as independent spheres. The reality is that they are not sperate but very closely interwoven. The British Army of the mid-eighteenth century was a product of British politics with the differences between the British and Irish Establishments being a case in point. Equally, military activities take place within a political context. Britain's reluctance to engage in military action against France and Spain over Corsica and the Falkland Islands was seen as a weakness which encouraged colonial opposition.[2] Once the threshold into war has been crossed and overt military operations commenced, political history can appear even less relevant. This is not the case. A government needs to maintain domestic political support to pursue a war. Coalition politics occupies the time of any commander in a multi-national environment. Neutral powers need to be wooed if only to keep them away from the opponent's sphere. Britain failed to achieve this in the European context during the American War of Independence but was successful in preventing the Native American tribes siding with the rebels. The war was a civil war and therefore domestic politics on both sides of the Atlantic were an important consideration, especially for a regiment like the 47th which was posted to North America before the outbreak of open hostilities. Ensign John Pitt was forced by his family's political views to resign his commission in the 47th rather than fight the rebels, but then joined another regiment after the French entered the war. Loyalties are nuanced, and that applied to all participants in the war, on both sides.

---

1 Wylly, *Loyal North Lancashire*, vol.I, p.35.
2 Robinson, 'Britain Between Continents', pp.52–56.

The orders given to Lieutenant Colonel William Nesbit when he sailed with the 47th to New York and New Jersey have not survived. On his arrival he might have expected to have been briefed by the governors, William Tryon of New York and William Franklin of New Jersey, on the local political situation. The latter was the illegitimate son of Benjamin, who remained loyal to the crown despite his father's rebellion. Only one muster roll exists for the regiment's time in New Jersey, for January 1774. The regiment was distributed between Perth Amboy (sometimes referred to as Port Amboy at the time), Elizabeth Town and (New) Brunswick. New Jersey colony was sometimes still referred to as The Jerseys because, until 1702, there were East and West Jersey. Elizabeth Town, now Elizabeth, founded in 1668, was the original capital of East Jersey until 1686 when replaced by Perth Amboy. With the unified royal colony, the capital alternated annually between Perth Amboy and Burlington, the capital of West Jersey. Perth Amboy is unique in possessing the only original governor's mansion from the colonial period, Proprietary House. The general's company and Captains Craig's, Sherriff's and Smelt's companies garrisoned Perth Amboy.

Elizabeth Town was located 11 miles north of Perth Amboy. The major's, and Captains Aubrey's and England's companies were garrisoned there. The remaining three companies, the lieutenant colonel's, and those of Captains Alcock and Irving, were stationed at New Brunswick, some 15 miles to the west. Located on the Raritan River and the King's Highway midway between New York and Philadelphia, New Brunswick occupied a strategic position in New Jersey. The 47th's dispositions in New Jersey were not dissimilar to those they had occupied in Ireland, with several companies in each of a number of garrison locations. Although the garrison locations were not as widely distributed as in Ireland, in New Jersey they were still 10–15 miles apart. None of these three garrison locations were capable mutually supporting each other. This does not look like a troop disposition into a hostile, threatening environment.

By the beginning of August 1774, the regiment was concentrated in New York. As was discussed in Chapter 3, the regiment experienced a sharp increase in desertions while in New Jersey and New York. There were clearly political tensions in the region. However, as will be shown, these tensions were by no means universal, and it would be inaccurate to portray open hostility to the regiment. Add to that the relatively short period of time which the 47th spent in New Jersey or New York and there was only limited opportunity for politically motivated enticement of a soldier to desert the colours.

New Jersey and New York were not immune to the political turmoil which followed the end of the French and Indian War. We tend to view this political opposition as being focused on Boston, Massachusetts, because of the events of 1775, but it can be found from Halifax and Quebec through to the West Indies, and in Britain and Ireland. In 1770, New York saw both the Battle of Golden Hill on 19 January between troops and 'Sons of Liberty', and also the unveiling of an equestrian statue to George III on 21 March, commissioned by the General Assembly. The Battle of Golden Hill occurred six weeks before the Boston Massacre and, although no one was killed in New York, both events coalesced around increasing tensions between civilians and soldiers. Opposition to the Townshend Duties provided a political justification. These would be repealed in March 1770, except for the duty on tea, but this was an era of slow transatlantic communications and so word was slow to reach the colonies. Another justification was that British soldiers were accustomed to working in their off-duty time, and this was clearly in competition with civilians. However, as we will see with the Convention Army, the economic output of British soldiers and their families was crucial to the Revolutionary economy. In the days before the Boston Massacre, Private Patrick Walker (29th) had been engaged in conversation with the offer of work, as a lure into an assault.[3] Finally, British soldiers were the personification of the crown and any misdemeanour on their behalf was potentially highly political. They were subject to both regimental discipline and to the courts, as occurred after the Boston Massacre. The mob knew it could taunt soldiers with impunity, because it was unlikely that the soldiers would retaliate. The mob also knew that its members were unlikely to face the courts, as was the case following the Boston Tea Party when no one was prosecuted. That the Boston authorities could not, or would not, charge and convict anyone from the Boston Tea Party and similar incidents provoked the government to pass punitive legislation against Boston and deploy increasing troop numbers there. This was precisely the response which the protagonists required in order to escalate tensions in the colonies.

It would be wrong to consider that this mob violence was reserved for the British Army, or even loyalists. In late-1778, ships of the French navy were in Boston harbour. A bakery was established to feed the crews. When the mob demanded that they were given bread and the French bakers refused, a disturbance broke out. Two French officers, Chevalier Gregoire de Saint-Sauveur of the *Tonnant* and one-legged George René Pléville le Pelley of the *Languedoc* with a party of grenadiers arrived and diffused the tensions. When returning to their ships, however, the officers were set upon by a gang of about 50 men, beaten, and left for dead. Saint-Sauveur died a week later. As followed similar incidents, no one was ever prosecuted.[4]

The 47th's time in New Jersey and New York coincided with the First Continental Congress, held at Carpenters Hall, Philadelphia. Representatives of 12 of the 13 colonies attended to debate their response to the government's actions; Georgia did not send delegates, while Quebec declined their invitation. The congress did not advocate independence. They adopted a trade boycott of British goods and produce unless certain 'Coercive' or 'Intolerable' Acts were repealed. They also adopted a petition to George III professing their loyalty but requesting that all parliamentary legislation dealing with the colonies enacted since the end of the last war was repealed.

---

3 Archer, *As If an Enemy's Country*, pp.182-183.
4 C.M. McBurney, 'Why did a Boston Mob kill a French Officer?', *Journal of the American Revolution* (23 October, 2014), <https://allthingsliberty.com/2014/10/why-did-a-boston-mob-kill-a-french-officer/>, accessed 20 September 2021.

The 'Intolerable Acts' were five acts of parliament passed in response to the Boston Tea Party of 16 December 1773 which was in response to the Tea Act of 10 May 1773, itself a response to the financial difficulties of the East India Company from the economic overexploitation of Bengal and famine. One of the acts, the Quartering Act, addressed the longstanding issue of housing soldiers in the colonies. Colonial assemblies objected to the cost of quartering troops and to the presence of a standing army in peacetime. This objection to a standing peacetime army is a well-established English liberty going back to the English Civil War. This liberty has to be balanced with the requirement for an army to provide defence. Capable armies that can wage war effectively do not simply materialise, as has been shown in Chapter 4.

This was the political background against which the regiment returned to North America. But how did the regiment interact with New Jersey society? The evidence is that the regiment's short stay there was amicable. Correspondence between the 'Mayor, Aldermen and Common Council' and Captain England suggests that their stay in Elizabeth Town was as enjoyable as could be asked for:

> Sir: The Mayor, Aldermen, and Common Council, of the free Borough and Town of Elizabeth, understanding that the 47th regiment are ordered to leave the province of New-Jersey, the Corporation considering the peaceable and orderly behaviour of the private soldiers of the said regiment under your command since they have been quartered in this place; which has been productive of the greatest harmony between them and the inhabitants, which is doubtless to be ascribed to the attention of their several officers; conceive you as the chief commander and the other officers of the said regiment intitled to, and accordingly embrace the opportunity of rendering you, and other Gentlemen their acknowledgments for such your attention and vigilance.
> By order, JOHN DE HART, Clerk
> Elizabeth-Town, July 25 1774.

This letter was re-printed in *Rivington's New-York Gazetteer* in August 1774, and so would have had wider circulation than just a piece of polite correspondence between the borough council and an officer of a departing regiment.

In reply, Captain England was equally courteous and complimentary:

> Gentlemen: The Gentlemen of the 47th regiment quartered at Elizabeth-Town, have desired me to express the sense they entertain of the high honour conferred on them, by the address I received from the Mayor, Aldermen, and Common Council, and to return their thanks for it. They consider themselves highly flattered, at their conduct meeting with the approbation of so respectable a body.
> The pleasing society which they are happy to say they have enjoyed, with the principle gentlemen since their arrival here, must naturally be looked on as one of the chief causes of the harmony and unanimity which they are equally happy to observe, has subsisted between the rest of the inhabitants and the soldiers, – they quit that society with regret, and beg me to assure you, they shall always think on it with the greatest satisfaction.

> I have the honour to be, Gentlemen, With great esteem, Your very humble and obedient servant,
> RICHARD ENGLAND, Capt. 47th Regt.
> Elizabeth-Town, July 25th.[5]

This hardly gives the impression of a tyrannical redcoat occupation.

On 15 November 1774, the 47th Foot disembarked in Boston, but only after being abroad their transports in the harbour for three weeks while their accommodation was arranged. Meanwhile, in Massachusetts, a political coup had also taken place which limited crown control to the reach of the army, which was effectively Boston. The arrival of additional regiments to support Lieutenant General Gage in his attempts to restore royal authority in the colony did not bode well.

What members of the 47th Foot thought of this state of affairs is not recorded. Long serving members may have recalled horrific deaths in the forests of Canada, or freezing and starving in Quebec City during the winter of 1759 to 1760. They were about to enter siege conditions in a North American winter once again. Did they now curse the ingratitude of colonial society, or sympathise with the rebels? While we cannot ascertain the political views of the private solider, those of three officers can be ascertained: Major General Carleton, Captain Craig and Ensign Pitt.

Carleton's career has been described previously which includes his relatively liberal attitude with respect to the Quebec Act. He took a pragmatic approach to the Continental Congress' attempts to drum up anti-British sentiments amongst the Québécois by doing nothing to provoke a reaction. He also faced opposition from British merchants from the Thirteen Colonies who had settled in Quebec and who adopted a pro-Congress stance. He could have dismissed these as opportunistic actions from within the domestic opposition which would have opposed his rule regardless. The rebel's 1775 invasion of Canada, however, was another matter. It would be understandable if he were humiliated by the failure of the British Army garrisons, especially Fort Chambly's failure to resist for longer, and angry at the failure of the militia to make a stand. He was forced into another humiliation when he fled from Montreal, with the associated risk to his life. He must have contemplated an ignominious return to London to face a public enquiry following the loss of Quebec to the rebel army. In Quebec, he and his family risked their lives in a city under siege which could be ended by being stormed from without or an uprising from within. The prospects for the defenders of the city, their families and supporters were not good. His 1776 campaign was slow and methodical, bringing overwhelming resources to bear so that victory was not left to chance. Carleton's vigour has been questioned. Did this imply a sympathy to the rebel cause? This is unlikely because his responsibility to the crown, for his future career and even the safety of his family was bound up with the security of Quebec. He ensured that his army was never jeopardised

---

5   W. Nelson, (ed.), *Documents Relating to the Colonial History of the State of New Jersey*, First Series (Paterson, NJ: Call Printing and Publishing, 1917), vol.XXIX, p.444, De Hart's letter and England's reply. I am grateful to Vivian Davis for bringing these documents to my attention.

unnecessarily which would have opened the province to another invasion; although this never occured, it was remained a threat for the remainder of the war. Whatever Carleton's private sympathies and personal inclinations towards the rebel cause, he executed his difficult duties with the limited resources available and saved Canada.

Ensign John Pitt was in a very different position to Carleton. Independently wealthy and politically well connected, he was in a position to abandon an advantageous military career for political principles. He was the son of William Pitt 'the Elder', Lord Chatham. Chatham, who dominated the middle of the century, was especially noted for his conduct of the Seven Years War. He resigned his last ministry in 1768 citing ill health, but was well enough to resume his seat in the House of Lords from 1770. He took a conciliatory stand towards the growing American crisis. Ensign Pitt was commissioned on 14 March 1774 and shortly afterwards was serving as Aide-de-Camp (ADC) to Major General Guy Carleton, newly appointed to both Colonel of the 47th and Governor of Quebec; there were no vacancies for ensigns in the 47th, but the Secretary-at-War, Viscount Barrington, persuaded Ensign Milbourne West to transfer to the 29th Foot, with the usual purchase fees being waived.[6] This was a politically advantageous appointment for Carleton while providing Pitt with a political position upon which he could build a future career.

John Pitt's early career as an ensign in the 47th was curtailed by family politics. This did not adversely affect his military career, as shown in this 1799 portrait of him as a major general. (National Portrait Gallery)

As Carleton's ADC, Pitt shared all of the Governor's escapes from the rebel's 1775 invasion of Canada but returned to Britain carrying despatches in October 1775 thereby missing the siege and battle of Quebec, followed by the opportunity to gain glory in driving the rebels out of Canada. Despite the rebel's aggression beyond the boundaries of their home colonies, Pitt's involvement was unacceptable to the family. On 14 February 1776 Lady Chatham wrote to Carleton:

---

6   TNA: WO 65/24 Army List 1774, 29th Foot, p.83; WO 65/25 Army List 1775, 29th Foot, p.83, 47th Foot, p.101; J. Reiter, *The Late Lord: the Life of John Pitt-2nd Earl of Chatham* (Barnsley: Pen & Sword, 2020), p.17. In 1775, West resigned his commission, and his place was taken by John Enys whose account of the war in Canada is cited in this work

> Sir
>
> The weakness of my Lord's health [he would die in 1778] will not admit of his expressing at large the sense he has of the extent of your goodness to his son. It has made an impression on him which will always remain in his mind, attended with the sincerest gratitude. The advantages Pitt has received, from the time he has been honoured with the eye and protection of General Carleton, have been such as my Lord had persuaded himself, from every reason, he must receive.
>
> Feeling all of this, Sir, as Lord Chatham does, you will tell yourself with what concern he communicates to you a step that, from his fixed opinion with regards to the continuance of the unhappy war with our fellow-subjects of America, he has found it necessary to take. It is that of withdrawing his son [in the 47th Regiment of Foot] from such a service. He honours the service; and, under the military auspices of General Carleton, he had flattered himself that his might one day have arrived at some degree of merit in the profession. Though, from particular circumstances, he must cease to have the honour of attending you as aide-de-camp, my Lord will nevertheless hope for the continuance of your favourable opinion and protection to him, and trust that you will accept his sincere wishes for your return to England, and for the happiness of yourself and your whole family; – in which allow me to join.
>
> I am, Sir, with every regard, etc…
>
> Hester Chatham.[7]

Pitt landed in England on 2 November 1775. In the January 1776 muster roll and officer's absent list, Pitt is listed as a serving in the lieutenant colonel's company, but as absent serving as Carleton's ADC. By September 1777, his name has been removed from the regiment. Pitt's biographer, Jacqueline Reiter, is of the opinion that it was Lady Chatham who applied pressure on Pitt when his position as Carleton's ADC was 'embarrassing' given Lord Chatham's opposition to the war.[8] Following France's entry into the war, Pitt had no such qualms fighting this foe and joined the 39th Foot in February 1778. After just over a year serving in Gibraltar, he obtained six month's leave and returned to Britain, thereby missing out on the Great Siege of Gibraltar which commenced in June 1779. Pitt remained in Britain, transferring to the 86th Foot as a captain in September 1779. When that regiment was ordered for overseas service, there was again the concern that he might have to fight the American rebels. Relief that the 86th was not destined for America was short lived; the mortality rate on the Leeward Islands was infamous. Pitt's younger brother, James, died on Antigua about this time. Pitt did not remain on the Leeward Islands long, obtaining leave between September 1780 and January the following year, but did not rejoin his regiment and transferred to the 3rd Foot Guards in London in December 1782.[9]

---

7   Quoted in Ruppert, 'Those Who Could Not Serve'.
8   TNA: WO 12/5871: Muster Rolls, 47th Foot, January 1776; Volunteer George Stephenson was promoted Ensign *vice* Pitt on 10 July 1776, WO 65/27: Army List 1777, 47th Foot, p.101; Reiter, *The Late Lord*, pp.19–21.
9   Reiter, *The Late Lord*, pp.22–23, 25, 27–28; WO 65/30: Army List 1780, 86th Foot, p.163; WO 65/32: Army List 1782, 86th Foot, p.163.

Private of the 47th Foot charging at the Battle of Trois-Rivieres, Quebec, 8 June 1776. He is still in his Regulation 1768 uniform as the subsequent uniform modifications had not yet been introduced. (Giorgio Albertini, © Helion & Co.)

Reconstruction of a private, centre company, 47th Foot. This reconstruction is based upon the 1768 Royal Warrant and examination of the inspection returns. The evidence is not always conclusive, and research is a constant process. In the case of 'The 47th Regiment of Foot', this has been a 30 year long process. (Author's Collection)

A private soldier of the 47th Foot takes aim.

Reconstruction of a private, light company, 47th Foot. The light company's uniform included a shorter coat with wings, red waistcoat, belly box for additional ammunition, powder horns, a pouch for spare musket balls, black leatherwork and a cap. (Bob Fry)

1777 Campaign Uniform. This reconstruction has incorporated variations seen in 'A View of Ticonderoga from a Point on the North Shore of Lake Champlain'. This offers a different impression from the von Germann illustration overleaf. (47th Regiment of Foot, Aubrey's Company 1780)

Re-enactors of the 47th and 60th Foot, Fort Mackinac, in modern day Michigan, some 3,300 miles from Fort Charles. Mackinac was just one of the Great Lake forts the survivors of the 47th became familiar with after Saratoga. (47th Regiment of Foot, Aubrey's Company 1780)

47th Foot in 1777. Friedrick von Germann was an officer from Hesse-Hanau who served in Quebec and New York in 1776 and 1777, until becoming part of the Convention Army. His illustration of the 47th Foot is an important source for interpreting their uniform during the 1777 Campaign. (Stadtarchiv Braunschweig, H VI 6: 27 Seite 15)

24th Foot in 1777. In his watercolour of the 24th Foot, von Germann shows them still wearing stockings and breeches in 1777. They can also be seen being worn in one of James Hunter's paintings of Fort Ticonderoga. (Stadtarchiv Braunschweig, H VI 6: 27 Seite 13)

A stylised Grenadier of the 47th Foot from *Uniforms of the Several Regiments of Foot in his Majesty's Service* (1771). Other Grenadiers in the same work look similar which questions the reliability of these illustrations. (The Society of the Cincinnati, Washington, D.C)

Von Germann's image of a British solider in the Canadian Winter (New York Public Library)

The British Army's ability to adapt to winter warfare conditions speaks volumes for their tactical flexibility. The 47th Foot mastered conventional tactics for the open battlefield and woodland tactics, but they also had to learn to operate in the extremes of a Canadian winter. Reconstructed here by a member of the '8th the King's Regiment of Foot - Light Company'. The clothing shows similarities with the von Germann illustration but the 8th had been garrisoning the frontier since before the outbreak of the American War of Independence and so had adapted to the prevailing conditions separately to the troops in Canada. (Marcio da Cunha)

A member of the '8th the King's Regiment of Foot - Light Company' demonstrates operating in the severe conditions of a North American winter. (Marcio da Cunha)

A View of Ticonderoga from a Point on the North Shore of Lake Champlain. This painting shows a range of uniforms being worn on Lake Champlain. An officer wears his cocked hat while three others wear the familiar cap associated with the 1777 campaign. All wear long leggings which are reconstructed on the bottom left of page iii. (Library and Archives Canada/James Hunter collection/c001524k)

A South-West View of St. Johns, Quebec, with Plan. Fort St John's was a key objective for both rebels and General Carleton. It was also the base from which Carleton could construct, provision and launch his fleet. (Library and Archives Canada/James Peachey collection/c001507k)

Plan of Manouvres ... Phoenix Park, Dublin 1775. Phoenix Park allowed the Irish Establishment to conduct divisional-sized exercises which provided the exercising troops with a far more realistic experience than could be conducted in Britain. All six regiments exercising in June 1775 would soon follow the 47th Foot to fight in the American colonies. (Royal Collection Trust / © Her Majesty Queen Elizabeth II 2021 RCIN 734007)

Captain Thomas Aubrey, by Nathaniel Hone. One of two company commanders who would avoid captivity following Saratoga and continue to fight from Canada. In this portrait he is wearing the 1768 Royal Warrant uniform of the 4th (King's Own) Foot in which he served between 1766 and 1771, before joining the 47th. (National Museum of Wales)

General Sir Guy Carleton. Colonel of the 47th Foot following General Lascelles' death, Carleton's role in the defence of Canada was flawed, especially sending two regiments to Boston, but his subsequent actions were slow and methodical, ensuring that Canada was never again seriously threatened from the rebellious colonies. It is the author's opinion that Carleton would not have become trapped at Saratoga had he still been in command. (Library and Archives Canada/Mabel Messer collection/c011165560)

James Henry Craig represents the bulk of the regimental officers who served resolutely and loyally whatever their political opinions were. Born on Gibraltar to a Scottish father in 1748, he was educated there and then at a military academy in Modena, Italy before commissioning into the 30th Foot at Gibraltar. Although officers received no formal military training, his time at Modena would have made him stand out amongst his contemporaries as would any languages he had acquired while in Gibraltar and Italy. He was promoted to captain in the 47th in 1771 and was commanding the Light Company by January 1774. He travelled to North America with the regiment and served at Lexington, Concord and Bunker Hill. Some later sources state that he was wounded at Bunker Hill but this does not appear in any contemporary records. During their retreat following the Battle of Trois-Rivières (8 June 1776), on the 21st a party of 30 men of the rebel 6th Pennsylvania Regiment under Captain James Armstrong were sent to Ile aux Noix on the Richelieu River, just eight miles from Lake Champlain. There they 'fell in with a party of the enemy's light infantry and a number of Indians' commanded by Craig. After two were killed on each side the rebels surrendered. Craig was still commanding at the Ile aux Noix when he received Major John Bigelow, sent from Fort Ticonderoga with a petition from Congress for an exchange of prisoners and to protest about the killing of a rebel officer by Native Americans after his surrender. Bigelow was treated civilly by Craig. When asked whether there were more British officers with the Native Americans, Craig stated that there were, to which Bigelow was appalled that such actions could be allowed where British officers were in command. Craig replied that it was not always possible to control the Native Americans as they would fight in the own way. He showed far more realism and understanding of the realities of war after just a few months in Canada than did Bigelow.

In 1777, Craig and his company was part of Brigadier General Simon Fraser's composite light battalion. On 4 July, it was Craig and 40 soldiers which reconnoitred Sugar Loaf Hill (now known as Mount Defiance) and confirmed that cannon could be placed there. Their subsequent placement forced the rebels to evacuate Fort Ticonderoga.[10] Three days later he participated in the Battle of Hubbardton where he was one of 148 British wounded, having been shot in the arm. As a result of his injury, he undertook headquarters duties, which included participating in the negotiations resulting in the Saratoga Convention. Craig was chosen to take despatches to London and thus avoided the trials faced by the Convention Army. Burgoyne was able to do Craig one last favour by recommending him to Lord Germain: '[he] is an officer of Great Merit, and is particularly worthy of Notice for having Served with unablated Zeal and Activity thro' this labourious Campaign notwithstanding a wound thro' his Arm which he received at Hubbardton.'[11]

Craig was promoted to major in the newly raised 82nd Foot. They sailed for Halifax, Nova Scotia and then, on 30 May 1779, with the 74th

---

10 Stanley, *For Want of a Horse*, p.108.
11 D.R. Cubbison, *Burgoyne and the Saratoga Campaign: his papers* (Norman, OK: University of Oklahoma Press, 2021), p.332.

Foot, sailed to Castine, Maine which they captured without opposition. This expedition intended to establish a new colony for loyalists, New Ireland. The rebel reaction was to launch their largest naval expedition of the war, the Penobscot Expedition. The two British regiments, although outnumbered, withstood a 21-day siege until relief arrived in the form of the Royal Navy. Their blockade of the Penobscot Expedition's ships resulted in the US Navy's greatest defeat until Pearl Harbor. New Ireland remained British until the 1783 Treaty of Paris. The 74th garrisoned Fort George at Castine but the 82nd were withdrawn to Halifax again until, in January 1781, they were part of the expedition to North Carolina. Craig captured Wilmington, North Carolina, where he received 'a ready welcome' from the loyalists. He set about creating a secure base and conducting operations in the region. It would be to Wilmington that Cornwallis withdrew after Guilford Courthouse. Craig also fully supported the loyalist militias in what was an increasingly vicious and fratricidal civil war.

With Cornwallis' surrender at Yorktown, the British position in the south became untenable. On 18 November 1781, Craig, the 82nd and all of the loyalists who wished to departed for Charleston; those who remained lost their property and some were executed. An evacuation fleet of 150 ships departed Charleston on 14 December 1782 and with it all hope of restoring British rule in the south.

Defeat of Britain's war aims did not end Craig's career. He was promoted to lieutenant colonel and commanding officer of the 16th Foot. Promoted to colonel he visited Persia to study their military training. He was a staff officer to the Duke of York during the failed Flanders Campaign and then in 1795 participated in the capture of Cape Town, where he served three years as governor, for which he was knighted. He served briefly as Commander-in-Chief in India and then in the failed 1805 Anglo-Russian expedition to expel Napoleon from Italy. His final appointment was as Governor-General of the Canadas in 1807. He was not a wise choice. He alienated the Québécois. His hostility to the United States was inopportune at a time of increasing tension in the aftermath of the Chesapeake-Leopard Affair. He also hired Irish-born former US Army officer, spy and adventurer, John Henry. Henry opposed the republican government and intrigued that in the event of war, Massachusetts and New England might be persuaded to break away into a separate federation, possibly even allied with Britain. On 1 January 1812, Craig was promoted to full general. He died on the 12th.

Following Craig's death, James was unable to gain the rewards he had been promised, so sold their correspondence to the US President for $50,000. These papers would be used as evidence in support of the War of 1812.

Chaim Rosenberg's article on Craig includes the following quote from Henry Bunbury which highlights Craig's character, and the complexities of human nature:

> [V]ery short, broad and muscular, a pocket Hercules, with sharp, neat features, as if chiseled [sic] in ivory. Not popular for he was hot, peremptory and pompous; yet extremely beloved by those whom he allowed to live in intimacy with him;

clever, generous to a fault, and a warm and unflinching friend to those he liked …
one of the kindest men I have ever had to transact business with.[12]

As an officer apparently without great wealth or the patronage of great men, Craig seems to have progressed through ability and determination. In this respect, Craig was similar to Carleton. He was noticeably unsympathetic to the rebels, demanding complete loyalty to the king. By the time he landed in North Carolina the persecution of loyalists was well established. He had experienced their fates in Boston, Canada and Castine for simply wishing to remain loyal to the crown.[13] Thus, regardless of his personal political views pre-1775, his opposition to the rebels most likely grew from his experiences of the victimisation suffered by loyalists by the rebels.

This 10 percent sample of the regimental officers shows the range of political views we would expect in any organisation. There was the independently wealthy and politically connected Pitt who could (or maybe had to) follow the family political line, or arrange his leave from an inconvenient posting without harming his military and political career. This was not an option which was open to many in the 47th. Carleton and Craig lacked independent wealth or patronage, so had to rely on their own ability for advancement. They too could have resigned their commissions or transferred to other regiments as a number of other officers did.[14]

Craig was not the only one of the regimental officers in 1775 to reach the rank of general. Paulus Aemilius Irving would become both commanding officer of the 47th and colonel of the regiment before retiring as a general. Robert Douglas would command the 47th after Irving. There was also Carleton but setting him aside, three of the remaining 29 regimental officers achieved general rank. The regiment's fate at Saratoga did not hamper their careers.

The Siege of Boston

Although the 47th's time in Boston was dominated by two major actions there is in any siege environment a constant low-level skirmishing to dominate the surrounding countryside. The diary of Lieutenant William Bamford (40th Foot) for January to March, 1776 describes this level of military action which is often overlooked when, for example, on 5 February, a small party from Charlestown raided and returned with four of the rebel's bullocks, although one man was wounded in the neck.[15]

---

12 C.M. Rosenberg, 'James Henry Craig: the pocket Hercules', *Journal of the American Revolution* (30 October, 2017), <https://allthingsliberty.com/2017/10/james-henry-craigpocket-hercules/>, accessed 20 September 2021.
13 Baule and Gilbert, *British Army Officers*, p.43; Hadden, *Journal*, p.88, Appendix No. 22, pp.557–558; O'Callaghan (ed.), *Orderly Book*, p.69, 10 August 1777; Cubbin, *Burgoyne*, p.332.
14 See Urban, *Fusiliers*, pp.58–61 for the difficulties experienced in the 23rd Royal Welch Fusiliers.
15 J.B. Hattendorff (ed.), *A Redcoat in America: the diaries of Lieutenant William Bamford, 1757–1765 and 1776* (Warwick: Helion, 2019), pp.171–182.

Despite this, Lieutenant General Gage attempted to run a civilian administration to keep both sides of the political divide content. Courts of enquiries were held to investigate officers and soldiers accused of offenses against the populous; soldiers were ordered not to appear in public with their 'sidearms' and guards were to arrest all soldiers involved in disturbances. On 5 March 1775, the townspeople commemorated the fifth anniversary of the Boston Massacre, despite concerns that it would lead to further disturbances. In the end, the event passed peacefully. It would not be until after Lexington and Concord that an exodus of rebels, or those wanting to avoid being caught up in a siege, was noted. At the same time, loyalists from the countryside, where they were no longer welcome, moved into Boston and the crown's protection.[16]

The Boston Garrison was structured into three brigades:

1st Brigade (Lord Percy)	4th, 23rd, 47th Regiments; 1st Marines joined later.
2nd Brigade (Pigott)	5th, 38th, 52nd Regiments.
3rd Brigade (Jones)	10th, 43rd, 59th, detached companies 18th/65th Regiments.

On 12 March 1775, the strengths of the battalions in 1st Brigade were:

4th Foot	315
23rd Fusiliers	314
47th Foot	296
1st Marines	336
Total	1,261[17]

Lieutenant Frederick MacKenzie (adjutant, 23rd Fusiliers), noted on 14 January 1775 that the men were to receive four days salt rations and three days fresh per week. The Marines and the hospitals were on fresh rations throughout. The arrival of several ships on 17 February with provisions and coal must have been a great relief. The soldiers received fresh rations and 'food [and] porter 3 times a week'.[18] William Bamford recorded that the weather for 18 January 1775 was an 'extream [sic] hard frost, very cold.'[19] In May 1775, women and children were also added to the ration strength. On the 3rd, this was half a ration, but for women with more than one child, they received a full ration. Three days later the calculations were adjusted to half a ration for a woman and a quarter ration for each child. At least the soldiers received rations, which they paid for with deductions from their pay. Officers had to provide their own food and were vulnerable to price rises in siege conditions. Contrary to popular opinion, officers were not normally independently wealthy. Mark Urban paints a sorry picture of junior officers unable to live, and maybe support a family, under these conditions and forced to sell their commissions. One officer wrote home asking for food to be sent to him. It was a

---

16   MacKenzie, *British Fusilier*, p.36, 5 March 1775; Barker, *British in Boston*, pp.3, 6–7, 24; Tanner, *Instruments of Battle*, p.96.
17   MacKenzie, *British Fusilier*, p.41, 12 March 1775; Barker, *British in Boston*, p.9, 29 November 1774.
18   Hattendorff, *William Bamford*, p.176, 17 February 1776.
19   Hattendorff, *William Bamford*, p.176, 18 February 1776.

precarious existence.[20] The winter of 1775/1776 was little better. To heat the billets, Boston required 336 tons of coal a week imported on colliers which could fall victim to rebel privateers. In January 1776, the arrival of a coal shipment allowed Howe to cancel an order for taking firewood from old houses and wharves, but by March the non-arrival of supply convoys had reduced supplies to just five weeks.[21]

Ill-discipline was a problem in the Boston garrison, as illustrated by Lieutenant Frederick MacKenzie's (23rd Fusiliers) diary entries for 1 and 4 February 1775. A court martial was held for soldiers accused of selling firelocks to 'the Country people.' A soldier of the 4th Foot was found guilty and sentenced but a sergeant and two privates of the 38th were acquitted. However, on 8 March a 'Country fellow', Thomas Ditson of Billerica, was caught trying to buy a musket off a soldier of the 47th. He was tarred, feathered and paraded round the town to The Neck.[22] Evidently, the punishment had the full support of the officers, although not their participation, but incurred the displeasure of the townspeople and Gage. MacKenzie appears to have approved as a deterrent to future attempts. This incident gained some notoriety amongst the rebels as Lieutenant Colonel William Nesbitt was accused of being an advocate of tarring and feathering.[23]

Alcohol abuse became a particular problem which MacKenzie mentioned on 2 and 10 February 1775. The sale of rum in such quantities and so cheaply by 'Soldier's wives and others' resulted in numbers of soldiers being intoxicated each day. The civilians also encouraged excessive drinking because, once drunk, soldiers were induced to desert. Some of the rum being sold was 'of so pernicious a quality' that two men had died of drinking it. Gage even ordered those women found selling rum be put on board a ship, however Lieutenant John Barker (4th Foot) observed 'but was taken little notice.'[24]

January 1776 saw a call to establish a tradition which is now a mainstay of Boston life, the St Patrick's Day Parade. Captain Craig of the 47th published a notice in the *Massachusetts Gazette and Boston Weekly News-Letter*:

> The ancient and most benevolent of the Friendly Brothers of St. Patrick. The Principal Knot of the 47th Regiment is to meet at the Bunch of Grapes on Thursday the 29th inst. at eleven o'clock in the forenoon. ... All the Friendly Brothers in the army are requested to meet at the same place at one o'clock, on business relating to the order in general.[25]

---

20   MacKenzie, *British Fusilier*, p.28, 14 January 1775; Hattendorff, *William Bamford*, p.176, 17, 18 February 1776; Urban, *Fusilier*, p.58; Atkinson, *The British are Coming*, pp.219, 223; Barker, *British in Boston*, p.20, 14 January 1775; p.43, 3 May 1775; p.43, 6 May 1775.
21   Hale, Stevens & Howe (eds), *Orderly Book*, p.200, 19 January 1776; Huntingdon Library (HL): MSS HM 66: Journal of an Officer of the 47th Regiment of Foot, f.22, 2 March 1775.
22   MacKenzie, *British Fusilier*, p.32, 1 February 1775; p.33, 39–40.
23   Atkinson, *The British are Coming*, p.48; Hagist, *Noble Volunteers*, p.8. I am indebted to Thomas Tringale for information on this incident.
24   MacKenzie, *British Fusilier*, pp.32, 33, 10 February 1775; Barker, *British in Boston*, pp.9, 17, 44. See also Hale, Stevens & Howe (eds), *Orderly Book* which mentions alcohol abuse on pp.11, 14, 33 but then is silent until p.229; *The British are Coming*, p.263; Hagist, *Noble Volunteers*, pp.60–64.
25   *Massachusetts Gazette and Boston Weekly News-Letter*, Jan. 22, 1776, quoted in Richard Frothingham. 'Siege of Boston', *Proceedings of the Massachusetts Historical Society*, vol.14

On 26 April 1775 the 47th moved out of the winter quarters they had occupied since disembarking in Boston and moved into a tented camp on Boston Common.[26] Finally, a calamity befell the 47th when, on 17 May 1775, a fire broke out at Treat's Warf, destroying 41 houses and warehouses. Stored in the warehouses were the uniforms, arms and accoutrements of four companies of the 47th and all of the 65th Foot. As there are no references to members of the 47th or 65th going about naked, it is assumed that these were spare or unissued items.[27]

Tactical Application in Massachusetts

Detailed narratives for both major actions around Boston are covered in many other accounts and will not be repeated here in detail. The raid on Lexington and Concord of 19 April 1775 was aimed at seizing and destroying military stores which were intended for use against the British Army. With this action the army's role transitioned from assisting the civil authorities to quelling open rebellion. By the time of the Battle of Bunker Hill on 17 June 1775, there was no such transition and therefore no such confusion.

The Portsmouth Alarm

Lexington was not the first shot of the American War of Independence. That was the Portsmouth Alarm. The previous December, rebels in New Hampshire had attempted to storm Fort William and Mary and seize weapons and munitions stored there. On one side was New Hampshire-born Governor John Wentworth and also New Hampshire-born regular army Captain John Cochran with five soldiers to garrison a fort in poor state of repair. Their cannon and munitions were intended for defence against ships rather than an infantry assault. On the other side was some 400 rebels led by local merchant ship captain, John Langdon. The outcome of 400 versus six was a forgone conclusion, and mercifully no one was killed, but a King's officer and his soldiers had been assaulted, his banner removed and gunpowder seized. Earlier, and generally better known, actions like the Boston Massacre could be glossed over with the veneer that it was the 'lower orders' engaged in 'mob violence' based around loosely defined economic and political grievances which did not constitute a rupture of government by the colonial elites. The Portsmouth Alarm was a clear act of open rebellion, but did not initiate open warfare. For the ordinary soldier in Boston, this situation allowed uncertainty to develop. For the regimental officer who might have to give the order to fire, any uncertainty and indecision gives the initiative to the opponent. In a combat situation, the resultant delay can be fatal.

(1876), pp.229–316.
26   MacKenzie, *British Fusilier*, p.75 and Barker, *British in Boston*, p.39, 26 April 1775.
27   HL: MSS HM 66: Journal of an Officer of the 47th Regiment of Foot, ff.13–14, 17 May 1775; Atkinson, *The British are Coming*, p.86; Barker, *British in Boston*, p.47, 18 May 1775.

NEW JERSEY, NEW YORK, NEW ENGLAND

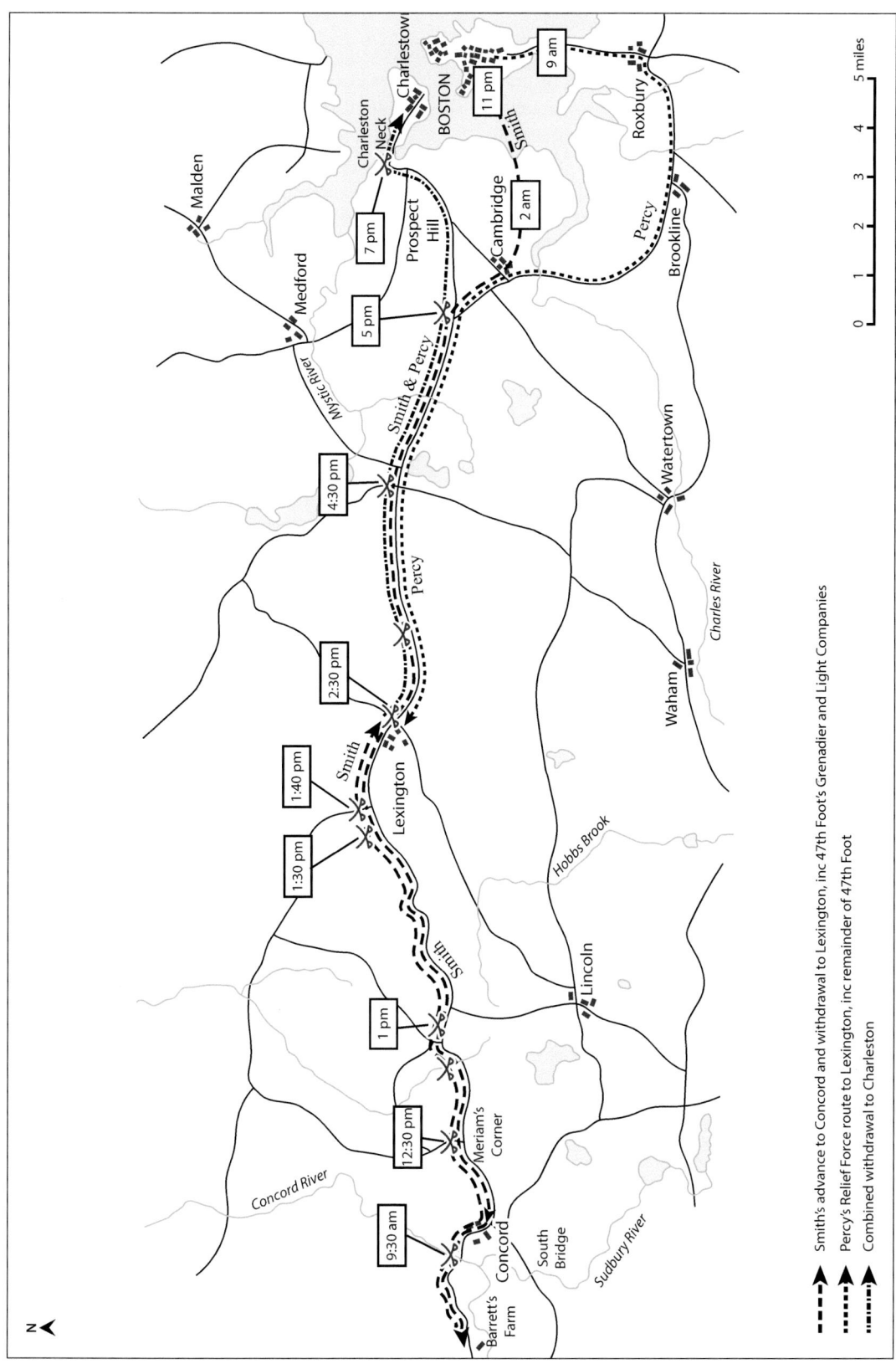

The Raid on Concord.

Lexington and Concord

On 15 April, Lieutenant General Gage ordered all the flank companies off routine duties to practice 'the Grenadier Exercise and some New Evolutions for the Light Infantry.'[28] This included the 47th's Captain Richard England's grenadier company and Captain James Craig's light company. This was part of a deception plan so that their presence would not suddenly be missed; Lieutenant John Barker (4th Foot) called it a 'blind'.[29] Lieutenant Colonel Francis Smith (10th Foot) commanded the main force composed of the infantry and Marines (the Royal title was not added until 1802). Company officers were given orders at 8:00 p.m. that their soldiers were to be at the beach at 10:00 p.m. on the 18th. Smith would command the grenadiers while Major John Pitcairn (Marines), commanded the lights. There were delays and confusion before the 700-strong force was transported across Back Bay to Lechemere Point. Having had to wade ashore which made them 'wet up to their knees', they then had to wait until 2:00 a.m. for food (a lot of which was discarded as they brought rations with them) and ammunition to arrive before starting their march through Menotomy, Lexington and onto Concord.[30] The two lead light companies, 4th and 10th, arrived at Lexington. The rebels were famously aware that the 'The regulars are coming out'.[31] Captain John Parker had formed up his militiamen in two ranks to receive the redcoats, but on realising that they were outnumbered, ordered his men to lay down their arms and withdraw. At some point, a shot was fired. The redcoats released pent up frustration on the militiamen responsible. Smith arrived with the main body and restored order. Parker's men suffered eight killed and 10 wounded, while Smith's force suffered two wounded, a sergeant and Smith's horse. It was 5:00 a.m.

Smith then marched on to Concord. About a mile outside the town at Meriman's Corner, the regulars were met by some 200 militiamen who, realising they were outnumbered, fell into a column and marched into Concord with drums and fifes playing. Militiaman Amos Barrett recalled 'We had grand music.'[32] Smith observed militiamen on a ridge on his right flank. He despatched some light companies to drive them off, and militia withdrew to a second ridge to the north of Concord.[33] This is a good example of the light companies performing their tactical role, in this case preventing enemy forces from interfering with the commander's intent, to use the modern expression.

On arrival in Concord, the 47th's light company occupied the high ground of Lee's Hill to the north west of the town.[34] Captain Munday Pole (64th Foot, light company) took three light companies to South Bridge while Captain Lawrence Parsons (10th Foot, light company) took the remaining seven to North Bridge. At North Bridge, Parsons took four companies to

---

28   MacKenzie, *British Fusilier*, p.48, 15 April 1775.
29   Barker, *British in Boston*, p.29, 15 April 1775.
30   Barker, *British in Boston*, p.31, 19 April 1775.
31   Atkinson, *The British Are Coming*, p.59.
32   Atkinson, *The British Are Coming*, p.66.
33   Morrissey, *Boston 1775*, pp.36–38.
34   Morrissey, *Boston 1775*, p.42.

search Barratt's Farm, two miles away. The remaining three light companies under Captain Walter Laurie (43rd) were deployed 'two up' with the 4th and 10th on the far bank and his own 43rd on the near bank. Around 9:00 a.m., Colonel James Barrett commanding the 500-strong Concord Militia saw smoke from the town, feared that the town was being put to torch and advanced on North Bridge. Outnumbered, Laurie called for reinforcements and withdrew his two forward companies. Smith brough up the grenadier companies of the 5th, 23rd and 47th to Laurie's assistance.[35] Bridge crossing was a manoeuvre which the 47th and other regiments had practiced in Ireland. Now, this manoeuvre appears to have become panicked with the retiring companies masking the fire of the covering company and no thought being given to taking up the bridge's planks. Laurie was forced to withdraw some 400 yards until reinforced by three grenadier companies under Smith, at which point the militia withdrew. The regulars suffered two killed and 10 wounded.

Meanwhile, the grenadier companies' searching of Concord revealed very little due to careful preparation by the rebels, with 500 pounds of musket balls being dumped in the Mill Pond and later largely recovered. Pole found and damaged three iron 24-pounder cannons. He also set fire to the carriages and tools. The smoke from this fire would be misinterpreted with fatal consequences. Fires were also lit in two nearby houses but were extinguished when the inhabitants objected.

Smith left Concord around midday. As they departed, more militia companies were converging on the withdrawal route. At Merriman's Corner, militia fired on the deployed flank companies killing two and wounding more. The conditions were set for the next 18 miles. It was not all one sided, as was shown at Tanner's Brook where the Bedford Minute Company was attacked from the rear by a light company, killing the captain and two others. Brendan Morrissey considered that this tactic accounted for two thirds of the militia casualties that day.

Back in Boston, Brigadier General Lord Percy (5th Foot) received permission to support Smith with his 1st Brigade (4th, 23rd, 47th Foot and Marines) and two artillery pieces at 4:00 a.m. Orders were issued at 6:00 a.m. and received by the three infantry regiments at 7:00 a.m., but the instructions for the Marines were delayed because the messenger was unaware that Major Pitcairn was with Smith, not his battalion. It would be 9:00 a.m. before they departed. At a bridge over the Charles River they found that the planks had been taken up, but stored nearby. Fortunately, on 30 March, Percy had conducted a brigade route march to familiarise the populous with troops on routine marches. Lieutenant John Barker (4th Foot) reported that this 'alarmed the people a good deal' so that at Watertown, they loaded two cannons (but refrained from firing them) and at Cambridge the inhabitants pulled up the bridge.[36] Forewarned, Percy had brought tools and nails for just such an eventuality and a repair was effected. Percy reached Lexington about midday and, around 3:00 p.m., bodies of militiamen were seen around

---

35   Morrissey, *Boston 1775*, p.42.
36   Barker, *The British in Boston*, p.29, 30 April 1775.

the town. Smith's men met up with Percy's and both bodies departed from Lexington at around 3:30 p.m., with Percy providing the rear guard, rotating the Marines, then 47th, and then 4th Foot in this position. Smith's force led the way where, according to MacKenzie (23rd Fusiliers), 'the fire was nearly as severe as at the rear.'[37] The attacks continued, and one mile beyond the Menotomy River another ambush was disrupted by a flank attack which killed three of the rebels, including Major Isaac Gardner from Brookline, the most senior militiaman killed that day.

Percy correctly surmised that the Charles River bridge would have been dismantled and would be provide a focal point for militia companies, so he chose a different route to Bunker Hill where his force took up positions while Smith's force was ferried to Boston. A truce was agreed with the town of Cambridge who did not call out their militia and who assisted in ferrying Smith's men into Boston.[38]

There is usually very little positive to say about the Lexington and Concord raid. Rick Atkinson, most recently, was scathing in that 'The British combat performance, if often courageous in the ranks, had been troubling, with miserable staff work and inert commanders, Percy excepted.'[39] The staff work was poor, with both Smith and Percy delayed unnecessarily. The plan itself was overly ambitious although based on good intelligence because the troops did know what they were looking for and where.

Let us examine what we know of the tactics being employed on the day. There was a composite battalion of grenadiers marching along the road with light companies providing flank protection. Three examples of this have already been provided where they successfully drove of or disrupted militia actions. This is what a light company was supposed to do. There was the incident around North Bridge where the retirement of two companies back across the bridge was disorganised. This was disappointing because this was, again, a manoeuvre which the 47th had practiced in Ireland and so should be within the competencies of those three light companies. Criticism of the performance of the soldiers have been made by their own officers, especially in relation to their lack of discipline and fire control. Youth and inexperience are usually blamed, but their own officers have to take responsibility for this.

Who were the private soldiers on that afternoon of 19 April 1775? He had just spent a North American winter besieged in Boston living off preserved rations and fuel which had to be shipped across the Atlantic. He had taken part in practice marches around five to eight miles out of Boston and into the surrounding area. On the night of 18/19 April 1775, he was rowed from Boston, across Back Bay to land at Lechemere Point. From there to Concord was a march of about 20 miles which was unopposed. He then had to march a similar distance under constant sniping fire from Concord back to Boston. Even with the experience of previous training marches, 19 April was going

---

37 MacKenzie, *British Fusilier*, p.56, 19 April 1775.
38 Morrissey, *Boston 1775*, pp.35–48; Atkinson, *The British are Coming*, pp.55–82; HL: MSS HM 66: Journal of an Officer of the 47th Regiment of Foot, ff.6-12, 18 April 1775; Barker, *British in Boston*, pp.31–37, 19 April 1775.
39 Atkinson, *The British are Coming*, p.79.

to be a challenge. He had been ordered at 10:00 p.m. on the 18th to prepare for an operation. Hopefully, he will have been in bed asleep, if not he will have been up all day and was about to start a 24-hour mission. Our sample private soldier is young, probably two years' service, in his first action, having endured a North American winter on inadequate rations, accommodation and heating, limited opportunity for exercise, has been awake for at least 24 hours and has to march 20 miles to Concord in full knowledge that he has to complete 40 miles that day to return to the safety of Boston. He had been fired upon by some militia, seen others observing him from a distance, and marched with others while fifes and drums played. To use the modern army vernacular, he was chin-strapped; he was physically and mentally exhausted. That his drills were not as slick as on the parade square is hardly surprising. His detractors, including some of his officers, also claim that he had sufficient time and energy for looting, arson and other atrocities. He has not yet found his warfighting *ethos*, but then the war was only hours old. The building blocks are there, but in need of significant refining and polishing.

The rebels, for that is what they are now, had proved their metal. This should not have been any surprise because they were defending their homes on familiar terrain. They had proved highly effective at company level, but lacked good command and control beyond that. Estimates of number of rebels involved are as high as 20–30,000. This to inflict 273 dead, wounded and missing on the regulars. That is about 100 participants per loss inflicted. Other calculations estimate that 75,000 shots were fired requiring over a ton of gunpowder: only one in 300 shots found its mark.[40]

The British Army intended to conduct a raid against rebel supplies in Concord. They achieved, to use the modern expression, their 'Commander's Intent'. What of the rebels? It is more difficult to determine their Commander's Intent because there was no central direction. But they did not prevent the raid, they did not protect their property (in fact, by firing from houses, they made those houses legitimate targets), they did nothing to make the British Army return to Boston because that was always their intention, nor did they prevent that return to Boston. They killed, wounded and captured some Regulars, but not many for the number of rebels involved.

Bunker Hill

The main change in the Boston garrison's command structure occurred 25 May 1775 when Major Generals John Burgoyne, Henry Clinton and William Howe arrived on HMS *Cerberus*.[41] Together with Gage they planned a four-pronged offensive to commence on 18 June. Intelligence of this reached the rebels who planned their own pre-emptive strike to disrupt the plan. They aimed to occupy Bunker Hill, although in the end they entrenched Breed's Hill. The rebels marched over the same terrain which Percy's 1st Brigade halted on 19 April. Had Percy established permanent positions there, all that was to come would have been avoided.

---

40 Atkinson, *The British are Coming*, p.79; Morrissey, *Boston 1775*, p.47.
41 HL: MSS HM 66: Journal of an Officer of the 47th Regiment of Foot, f.14, 25 May 1775.

A VERY FINE REGIMENT

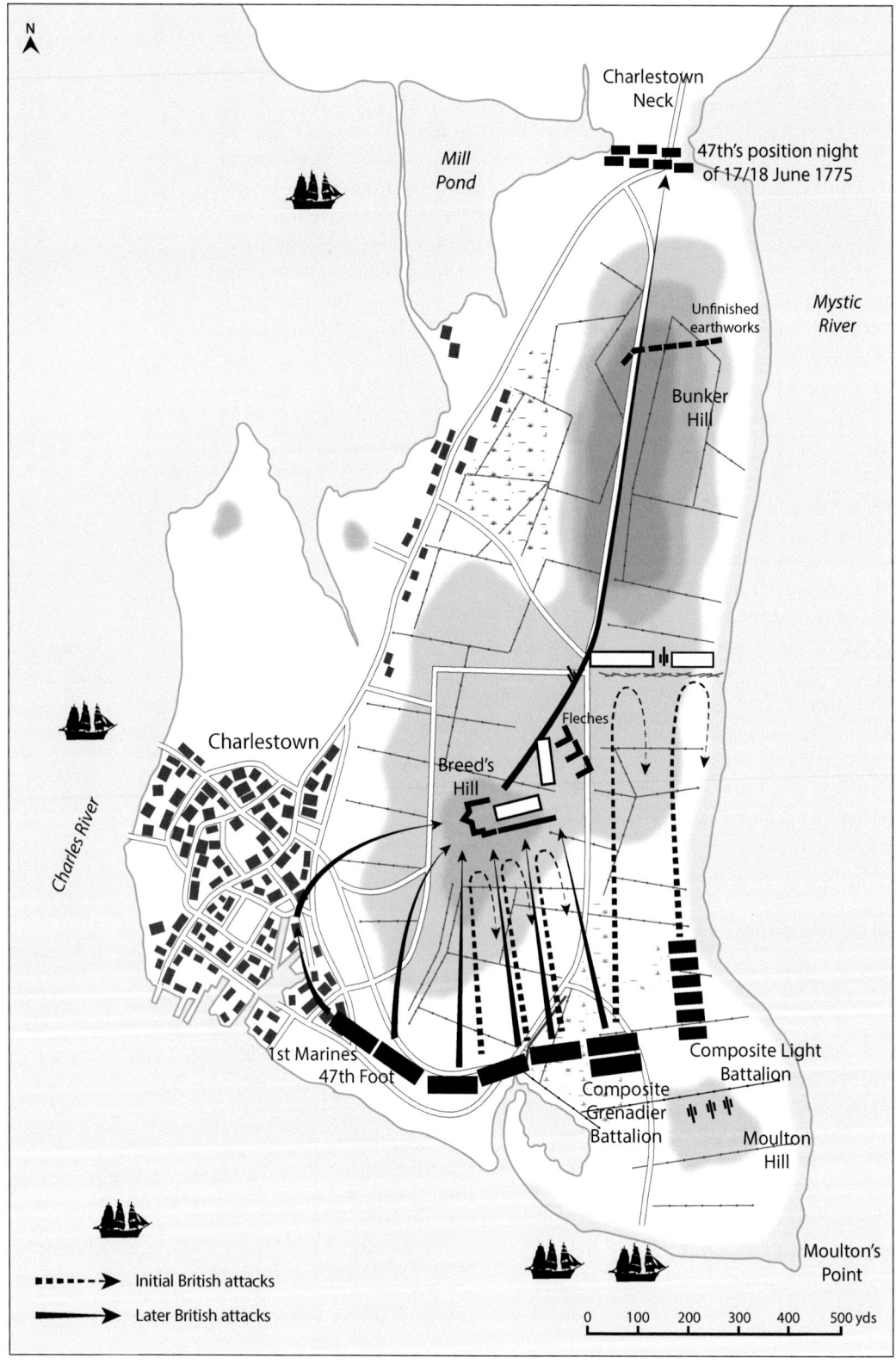

The Battle of Bunker Hill.

Overnight on 16/17 June, rebels under Colonel William Prescott occupied Breed's Hill and started the construction of a redoubt. At 4:00 a.m. on the 17th, the Royal Navy observed the entrenchments and opened fire while other vessels targeted the Charlestown Neck to prevent reinforcements arriving. Naval and artillery fire did little damage against the earthworks but did inflict some casualties. Lack of sleep, rations and water coupled with the occasional casualty appears to have cooled the revolutionary ardour by midday with some taking the opportunity to slip away. The British generals decided to attack while the redoubt was still incomplete. It would be 1:00 p.m. before the first wave landed and 3:00 p.m. before the second arrived. In the meantime, more rebel infantry and artillery had crossed the Neck.

Howe's plan was for Pigott's 2nd Brigade (38th and 43rd Foot, flank companies of the 35th, 2nd Marines and 63rd Foot) to make a frontal assault against the redoubt which would fix the rebels in place. This would be the left wing. Howe would command the right wing of the grenadier and light battalions, with artillery support. They would advance to the north of Breed's Hill in a right flanking move to envelope the rebels and cut of their retreat. The 47th's flank companies were part of the grenadier and light battalions. The remainder of the 47th formed a reserve with the 1st Marines. Critically, Howe knew that he had to clear the rebel redoubt by the end of the day which meant that time was of the essence. Unfortunately, he was not aware that a rail fence extending northwards from Breed's Hill to the Mystic River had been occupied and strengthened.

There would be three assaults against the rebel redoubt, with the rail fence providing an impassable obstacle. It was here that the 47th's grenadiers would suffer seven deaths and the lights another fatality. The anonymous journalist of the 47th Foot described the action: 'The approach was likewise obstructed, every 20 or 30 yards, by strong rails and fences, over which the troops was obliged to climb, exposed to the whole fire of the redoubt, and a breastwork of considerable extent, which could not be perceived from the Shipping. These difficulties were overcome with the utmost intrepidity and Valour.'[42]

It was during the third assault that the reserve (47th Foot and 1st Marines) were able to move to the south of redoubt and deliver a flanking attack. This would cost the 47th another 11 dead. By now the rebels were running low on ammunition. Lieutenant John Waller (1st Marines) described the scene: 'Nothing could be more shocking than the carnage that followed the storming of this work …We tumbled over the dead to get at the living who were crowding out of the gorge of the redoubt. … 'Twas streaming with blood & strewed with dead and dying men, the soldiers stabbing some and dashing out the brains of others.'[43] Afterwards, the 47th occupied Charleston Neck and while the rest of the army 'lay on their arms, on the heights, and began to entrench', but 'The 47th were exempt from work, as being in the post of honour, and uncovered.'[44]

---

[42] HL: MSS HM 66: Journal of an Officer of the 47th Regiment of Foot, ff.15 – 19.
[43] Lieutenant Weller quoted in Atkinson, *The British are Coming*, p.108.
[44] Morrissey, *Boston, 1775*, pp.51–67; HL: MMS HM 66: Journal of an Officer of the 47th Foot, f.18

Bunker Hill was a pyrrhic victory. It was essential that the redoubt was captured by the end of the day which limited the time for any form of operational finesses. The casualties were a shock to all, more so than following Lexington and Concord. The most profound impact on the conduct of the 47th's war would be through one of the observers, safe in Boston, but who nevertheless observed and learnt the lesson of infantry assaults against entrenched rebels. That was Major General Burgoyne.

Could Bunker Hill have been fought any better? Time was of the essence if the rebels were to be evicted before their entrenchments became more developed, necessitating a more costly assault. The British commanders acted with speed and aggression, unlike at Lexington and Concord. A frontal assault fixed the rebels in their positions while the flank companies executed an envelopment which would have encircled the rebels, forcing their surrender. The envelopment failed because the rail fence position occupied by the rebels proved to be impregnable. This meant that the main effort was now with the frontal assault as an unintended consequence. The objective, which was the clearing of the rebels from Breed's Hill by the end of the day, was achieved, but at great cost; the rebel commanders, however, failed, at great cost, to achieve their objective.

The Impact of 1775

The muster roll for 20 September 1775 shows a regiment undergoing the reality of operations. A list of officers absent included with the muster rolls shows that of the 30 regimental officers, almost half, 13, were in some way removed from regimental duties. Two were in Quebec, Major General Carleton and Ensign John Pitt, his ADC. Six were sick and three on extra-regimental duties. Two new ensigns were appointed but unavailable, Joseph Dowling had yet to join the regiment while John Rotton was a prisoner of the rebels. This document does not show the whole picture as two officers, Lieutenant Christopher Hillard of the grenadier company died at Bunker Hill and Lieutenant Richard Gold of Captain Aubrey's company died two days later. Captain Smelt's company suffered most with Smelt on duty in Boston as a Brevet Major, Lieutenant Gerrard Irving sick and Ensign John Rotton as a prisoner of the rebels, leaving the company in the care of the two sergeants and three corporals. Nineteen British Army officers died at Bunker Hill, of which two were from the 47th.[45]

Lieutenant Gold's misfortune went beyond just the death in service of an officer. Gold's wife, Maria, had died before the regiment had sailed for America and now their two children, Charles, aged nine, and eight year old Joyce, were left destitute and alone in Boston. The King was petitioned to bring them home and to enter Charles as a cadet in the Royal Artillery and Joyce, when old enough, at the Drawing School at the Tower of London. Gold

---

45 TNA: WO 12/5871: Muster Rolls, 47th Foot, February 1777; S.R. Frey, *The British Soldier in America: a social history of military life in the Revolutionary period* (Austin: University of Texas Press, 1981), p.125.

had been commissioned into the 47th in 1755 and promoted to lieutenant in 1758, but had failed to obtain promotion since then. He had served in Canada and the West Indies. In 1768 he had petitioned for a grant of land in Cape Breton, but this does not appear to have been successful. His estate was valued on his death at about £300, so his children were not entirely destitute, but they were now orphaned and left to make their own way in the world.[46]

Of the other ranks, recruiting, drafting, sickness and deaths were changing the nature of the regiment. By 20 September, the regiment had suffered 27 died, killed or missing. Most of these occurred around 19 April (Lexington and Concord) and 17 June (Bunker Hill) 1775. Captain Craig's light company reported two soldiers missing for 19 April, and Captain England's grenadier company reported one died. The figure usually given is five killed and 22 wounded, although this not born out by the muster rolls which only record three missing or killed. Two of the wounded were Lieutenant Henry Baldwin (in the throat) and Donald McLoed (breast).[47] On 17 June and the days immediately following accounted for 18 deaths, with almost half (seven) of the deaths falling on the grenadiers and one more for the lights. Of the remaining eight companies, Captain Sherriff's fared worse with three fatalities; two (Robert Marrett and Roger Kenyon) are listed as 'Died' on 17 June while the third, Hugh Corbett, 'Died' on 26 July which could have been from wounds sustained at Bunker Hill, or from some unrelated incident or illness. It could be that more of the deaths later in the summer also died of wounds sustained at Bunker Hill, but it is difficult to be certain. What this does indicate is which company was in the thickest of the fighting – the grenadiers. There were also 48, or about 10 percent, of the regiment listed as sick. This was before the winter had begun. The overall health of the 47th Foot after less than 12 months in Boston was not good.[48]

To replace these losses, 15 recruits were 'entertained', all on 3 April 1775 and arriving in Boston on the same convoy. More significant were 38 soldiers drafted in from 20 different regiments. This was a not uncommon practice, especially for young men keen to satisfy their 'ardent disposition for adventure', as William Crawford justified his transfer from the 12th Light Dragoons to the 20th Foot.[49] These were trained soldiers so of more use than the recruits. Some, like the pair drafted from the 3rd Foot, came from regiments which remained in Britain for the duration of the war. Others were from regiments which would serve alongside the 47th in Canada, like the 20th, 21st and 34th, while others were from regiments which would see extensive service in the middle and southern colonies, like the 17th, 33rd and 40th. The regiments to provide the most numerous draftees were the 33rd (four) followed by the 55th (three), both of which would see extensive service from 1776, but in 1775, Boston was where the fighting was and where the casualties were being suffered.

---

46 Baule and Gilbert, *British Army Officers*, p.74; TNA: PROB 30/55/194: petitions for Charles and Joyce Gold, minors, 18 March 1777; PROB 30/55/195: affidavit by Robert Munday, 10 March 1777; PROB 31/651/771: Will of Lieutenant Richard Gold, 13 October 1777; TNA: PC 1/59/6/1/27: Lieutenant Richard Gold Petition for land in Cape Breton, 2 July 1768.
47 MacKenzie, *British Fusilier*, p.61, 19 April 1775.
48 Frey, *British Soldier in America*, pp.33, 41
49 Hagist, *British Soldiers, American War*, pp.51–72 especially p.62.

6

With Carleton in Canada

The evacuation of the Boston Garrison on 17 March 1776 was a disaster for Washington and the rebellious colonies. The only British Army in the American colonies had been allowed to escape. There were now no British Army units in the Thirteen Colonies. The only other field army in North America had been Governor Carleton's limited forces in Canada, and they had suffered a series of defeats which pushed them back to their final stronghold in the capital, Quebec. Although Carleton was shortly to begin the process of driving the rebels out of Canada, it had been a very close-run thing and Canada was far from safe. General Howe successfully evacuated 17,000 troops and 1,000 Loyal Americans from Boston to Halifax, Nova Scotia. Most of these troops under Howe, reinforced from Britain, Ireland, and Germany, would extract their revenge by humiliating Washington around New York later in the year. That city and environs would be returned to Royal governance and remain so until the end of the war. The 47th were almost part of Howe's revenge. However, on 20 April 1776, they were despatched from Halifax, to support Carleton. Their revenge would be to drive the rebels out of Canada and across the border into New York. They travelled to Quebec on three transports escorted by the frigate *Niger* and arrived on 8 May. Howe had detached the 47th without instructions from the War Office and the regiment's recall was ordered on the 11 June, only to be rescinded 10 days later.[1] It was commonplace for a colonel to have his regiment on campaign with him so the despatch of the 47th to Carleton was not out of the ordinary.

The Defence of Quebec

In the early hours of 10 May 1775, the sleeping garrison of Fort Ticonderoga, numbering less than 50 and blissfully unaware that hostilities had broken out, were captured in their beds by 83 'Green Mountain Boys' led by Ethan Allan and Benedict Arnold. A smaller and equally unaware, 10-strong garrison at Crown Point was also captured. Both forts were located on Lake Champlain,

---

1　Hadden, *Journal*, p.lxviii.

WITH CARLETON IN CANADA

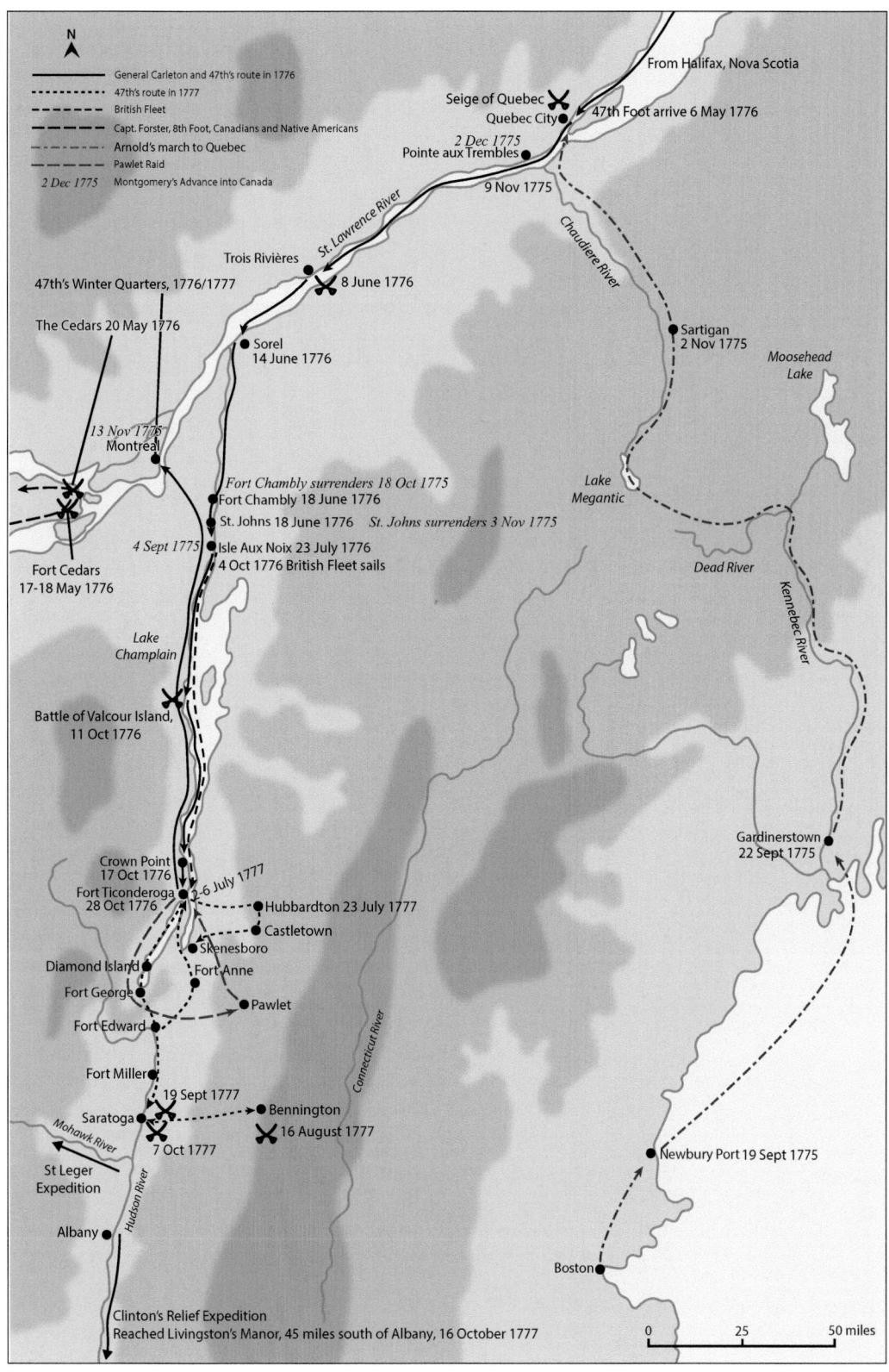

Quebec to Saratoga, 1776–1777.

in upper New York. This was the traditional invasion route between Quebec, and New York and New England, was the reason for the fort's existence and had been the objective of Major General James Abercromby's bloody failure in 1758. The skill in executing the bloodless capture of the forts is rightly to be applauded, and fits within the context of a *coup d'état* in 1775 whereby the means of government were seized by the rebels from an unsuspecting and unprepared administration.[2]

General Carleton was right to have been alarmed about the rebel's intentions towards Quebec.[3] Of the five regiments allocated to Canada's defence, two (the 10th and 52nd Foot) had been sent to Boston while the 8th Foot was widely distributed around the Great Lakes leaving just the 7th and 26th Foot, some 750 men, spread over 250 miles between St Johns, Chambly, Montreal, Trois-Rivières and Quebec. The political position of the Québécois was mixed. The effects of the Quebec Act had yet to be disseminated across the province and there were elements who opposed aspects of it, but equally there was no love lost with the New Englanders, and they had not sent delegates to the Continental Congress. Like the rebels around Boston, the Québécois could be expected to fight in defence of their homes in a campaign which was likely to be successful, but would be increasingly unreliable away from their community and if the campaign was going against them.

In the summer of 1775, the Continental Congress authorised two armies to be paid for by all of the colonies. One, at Boston, under George Washington, was to be 10,000 strong but later grew to around 22,000. The Separate Army, later known as the Northern Army, would operate against Canada. The irony of all of this was that it was precisely what the British government had asked of the colonies for the last 20 years – raising and funding an army for their own defence – and if they had done it then, the intervening 20 years of division and hostility may well have been avoided.

The rebels planned a two-pronged attack. The main force of about 2,200 troops entered Quebec at the beginning of September, 1775 and targeted the isolated British garrisons at St Johns and Chambly, with the city of Quebec as its final objective. It was commanded jointly by former British officer turned rebel, Brigadier General Richard Montgomery and New York magnate Major General Philip Schuyler. During the campaign, Montgomery would command the troops in the field while Schuyler provided the rear area support functions from New York. The second thrust through the Maine wilderness to arrive opposite Quebec City ahead of Montgomery was a feat of super-human endurance, which came close to military disaster. This force of about 1,000 men was commanded by Major General Benedict Arnold, although only about 650 men completed the arduous journey.

Montgomery's force crossed into Canada to capture St Johns. The first two attempts failed but in the middle of September he initiated a formal siege with some 2,000 men. The British commander at St Johns was Major Charles Preston (26th Foot) with some 700 from the 7th and 26th Foot,

---

2   Atkinson, The British are Coming, pp.84–85

3   Carelton, along with Howe, had been given the local rank of general. *The Gazette*, 23 March 1776, issue 11651, p.2

Royal Artillery and Royal Navy, Royal Highland Emigrants, the Montreal Militia, Canadian volunteers and Native Americans. The garrison contained, and was supported by, its wives and children. Also caught in the siege was the then Lieutenant John André. Preston was well aware that his only chance of success was to hold out until relieved by Carleton, in the hope that it would happen before his food and powder supplies ran out. Carleton requested the return of the 10th and 52nd Foot from Boston, which would have provided him with a manoeuvre force to raise the siege, but they were not released. Not for the last time were Canada's interests subordinate to those of the main army in America. St Johns was linked to Fort Chambly just a few miles away. The garrison there was commanded by Major Joseph Stopford (7th Fusiliers). His defence was nowhere near as vigorous as Preston's, and he surrendered on 18 October. Critically, he did so without destroying the garrison's supply of gunpowder. Chambly's artillery would now be turned against St Johns. To crown Stopford's humiliation, the colours of the 7th Fusiliers were captured and presented to Congress. With news of Chambly's surrender and his own supplies running low, Preston negotiated terms of surrender with Montgomery on 3 November. Preston had delayed Montgomery for almost two months which had seen the strength of his Northern Army drastically reduced through death and illness. Critical time had been bought to save Canada.

Montreal was not a defensible city and Carleton had significant concerns about the steadfastness of its inhabitants to stand against the rebels. He left on 11 November making for the provincial capital, Quebec City, where he could make a final stand until reinforcements arrived from Britain in the spring.

Benedict Arnold arrived opposite Quebec City out of the wilderness on 3 December, the day after St Johns surrendered. Montgomery arrived about a fortnight later with some 300 men. His force had been significantly reduced when their enlistments expired, and he also had had to leave a garrison at Montreal. Even combined, Arnold's and Montgomery's forces were inadequate and lacked the artillery required to reduce Quebec's fortifications. Carleton created a garrison of some 1,800 from regulars, sailors, Marines, militia and Royal Highland Emigrants. All three commanders knew that all Carleton had to do was wait out the winter, safe behind the walls, while the rebels suffered outside in the Canadian winter. To force the issue, Montgomery and Arnold attempted to storm Quebec by stealth overnight on 31 December 1775. The assault was spotted by guards and the attack failed with the death, injury or capture of several commanders and a significant number of their men, including the death of Richard Montgomery.[4]

The Tide is Turned

Following Montgomery's death, command of the Northern Army besieging the city was passed to Brigadier General John Thomas. Thomas arrived on 1 May 1776 to find a disaster. The 'besiegers' consisted of about 1,000 men, far fewer than Carleton had within the city, and they were ravaged

---

4   Atkinson, *The British are Coming*, pp.207–211; Morrissey, *Quebec, 1775*, pp.51–62.

by smallpox. A few days later, the 47th arrived to raise the seige. Thomas organised a withdrawal to Trois-Rivières starting with the sick, but he would himself die of smallpox on 2 June. The next commander was Major General John Sullivan who arrived at Sorel on 5 June. Brigadier General William Thompson had already despatched Colonel Arthur St Clair and 600 men to Trois-Rivières where it was intended to make a stand. On his arrival, Sullivan despatched Thomas and a further 1,600 men to join St Clair. The arrival of reinforcements allowed Carleton to drive the rebel forces away from the defences of Quebec, but he was a cautious commander. He waited for the arrival of Lieutenant General Burgoyne, the 9th, 20th, 29th and 53rd Foot, *Generalmajor* Baron Frederick von Riedesel and his Germans. Carleton now moved with speed and decisiveness. On 22 May, he sailed with the 29th and 47th Regiments to Trois-Rivières where he was joined by Burgoyne and further British and German regiments.

The Battle of Trois-Rivières
Fought on 8 June 1776, Trois-Rivières was intended to halt and defeat Carleton's advance. On the 7th, Thompson and St Clair crossed the St Lawrence River at Point du Lac just above Trois-Rivières but their move was observed and reported to the British. Leaving 250 men to guard the landing place, Thompson then persuaded local farmer, Antoine Gautier, to guide his army to Trois-Rivières. Gautier deliberately led the rebels into a swamp which delayed their advance by hours. In the meantime, British troops had disembarked from the fleet and taken up positions south of the village. The ships then sailed to Point du Lac and drove off the rebels from the landing place.

Thompson's men finally extracted themselves from the swamp, only to be fired upon from by British warships in the river. Another rebel force under Colonel Anthony Wayne emerged from the swamp only to face British troops, and quickly fled the field. Thompson managed to extricate a party back to the landing site, only to find it occupied by British troops under the command of the 47th's commanding officer, Lieutenant Colonel Nesbit. Wayne realised that only in the swamp were they in a secure position; from there about 800 were able to extract themselves back to Sorel.

Corporal George Fox was one of the survivors of the 7th Fusiliers after the majority, including his brother, had surrendered at St Johns. He was one of 52 drafted into the 47th and would serve with the regiment until discharged in Lancaster, England at the end of the war.[5] Another combatant was Corporal Roger Lamb (9th Foot), who we last met in Dublin undergoing training in light infantry tactics. Lamb recorded how the drums were beaten at 3:00 a.m. and they marched out to meet Thompson; his description of his first experience of combat has been given previously. Fox described how they lay at anchor for four days before 'the rebels came down by the woods intending to bourn [sic] the town call'd the three rivers. on the 7th we landed and drew up in line of battle. our left wing engaged them [and] we took

---

5   J.A. Houlding, and G.K. Yates, 'Corporal Fox's Memoir of Service, 1766–1783', *Journal of the Society for Army Historical Research*, vol.68, No. 275 (Autumn, 1990), p.154, n.50.

and kill'd several of them particularly G. Tomson [Brigadier General William Thompson] their Chief.[6]

An anonymous 47th officer expanded on Fox's account:

> About 4 in the Morning an Alarm was given by an out Picquet of the approach of a Strong Body of the Rebel Army. The greatest part of the Troops still remained on Board as they had arrived but late the preceding night. A short time after the Alarm had been given, some Shots were heard from one of the King's Frigates which was Station'd a little above the Town: these Shots were fired on part of the Rebels, who were advancing between the Skirts of the Wood and the River. They immediately threw themselves into the Wood. In the meantime the Troops, who were on Shore, were ordered to line ev'ry Avenue leading from the Town to the Wood, and take post in the best manner possible. Those who were on Board their Ships received orders to Land with the greatest Expedition. About 5 o'clock strong advanced Parties were sent towards the Wood; they saw the Rebels advancing in three Columns, who began a heavy Fire, with their small Arms, which was instantly returned by two Centre Companies of the 9th Regt. Grenadiers and Lt Infantry of the 20th and 62d Regiments. In the meantime a strong reinforcement of our Troops with some Field pieces arrived, which soon swept the Woods, and broke the Rebel Columns, the broken remains of which were pursued by the above mentioned Grenadiers and Lt. Infantry Companies, as far as prudence seemed to direct. The Rebels from that time did nothing regular; but broken and dispersed fired a Few scatter'd Shots, which did little execution.
>
> The Surprize the Rebels felt at finding us so prepared to receive them, contrary to their Expectations, and the Alertness and Steadyness of the King's Troops on the Occasion, I believe occasioned their precipitate Flight tho' the Province, for they never after dared shew a Countenance, tho' in some places strongly Intrenched, particularly at Sorrel, and St John's.
>
> A Strong Detachment of 1,200 Men under the command of L[ieutenant] C[olonel] Frazier, marched up the River, to try if possible to get between the Rebels & their Batteaux; the Attempt did not succeed, thro' the very precipitate Flight of the Enemy.
>
> Prisoners taken that Day – 280 – besides B[rigadier] G[eneral] Thompson who commanded the expedition, with 6 other Officers.
>
> Killed were found in the Woods, upwards of 50. 'Tis supposed many of their Wounded and Stragglers must have lost and perished in the Woods, as the Rebels themselves acknowledged on that day to have lost 630 men.
>
> Of the King's Troops – Killed in the Field – 3
> Of Do.   Wounded   14 of which 2 died.
> Killed and Wounded   Total 17
> No Officer hurt
> The Generals were still at Quebec.[7]

---

6   Houlding and Yates, 'Corporal Fox', p.154.
7   Stanley, *For Want of a Horse*, pp.71–72. For an almost identical passage, see Baxter, *British Invasion*, pp.106–108.

Lieutenant Colonel Nesbit then crossed the river to get behind the rebels. The British advanced to try and capture the boats and cut off their escape, but only two were seized. Lamb described the number of rebels killed and wounded as 'considerable'.[8] The prisoners would be paroled and evidently had nothing but good words for the conduct of General Carleton.[9]

It is not very often that named women appear in accounts in independent actions which portray them in a positive light. One who does is Mrs Middleton, the husband of Private Robert Middleton of Captain Gamble's company. Her exploits reached the attention of Captain Sir Francis Carr-Clerke, ADC to Burgoyne:

> Before I close my letter I must not omit telling your Lordship of one Instance of Courage that was shown at Trois Rivieres by a fair Country woman of yours, that deserves to be recorded. The wife of Middleton Soldier in the 47th Regt. Quiet alone took & disarmed six Provincial Soldiers, & was the means of two more being taken also. The Circumstances are thus, which [she] related to Genl. Burgoyne in my Presence. She said she went to a House about a quarter of a Mile from the River near the Wood, for some Milk to carry to her Husband the 8th of June during the Engagemt [sic]. That on opening the Door she saw six Rebel Soldiers armed, that this daunted her a little, however she took Courage, & rated them saying, 'Ay'nt ye ashamed of yourselves ye villains to be fighting agst. Your King & Countrymen' that they looked sheepish, therefore she said, you are all Prisoners give me your Arms, that two more remained at the Outside of the back Door, which she was more afraid of than all the rest, that however standing between them, & their Arms, she called to some Sailors at the River Side, to whom she delivered the Prisoners, & who presently took the other two.
>
> This is exactly true, & she is, contrary to what you wou'd imagine her, a very modest, decent well looking woman.[10]

The rebels lost some 200 prisoners at Trois-Rivières. Mrs Middleton single-handedly accounted for 4 percent of that haul. Trois-Rivières was another disaster for the rebels. Thompson was amongst those captured. In an ironic twist of fate, he was later exchanged for *Generalmajor* Frederick von Riedesel in 1779.

For the British, it was an equally crucial victory. Carleton's caution had paid off. He now had sufficient troops to drive the rebels out and liberate Quebec. For the 47th, this minor victory must have provided a great boost to their confidence after the previous 14 months. Trois-Rivières deserves greater recognition than it has received. It was a relatively small action, but in the American War of Independence, such actions had repercussions well beyond their size. Like Washington's crossing of the Delaware, Trois-Rivières

---

8   R. Lamb, *An original and authentic Journal of occurrences during the late American War, from its commencement to the year 1783* (Dublin: Wilkinson & Courtney, 1809), pp.107–108.
9   Lamb, *Journal*, pp.107–108; Baxter, *British Invasion*, p.132, 29 July 1776.
10 Quoted from British Soldiers, American Revolution: Robert and Mrs. Middleton, 47th Regiment of Foot, <https://redcoat76.blogspot.com/2009/12/robert-and-mrs-middleton-47th-regiment.html> accessed 20 September 2021.

was an essential victory to restore faith in their arms; unlike Washington's raid, Trois-Rivières was a key action in a campaign which secured Quebec and drove the war back into New York. It also occurred before Howe's more well-known actions around New York, which commenced a month later.

The Pursuit Beyond Trois-Rivières

Carleton appointed Lieutenant Colonels Nesbit (47th Foot), Fraser (24th), Powell (53rd) and Gordon (29th) to be Brigadier Generals on 10 June 1776. Nesbit was to command the 1st Brigade consisting of the 9th, 31st and 47th Regiments. Lieutenant Thomas Story, of the 47th, was appointed Nesbit's Major of Brigade. The 21st Fusiliers would be added on the death of Gordon and the disbandment of his brigade. On 26 July, it was reported that Gordon had been 'dangerously' (mortally, as it transpired) wounded by an 'infamous Skulker', 'lurking in small Parties' commanded by one Lieutenant Whitcombe of Connecticut. The killing of Gordon was controversial at the time.[11] Brigadier General Simon Fraser commanded the Advance Corps consisting of the grenadier and light battalions plus other irregular formations.

Corporal Roger Lamb (9th Foot) described 1st Brigade's pursuit of the rebels. They boarded ships on the 9th and landed at Sorel on the 14th but missed the rebels by just two hours. The following day, the pursuit resumed on land in three columns with Burgoyne taking the lead. On the 16th, the panic which the rapid British advance was causing was self-evident:

> Continued our march day and night, expecting every hour to come up with them, however, in all their haste, they took care to set on fire their Batteaux, ships, military stores, &c. It must be confessed that their distress at this time was very great. A British army lose on their rear, and threatening them with destruction; their men obliged to drag their loaded batteaux up the rapids by mere strength, often to their middle in water. They were likewise encumbered with great numbers labouring under [smallpox].[12]

Lieutenant William Digby (53rd Foot) elaborated on the journey:

> About one in the morning, his excellency, [Carleton], came up and immediately ordered the fleet to get under way; the wind then turning fair, but soon after an express arriving and some shots being heard fired on shore [he] ordered them to anchor. The appearance of such a fleet so great a distance from the sea, was well worth seeing, also the beauty of the river, many villages being scattered on its banks, with the mildness of the weather and the verdure of the country, (the trees being then in bloom), formed a most romantic and charming prospect, particularly after being so many weeks at sea. In less than an hour, [Carleton's]

---

11   Hadden, *Journal*, pp.236–237, 26 July 1776; Baxter, *British Invasion*, pp.128–131; M. Berbieri, 'Infamous Skulkers: the shooting of Brigadier General Patrick Gordon', *Journal of the American Revolution* (11 September, 2013), <https://allthingsliberty.com/2013/09/infamous-skulkers-shooting-brigadier-general-patrick-gordon/>, accessed 20 September 2021; J. Kelly, *Valcour: the 1776 Campaign that Saved the Cause of Liberty* (New York: St Martin's Press, 2021), Ch.8.
12   Hagist, *British Soldier's Story*, p.27.

ship got under way, [and] sailed ahead towards the frigate, when the whole fleet weighed, and at day light, were ordered to form a line of battle as near as the channel would admit. On our opening [upon] the fort Sorrel, the troops got orders to be in readiness to land on the shortest notice, the signal being a blue ensign at the frigate's mizzen picue. Soon after we received orders for the light infantry and grenadiers of the army, with the first brigade only, to land, and about 9 in the evening, reached the shore under the command of brigadier general Nesbit, lieutenant colonel of the 47th regiment.

We found the enemy had deserted their lines and about 10 o'clock the troops took post and lay all night on their arms.[13]

On the 18th at 2:00 a.m., the army departed Sorrel for Chambly, a distance of 13 miles which they reached around 9:00 a.m. The rebels had withdrawn to St John's, 12 miles further on:

The army marched in the greatest regularity, as from intelligence received, [Carleton] had no doubt but he should be attacked on his march, our road leading thro thick woods. When we got within about a league of St John's, [Carleton] was informed that a party which had been taken for an advance guard of theirs coming out to meet us, was their rear guard, covering their retreat, on which three companies of light infantry were ordered on, which they did on a trot, and reached the fort about dark, finding it abandoned and on fire. The army came up about half an hour after and lay on their arms all night.[14]

The advance of the light infantry was led by the 47th's light company under Captain James Craig.[15]

Brigadegeneral Johann von Specht (Regiment Specht) described the remains of St John:

Fort St. Jean only consists of a rampart hemmed in by palisades and a dry trench and not far from it, there is an entrenchment provided with earthwork and another dry trench. In the middle, there is a small house, which was assigned to Brigadier Specht as his quarters. The magazine, houses, barracks etc. that had been burned by the Rebels last year have been rebuilt.[16]

Lieutenant James Hadden (RA), who arrived in Quebec on 12 July, described the ruins of Chambly as:

… the shell of a large square House *loop holed,* is an ancient structure raised about 50 Feet, totaly [sic] of Masonry and intended as a defence against the sudden attack of the Savages. It was surrender'd by *Major Stopford* (last year) to the *Rebels* (who brough 1 Gun & a Horse load of powder against it,) after firing a few Shot:

---

13 Baxter, *British Invasion*, pp.113–114.
14 Baxter, *British Invasion*, p.118.
15 Stanley, *For Want of a Horse*, p.75.
16 H. Doblin, (trans.). *The Specht Journal: a military journal of the Burgoyne Campaign* (London: Greenwood Press, 1995), p.46, 14 June 1776.

he neglected to destroy a large quantity of powder then in the *Fort*, they were enabled to return and attack Fort St. John. The powder might have been thrown into the *Rapids* as the Fort is immediately above them … *Timidity* and *Folly* in this instance seems to have been the cause of all the succeeding misfortune in Canada.[17]

Corporal George Fox of the 47th takes up the pursuit: 'They retreat to St Johns. then we set sail and landed at Sorell and march'd to St Dennies and from there to Chamablee 18 miles about St D[ennies]. we halted there for fou[r] hours to Victule and then pursued to St Johns 24 m[iles]. they had set fire to the fort and gone in their batoo up the Lake'.[18] The advance halted on 26 June when the rebels escaped across the lake to Crown Point but, as Lamb writes, 'We could not for want of boats urge our pursuit any further'.[19]

During this pause, small scale operations continued. On the 23rd, Captain Lieutenant Alexander Fraser (9th Foot) set out to raid along the lake. Fraser had been given the task of liaising with the Native Americans by Burgoyne. He had originally been commissioned into the 78th Highlanders during the Seven Years War. Afterwards he had been employed on missions along the frontier. His experience made him well suited to frontier operations. He was also the nephew of Lieutenant Colonel Simon Fraser (24th Foot), who would be given the command of a brigade later in the year.[20] Fraser was accompanied by Lieutenant Thomas Scott (24th Foot) as his second-in-command, 30 Native Americans, a few Canadians and a sergeant, corporal and 12 privates from the 47th's light companies. They encountered a party of rebels on the lake which they engaged and captured, returning to St Johns with 34 prisoners for the loss of one Native American killed, and two Canadians and one 47th private wounded.[21]

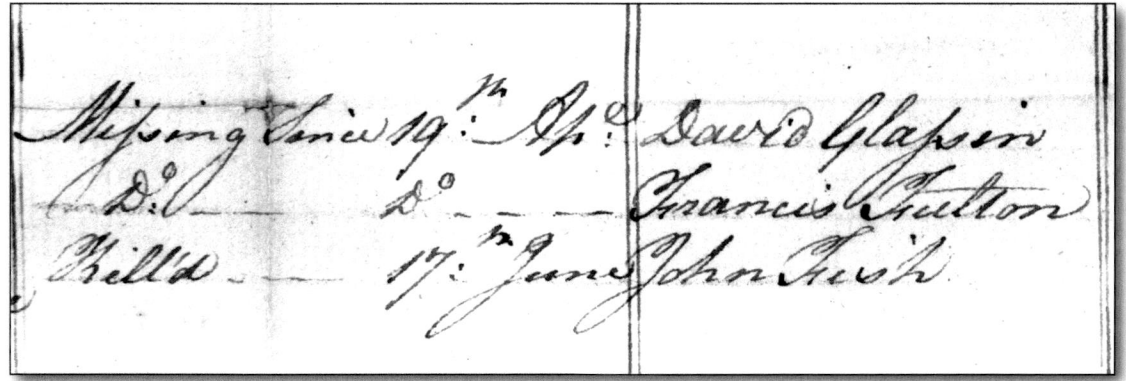

Detail of Captain Craig's company muster roll at Charlestone on 20 September 1775: Missing since 19th April David Glasson; D[itt]o D[itt]o Francis Sutton. (The National Archives)

---

17 Hadden, *Journal*, pp.2-3.
18 Houlding and Yates, 'Corporal Fox', p.154.
19 Hagist, *British Soldier's Story*, pp.27-28.
20 S.G. Strach, 'A Memoir of the Exploits of Captain Alexander Fraser and His Company of British Marksmen, 1776–1777' Part I, *Journal of the Society for Army Historical Research*, vol.6, No. 254, (Summer 1985), pp, 91–98, especially p.94; TNA: WO 65/27: Army List 1777, 9th Foot, p.63.
21 Strach, 'Captain Alexander Fraser,' Part. I, pp.94–95; Baxter, *British Invasion*, pp.122–125; Stanley, *For Want of a Horse*, pp.77–81.

The Construction of a Fleet

It would take three months to construct the Lake Champlain fleet; rapids prevented ships on the St Lawrence River entering the lake. In mid-September, Nesbit became seriously ill so that Lieutenant Colonel James Hamilton (21st Fusiliers) was appointed to command the brigade. Nesbit died on 3 November.[22] Lieutenant James Hadden (RA) recounted two tales of Nesbit, neither of which reflected well on him. In the aftermath of the failed invasion of Canada, Brigadier General William Thompson and another officer prisoner, Colonel William Irvine, surrendered to Nesbit 'by whom we were cruelly treated', they:

> … had the honour of being marched for six miles in the common crowd, without further distinction than being placed near the front. The commanding officer would neither allow us horses or a carriage, though we requested it, and represented to him our miserable condition. Notwithstanding, we were hurried off in a few minutes, and pushed exceedingly fast for six miles…[23]

They then arrived at headquarters where Carleton and Burgoyne treated them better. Thompson, Irvine, and the rest of the prisoners were rebels which meant that they were not entitled to the rights and protections which a prisoner of war was entitled to. In an earlier example, Nesbit was described as a 'master of the art of tarring and feathering, as he tried his hand on a poor countryman' in Boston before Lexington.[24] This is probably a reference to the taring and feathering of the man who attempted to buy a soldier's musket which was recounted in the previous chapter.

Lieutenant Thomas Story's career as major of brigade appears to have ended with Nesbit's death. He had been serving in Captain James Craig's light company in January 1776, and was there again in February 1777. Story had been a half-pay officer in the 99th Foot until appointed to the 47th's light company when it was raised in 1770. He petitioned Carleton sometime after Lieutenant Colonel Nesbit's death for the next available captaincy because after 14 years in his rank, he was the oldest lieutenant in Canada. As part of the Convention Army and listed in the Cambridge Parole, he was promoted to captain lieutenant in 1778 and transferred to the 20th Foot in 1780 as a captain.[25]

The retreat of the rebel forces now also meant their abandonment of those Canadians who had supported them during the invasion, despite Congress's promise never to do so. Carleton's treatment of rebel prisoners, both American and their Canadian supporters, is noted for its leniency.[26]

---

22   TNA: WO 32/3102: Petition of Widow of Lt Col Nesbitt; Hadden, *Journal*, pp.175–176, 282.
23   Hadden, *Journal*, p.176, n.ee.
24   Hadden, *Journal*, p.176, n.ee.
25   Baule and Gilbert, *British Army Officers*, p.171; TNA: WO 28/9-31: Lieutenant Story's Memorial to Carleton.
26   T.C. Jones, *Captives of Liberty: Prisoners of War and Politics of Vengeance in the American Revolution* (Philadelphia: University of Pennsylvania Press, 2020), pp.73–74.

Lieutenant Hadden (RA), escorted across the Atlantic 53 recruits who, when they arrived at St. Thérèse, Montreal, were ordered distributed between the two weakest regiments, the 47th and 53rd. They received 48 and five respectively. The recruits were organised into 'Sizes and Lots' for the 'impartiality of the Distribution' to ensure the fair distribution of the recruits.[27] The 8th and 47th also expected to receive 150 German recruits. Some of these were serving soldiers because the receiving regiments were ordered that the sergeants and corporals were to keep their rank, clothing and pay, but that they were to be mustered as private soldiers until a suitable vacancy arose which they were to receive. It later transpired that the ships carrying these soldiers had been blown off course and made landfall in the West Indies. They then made their way to New York where they had been appropriated into Howe's army. There are two interesting points here. One is the recruitment of Germans directly into the British Army, an example of this is Georg Hundertmark a German by birth but serving in the 9th Foot who would be executed for desertion the following year. This also shows once again the 'Main Army' ignoring the requirements of the army in Canada.[28]

Promotions continued as usual. Ensign John Rotton was promoted Lieutenant *vice* Lieutenant French. Hadden believed that Rotton was a nephew of Carleton, whose sister Catherine had married one John Rotton of Dublin. Ensign Rotton was commissioned on 28 January 1775 and sailed in the *Hope*, from Cork. The ship made landfall at Gloucester near Philadelphia in early August, unaware of hostilities, and the passengers and crew were taken prisoner by the Pennsylvania Committee of Safety. The muster roll of Brevet Major Thomas Smelt's company at Charlestown on 28 September 1775, lists Ensign Rotton as 'Prisoner with Rebels'. Paroled in Hartford, Connecticut, the officers considered themselves to be ill-used, and petitioned Congress to move them elsewhere. At some point he was exchanged and finally joined the regiment, as he was part of the Convention Army in 1777 and is listed on the Cambridge Parole. Hadden's footnote sheds light on Rotton's misadventures which otherwise would suggest that he had been captured around Boston. In the February 1777 muster rolls, Rotton is recorded as being promoted to lieutenant and posted to Captain Aubrey's company where he was again listed as a 'Prisoner with the Rebels'.[29]

Ensign Arthur French was part of the major's company in Morristown, Ireland in May 1773 and Elizabeth Town, New Jersey, in January 1774, and was listed as being on leave on both occasions. By August 1774 he was back on duty when the company was based in New York and Boston. His promotion to lieutenant was recorded in January 1776 and he was posted to Captain Craig's

---

27 Hadden, *Journal*, p.234, 25 July 1776.
28 TNA: WO 4/98: Secretary-at-War, Out Letters, General Letters, 3 August 1776; WO 4/100: Secretary-at-War, Out Letters, General Letters, 18 July 1777; O'Callaghan (ed.), *Orderly Book*, p.81, 24 August 1777; p.127, 6 October 1777; Hagist, *Noble Volunteers*, pp.110, 219–220.
29 TNA: WO 12/5871: Muster Rolls, 47th Foot, February 1777; see also G. Shattuck, 'Major Christopher French, Prisoner of War', *Journal of the American Revolution* (5 May, 2015), <https://allthingsliberty.com/2015/05/major-christopher-french-prisoner-of-war/> accessed 19 October 2021. French was the senior office captured on the *Hope* and set out to make difficulties for his captives. I am indebted to David Babington-Smith for bringing this article to my attention.

light company and was still serving there in February 1777 but thereafter the muster rolls are missing. Hadden is incorrect when he suggests that French left the regiment about 10 July 1776 when Rotton was promoted. French was attached to Fraser's Company of Marksmen in 1777, and is listed in the Cambridge Parole. He appears in the Army List until 1783.[30]

Two Volunteers also gained commissions in the 47th at this time. 'Gentlemen Volunteers' where men of the right character and background, but who lacked the financial resources to purchase a commission. By volunteering, they served in the ranks until a vacancy arose and they were selected to fill it. Volunteer Gustavus Hamilton was commissioned ensign on Rotton's promotion. Hadden believed that Hamilton was with either Aubrey's or Gamble's company on Diamond Island as he was not part of the Convention Army. He was actually commissioned into Captain Sherriff's company (according to the February 1777 muster roll) but the following March was listed in Captain Richard L'Estrange's company at Belle Isle and 'On Command', that is that he was engaged on duties away from the regiment. He was subsequently promoted Lieutenant in 1780 and is listed as recruiting for Captain Aubrey's company at Whitehaven in August 1783. He went onto half-pay in 1784.[31]

The final promotion was another volunteer, George Stevens, *vice* Lord Pitt who had, as has been discussed, resigned his commission. Stevens was commissioned on 10 July 1776 and was still an ensign four years later.[32] Captured and part of the Convention Army, Stevens was part of the Cambridge Parole but still an ensign in the colonel's company in Lancaster in February 1782. He was promoted the following May, but the muster rolls are incomplete making tracking his movement within the regiment difficult.[33]

Introduction of Light Infantry Tactics in Quebec

A great deal is made of the innovations in the light infantry tactics principally around the campaigns in the middle and southern colonies, most recently in MacNiven's *British Light Infantry in the American Revolution*.[34] Exactly the same process occurred in Canada as soon as there was a pause in the operational tempo. In Chapters 4 and 5 we examined the intellectual space in which the innovators worked. What we see in Canada is the same intellectual process but chronologically and geographically isolated from the main army at Halifax or New York under Howe and his successors. Indeed, the two commands operated independently throughout the war. We have

---

30 Hadden, *Journal*, pp.213–215, 10 July 1776; Baule and Gilbert, *British Army Officers*, pp.69, 156; O'Callaghan (ed.), *Orderly Book*, Parole of Burgoyne's Officers, p.179.
31 Hadden, *Journal*, pp.214–215, 10 July 1776.
32 TNA: WO 65/27: Army List 1777, 47th Foot, p.103; WO 65/30: Army List 1780, 47th Foot, p.114.
33 Hadden, *Journal*, p.215, 10 July 1776; O'Callaghan (ed.), *Orderly Book*, Parole of Burgoyne's Officers, p.179.
34 R. MacNiven, *British Light Infantry in the American Revolution* (Oxford: Osprey, 2021).

already seen this with Howe's retention of two of the regiments provided for Canada's defence in Boston and then New York, and we will see the disastrous consequence of this approach in the next chapter.

Hadden's *Journal* describes the introduction of simplified, light drills while the construction of the Lake Champlain fleet provided an operational pause. On the 29 June 1776, all regiments were to drill for two hours per day in the cool of the morning:

> No Exercise need be practiced, except Loading, Levelling, charging with Bayonets, and marching, in which it is meant to comprehend changing front by Divisions, and by Files; suffering the Regiment to break and form upon one given point, either by a file from Right, Left or Centre: The Order of forming is to be at two deep, and the Files 18 Inches asunder.[35]

And on the 3 July 1776, on firing:

> The Brigades may use Cartridges for Exercise, but the Ball is to be most carefully preserved except *twenty* for each Recruit, and *ten* for every other Soldier of each Regiment, which may be expended for firing at marks, or otherwise, at the orders of the Brigadier General.
>
> A Return to be given in from each Regiment to Major General Phillips on Saturday next of the number of Ball instore, that Powder, Paper and Twine may be ordered for the Regiments to make into Cartridge.
>
> The Brigades will take care to preserve eighteen Rounds for Service.[36]

On August 8, one hundred rounds per man to be made up:

> Every Regiment to demand of the Commanding Officer of Artillery in Camp of Powder, Ball, and Paper necessary to complete to one hundred Rounds a Man, which are to be directly made up, and are to be kept in Store by each Regiment with the greatest care. The Artillery will lend the Powder Barrels (which will be delivered with Powder) to pack up Musquet Cartridges when made, but these Barrels are to be accounted for, or returned after the Campaign.
>
> The number each will hold, will put in, is nearly 2000 Cartridges.
>
> Whenever the Number of Cartridges of any Regiment is diminished by 15 Rounds a Man, a fresh demand is to be made, so as to keep the 100 Rounds *always complete*. The Commanding Officer of each Regiment will sign the Demand, and the Officer who is sent with the Party, will give a receipt for the Powder &c.[37]

And three weeks later the Order was followed up:

> The Order of the 8th Instant for competing 100 rounds a Man of Musket Cartridges should by this time be perfected. It is therefore directed that small

---

35   Hadden, *Journal*, pp.197–198, 29 June 1776.
36   Hadden, *Journal*, p.205, 3 July 1776.
37   Hadden, *Journal*, p.245, 8 August 1776.

Barrels, or well secured Boxes covered with painted Canvass, be provided by each Regiment, to pack these Cartridges very carefully against Damp.[38]

At the end of August, Brigadier General Simon Fraser proposed the formation of a 'Company of Marksmen' under Captain Lieutenant Alexander Fraser. This was to consist of 100 men 'chosen for their strength, activity and being expert at firing … Each man to be furnished with an excellent firelock, the lock in good order and the hammer well steeled.' He also proposed that the Canadian Volunteers were augmented to 70 or 80. The two corps would operate on the flank of the main body, and could be augmented with Native Americans as required. On 6 September, Carleton ordered for one sergeant, one corporal and eight privates from each regiment in Nesbit's and Powell's brigades to form Fraser's Company. Having spent the period 7–10 September organising his company, Fraser departed over the next few days with 150 Native Americans to establish posts and gather intelligence. They do not appear to have been involved in any significant action, and at the end of the campaigning season the company was broken up with the men returned to their parent units, to be reformed in 1777. Fraser was rewarded with a promotion to captain in the 34th Foot on 11 November 1776.[39]

Uniform Modifications

One of the characteristics of the army in Canada during the 1777 campaign was their distinctive uniform which was captured by *Hauptmann* Friedrich von Germann, from Hesse-Hanau, in a series of watercolours. There is evidence that similar unform modifications were being introduced in 1776. In July 1776, Lieutenant William Digby (53rd Foot), described an alternative to breeches and stockings: 'Though we all went as thinly clothed as possible, wearing large loose trousers to prevent the bite of the moscheto.'[40] In the spring of 1777, *Hauptmann* Pausch also described their design and practicality:

> There was ordered for the English artillery long, loose, and wide linen overalls – such as the sailors wear – to be made in one piece from one end to the other; and to be of the same length as leggings. They were mostly made of old tents. I found this kind of clothing to be very well adapted to this climate and our present situation. They were particularly convenient not only for marching, but as a protection against the insects which are especially annoying to the men both in the field and in the camp. Lieut. Defais and myself amply tested the merits of this clothing *last year*, while on our journey to and from Three Rivers and Chambly … Accordingly, as I had no old tents which would serve the purpose, I did not

---

38 Hadden, *Journal*, p.263, 29 August 1776.
39 Strach, 'Captain Alexander Fraser', Part 1, pp.96-98; C.T. Atkinson, 'Some Evidence for Burgoyne's Expedition', *Journal of the Society for Army Historical Research*, vol.26, No. 108 (Winter, 1948), pp.132-142, especially pp.134-135; WO 65/30 Army List 1780, 34th Foot, p.104.
40 Baxter, *British Invasion*, p.122.

hesitate, but bought, at the lowest price, Russian linen and had it made up into pants. … These pants are now all finished, and are worn by the men not only in the barracks, but when of duty and at drill.[41]

Not all of the illustrations show gaiter overalls being worn, some regiments are shown in breeches and stockings. Similarly, a detail of a painting of Lake Champlain in 1777 shows a Royal Artillery officer in breeches and stockings, and three soldiers wearing Indian leggings over breaches. So, when Carleton wrote to Secretary at War, William Viscount Barrington on 17 November 1776 '… the clothing of many of the regiments … has not been sent out … I have learnt that schemes are pursued, in the furnishing of the clothing of some regiments which are by no means conformable to any orders of His Majesty … which I have ever seen, or to the usual practice of the Army',[42] he was acknowledging what was already an established practice, that of altering the uniforms to meet the existing conditions. His use of plurals throughout is interesting, suggesting that regiments were undertaking their own schemes rather than following a centralised direction. By March the following year the clothing had still not arrived. The transport, *Mellis*, with the 16,000 uniforms and 30,000 pairs of shoes was captured by rebel privateer John Paul Jones, being the most valuable cargo seized at sea during the war.[43] In April 1777, Lieutenant Thomas Anburey (29th Foot) implied that the non-arrival of the *Mellis* had necessitated an official policy:

> The cloathing for the army not being sent out last year, and as it will be too late to fit it to the men when it arrives, the commanding officers of the different regiments have received orders to reduce the men's coats into jackets, and their hats into caps, as it will be the means of repairing their present cloathing, and be more convenient for wood service, that when the army take the field, they will in a manner be all light infantry. The regiments have the hair that is affixed to their caps of different colors; ours is red …[44]

Cocked hats were cut down and converted into caps with a false front and a horsehair comb. Again, however, the Lake Champlain 1777 detail shows a Royal Artillery officer wearing a cocked hat. Captain Sir Francis-Carr Clerke, ADC to Burgoyne approved of the new style: 'The Cloathing of Some of the Regiments not being arrived, the Army have cut their Skirts to light Infantry measure, in order to repair the Coat, & old hats cut up into light Infantry Caps, which I think gives them a lively smart appearance.'[45]

In terms of equipment carried, Corporal Roger Lamb (9th Foot) summarised his usual load: '… a knapsack, blanket, haversack containing four day's provision, a canteen for water, and a proportion of his tent

---

41   Pausch, *Journal*, pp.106–107. Present author's italics.
42   TNA: WO 1/11: Letter 17/18, Carleton to Barrington, 17 November 1776. I am indebted to Matthew Zembo for bringing this document to my attention.
43   Atkinson, *The British are Coming*, pp.467–468.
44   Anburey, *Travels*, vol.I, pp.197–198, Letter XVII, 6 April 1777.
45   'Letters to Lord Poleworth from Sir Francis-Carr Clerke, Aide-de-Camp to General John Burgoyne' *New York History* (October, 1998) quoted in Hagist, *British Soldier's Story*, p.xlv.

furniture, which, supperadded to his accoutrements, arms and sixty rounds of ammunition, made a great load and large luggage, weighting about sixty pounds.'[46] Right at the end of the 1777 campaign, the 47th's Corporal George Fox would still have his knapsack, when the bottom of it was taken off by a cannon ball.[47] He does not elaborate where it was in relation to his body at the time.

On occasions, wagons were made available to transport the tents, but as the troops advanced south of Ticonderoga, logistics became a growing problem. As early as May 1777, Thomas Anburey was concerned about the provision of horses for his baggage 'if not, I shall be compelled to send back my baggage, and then, hey for courage and a knapsack!'[48] In a later letter, he quoted Burgoyne's order that some regiment's officers were encumbered with more baggage than they could transport, and in the last war officers 'took up with soldiers tents, and often confined their baggage to a knapsack, for months together.'[49]

Roger Lamb provides a generic, bucolic description of life on campaign in an encampment which is timeless to all campaigning soldiers:

> The Bivouack of an Army. It is a pleasing sight to see a column arrive at its halting ground. The Camp is generally marked out, if circumstances allow of it, on the edge of some wood, and near a river or stream. The troops are halted in open columns and arms piled, pickets and guards paraded and posted, and in two minutes all appear at home. Some fetch large stones to form fire places; others hurry off with canteens and kettles for water while the wood resounds with the blows of the tomahawk. Dispersed under the more distant trees you see the officers, some dressing, some arranging a few boughs to shelter them by night, others kindling their own fires. How often under some spreading pine tree which afforded shade, shelter and fuel have I taken up my lodgings for the night. Sitting in the midst of my comrades, men whom I loved and esteemed partaking of a coarse but wholesome meal, seasoned by hunger and cheerfulness. Wrapt up in a blanket, the head reclining on a stone or a knapsack coved [sic – covered] with the dews of the night or drenched perhaps by the thunder shower sleeps many a hardy veteran. A bivouack in heavy weather does not I allow present a very comfortable appearance. The officers sit shivering in their wet tents idle and angry. The men with their forage caps drawn over their ears huddle together under the trees or crowed round cheerless smoky fires – complaining of their commissaries, the rain and the Americans.[50]

The army in Canada developed its own, unique style by adopting the uniform to meet the prevailing conditions. Matthew Zembo in his research believes that the orders referred to by Pausch and others was simply an

---

46 Hagist, *British Soldier's Story*, p.42.
47 Houlding and Yates, 'Corporal Fox', p.160.
48 Anburey, *Travels*, vol.I, p.211, Letter XVIII, 20 May 1777.
49 Anburey, *Travels*, vol.I, pp.353–354, Letter XXXIII, 14 July 1777.
50 D. Hagist, 'Unpublished Writings of Roger Lamb, Soldier in the American War of Independence', Part 1, *Journal of the Society for Army Historical Research*, vol.89, No. 360 (Winter, 2011), pp.283–284.

official recognition of existing practice, and that the variation within and between units was probably far greater than we realise. Similar changes were occurring in Howe's army in New York with the adoption of slouch hats, sleaved waistcoats, and gaiter overalls. As with the tactical innovations, both armies were conducting the same exercise in uniform modification simultaneously yet independently, although reaching different conclusions due to the differences in topography. This simultaneity speaks volumes for the army's ability to adapt rather than being hidebound to tradition and regulation.[51]

Taking the War into New York

While the fleet was being built on Lake Champlain, Captain Fraser's Company of Marksmen was acting in the tradition of rangers from the French and Indian War, patrolling up the lake, gaining intelligence and denying the same opportunities to the enemy. In late August he moved his company and three light companies to the Lacolle River, on the left bank of the Richelieu River. A patrol at the end of August under Fraser returned with nothing of significance. On 6 September, a patrol under Lieutenant Thomas Scott (24th Foot) of one sergeant, one corporal and 12 volunteers from the light companies, accompanied by Canadians and Native Americans got above the rebel fleet under Benedict Arnold and was able to inflict some casualties on a shore party from the *Enterprise*, gathering wood. The rebels were supported by fire from the ship and reinforcements were landed which forced the British to withdraw. Rebel losses were two killed, one mortally wounded and four injured; Scott reported 16 enemy killed. The rebels recovered what was described as an officer's hat with a 47th button. Scott from the 24th Foot was the only known officer to have participated in the patrol, so the assertion that it was an officer's hat can be questioned, but it does testify to the presence of the 47th in the patrol.[52]

By the autumn, the army was on the move again. On 22 September, the 47th was ordered to march to St John.[53] Lieutenant James Hadden (RA) described the state of the roads on the final 19 miles to St Johns, which was a foretaste of what was to come: 'Being incumber'd with many Carts &c destined for the expedition our march was much retarded by the badness of the Roads, which were uncommonly so notwithstanding the late fine weather: more than half the Carriages were broken & we did not get to St. John's 'till late night.'[54] It was during this pause in the campaigning that the worst incident of indiscipline occurred associated with the 47th Foot in Canada occurred. On 4 October 1776:

---

51 M. Zembo, 'The Training and Tactics of the British Army in Preparation for the Burgoyne Campaign and the Invasion of New York in 1777: The Case for the Battle of Fort Anne', presented at 85th Annual Meeting of the Society for Military History (April, 2018).
52 Stanley, *For Want of a Horse*, pp.86–87; Baxter, *British Invasion*, pp.143–144, n.112; Strach, 'Captain Alexander Fraser,' Part. I, pp.94–95; Kelly, *Valcour*, pp.104–105.
53 Hadden, *Journal*, p.288, 22 September 1776.
54 Hadden, *Journal*, p.51.

> The Commander in Chief delayed to reprimand in Orders, the insolent, shameful, and ungrateful Clamour made at the Evening Parade of Tuesday last, by the 31st and 47th Regiments, in hopes, and in expectation that the Displeasure he expressed to the Commanding Officers of those Corps, with his Orders to communicate the same immediately to the Officers of Companies, would have produced such visible and equal marks of Contrition, as might have justified him in suffering the matter to rest thenceforward in Silence. His Excellency has been in some measure disappointed, and he has therefore in justice to both Regiments, left it in charge to take public notice of the difference of their behaviour.
>
> The 47th Regiment have not ceased through their Commanding Officer to acknowledge their offence and to testify their penitence, and in such terms of Decency and respect, as make due atonement, and restore them to the good opinion they before deserved.

He then went on to admonish the 31st Regiment:

> It is a painful necessity to include other Officers in this regimental Censure, but it can hardly be supposed, if the Subject of Rum had been properly explained, that men could be so devoid of Duty and Reason as to expect indulgencies never granted to any Army; absolutely impossible to be complied with in the present service, and were it otherwise, improper and prejudicial.
>
> The Officers are required and ordered these truths known to the men, and those who want recollection are to be taught to reflect on the numerous and unprecedented favours already heaped upon this Army, by the King, their Countrymen at Home, and their own Officers.
>
> The impression of just principles carefully instilled, soon becomes visible and certain, and Solder is so prepared, will ever consider that Decency, Regularity, Subordination and respect to their Officers, when out of Action, are the best and most honourable pledges they can offer to their Superiors for trusting to their hands, when they shall meet the Enemy, the Glory of His Majesty's Arms, and the Vindication of the Rights of Great Britain.
>
> Rum will be allowed to the Regiments to Day, the 31st Regiment excepted.[55]

Alcohol was a perennial problem in the army as a source of insubordination, as in this example and also as has been shown in the Boston Garrison. A month earlier Lieutenant Hadden recorded that: 'The Soldiers are to be strictly enjoined not to give any Drink to the Indians, and any Women who shall be detected in having given or sold Rum to the Indians, shall be directly turned out of the Camp.' The order was repeated five days later, so the first instruction had clearly not been adhered too, as we saw in Boston.[56]

After three months of shipbuilding, the fleet was ready to set sail. The rebel fleet was commanded by Benedict Arnold, now returned and recovered from his Quebec escapade. His vessels had either been captured in Canada, or built at their own shipyard in Skenesborough near Fort Ticonderoga. The ensuring Battle of Valcour Island on 11 October was amongst the strangest

---

55   Hadden, *Journal*, pp.299–302, 4 Oct 76, After General Orders.
56   Hadden, *Journal*, pp.277–278, 8 Sept 76; pp.280–281, 13 Sept 1776.

of the war as it was principally fought by land soldiers on water. Corporal George Fox (47th Foot) provided a narrative of the action, but it is unclear whether or not the 47th participated:

> Our Army stayed there till the begining of September repairing the fort and building near 200 batooes to pursue them, we advac'd in our batooes [and] they kept retreating, from the Isle Le knower we went up the river La-cool. we continued our expedition over the Lake Champaness 250 [miles] from Quebeck, 150 m over the lake and there we over took them on the further side of the lake under Arnold he was wounded, [and] we destroyed several of thir vessels. they were in Schoners floating batterys and gun boats (we had Batooes gun boats) then we followed them to Chimney point our old fort opposite Crown point (which is 400 miles from Quebeck) the river that parts them runs from the Lake C[hamplain] [and] there we encamp'd till Oct. the rebels when [i.e. went] up to Ticondarago to winter Quarters, now winter approaching we were oblig'd to retreat down into Canada for winter quarters in different cantoonments.[57]

The rebel fleet consisted of 15 vessels which ranged from two 12-gun ships (the sloop *Enterprise* and the schooner *Royal Savage*) to eight three-gun 'gundalows' or 'gondolas'. These were flat-bottomed, 50-foot long armed barges with a single square sail and oars for propulsion. They were armed with three cannons, one projecting forward and one on each side. Critically, they were quick to build.[58] Arnold realised that he would be outgunned by Carleton and positioned his fleet in a crescent to the west of Valcour Island. The island is located close to the west bank of, and about a third of the way down, Lake Champlain.

Facing the rebels was a far larger British fleet of some 33 vessels. The four largest vessels matched or outgunned Arnold's largest ships. *Inflexible* carried 22 guns, followed by *Thunderer* (18 guns), *Maria* (an 18-gun schooner named after Lady Carleton) and *Carleton* with 12 guns. *Loyal Convert* was a seven-gun gundalow and the remainder were gunboats carrying a single gun each. Furthermore, Carleton's fleet was commanded by Captain Thomas Pringle, RN, and assisted by other naval officers including James Dacres, Edward Pellew and John Schank. All four pursued successful careers and became admirals. Certainly, a pool of exceptional talent.

Captain Pringle set sail on 9 October to find and destroy the rebel fleet. On the 10th, he sailed past Valcour Island, unaware that his enemy were anchored on the far side. Arnold despatched *Congress* and *Royal Savage* to gain the attention of the British. As they attempted to rejoin their lines, *Royal Savage* went aground off the southern tip of Valcour Island. She was boarded by the *Loyal Convert*, capturing 20 men in the process, but had to

---

57 Houlding and Yates, 'Corporal Fox', pp.154–155. Fox served in one of the centre companies. The anonymous author of *For Want of a Horse*, who is believed to be an officer in one of the 47th's detached flank companies, does not mention participating in the battle either. He has no entries between 7 and 17 October 1776, pp.89–90.
58 Kelly, *Valcour*, pp.38, 259.

be abandoned due to heavy fire from the remaining rebel fleet. *Royal Savage* was burned and abandoned.

It was now 12:30 p.m. The British fleet manoeuvred to attack, led by *Carleton* and the smaller vessels. *Thunderer* and *Maria* struggled to make headway against the wind and would not participate in the battle while *Inflexible* made only slow progress and joined the battle late. By 6:30 p.m., the rebel eight-gun schooner *Revenge* had been sunk and gundalow *Philadelphia* irreparably damaged and later sunk. The rebels focused their fire on *Carleton* which was disabled and badly damaged before it could be towed to safety. Midshipman Edward Pellew distinguished himself by taking command after the captain, Lieutenant James Dacres, was injured.

Inflexible finally arrived at sunset and her guns quickly silenced the remainder of Arnold's fleet. The British also landed Native Americans on the lakeshore and island to prevent the rebels from abandoning their vessels and making an overland escape. With dusk, the rebels withdrew and the British called off the battle. However, Arnold observed a mile-wide gap between the British vessels and the lake shore, and skilfully extricated his surviving vessels. By morning Arnold was at Schuyler Island, eight miles to the south. Carleton erroneously ordered his fleet northwards around Valcour Island before sending scouts out to locate the enemy. Despite making good his escape, Arnold's fleet was severely damaged. Two vessels were scuttled on Schuyler Island, and *Lee* was abandoned on the shore where it was recovered by the British. The British pursued them southwards. *Washington*'s damage slowed her escape and she surrendered with 110 crewmen. Finally, Arnold directed his remaining vessels to the now named Arnold Bay which was too shallow for the larger British vessels to enter. There, the remaining vessels were torched; Arnold performed the task himself on his flagship, *Congress*. The 200 surviving crewmen now made their escape overland, narrowly escaping the Native Americans, and reached Crown Point where they found the last five surviving vessels. Realising that Crown Point could not be held while the British had control of the lake, the fort was burned, and they made their escape for Fort Ticonderoga.

Carleton had one final card to undermine the rebels left to play. He had in his possession some 200 rebel prisoners. Rather than returning them to Quebec where they would have to be housed, guarded and fed, he released them under a flag of truce at Fort Ticonderoga with the observation that he had never invaded their property nor sent a single soldier to distress them. Tales of British humanity soon spread amongst the rebel garrison, so the grateful prisoners were quickly sent away from the fort.[59]

Winter 1776–1777

Winter in Canada can be tough, even today. In 1776, those regiments which had arrived in the summer from the milder climes of the British Isles may

---

59 Atkinson, *The British are Coming*, pp.405–429; Morrissey, *Quebec 1775*, pp.73–86; Hadden, *Journal*, pp.22–33; Hagist, *British Soldier's Story*, pp.28–30; Kelly, *Valcour*, pp.219–220.

well have faced the coming winter with dread. For those members of the 47th who had spent the previous winter besieged in Boston, the prospects for the coming winter were probably relatively good. Many of the interesting accounts from this winter would come from the German sources whose experiences of winter would have been closest to that of Canada.

The 47th was dispersed in several communities around Montreal. According to Specht, their winter quarters were in Lachine, at the Ille-de-Montreal, now a suburb of the city, while the grenadier and light companies were quartered between Chateauguay and St Ours, on the opposite bank of the St Lawrence River.[60] During the winter, the 47th received a new commanding officer. Nicholas Sutherland was promoted lieutenant colonel and appointed commanding officer on 5 November 1776 to replace Lieutenant Colonel Nesbit, who had died a month earlier. Sutherland was initially commissioned into the 62nd Foot, later the 60th (Royal Americans), in 1755. He transferred to the 77th (Montgomery's) Highlanders on promotion to lieutenant in 1757. As captain lieutenant he was wounded during the Cherokee War of 1760. Further service took him to the Caribbean and Havana before returning to New York in 1762. The 77th took part in the Battle of Bushy Run in 1763 which was part of Pontiac's Rebellion. It was disbanded later in the year. After a period on half-pay, Sutherland joined the 21st Fusiliers in 1765 which was then posted in North America. He remained with the 21st until he moved to the 47th. When Sutherland took command of the regiment, his entire military service except for 1773 to 1776 had been in North America. That would have placed him amongst the most experienced commanding officers under Carleton and Burgoyne. In 1777, he would command the regiment throughout the Saratoga Campaign, lead the belated breakout back towards Fort Ticonderoga and was instrumental in the negotiations leading to the signing of the Saratoga Convention. He was paroled at some point before February 1779, although exactly when is unclear, for he was commanding a Fencible Regiment in Scotland at that date. He died on 18 July 1781.[61]

Hauptmann Pausch of the Hanau Artillery appears to be very content with the winter accommodation he and his men received, which was as good as the Royal Artillery received. There is nothing to suggest that the 47th Foot fared any differently. Pausch writes:

> My company was allotted to it six large rooms in the barracks with fire-places; and to my subalterns were given two tooms. All Captains of Artillery, including myself, are billeted in the city. Each room, occupied by my men, contains ten beds – every bed holding two persons. Every Saturday, wood, coal, and lights are distributed among them from the magazine; and, on every eighth day, provisions are dealt out to them fairly and equitably. Nearly all the winter they were furnished with fresh meat and very good bread. Each man, with the exception of those who are sick, draws salt beef and pork, and very good butter. The latter article is served out at the rate of one pound per man for eight days; and every time that salt meat

---

60 Specht, *Journal*, pp.36, 38.
61 Hadden, *Journal*, Appendix No. 22, pp.556–562; Baule and Gilbert, *British Army Officers*, p.173; TNA: WO 65/27: Army List 1777, 21st Foot, p.77; 47th Foot, p.103.

is given out, pease and oat-meal are also furnished. For all this, the company have to thank solely the kind care of Gen. Phillips, who is just as solicitous concerning our rations and treatment [as the RA].⁶²

He elaborated further on the provisions: 'We were supplied the same in every respect as the Artillery of the King, having fresh meat and very good bread.'⁶³

The other item which was essential to survive the winter was clothing. Again, Pausch is descriptive of the cold weather items which he and his men received. First of all was:

> One pair of long blue cloth over-alls such as are worn by sailors, which come high up above the hips and way down to the shoes. These are fastened under the feet with a leather strap, and have five buttons on the outside of each leg and extend about a quarter the way up from the ankle, also:

> One large blue woolen [sic] cap.
> One pair of blue mittens lined with corduroy material
> One capacious under-jacket, the sleeves being made of strong white corduroy.
> One Canadian over-coat with a cape and facings of white sheeps wool, and bound with a light blue broad. The cape itself is made out of a whitish gray cloth a kind of melton. It is bound with light blue woolen ribbon, and in three places extending down in front to the waist it is fastened with rosettes – these later being made out of this same blue ribbon. This garment is called thought all Canada a *capot*.⁶⁴

All of which met with his approval: 'These outfits – so necessary in this part of the world – are of great service to my men, especially those who are sick. Of the latter, there are over thirty who are suffering from a kind of scorbutic itch.'⁶⁵ Lieutenant William Digby (53rd Foot) also seemed content with the situation: 'Thus situated we passed the Winter in as agreeable a manner as was in our power, with an expectation of opening the campaign early the ensueing season.'⁶⁶

Conclusion

The 1776 campaign in Quebec deserves more recognition than it has received, occurring as it did at the end of the Boston campaign and the beginning of Howe's New York campaign. The loss of Canada would have been catastrophic, potentially war-ending, in a way that the loss of Boston was not. Canada provided the secure base from which British forces could strike into the rebellious colonies and which Congress never neutralised. This contrasts with New York which largely became a super-garrison especially

---

62   Pausch, *Journal*, pp.92-93.
63   Pausch, *Journal*, pp.72-73.
64   Pausch, *Journal*, pp.93-94.
65   Pausch, *Journal*, p.95, see also pp.106–107.
66   Baxter, *British Invasion*, p.184.

when the active campaigning switched from the central colonies to the south after 1778. Canada also provided a safe refuge for loyalists both during and after the war. The securing of Canada within the British Empire clearly had significant long-term implications.

Carleton showed what professional officers with a professional army could achieve when placed on a clear war-footing. In 1776, his army moved rapidly in pursuit of the rebels and executed an impressive deployment at Trois-Rivières. Washington's Crossing of the Delaware is often described as an action essential to restore the morale of the Continental Army. Trois-Rivières should be viewed in the same context, as a small yet vital action in restoring confidence in British arms after Boston and the rebel's 1775 invasion of Canada. The confidence gained at Trois-Rivières would be carried forward into 1777.[67]

Valcour Island was another spectacular British success. Control of the lake was secured and remained so for the remainder of the war. The destruction of Crown Point meant that the most northerly rebel fort was Ticonderoga at the southernmost tip of the lake. The threat to Canada had now greatly receded and in that, Carleton had successfully discharged his duties. Winter was now approaching and the campaigning season ending. He wisely decided not to attack Fort Ticonderoga, confident that it would fall the following spring, as indeed happened. However, his political masters in London were displeased. This failure would result in his recall the following year. *Generalmajor* Baron Frederick von Riedesel thought that if they had reached Fort Ticonderoga a month earlier, it could have been captured. There is something in this because Lieutenant James Hadden considered that a third of the British ships were not engaged at Valcour Island. Carleton's fleet was clearly constructed on an excessive and time-consuming scale. Carleton was, however, a cautious commander who ensured that he had superiority before attacking. Fort Ticonderoga would still be there in the spring and British control of the lake was unlikely to be challenged. The rebels at Ticonderoga could do nothing to threaten Canada. Had Arnold's fleet achieved superiority over the lake, then the 1777 campaign may well have been fought in Quebec, not New York.

Benedict Arnold fared little better. As well as losing control of the lake north of Fort Ticonderoga, the burning of the *Royal Savage* had also destroyed his personal papers. Congress' refusal to reimburse him for his expenditures would become one of the factors leading to him returning his allegiance to the crown.

Carleton's unwillingness to attempt to recapture Fort Ticonderoga is usually portrayed as a factor in the failure of the 1777 Campaign. While this is the subject of the next chapter, it is worth examining this view from both the 1776 and 1777 campaign positions. In 1776, it was the right decision as the winter weather was expected from the middle of the month. Canada and Lake Ticonderoga were secure so why risk the health of his army in a winter siege? It may have been possible to capture the fort if they had arrived a month earlier, but that would have meant deploying a smaller fleet sooner

---

67 Frey, *British Soldier*, p.128 comments on the high morale of British troops in a range of challenging circumstances.

with a smaller margin of success. Counterfactual history should always be approached with caution, but let us examine a scenario in which Fort Ticonderoga was captured in late-1776 without inflicting undue damage on the British forces.

It would have been impossible to accommodate and feed the entire army at Fort Ticonderoga over the winter, deep inside enemy territory, so the majority of the army would still have been withdrawn to Canada. It would still have been necessary to collect and transport the army down Lake Ticonderoga in the spring of 1777. This could have been carried out quicker if they were transported directly into a friendly port and without the need to prepare for a siege which would have been advantageous. The fort itself should have been able to resist a siege and thus delay Burgoyne's juncture with Howe and St Leger at Albany, as Major Preston had done at St Johns the year before. This is the scenario which Burgoyne anticipated, so the precipitous evacuation was an unexpected bonus.

The recapture of Fort Ticonderoga would have been a crowning glory to the 1776 campaigning season. However, such a siege risked weakening Carleton's forces and jeopardising the security of Canada. As it was, Carleton had successfully recovered from a situation verging on the catastrophic for British rule in North America to secure a firm base for future operations. This was no mean feat, and one worthy of far more acclaim than it currently receives.

7

With Burgoyne to Albany

Lieutenant General John Burgoyne returned to Quebec on 6 May 1777 after a winter in London during which he had proposed a three-pronged strategy which would isolate the radical New England colonies from the more moderate middle and southern colonies, and to which the government agreed. Once isolated, the New England colonies could be defeated. This strategy required a main force to descend along Lake Champlain, to capture Fort Ticonderoga and head for Albany, New York. This axis would be joined by a secondary force under Lieutenant Colonel Barry St Leger from the Great Lakes, capturing Fort Stanwix and advancing along the Mohawk River to affect a juncture at Albany. The third axis would be General Howe advancing from New York up the Hudson to Albany. There was considerable merit to this plan.

In a paper of 30 November 1776, Howe listed six objectives for 1777. Holding New York City was, naturally, first, followed by 'To attack Albany from New York City'. The sixth priority was 'to threaten Philadelphia.'[1] This preceded Washington's crossing of the Delaware and the subsequent actions at Trenton and Princeton over Christmas and New Year of 1776 to 1777. Clearly Howe's priorities changed, but these were not communicated to London or Quebec.

Burgoyne also brought with him from London news which was disappointing to Carleton. Despite Carleton's successes in 1776, he was not to lead the army into New York. His failure to capture Fort Ticonderoga the previous autumn had led to him falling out of favour with his political masters. Carleton's responsibility as Governor and Commander-in-Chief of Quebec was the defence of Canada, which he had achieved. It would not be appropriate, therefore, for him to go campaigning outside of Canada for purposes other than its immediate defence.

Howe's decision to march on Philadelphia rather than Albany fundamentally undermined the 1777 strategy as Burgoyne understood it and led to Burgoyne being left isolated and surrounded at Saratoga. The only

---
1   Cubbison, *Burgoyne*, p.40.

A VERY FINE REGIMENT

Spitfire in Lake Champlain by Ernest Haas. This atmospheric painting of underwater archaeologists examining the apparently intact and upright Spitfire illustrates a vessel typical of the 1776 campaign. (Lake Champlain Maritime Museum, gift of Ernest Haas)

person who could have directed Howe to march on Albany was George, Lord Sackville, the Secretary of State for the American Department. He did not.

The distance from Montreal, where the 47th wintered, to Albany is some 220 miles, but from Fort Ticonderoga, which was the first hostile defensive position, to Albany is just 100 miles. This was a reasonable advance in a campaigning season. However, Burgoyne's forces in Canada experienced difficulties at an operational level throughout, particularly in terms of logistics and rebel counter-mobility activities. Burgoyne correctly identified the logistic requirements of his army. He knew that he needed 500 carts to carry 14 day's supplies. Despite the best efforts of Carleton, this was beyond Canada's resources. Logistics was a perennial problem throughout the war and one in which the rebels invariably performed worse. Nevertheless, with the exception of the Battle of Bennington on 16 August 1777, Burgoyne's campaign was a series of highly successful tactical combats until the final desperate actions around Saratoga. Burgoyne suffered from the same difficulties as the British Army in general; operating in regions with inadequate communications, an ambivalent or hostile local population, and the inability to replenish lost men and material.[2]

The terrain which Burgoyne's army would fight through as it pressed on to Albany was heavily wooded. Woodland fighting is one of the most challenging environments encountered by the soldier. Erwin Rommel described the confusion almost 150 years later:

> The fighting in Doulcon woods emphasizes the difficulties of forest fighting. One sees nothing of the enemy. The bullets strike with a loud crash against trees and branches, innumerable ricochets fill the air, and it is hard to the direction of the enemy fire. It is difficult to maintain direction and contact in the front line; the commander can control only the men closest to him, permitting the remaining troops to get out of hand.[3]

Structure of the Army

At the opening of the campaign, Burgoyne's infantry was organised into two wings, each containing several brigades:

Right Wing – Major General William Phillips, RA.

Advance Corps – Brigadier General Simon Fraser, 24th Foot.
    Corps of Marksmen – Captain Alexander Fraser, 34th Foot
    24th Foot – Major Robert Grant
    Grenadier battalion – Major John Acland, 20th Foot
    Light battalion – Major Alexander Lindsay, 53rd Foot[4]

---

2   Cubbison, *Burgoyne*, pp.44–46, 79, 90–91.
3   E. Rommel, *Infantry Attacks* (Barnsley: Pen & Sword, 2006), pp.20–21.
4   The flank companies were drawn from the seven battalions of the army in Canada, plus those of the 29th, 31st and 34th Foot.

A VERY FINE REGIMENT

Canada and the West.

1st Brigade – Brigadier General Henry Powell, 53rd Foot.
    9th Foot – Lieutenant Colonel John Hill
    47th Foot – Lieutenant Colonel Nicholas Sutherland
    53rd Foot – Major Paul Irving

2nd Brigade – Brigadier General James Hamilton, 21st Foot
    20th Foot – Lieutenant Colonel John Lind
    21st Foot – Major George Forster
    62nd Foot – Lieutenant Colonel John Anstruther

Left Wing – *Generalmajor* Frederick von Riesdesel

Advance Corps – *Oberstleutnant* Heinrich von Breymann
    Grenadier battalion – *Major* Otto von Mengen
    Light battalion – *Major* Ferdinand von Barner
    Jäger company – *Hauptmann* Carl von Geyso

1st Brigade – *Brigadegeneral* Johann von Specht
    Regiment von Rhetz – *Major* Balthasar von Lucke
    Regiment von Riedesel – *Oberstleutnant* Ernst von Speth
    Regiment von Specht – *Major* Carol von Ehrekrook

2nd Brigade – *Brigadegeneral* Wilhelm von Gall
    Regiment Prinz Freidrich – *Oberstleutnant* Christian Praetorius
    Regiment Erbrpinz – *Oberstleutnant* von Lentz[5]

The army's strength was 6,904. Fifty soldiers per regiment were ordered to remain in Canada. In accordance with what was by now common practice, the flank companies were detached to the grenadier and light battalions. At some point before 2 July Fraser's Company of Marksmen was reformed, presumably with the same personnel as in 1776.[6]

The respective regimental strengths of the right wing's 1st Brigade were:

9th Foot	24 Officers	374 Other Ranks
47th Foot	24 Officers	356 Other Ranks
53rd Foot	24 Officers	369 Other Ranks[7]

Burgoyne's papers list the 47th's strength at 503 rank and file on 1 May 1777, including two 'Prisoners with the Rebels'.[8] This higher figure probably includes the grenadier and light companies. *Hadden's Journal* gives their

---

5 Morrissey, *Saratoga 1777*, pp.19–20.
6 Hadden, *Journal*, p.140; S.G. Strach, 'A Memoir of the Exploits of Captain Alexander Fraser and his Company of British Marksmen, 1776–1777, Part II', *Journal of the Society for Army Historical Research*, vol.63, No. 255 (Autumn 1985), pp.164–179, especially p.166.
7 Morrissey, *Saratoga 1777*, p.20.
8 Cubbison, *Burgoyne*, p.212.

strength as 524 on 1 July, again this is likely to include the grenadier and light companies.⁹

On 16 June, Burgoyne's force departed and sailed past the Isle au Noix and Point de Fer, the former being garrisoned by the 20th Foot and described by Lieutenant James Hadden (RA):

> Here we found several *Block Houses* finish'd and the island in a tolerable state of defence. The 20th Regiment, in Garrison at this place were compensated for a scarcity of Fresh Provision by the immense quantities of all kinds of Fish taken every where round the Island, which in itself is extremely barren affording a bare subsistence for a few Horses and Cows: before this supply of Fish was to be had (The Lake being Frozen) the Men were much afflicted with the Scurvey and many of them were brought to a *General Hospital*, which during the last year was quarter'd at Montreal: A few Men died, but the majority recover'd, and supplies of Fresh Provisions were latterly sent to them across the *Ice* from *St. Johns*: The *Spruce Beer* was also served to them & with success.¹⁰

While Specht described the island as 'covered with barracks, magazines and several blockhouses; various redans have been cast up here and there on its shores.'¹¹

Fraser's Advance Corps reached the Bouquet river ahead on the main body on the 20th, and on the 25th landed at Crown Point. Stormy weather gave way to hot, muggy weather, and blackflies. The following day the main body arrived. On the 30th, Burgoyne delivered his intent:

> The Army embarks tomorrow, to approach the Enemy. We are to contend for the King, and the constitution of Great Britain, to vindicate Law, and to relieve the oppressed – a cause in which his Majesty's Troops and those of the Princes his Allies, will feel equal excitement. The Services require of this particular expedition, are critical and conspicuous. During our progress occasions may occur, in which, no difficulty, nor labour, nor Life, are to be regarded. This Army must not retreat. The General [drum call] to beat tomorrow in place of the Revalley [Reveille] at dawn of Day, the Assembly to beat an hour afterwards at which time the whole will embark. A Field Officer with 100 British, and 100 Germans to remain at Chimney Point to take charge of the provisions & Stores at that place. The Wings are to take up their new encampment in Two Lines. So soon as the Regiments are encamp'd a working part of 20 Men and a Subaltern from each will parade in front of their respective Regiments.¹²

To his Native American allies, fully aware of the controversy which their unrestricted warfare would provoke, he said:

> [The] necessity of restraint and their passions, and that they must be under control, in accordance with the religion, laws of warfare, principles and policy

---

9   Hadden, *Journal*, p.lix.
10   Hadden, *Journal*, p.54.
11   Specht, *Journal*, p.46, 16 June 1776.
12   Hadden, *Journal*, pp.81-82.

which belonged to Great Britain … positively forbidding bloodshed, when not opposed in arms, [declaring] aged men, women, children, and prisoners sacred from the knife, even in time of conflict; … the war must not be made as when they went forth alone, but under the absolute will and control of the army of the king.[13]

The army departed for Fort Ticonderoga the following day.

Fort Ticonderoga 2–6 July

Sailing down Lake Champlain was a pleasant experience. It was about a mile wide and covered with vessels of all types. The musicians of each of regiment played throughout.[14]

Against this pleasant backdrop came rebel propaganda. Corporal Roger Lamb (9th Foot) objected to reports in *Saunder's News-Letter* of 14 August 1777 which described alleged atrocities 'that seven hundred men, women, and children, were scalped on the sides of Lake Champlain; that the light infantry and Indians scoured each bank, women, &c flying in turns before them.' Lamb believed that between St Johns and Crown Point, there were not more than 10 dwellings in 80 miles, 'Could inhabitant, *which never existed in a country*, be scalped, or fly before their enemies?'[15] This appears to be an early attempt to demonise the 'Light Bobs'.

Fort Ticonderoga was, and remains, an impressive fortification. Designed to protect Canada from an invasion from the British colonies, it was facing the wrong way for an attack from Canada. It had also suffered from a lack of investment since the end of the previous war, which Carleton had recognised. Rebel Brigadier General Arthur St Clair, following his defeat at Trois-Rivières, took command of the fort on 12 June 1777. He was supported by three Brigadier Generals: Benjamin Poor, John Paterson and Roche de Fermoy. Colonel Jeduthan Baldwin was the fort's engineer. Both St Clair and Major General William Schuyler were shocked by the state of the defences and the lack of progress in making the fort defensible. The extensive defences required an estimated 10,000 men. The garrison of 2,800 Continental line infantry would be joined by Lieutenant Colonel Pierce Long and 700 New Hampshire militiamen on 4 July. With well-stocked storerooms, St. Clair should have been able to inflict a significant delay on Burgoyne.[16]

To the southeast of Fort Ticonderoga, across the lake, was a second camp and fortifications called Mount Independence. A 400-yard pontoon bridge linked the two sites which was protected by a boom intended to halt and negate Burgoyne's fleet. Northwest of Fort Ticonderoga stood Mount Hope which was fortified, but the artillery had been withdrawn before the British arrived leaving only unsupported infantry. To the south of the fort ran the

---

13 Quoted from H.B. Carrington, *Battles of the American Revolution 1775–1781: Historical and Military Criticism, with Topographical Illustrations* (New York: A.S. Barnes, 1876), p.306; see also Lamb, *Journal*, pp.135–137.
14 Hadden, *Journal*, p.82.
15 Lamb, *Journal*, p.158.
16 S. Clay, *Staff Ride for the Saratoga Campaign, 13 June to 8 November 1777* (Fort Leavenworth: CSI Press, 2018), p.79; Cubbison, *Burgoyne*, pp.56–57.

outlet to Lake George; La Chute River. Colonel Baldwin had built blockhouses to defend the portage across the waterway. On the other bank of the river lay Mount Defiance (also known as Sugar Loaf Hill). This peak overlooked both Fort Ticonderoga and Mount Independence. It was not defended because the rebels believed it was impossible to mount artillery there. On 20 June, the five rebel generals prepared a plan whereby the fort should be held as long as possible, before withdrawing to Mount Independence, with the option of then falling back to Skenesboro if necessary. Thus, a contingency plan was prepared, in which a mind-set of defeat and withdrawal was already established.[17]

Burgoyne landed on the west bank of Lake Champlain on 1 July while Riesedel's wing landed on the east bank. The following day Fraser's Advance Corps captured Mount Hope by enveloping it from the west. The rebel defenders skirmished back to the protection of the 'old French Lines', part of Fort Ticonderoga's outworks. The Advance Corps then probed forward to test the strength of the rebel defences, before withdrawing to consult with Burgoyne about the next stage. One of the 47th soldiers in the Company of Marksmen was captured around this time. Riesedel, meanwhile, was advancing down the east bank to approach Mount Independence from the northeast, threatening to trap St Clair in a pincer movement. The going on the east bank was considerably slower than on the west, with Riesedel's men having to contend with thick undergrowth in a swampy forest cut by many watercourses. Specht described the weather as being 'exceedingly hot these days and the regiment greatly benefited from camping in the woods.'[18]

The 1st Brigade disembarked at Three Mile Point and set up camp for two or three days. They found rebel artillery fire from the fort 'so hot we were obliged to move our camp into the valleys' so that the shot passed safely overhead.[19] During the 4th, Lieutenant William Twiss, Burgoyne's chief engineer, examined Mount Defiance, and decided that it was perfectly possible to drag guns to the summit. Phillips' gunners spent the following day doing just that. Their force protection was provided by the 47th's light company, their activities were described by the regiment's Corporal George Fox:

> … strongly, we began to clear suger loaf hill a large hill s.w. of the town and forts on the opposte side of the river that command the town and forts a m[ile] distance, where they [thought] it was impossible for us to get any Cannon up. it was so steep and high twas with great fatigue with horses we got 9 32 pounders up. after clearing the hill and building a battery, we mounted 2 [and] should have mounted the other seven in the morning[20]

Alerted, St Clair realised that neither the Fort nor the Mount Independence site were defensible and ordered an evacuation that evening. Corporal Fox described how 'they under [Major General Philip Schuyler] left the fort

---

17 Clay, *Saratoga Campaign*, pp.79–80.
18 Clay, *Saratoga Campaign*, p.81; Specht, *Journal*, p.52, 4 July 1777; Strach, 'Captain Alexander Fraser, Part II', n.62; Cain, *Horrors of a Civil War*, p.105, n.142.
19 Baxter, *British Invasion*, pp.203–204.
20 Houlding and Yates, 'Corporal Fox', p.155.

stores &c in the night. In the morning we took possession, they [abandoned] 100 pieces of cannon and all the heavy baggage with stores of provission and Spirits.'[21] Evacuation vessels sailed for Skenesboro while the remainder of the garrison would retire over the bridge to Mount Independence then by land to Fort George via Hubbardton and Castleton.

Initially, the rebel evacuation was conducted smoothly with the British unaware of events, despite a full moon. That was until Brigadier General Matthias La Roche de Fermoy not only failed to evacuate his brigade, but became drunk and set fire to his headquarters, the smoke from which alerted Riesedel while the light of the flames revealed the evacuation to British sentries on Mount Defiance. At dawn, two deserters informed Burgoyne of the evacuation. Fraser's Advance Corps was ordered to seize the pontoon bridge Corporal Lamb (9th Foot) scathingly dismissed the rebels efforts to blockade the river with a boom 'composed of very large pieces of timber, fastened together by rivetted bolts, and double chains. This bridge, on which the Americans had bestowed so much labour for ten months, and which was deemed by them to be impregnable, was cut through in less time by the British seamen, than it would have cost time, to have described its structure.'[22]

Over confidence in the boom's ability to hold back the British fleet meant that the waterborne evacuation was not pursued as vigorously as it should have been. Reaching Skenesboro around midday, the women and sick continued to Fort Anne while the able-bodied men either manned the fortifications or started to unload the vessels. By 9:00 a.m., the British fleet with Powell's 1st Brigade aboard was through the boom and in pursuit to catch the rebels by surprise. The 47th landed and moved into the town to seize vessels and stores, while the rebels burnt and sunk them to prevent their capture. They also burnt a block house and iron works before withdrawing. Corporal Fox described the chaos which greeted the 47th:

> … they went up the river in their shipping &c &c [and] ours follow'd them to Skenbury [Skenesboro] & destroyed them &c w[h]ere they could not go any higher. there was one of their capital ship was blown up by a shell when it got amongst their powder. the report was heard 25 M[iles] and we saw the smoke above 20 m[iles]. like a Cloud in the sky. the rebels burnt their batoos and took to the woods. Their provision they had sunk and out men went down and see'd there was a deal sunk, then we got our grappling irons to hook up their barrels of pork and flour, but we had such quantities of pork that we were sick at the sight of it. Then encamp'd there.[23]

The remainder of 1st Brigade pursued the rebels as far as Fort Anne where they overtook the vessels carrying the women and sick. The rebels burned Fort Anne and withdrew to Fort Edward, 40 miles south of Fort Ticonderoga. Fort Anne to Albany is just 70 miles.

---

21 Houlding and Yates, 'Corporal Fox', pp.155, 157.
22 Hagist, *British Soldier's Story*, p.38; Baxter, *British Invasion*, p.215.
23 Houlding and Yates, 'Corporal Fox', p.157.

Two separate battles would be fought over the next few days as the fleeing rebels were pursued. The 9th Foot departed Skenesboro on the 7th and were engaged the following day. The 47th were not involved in this action although George Fox says that they were sent to help the wounded.[24] The second action at Hubbardton involved the light company and those of the 47th serving in Fraser's Company of Marksmen.

The Battle of Hubbardton 7 July

Fraser departed Mount Independence with half of his Advance Corps in pursuit of St Clair, who reached Hubbardton by the end of the 6th, where Colonel Nathan Hale (2nd New Hampshire Regiment) remained to round up stragglers and Colonel Ebenezer Francis (11th Massachusetts Bay Regiment) formed a rear guard. Colonel Seth Warner of the Green Mountain Boys remained to bring Hale and Francis on to Castleton, 11 miles further south. Francis informed Warner that he had no intention of pushing his men, or the stragglers, any further that evening as they needed rest. Warner agreed, despite this contradicting St Clair's orders and they remained in Hubbardton overnight. Fraser's Advance Corps camped just three miles from Hubbardton.

Overnight, Native American guides located the rebel camp. Before dawn on the 7th, the Native Americans and loyalists set off to attack, followed by Fraser and two companies of the 24th, the grenadiers and lights. A piquet was overwhelmed and from a saddle above Sucker Brook, Fraser could see the rebel campfires. Fraser sent in the 24th under Major Grant and Captain Fraser's Marksmen first. The 47th's light company was deployed second from the left, after 62nd's lights. The 2nd New Hampshires were caught off guard and suffered casualties, but did not break and formed with sufficient order to return heavy musket fire. The 11th Massachusetts were already formed up for their march to Castletown and now formed up on Hales' right. Warner also brought his Green Mountain Boys to support Hale. Realising that he had encountered a larger force than anticipated, Fraser sent Acland and the grenadiers to execute a right flanking move over Zion Hill which dominated the Castleton road.

Meanwhile the 24th and light companies under Lindsay advanced directly on the Castleton road. In the middle of the battlefield was a feature, now known as Monument Hill, which provided a defensive position with a small amount of cover. The rebels reached it first, but in the process the New Hampshires crossed behind the 11th Massachusetts and now formed up their right. The British 24th and light companies charged at the rebel positions. There were casualties on both sides, including Colonel Hale, but the rebels forced the redcoats to retire. The grenadiers with two light companies seized Zion Hill and dominated the road, forcing Warner's men to defend Selleck Farm to prevent the grenadiers rolling up the New Hampshire line from their left. An assault by the grenadiers drove Warner out of the farm and he fell

---

24　Hagist, *British Soldier's Story*, pp.39–41; Houlding and Yates, 'Corporal Fox', p.158; Hagist, 'Unpublished Writings of Sergeant Roger Lamb', Part 1, p.283.

back to new positions across the Castleton road. At the same time, the rebels attempted to turn the British left flank and advanced, forcing back the 24th and the light companies. The British rallied and counter attacked, eventually forcing the rebels from Monument Hill to join Warner's men on a log fence on the opposite side of the road, where they held out for a further two hours.

Around 10:00 a.m., German reinforcements arrived on the battlefield, having manoeuvred to strike the rebel right. Riedesel ordered his men to sing as they approached which simultaneously heartened the British and disheartened their enemy. The rebels then started to break in disorder along the Castleton road, with Colonel Francis being killed in the process. Colonel Hale and 230 hundred prisoners were taken. At Castleton, St Clair heard the fighting and despatched two aides to report on the situation. He attempted, but failed, to march his men back to help Francis. Two other militia regiments also refused to march to their aid. The noise died down and the aides returned to report it was all over. St Clair continued his retreat. Fortunately for him, the British were in no position to resume their pursuit. They remained in Hubbardton, enduring a thunderstorm while they cared for the wounded and buried the dead.[25]

Table 7.1 Casualties from 2–7 Jul 1777[26]

	British			Rebels		
	KIA	WIA	MIA / POW	KIA	WIA	MIA / POW
Fort Ticonderoga	5			7	11	
Hubbardton (Clay)	60	168		41	96	230
Hubbardton (Hadden)	17 Officers and 109 Rank and File Killed and Wounded, making 126.					

Specht provides a breakdown for the British and German losses (see Table 7.2).[27] The light company of the 47th lost three rank and file killed, and one captain and two rank and file wounded. The grenadiers suffered one rank and file killed and one wounded.[28]

Table 7.2 Breakdown of British and German losses

	Wounded			Killed		
	Officers	NCOs	Pvts	Officers	NCOs	Pvts
English grenadiers	6	4	35	0	0	11
English light infantry	4	4	74	1	1	10
Jäger Company v. Barner	1	0	5	0	0	4
Light infantry	0	0	4	0	0	3
Braunschweig grenadiers	0	1	2	0	0	2
Total	11	9	120	1	1	30

---

25   Clay, *Saratoga Campaign*, pp.84–87, 152–158; Hadden, *Journal*, pp.85–89; Weddle, *Compleat Victory*, pp.130–133; Riedesel, *Memoirs*, vol.I, pp.118–119; Morrissey, *Saratoga 1777*, pp.35–41.
26   Clay, *Saratoga Campaign*, p.69 Fig. 7; Hadden, *Journal*, p.88.
27   Specht, *Journal*, pp.54–55, 7 July 1777.
28   S. Bradford, 'Lord Francis Napier's Journal of the Burgoyne Campaign', *Maryland Historical Magazine*, vol.57, No. 4 (December 1962), pp.301–302.

Hubbardton was another British victory but with about 20 percent casualties; such victories were unsustainable. The 47th suffered eight casualties with four killed but, with the exception of Captain Craig, it is unknown how many of the three other wounded were able to resume their duties. Lieutenant James Hadden (RA) states that there were 17 officer casualties and names 16 of them. Captain James Craig, commanding the 47th's light company was wounded there, as he had been at Bunker Hill. He was not sufficiently injured to have to return to Canada.

Hadden considered that the action brought Burgoyne's men 'nothing but honour' while 'the immediate movements of the Army were incumber'd or rather prevented, it being absolutely necessary to detail this Detachment as a cover for the Wounded, till they cou'd be removed to Tyconderoga [which] was not effected for some days, in which the Enemy recover'd from their panic.'[29] More recently, Clay described Hubbardton as 'the first indicator to the confident troops of the Army from Canada that the Americans would not be easily defeated' although this performance should be contrasted with those regiments who refused to march to their aid.[30] Burgoyne and the 47th already knew that the rebels could stand and fight. Caught in the open, the rebels' options were to stand and fight, or flight. After the ignominy of their flight from Fort Ticonderoga, a second flight was unlikely to be a realistic option. The real problem of Hubbardton for the British was that it was a distraction in the wrong direction, which achieved nothing militarily. They suffered losses they could not sustain, and casualty treatment delayed their onwards movement. Furthermore, there was no reserve to exploit the victory.

Beyond Fort Ticonderoga

South of Fort Ticonderoga, Burgoyne was faced by a dilemma about which route to pursue. The original plan had been to follow the La Chute River to Fort George Landing and a 32-mile lake journey to the Great Portage overland route to Fort Edward on the River Hudson. In the aftermath of Ticonderoga, the pursuit of the enemy had taken his troops further east, to Hubbardton, Skeneboro and Fort Anne. A westward movement could be interpreted as a withdrawal and a sign of weakness to embolden the enemy. Also, the La Chute turned out to be not as navigable as was anticipated. In just over 3½ miles, the fast-flowing river drops 230 feet. Another possibility was an overland route from Skenesboro to join up with Wood Creek which flowed into the Hudson. This was the shortest option. It was also the route taken by the retreating rebels to Forts Anne and Edward which made it susceptible to their counter-mobility actions. In the end, Burgoyne chose both options. On 10 July, Phillips was ordered to move the artillery with the majority of the bateaux and wagons to Lake George Landing via the La Chute while Riedesel and Powell were ordered to take the overland route to Fort Edward. It would take 19 backbreaking days to accomplish both tasks.

---

29   Hadden, *Journal*, pp.87–88.
30   Clay, *Saratoga Campaign*, p.86.

The retreating rebels conducted very effective delaying actions: bridges and causeways were destroyed; trees were felled across the road, with sometimes several overlapped to make clearing the debris even slower; streams and creeks were damned or had new channels dug to inundate the road. Burgoyne's troops were forced to build a two-mile long causeway and corduroy way, a backbreaking and time-consuming solution, as Corporal Roger Lamb described:

> The Americans, now under the direction of general Schuyler, were constantly employed in cutting down large trees on both sides of every road, which was in the line of march. The face of the country was likewise so broken with creeks and marshes, that there was no less than forty bridges as to construct, one of which was over a morass two miles in extent.[31]

While Lieutenant James Hadden (RA) described both the rebel's actions, and the effect it provided for them. They felled 'large *Tree's* across *Wood Creek*, and the *Road* leading by the side of it to Fort Anne. The clearing of which cost the Army much labour and time, and gave the enemy spirits & leisure to wait those reinforcements which enabled them to retire deliberately.'[32]

Now that the men were leaving the waterways, they had to carry all of their own equipment. On 18 July Major General Phillips ordered: 'The Men are to carry their Knapsacks, Haversacks and Blankets as is usual with the Troops; their Tents and Poles will be put into Country Carts appointed for that use.'[33] Burgoyne also realised that in order to reduce his reliance on supplies from Canada, which was slowing down his advance, he needed to acquire more supplies locally. However, a Congressional decree had initiated a scorched earth policy, as Specht describes:

> … whereby all the inhabitants of this region had to leave their houses and go further east taking along everything they could; all the damage they would incur from leaving their non-transportable effect and ungathered harvests would be refunded. Consequently, we found most habitations deserted and empty but, on the other hand, we took advantage of this by making much freer use of the garden fruits [and vegetables] in the field.[34]

This initiated the chain of events which would lead to the foraging raid on Bennington on 16 August. Burgoyne needed horses for his dragoons, recruits for the loyalists, and supplies and wagons for everyone. He chose to despatch a raid to Bennington, New Hampshire, where he believed all could be found in a depot guarded by just 300 militiamen. To lead the raid, he selected non-English speaker *Oberstleutnant* Friedrich Baum with loyalist Colonel Skene as a liaison officer. What Burgoyne was unaware of was the arrival in the area of Brigadier General John Stark with nearly 1,500 New Hampshire

---

31   Lamb, *Journal*, p.144,
32   Hadden, *Journal*, pp.94–95.
33   Hadden, *Journal*, p.309, 18 July 1777; p.312, 7 August 1777.
34   Quoted in Specht, *Journal*, p.60, 30 July 1777.

militia, or that Colonel Seth Warner had been reinforced and had returned to the region. Combined, they fielded some 2,350 men. Baum departed on 11 August with a mixed force of Germans, loyalists, Canadians, Native Americans and Fraser's Company of Marksmen; in all about 1,400 strong. On the 14th, Stark conducted delaying actions and withdrew in the face of Baum's advance to Bennington. Baum's force spent the remainder of the 14th and the following day constructing and improving defensive positions, but many were not ideal and often unable to provide mutual support. Around midday on the 16th, Warner and Stark deployed several columns to encircle Bennington and attack through the woods. Each of Baum's positions were broken. Concurrently, Burgoyne had despatched a further 700 men under *Oberstleutnant* Heinrich Breymann. Rain delayed their advance, until around 5:00 p.m. on the 16th when they met Skene and shortly afterwards Breymann's column was attacked. He lost 160 men killed and missing while extracting his force back to Burgoyne.[35]

The defeat at Bennington cost Burgoyne about 15 percent of his effective strength which would have significant ramifications over the next two months. Thirty-seven British soldiers were captured but it is unclear how many were killed; of the officers, one was killed and three wounded and captured. Captain Fraser evidently gave an order for his company of around 50 men to disperse and make their own way back to the British lines. Five returned on the night of the 16th to the 17th, and Fraser with two privates arrived on the 18th. Burgoyne issued orders to rebuild the company. One of the volunteers was Lieutenant Arthur French from the 47th's light company. Fraser's marksmen had been perfecting their skills for almost a year. The unit's capabilities could not simply be rebuilt with a new draft in the middle of operations.[36]

Lieutenant James Hadden (RA) with 1st Brigade reached Fort Edward on 31 July: 'the Ruins of a small Fort thrown up near the Hudson River to cover a part of it which is here *Fordable*. This is at present totally dismantled and does not appear ever to have been calculated for a further purpose than repelling a sudden attack being commanded on both flanks within Cannon Shot.'[37] Major General William Schuyler and his Northern Army of some 4,000 men had arrived at Fort Edward on 12 July, and had been in place for over a fortnight before Burgoyne's army resumed their move south. Schuyler withdrew to Stillwater, believing he had insufficient strength to hold Fort Edward. From Fort Edward it was just 60 miles to Albany. Schuyler did not halt at Stillwater. Two days later he withdrew to Van Schaik's Island at the confluence of the Hudson and Mohawk rivers. This is the river that the St Leger expedition planned to advance along to meet Burgoyne. St Leger's advanced guard would arrive at Fort Schuyler on 2 August. At this point, in

---

35 Morrissey, Saratoga 1777, pp.46–47, 49–53; Clay, *Saratoga Campaign*, pp.93–98, 177–196, 301–302; Weddle, *Compleat Victory*, pp.236–257.
36 Morrissey, *Saratoga 1777*, pp.46–47, 49–53; Strach, 'Captain Alexander Fraser, Part II', pp.170–171; O'Callaghan (ed.), *Orderly Book*, p.91, 2 September 1777; Cubbison, *Burgoyne*, p.93, 308.
37 Hadden, *Journal*, p.109.

mid-July, Burgoyne still expected to meet up with St Leger and also Howe. His advance continued in a leisurely, yet apparently unstoppable, fashion towards Albany.

It was in August that Burgoyne's troubles began. On the 3rd he received a letter from Howe informing him of his intention to capture Philadelphia rather than advance on Albany. On the 16th it was the loss of many of his German troops and the Marksmen at Bennington. Finally, on the 28th he received news that St Leger had failed to capture Fort Stanwix and would not be able to join him. Burgoyne lacked effective communications with Howe or St Leger. He also lacked clear orders from Howe, his superior in America, or London. Hanging over him were the fates of Gage in Boston and Carleton over Fort Ticonderoga. How would a retreat back to Fort Ticonderoga look? Despite the rebel victories at Bennington and Fort Stanwix, his main army had only faced weak resistance. A more cautious general may have retired to Fort Ticonderoga rather than risk an unsupported advance deeper into hostile territory. The threat of an 'Army in Being' was a potent weapon in its own right. Just by keeping his army intact in the Quebec border region with the ability to strike into New York would force Congress to maintain a strong Northern Army to counter this threat. This is what Carleton had done at the end of 1776. The removal of the threat from Burgoyne's army would allow Congress to redeploy troops away from the border region to threaten other British armies around New York City and Philadelphia.

Desertions also start to appear in August. The first reference to desertions in Burgoyne's *Orderly Book* occurs on the 6th when he stated that deserters from the 53rd Foot were believed to have been scalped by Native Americans. Lieutenant James Hadden (RA) mentions desertion for the first time on 24 August, when a deserter was shot, and a reward of $100 offered for evidence of the enemy enticing men to desert. This may have been the same event recorded by Specht on the 27th, a 'musketeer' from the 9th Foot, Georg Hundertmark, a German by birth, who had deserted his picquet. Specht puts an earlier date on the first execution, 11 August when one musketeer, Fasselabend, had deserted and served on a gun crew on a rebel sloop was caught near Skenesboro. Specht, on the other hand, noted rebel desertions going the opposite way from 1 August, although it appears that these had no desire to fight for the crown, rather to leave the rebel army and return home for their harvest.[38]

August also saw the worst case of indiscipline within the 47th that year. On the 7th, Captain John Alcock reported that two hardened and atrocious individuals who had robbed a gentleman that morning and threatened him with death were now in custody. He felt that the men would feel the same satisfaction as him at their capture because of the ignominy which the incident had brought on the regiment. On the 16th, Privates William Shehan and John Deering were convicted of assaulting Mr William Johnson at Fort Edward on the 7th, and awarded 1,000 lashes each. Shehan appeared before another court martial on 23 September, this time for desertion. He

---

38 O'Callaghan (ed.), *Orderly Book*, pp.65-66, 6 August 1777; Hadden, *Journal*, p.119; Sprecht, *Journal*, p.61, 1 August 1777, p.66, 11 August 1777, p.72, 27 August 1777.

was described as being in the 62nd Foot, so had been transferred from the 47th following the earlier offence. He received another 1,000 lashes. We will meet Deering again in Chapter 8 as part of the Convention Army following a successful escape to British lines at New York.[39]

The Artillery Park

A major change to the 47th's role occurred around 9 August. Lieutenant William Digby (53rd Foot) reported that day that they occupied Fort Miller, 9 miles closer to Albany. He also recorded the 'very disagreeable news of our regiment (53rd) being ordered back to garrison Ticonderoga and Fort George. I was much concerned at it, as in all probability I should not see them again during the war.'[40] Burgoyne had sent Brigadier General Henry Powell and the 53rd to relieve Brigadier General James Hamilton and the 62nd.[41] On the 17th, the 47th was ordered to Fort Edward where they were to take charge of the prisoners there.[42] From this point onwards, the centre companies of the 47th were not involved in combat until the attempted breakout of 8 October 1777. Lieutenant Poole England (47th Foot) was appointed Fort Major at Ticonderoga on 6 September.[43] On the 12th, the regiment were ordered to the camp at Batten Kill to 'cover the Provisions and assist in loading them' as the army was advancing. The following day, 'the six Companies of the 47th 'were to cover the Depot of Provisions' the British camp at Saratoga. They were positioned beside the river and their duties included preventing an attack from across the river which would have fallen on the army's rear areas.[44] Rear area security is one of the most thankless military tasks but a successful strike by an enemy against the rear area can devastate a campaign. The attack which Burgoyne feared did happen, although not against his camp at Saratoga, but against Fort Ticonderoga a fortnight later. By 20 September, the 47th were guarding the artillery park, which *Hauptmann* Pausch of the Hanau Artillery described: 'Behind our left wing, down on the plain [which borders the river] stands the Park of our heavy Artillery, our ammunition, provision and baggage train., and our hospital and batteaux. Together with a few companies of the 47th Eng. Reg. – partly in a fortified camp, partly not.'[45]

Diamond Island

On 8 September, *Generalmajor* Riedesel ordered Captain Aubrey and two companies (his and Gambles') of the 47th to march to Fort George the

---

39 FTM: Orderly Book of the 47th Regiment of Foot, 7, 16 August 1777, 23 September 1777.
40 Baxter, *British Invasion*, pp.244–246.
41 O'Callaghan (ed.), *Orderly Book*, pp.67–68, 9 August 1777.
42 O'Callaghan (ed.), *Orderly Book*, p.77, 17 August 1777.
43 O'Callaghan (ed.), *Orderly Book*, pp.95–96, 6 September 1777.
44 O'Callaghan (ed.), *Orderly Book*, p.101, 12 September 1777; pp.101–102, 13 September 1777; p.107, 15 September 1777.
45 Pausch, *Journal*, p.147.

following day. Lieutenant George Irwin and 30 men remained at the fort as a warning post, the remainder occupying the island, three miles away from Fort George. They were accompanied by *Fähnrich* Johann Heinrich Gödecke of the von Rhetz Regiment, and another unidentified officer. Two companies of the 53rd at Fort George were to go to Fort Ticonderoga.[46]

The role of these two 47th companies would have important consequences for the campaign and beyond, yet it was hardly likely to gain the regiment honour and glory at the time. It was normal for a commander to have 'his' regiment with him, as we see with Brigadier General Simon Fraser whose 24th was part of his Advance Corps or Brigadier General Powell with his 53rd Foot in his 1st Brigade during this campaign. Indeed, when Powell was sent to command Fort Ticonderoga, he took the 53rd with him. Morrissey in *Saratoga 1777* says that the decision to place part of the 47th in the rear 'has been cited as confirmation of both its poor reputation and its reliability!' without any further explanation or evidence.[47] For the previous almost three years, the 47th had been at the centre of all of the actions in Boston and between Quebec and Saratoga. Around Boston, the 47th's flank companies were with Lieutenant Colonel Francis Smith at Lexington and Concord, and at Bunker Hill, they were part of the flanking move attempting to encircle the rebels; the centre companies were part of Brigadier General Lord Percy's relief force and would be, with the 1st Marines, the first into the rebel redoubt at Bunker Hill. In 1776, the 47th was General Carleton's only regiment with operational experience.[48] They were closely engaged at Trois-Rivières, including Mrs Middleton, with Brigadier General William Nesbitt taking charge of the captured rebel commanders. Captain Craig led the rapid advance to recapture Fort St. John and similar multi-company tasks. In 1777, it was the 47th's light company which secured Sugar Loaf Hill which led directly to the rebel evacuation of Fort Ticonderoga and later fought at Hubbardton. The centre companies captured Skenesboro. Thereafter, growing lines of communications increased the demand for troops for security, a task which fell on the 47th and 53rd, but even there the two 47th companies on Diamond Island performed with credit. Finally, the 47th would lead the attempted breakout from encirclement in Saratoga and could have achieved a victory similar to the 'Paoli Massacre' if permission had been granted. Furthermore, Lieutenant Colonel Sutherland was extremely experienced in North American warfare. If anything, their record indicates a solid reliability. It is wrong to assign 'elite' status to Regular infantry regiments during the American War of Independence. The operations and tasks undertaken by the 47th show that they were a solid, reliable and trustworthy regiment.

Hadden, described Fort George as being indefensible, standing:

> … near the water at the end of the Lake, is a small square Fort faced with Masonry and contains Barracks for about a hundred Men secure from Cannon Shot. This

---

46 Specht, *Journal*, pp.74–75, 4, 10, 11 September 1777; FTM: Orderly Book of the 47th Regiment of Foot, R.A.O. 8 September 1777.
47 Morrissey, *Saratoga 1777*, p.21 n.10.
48 Hadden, *Journal*, pp.lxv–lxvi.

fort cou'd not stand a Siege, being commanded, & too confined not to be soon reduced by Bombardment. The Rebels before they abandon'd it had endeavour'd to destroy the *defences* and actualy blew up the Magazine on the side next the Water, which demolish'd that Face.[49]

Richard Cartwright (62nd Foot) described Diamond Island which:

… is very small is Nothing but a barren Rock, exposed on every side to the Wind, which at this Season made it disagreeably cold. Here we lay all Night in our Tent, and the next Morning the 1st of November, sailed from thence before a brisk southerly Breeze in a Barge, which arrived the Night before with orders to abandon that Post and at dark came to Ticonderoga Landing.[50]

Burgoyne was already concerned about his logistic tail and the provisions for his army. At the beginning of September, rebel commanders planned a strike against this weakness with the Pawlet Expedition. On 12 and 13 September, four rebel columns departed Pawlet and for five days made their way, undetected, to their objectives. Colonel Benjamin Woodbridge's 500 strong column of the 1st New Hampshire County Regiment, Massachusetts Militia were to strike at Skenesboro from the west. Colonel Samuel Johnson with 500 men of the 4th Essex County Regiment, Massachusetts Militia would travel through Hubbardton to seize Mount Independence as a diversionary raid for the main attack by Colonel John Brown and another 500 men of the Middle Berkshire Regiment, Massachusetts Militia against the northern tip of Lake George. Both Woodbridge and Brown were to defeat any troops they found, and destroy or remove any stores, equipment and machinery. Finally, Brigadier General Lincoln with 600–700 men would march to Skenesboro to reinforce the Woodbridge. With all four columns converging at Skenesboro, Burgoyne would be faced with a significant strike against Fort Ticonderoga.

On 18 September, the rebels arrived at their targets. Johnson seized Mount Independence and provided the deception to distract Powell, and to fix his garrison in the fort. Woodbridge found Skenesboro abandoned and nothing of significance to destroy. Brown seized the Lake George landing, at the northernmost part of the lake and overwhelmed the British forces there. He captured four companies of the 53rd (156 men), 119 Canadians and 63 artificers in addition to a brig, several gunboats and over 200 bateaux. Lieutenant Poole England of the 47th may also have been captured at this time. Brown also released over 118 rebel prisoners and seized a great deal of stores and foodstuffs. The British prisoners were despatched overland to Skenesboro, under the guard of the rebel prisoners turned guards. Brown then occupied Mount Defiance. For two days, Brown and Johnson attempted to persuade Powell to surrender Fort Ticonderoga. Surrounded, isolated from aid from the north and south, unaware of what support was en route to reinforce Johnson and Brown, Powell nonetheless did his duty, and resisted.

---

49   Hadden, *Journal*, p.107.
50   R. Cartwright, *A Journey to Canada* <http://62ndregiment.org/A_Journey_to_Canada_by_Cartwright.pdf> accessed 20 September 2021.

After two days, Johnson and Brown withdrew. On Diamond Island Captain Aubrey was alerted of the proximity of the rebel forces. He successfully resisted an attempt to capture the island. Defeated, the rebels burned their own vessels and retired to Skenesboro overland.[51]

The impact of this strike on Burgoyne's logistical train should not be underestimated. Although Powell held the fort and the 47th held Diamond Island, the loss of soldiers, labour (in the form of the rebel prisoners), stores and transport seriously impacted on the supply chain through to Burgoyne. When the survivors of St Leger's Expedition arrived on 27 September, Powell retained them to make good his losses and to secure his own logistics chain. There was, of course, no reason why this raid should be a one-off occurrence.

Burgoyne received reports from both Powell and Aubrey. Burgoyne's own report was dated 1 October 1777:

> *In consequence of authentic Letters received by [Burgoyne] from Brigadier General Powel at Ticonderoga, and Captain Aubrey of the 47th Regiment commanding at Diamond Island in Lake George.*
>
> *The Army is informed that the Enemy having found means to cross the Mountains between Skenesborough and Lake George, and having marched with another Corps from Hubbardton, a sudden and general Attack was made in the morning of the 18th upon the carrying Place at Lake George, Sugar Hill [Mount Defiance], Ticonderoga, and Mount Independence.*
>
> *The Enemy so far succeeded as to suprize the armed Boat, stationed to defend the carrying Place, as also the Posts on Sugar Hill and at the Portage, where a considerable part of four Companies of the 53rd Regiment were made Prisoners.*
>
> *A Blockhouse commanded by Lieutenant Lord was the only Post on that side that had time to make use of their Arms, and they made a brace Defence till Cannon (supposed to be taken from the Surprize Vessel) was brought against them.*
>
> *After stating and lamenting so fatal a want of Vigilance, [Burgoyne] has to congratulate the Troops upon the Event which followed.*
>
> *The Enemy having twice summoned [Powel], and received such answers as became a gallant Officer intrusted with an important Post, and having tried, during the course of four Days, several Attacks, and being repulsed in all, retreated without having done any considerable damage.*
>
> *[Powel] gives great commendation to the Regiment of Prince Frederic, and the other Troops stationed on Mount Independence. [Powel] also mentions with great applause the Behaviour of Captain Taylor of the 21st Regiment, who commanded 100 men in [Fort Ticonderoga], and that he was well supported by Lieutenant Beacroft of the 24th Regiment, who with the Artificers in Arms, in the Half Moon Battery, preventing the enemy from surrounding the Fort. On the 24th Instant the Rebels with the Gun Boats and Bateaux which they had surprised*

---

51   Weddle, *Compleat Victory*, pp.270–271; Clay, *Saratoga Campaign*, pp.102–104; E.A. Hoyt, 'The Pawlet Expedition, September 1777' *Vermont History*, vol.75, No. 2 (Summer/Fall, 2007), pp.69-100; M. Barbieri, 'Brown's Raid on Ticonderoga and Mount Independence', *Journal of the American Revolution*, 20 January 2022.

Regimental Morning Orders 9th September 1777 from the 47th Foot's orderly book, displaying details of the daily routine of regimental life: 'No Knapsacks or Baggage of any Kind is put upon the Carts on the march.' (Fort Ticonderoga)

at the carrying Place at Lake George, attacked in two Divisions, Diamond Island where Captain Auberry and a Detachment of the 47th Regiment were posted with some Cannon and Gun Boats: the Rebels were repulsed with great Loss, and pursued by the Gun Boats to the East Shore, where the principal Vessel and a Gun Boat were retaken, together with all the Cannon, except two which had burst; the Enemy, having had time to set fire to the other Batteaux, retreated over the Mountains.[52]

Hauptmann Pausch did not believe the reports writing in his diary 'N.B. This can be nothing but a lie,'[53] while Lieutenant Digby (53rd Foot) who had been so concerned about the departure of his regiment to Ticonderoga simply comments 'but this was not properly authenticated.'[54]

At the beginning of September, Burgoyne discussed the options for an advance. According to Specht, they expected more posts to be established as the lines of communications were extended. Burgoyne had other ideas. He wanted to advance against the rebels with 40 days supplies to affect a junction with the other British Army expedition. To achieve this, he would sever his communications back to Canada, leaving just the two 47th companies with four guns at Fort

---

52 Hadden, *Journal*, pp.321–325, 1 October 1777; Specht, *Journal*, p.86, 2 October 1777; Cubbins, *Burgoyne*, p.331, n.221; Hagist, *Noble Volunteers*, p.141 notes sickness at the fort as a significant cause for the losses, see also p.217.
53 Pausch, *Journal*, p.149.
54 Baxter, *British Invasion*, p.284.

Edward.[55] Burgoyne still believed, or appeared to believe, that Albany was within his grasp where he could gain the relief he needed by joining with other British forces. However, this could only be achieved if he severed his links to Canada.

Saratoga

While Brigadier General Powell and Captain Aubrey were defending the army's rear area and supply routes, Burgoyne fought the first of his two actions at Saratoga. His army had crossed the Hudson and then dismantled the bridge behind him. In the Northern Army, Schuyler had been sacked for failing to stand and halt Burgoyne's advance. He had been replaced by Major General Horatio Gates. Gates was born in England and had been commissioned in the 20th Foot and later served in the Seven Years War. He sold his major's commission in 1769 and bought a plantation in Virginia a few years later. Around Saratoga, he conducted reconnaissance for suitable locations to position his growing army to halt Burgoyne, while simultaneously launching the Pawlet Raid. Gates selected the Bemis Heights, a 100-foot bluff which dominated the 200–300-yard-wide flood plain. From the heights, a few well-placed cannon could interdict traffic on the river road, or on the river. Inland, however, the bluff petered out without a feature to secure the rebel left on. This area would have to be well observed by piquets to prevent any flanking moves by the British. It was here that the majority of the subsequent fighting would take place. Gates placed Brigadier General Benjamin Poor's brigade on the far left, with Brigadier General Ebenezer Learned's brigade on his right and Brigadier General Abraham Ten Broeck's New York Militia brigade either on the far left, or behind in support. This left wing was under the command of Major General Benedict Arnold. In the centre, between the two wings of Gates' army was positioned Colonel Daniel Morgan's Corps of Riflemen and Major (promoted to lieutenant colonel during the campaign) Henry Dearborn's light infantry. The rebels started constructing defences there on 12 September. Three days later, 150 Oneida Native Americans joined Gates. These would be his last reinforcements and were primarily used for scouting. By the 16th Burgoyne had reached Sword's House, just four miles from Bemis Heights. Facing a deteriorating supply situation and still uncertain of the exact rebel disposition, Burgoyne opted for a foraging expedition combined with a reconnaissance in force which, it was hoped, would bring the generals close enough to the rebel lines to observe them.[56]

Freeman's Farm – 19 September
During this action, the majority of the 47th were engaged in rear area security (guarding the artillery park) or line of communications (Diamond Island) duties. Members of the regiment participated in composite units like Fraser's Company of Marksmen, for example Lieutenant Arthur French, or the detached

---

55   Specht, *Journal*, p.74, 4 September 1777.
56   Clay, *Saratoga Campaign*, p.218.

flank companies in Acland's grenadier or Lindsay's light battalions which means that the 47th is not referred to in narratives of the battle in their own right. These three units were deployed on Burgoyne's right flank near McBride Farm. As the battle developed, the majority of the action, and therefore the surviving accounts, focused on the middle sector, facing Freeman's Farm.

Immediately due south, along the river road, were the main rebel defences. Extending inland was a gorge, known as the 'Great Ravine' which would be extremely slow going for any army. It was believed that a suitable crossing over the Great Ravine could be found further away from the river, where it was undefended, and which would allow a flanking move to strike the rebel left and roll it up. Burgoyne chose Fraser's Advance Corps from his right wing to find that passage, composed of the grenadier and light battalions, and the 24th Foot. Hamilton commanded the second brigade (centre) composed of the 9th, 20th, 21st and 62nd Foot, which was to follow Fraser, but turn south sooner and force a passage through the Great Ravine. Finally, Riedesel would command the left with the Riedesel, Specht and von Rhetz Regiments, and would advance along the river road. They would avoid the Great Ravine, repair broken bridges and other obstacles, and by a demonstration fix the rebel defenders by the river while Fraser made his turning move. This would be a reconnaissance in force, and Burgoyne's largest action since landing at Fort Ticonderoga two and a half months earlier.

Riedesel's advance was slowed by obstacles left by the retreating rebels. In the centre, Hamilton's brigade forced their way through the Great Ravine and turned to the right (westwards) toward where Fraser's Advance Corps would appear. Spying the buildings of Freeman's Farm, Major Gordon Forbes, and a detachment of about 100 men of the 9th, advanced in open order to search the farm buildings. Waiting for them were Daniel Morgan's riflemen of the 11th Virginia and Henry Dearborn's light infantry. The rebels opened fire on the 9th's skirmish line, which froze and then retired under orders from the wounded Forbes; as his small force was in the open, without cover and probably outnumbered, this was the only option open to Forbes. The remainder of Hamilton's brigade deployed along the treeline to the north of Freeman's Farm while Forbes' men withdrew on their supports. The rebels at Freeman's Farm, with their attention fixed on Forbes' retirement, charged after them and were stopped in their turn by fire from Hamilton's brigade; it also appears the fire from Hamilton's brigade against the Virginians also caused casualties amongst Forbes' men. Attracted to the noise of battle Fraser's Company of Marksmen with a cannon, joined the right of Hamilton's brigade, and fired upon the Virginians.[57]

A few moments later, the rest of the Advance Corps crossed the Grand Ravine and formed a second battle line opposite McBride's Farm. Dearborn had restrained his light infantry from joining the charge at Freeman's Farm and kept them in a position where he could see the Advance Corps forming up. Gates despatched Poor's brigade which formed up to the left rear of Morgan's troops, extending the rebel line to the left, and covering the Advance Corps. Over the next two hours, multiple attacks across the open

---

57 Hadden, *Journal*, p.163; Hadden says that the Marksmen were sent to aid Hamilton, rather than being drawn there by the sound of the fighting.

fields of both farms were executed, and driven back, on each occasion leaving more dead and wounded in the open spaces.

Fraser's Advance Corps on the right held its line. To support Dearborn in the rebel centre and to extend the line to the left, Arnold sent his remaining battalions – Colonel Jonathan Latimer's Connecticut Militia battalion and the remaining two from Poor's Brigade, the 2nd and 4th New York Continental Regiments – into battle. The 2nd New York ran into Lindsay's light battalion, who forced the New Yorkers back. The last to join the battle was Learned's brigade who, without any orders, engaged the Advance Corps' right and the Germans. The fighting was inconclusive.

Corporal Roger Lamb (9th Foot) described what would appear to be both of these encounters combined:

> The Americans being unable from the nature of the country, of perceiving the different combinations of march (as the country is thickly covered with woods, movements may be effected without a possibility of being discovered) advanced a strong column with a view of turning the British right, here they met the grenadiers and light infantry, who gave them a tremendous fire. Finding it was impossible to penetrate the line at this point, they immediately counter-marched and directed their principle effort to the centre.[58]

Hamilton's brigade in the centre was subjected to a heavy battering, particularly against the 62nd Foot and the Royal Artillery, which was unable to crew all of their guns. The 62nd would parade just 60 men the following day.

Generalmajor Baron Frederick von Riedesel had received no further orders from Burgoyne until about 4:30 p.m., when he was ordered to support Hamilton. Riedesel took his regiment, two companies from the von Rhetz Regiment and two 6-pounder guns under *Hauptmann* Pausch, and led them towards the fighting. They advanced for a mile, up the hill, through dense woodland. Rhetz's two companies arrived, singing hymns, to strike Morgan's Virginian riflemen of the rebel right at about 5:00 p.m. The effect of their arrival, as at Hubbardton, both shocked the rebels and emboldened the redcoats, who advanced to conform with the German line. Pausch brought his guns into the middle of Hamilton's formation. When he arrived:

> The entire line of [the 9th and 21st] faced about and, [with their assistance dragging the guns] my cannons were soon on top of the hill. I had shells brought up and placed by the side of the cannon; and as soon as I got the range, I fired twelve or fourteen shots in quick succession into the foe who were within good pistol shot distance. The firing from the muskets was at once renewed. … Presently, the enemy's fire, though very lively at one time, suddenly ceased. I advanced about sixty paces sending a few shells after the flying enemy, and firing from twelve to fifteen shots more into the woods into which they had retreated. Everything then became quiet and about fifteen minutes afterwards darkness set in.[59]

---

58 Hagist, *British Soldier's Story*, p.45.
59 Pausch, *Journal*, pp.134, 137–138.

The Virginians did not break, but refused their flank and were supported by New Hampshire soldiers. The arrival of Regiment von Riedesel brought their firepower alongside that of the British. Now it was the turn of the rebel line to become untenable, and they started to conduct a controlled withdrawal across a stream to their rear, and away from the battlefield. The battle ended around 6:30 p.m.[60]

Uncertain where the rebel lines were, or indeed where their forward troops were positioned, Burgoyne had planned to conduct a renaissance in force, but once in contact, no further advance could be made. Tactically, the new British light doctrines did not prove as successful as was anticipated. The British Army usually fought against superior numbers and did not engage in protracted firefights, but this is what Freeman's Farm dissolved into. The use of the bayonet charge was partially successful, but the terrain allowed the retiring rebels to regroup in the woodland and inflict casualties on the British, forcing them to retire. A successful bayonet charge would expected to drive the enemy off the battlefield, but here the enemy appear to have withdrawn out of the reach of the bayonet, but within range of their muskets enabling them to return fire. Of particular note is the performance, and losses, of the 62nd Foot. Captain John Money, the Deputy Quartermaster General, wrote how: '... the 62nd Regiment charged four times ... quitting their position each time... the rebels fled at every charge deeper still into the woods; but when the British troops returned to their position, they were slowly followed, and those who had been the most forward in the pursuit were the first to fall.'[61]

Burgoyne similarly lamented the failure of the British Army's trusted weapon, the bayonet:

> Few actions have been characterised by more obstinacy in attack or defence. The British bayonet was repeatedly tried ineffectually. Eleven hundred British soldiers, foiled in these trials, bore incessant fire for a succession of fresh troops in superior numbers, for above four hours; and after a loss of above a third of their numbers (and in one of the regiments above, two thirds), forced the enemy at last. Of a detachment of a captain and forty-eight artillerymen, the captain and thirty-six were killed or wounded.[62]

The other aspect of British tactical innovation – speed – was also lost here. Possibly, this arose because of the intention to keep all three brigades in alignment which could have cost one of them the benefit of surprise. Once both sides became engaged, there was no opportunity to use speed and manoeuvre to defeat the enemy. Regiments and companies were fed into the line but in a linear fashion, the most striking example of this actually came from the Germans at the end of the day, hitting Poor's brigade in the rear.

---

60 Morrissey, *Saratoga 1777*, pp.57–61; Snow, *1777*, pp.81-137; Clay, *Saratoga Campaign*, pp.104–109.
61 Quoted in Clay, *Saratoga Campaign*, p.229.
62 Quoted in Clay, *Saratoga Campaign*, p.229 and Spring, *With Zeal and With Bayonets Only*, p.257.

British losses were higher than those of the rebels. Both armies probably deployed a similar number in the field, but the rebels were not supported by artillery, so their achievement is quiet impressive. As ever, Burgoyne's army suffered casualties it could ill afford; 160 killed, 364 wounded and 42 missing. The rebels lost an estimated 100 killed, 200 wounded and 23 missing.[63] Burgoyne had had advanced a little closer to Albany and held the field, but he had not reached the rebel redoubts.

The Battle of Barber's Wheatfield 7 October 1777

Burgoyne remained inactive for three weeks hoping for the assistance which would yet turn his campaign into a victory. If a large force was advancing up the Hudson from New York, the best support he could provide would be to fix a significant portion of the rebel forces opposite him where they might yet be caught in a two-pronged attack. The weather was deteriorating, and food supplies were running low, both of which would have adversely affected the moral of his army.

The troops were not inactive though, and busied themselves fortifying the camp against attack, principally by creating redoubts in the open fields where Freeman's Farm had been fought: Balcarres Redoubt at Freeman's Farm, and Breymann Redoubt on McBride's Farm. While these works were commendable and necessary should the rebels attack, Burgoyne still needed to break through the rebel lines if he was to survive. Remaining in place would only see Burgoyne's force weaken until it ran out of supplies and was forced to surrender. Burgoyne was still uncertain of the extent of the rebel defences, but believed that they weakened as they extended away from the river. A right flanking movement by his best troops may yet produce the outcome he was seeking, he thought. There had also been no foraging parties in that direction. Foraging parties could follow behind the troops making the flanking move and alleviate the army's supply difficulties.

On the morning of 7 October, Captain Alexander Fraser's Marksmen with guides and Native Americans conducted a reconnaissance of the route to be taken, and reported back by 10:00 a.m. yet it would be 1:00 p.m. before Brigadier General Simon Fraser departed with his Advance Corps of some 1,700 men consisting of the grenadier and light battalions, the 24th, and the German grenadiers and jägers with 10 guns and 100 artillerymen in support. He was accompanied by Burgoyne, Phillips and Riedesel. The force moved westward past Freeman's Farm and Marshall's Farm to that of Simeon Barber where there was a standing wheatfield. The march took about 30 minutes. Rebel picquets were driven off and a defensive line was established on the far side of the field with the light infantry on the right (its right flank was secured in woods), the 24th and grenadiers with their left flank extending into woods. The Germans appear to have taken up positions in the wheatfield. Foragers and wagons were called forward to harvest the wheat. The generals took up a position on a cabin roof but were still too far away to see the main rebel lines.

63　Hadden, *Journal*, pp.325–326, 3 October 1777; see also Clay, *Saratoga Campaign*, p.233.

Receiving news of the British movement, Gates despatched his adjutant, Lieutenant Colonel James Wilkinson, to investigate, who observed the activities at Barber's Wheatfield and reported back. In the early afternoon, Morgan's Virginian riflemen and Dearborn's light infantry were ordered to deploy against Lindsay's light battalion, but they ran into Fraser's Marksmen and their deployment was delayed. Gates deployed Poor's brigade through Chatfield Farm opposite Acland's grenadier battalion at about 4:00 p.m. The grenadiers opened fire on Poor's brigade who responded with a volley, during which Major Acland was wounded, followed by a bayonet charge. Leaderless, surprised at receiving the charge which they would normally have delivered, and overwhelmed, the grenadiers retired, leaving behind the wounded Acland.

Meanwhile, Dearborn's light infantry had pushed through Fraser's Marksmen and took up a position on high ground to the right, and probably also to the rear, of Lindsay's light battalion. A bayonet charge by Dearborn's men hit the light battalion in the right rear, and forced them to retire to a new line behind the jägers. Lindsay regained control of his battalion but under intense fire, they started to falter again; and appear to have had difficulty identifying targets in the woodland while simultaneously themselves being easily identified in the open field. At this point, while rallying the 24th and light battalion, Brigadier General Fraser was mortally wounded.

Learned's brigade attacked the German units who held, and even drove off one attack, but the situation was becoming critical. Brigadier General Abraham Ten Broeck's New York Militia brigade also arrived on the battlefield and, although they took no part in the fighting, the psychological impact of their presence further demoralised the British and German troops. The grenadiers on the left were breaking, and their wavering infected the Braunschweigers. When *Hauptmann* Pausch, commanding the artillery, looked for the infantry to cover his retirement to the wood line, he found them already retreating. With his men he dragged the guns back to the trees before being overwhelmed and forced to abandon the guns. He described the panic of the broken army:

> Seeing that all was irretrievably lost, and that it was impossible to save anything, I called to the few remaining men to save themselves. I myself took refuge through a fence, in a piece of dense underbrush on the right of the road, with the last ammunition wagon, which, with the help of a gunner, I saved with the horses. Here I met all the different nationalities of our division running pell-mell – among them Capt. Schoel, with whom there was not a single man left of the Hanau Regiment. In this confused retreat all made for our camp and our lines.[64]

At this point, Benedict Arnold, appeared on the battlefield to inspire the rebels. Under their renewed attack, the rebels pursued the retreating British and Germans to the superficial shelter of the two redoubts, but that protection proved illusionary. With insufficient time or planning to effect a meaningful

---

64 Pausch, *Journal*, pp.171–172.

defence, these physically strong positions were soon overwhelmed, but not without cost. Poor's brigade advanced through a woodland trail into open fields which were dominated by the Balcarres Redoubt and an outer ring of smaller positions. They immediately attacked the first of these positions, now renamed 'Bloody Knoll'. They took it, but the name stands in testimony to the cost in seizing it. The main redoubt was manned by the survivors of the grenadier and light battalions, and the 24th Foot. The action at Bloody Knoll bought them sufficient time to catch their breath and organise a defence. Realising that this was a substantial position, Poor's brigade retired into cover where it could trade shots with the defenders. Colonel Phillip van Cortlandt, Commanding Officer of the 2nd New York Regiment, described the situation:

> I being yet with Poor's brigade and advancing, the British retiring towards their battery, as the Hessians towards theirs [Breymann's Redoubt]. General Arnold, now on the field and in sight of the nine gun battery [Balcarres Redoubt] send his aid to the right, ordering General Poor to bring his men into better order as we were pursuing. This order arrested our progress and prevented our taking the British battery in less than ten minutes; as we should have entered it almost as soon as the British. As Morgan did that of the Hessians, which Arnold discovered after sending the above order to General Poor, and as he has also sent another order by his aid, he now rode as fast as he could to counteract his own orders.[65]

While the assault on the Balcarres Redoubt paused, Learned's brigade and Morgan's riflemen marched behind Poor's brigade into position to assault the second redoubt, the Breymann Redoubt. The right of Learned's brigade quickly stormed three cabins which were held by Canadians. Their capture exposed the undefended rear of the Breymann Redoubt. The final assault against the redoubt was so quick and over such short distance that the defenders could only fire one or two rounds before trying to escape to the shelter of the woods behind them. Breymann was killed in his own redoubt and Benedict Arnold was wounded in the leg outside it, trapped for a while by his fallen horse. Meanwhile, the Balcarres Redoubt and its outer defences were too strong to be stormed directly by the rebels. Once the rebels occupied Breymann's Redoubt they were able to deliver harassing fire. The Balcarres Redoubt was held until dark and then evacuated. The rebels did not detect this move or, if they did, did not act to intervene or follow it up.

Barber's Wheatfield was nothing short of a disaster. Of the 1,700 of Burgoyne's troops participating, some 900 became casualties; a 50 percent casualty rate. Brigadier General Fraser and *Oberstleutnant* Breymann were killed, while Major Acland was wounded and captured. Both redoubts were lost, as was a great deal of artillery.

Gates was able to deploy some 7,000 troops of his Northern Army against Burgoyne's forage and reconnaissance expedition of about 1,700. Rebel losses

---

65   Quoted in J.F. Luzader, *Saratoga: a military history of a decisive campaign of the American Revolution* (New York: Savas Beatie, 2008), pp.287–288.

are estimated at 200 with just 30 killed.[66] With those odds, it is inconceivable that the outcome could be anything other than what it was: Burgoyne simply did not have the numbers to accomplish his mission in the face of growing rebel strength and in the absence of support. In addition to this, there was the deteriorating logistical situation facing the British versus the improving rebel position as they had retired on interior lines. Critically, Bemis Heights drove home the need to abandon the campaign and retire to secure winter conditions. Riedesel had already proposed this option. On 8 October, Burgoyne accepted the inevitable, but by this point it was too late, as the emboldened rebels were closing in on his fortified camp

During early October conditions continued to deteriorate. The weather turned for the worse and price increases made it impossible for common soldiers to purchase additions to their meagre rations, including rum:

> The soldiers both of the Engl[ish] and the German regts. had till now maintained themselves well with respect to desertion but it was now beginning to gain ground in both corps. Heavy duties, such as detachments, pickets and especially the work detachments, the fact that everything became more expensive; the daily, very tiring marches; the allurements and promises circulated by the enemy; finally an exaggerated idea of the rather bad situation of our cause and the fate of our army next winter when no good quarters could be expected – all these reason were the source of desertions.[67]

Burgoyne ordered rations to be cut by a third. He also attempted to bolster moral with the following message:

> There is reason to be assured, that other powerful Armies of the King are actually in co-operation with these Troops; and although the present supply of Provisions is ample, it is highly desirable to be prepared for any continuance in the Field that the King's Service may require, without the delay of bringing forward further Stores, for those purposed; the ration of Bread or Flour is for the present fixed at one Pound.[68]

On 9 October, Burgoyne received a message from Clinton stating his intent to march with 3,000 men against Fort Montgomery in 10 days' time. If successful, Lieutenant General Sir Henry Clinton would still be 100 miles south of Albany, twice the distance that Burgoyne was from Albany. Clinton did not specify whether or not he would advance further should his attack on Fort Montgomery be successful. Clinton had left New York on 3 October and three days later successfully captured Fort Montgomery and Fort Clinton. These forts guarded the Hudson and their capture opened the river to the British at least as far as West Point. However, news of General Howe's capture of Philadelphia would have been bitter to Burgoyne. It meant that Howe's army had moved southwards, away from Albany and therefore it was highly

---

66   Clay, *Saratoga Campaign*, p.117.
67   Specht, *Journal*, p.85, 2 October 1777.
68   O'Callaghan (ed.), *Orderly Book*, pp.125–126, 3 October 1777.

unlikely that anything other than Clinton's smaller force would be available to force its way through to Burgoyne. Albany was a small town of 3,000 inhabitants and so unlikely to have sufficient resources to accommodate and feed Burgoyne's men during the approaching winter. Even if he succeeded in reaching Albany, Burgoyne would need open communications to survive through to 1778. It would be almost three weeks before Burgoyne moved again, during which time inactivity coupled with reduced rations, had weakened both the strength and the morale of his army.

The 47th Leads the Breakout
Corporal George Fox described the aftermath of the battles:

> … the rest of our men were employ'd in raising works and bringing the baggage &c up. after burying the dead all men of duty were Employed in making batterys (they had works for 3 or four mile long of batterys and redouts which they had rais'd before we came to them) … After we had secured ourselves we built a bridge in the night and pass'd over in forage partys to get provinder for the horses … The Army lay still till the 7th Oct[o]ber (except a shell now and then) then our provision began to get short … [Then] we retreated to Saratago 18 m[iles] by night and took possession of the old french works, we began to cook our victuals by the fires [when] they fired and kill'd several of our men so that we put out our fires and lay upon ground all night, (they having got upon an small Island in the river) a detachment was sent and drove them off the Island and kept guard all night. the next day we pitch'd our tents and all hands of duty were employed in making ridouts and brest works to preserve us from their shot that came across the river. They had three batterys playing upon us, which drive us out of our works and obliged us to retreat 100 yds back between two hills and all upon one another to screen us from their fire … for ten day we liv'd on 4 buiscuits per man per day and then we had some flour serv'd out to us which we made dumplings of. we durst not go to our battooes for the little beef and pork. The time that we first retreated we fir'd 72 barrels rum and burnt the bridge and 450 battooes and Cannon sunk.'[69]

Burgoyne now knew that withdrawal to a secure base for winter quarters was the only option. The decision to withdraw was made on 8 October. Lieutenant Colonel Sutherland's six companies of the 47th were the strongest corps available, and would be supported by the 9th Foot, Fraser's Marksmen, Canadian volunteers and artificers. Sutherland departed around 9:00 p.m. Shortly afterwards, the heavens opened with torrential rain. Under normal circumstances, this would have covered any noise made, but one of their tasks was the re-construction of destroyed bridges. The rear guard, composed of the Advance Corps now commanded by Major General William Phillips (RA), did not set off until 4:00 a.m. on the 9th. Once the bridges that the 47th had built or repaired had been crossed by the Advanced Corps, they were destroyed. Some 400 sick and injured were left in the hospitals, in the care of

---

69   Houlding and Yates, 'Corporal Fox', pp.159–161.

surgeons and their mates and Burgoyne provided them with a letter to Gates asking him to take care of them.

Rebel troops entered the abandoned camp on the 9th and took responsibility for the sick and wounded. Gates did not closely pursue Burgoyne. He commanded eight brigades and knew that there were six more in the vicinity of Burgoyne's line of retreat. Three miles ahead of Burgoyne guarding the point where he had to cross the Hudson was John Stark's militia brigade of about 2,500 men. This would be sufficient to fix and hold the retreating army until Gates could bring the remainder of his army into action. Burgoyne's defeat was simply a matter of time.

The Advance Corps (bringing up the rear) halted an hour later to eat, and then formed up in preparation for a battle. Burgoyne still hoped that Gates would attack or that the matter could be settled on the field of battle. Sutherland, meanwhile, had pushed forward his reconnaissance, and found the entire of Brigadier General John Fellow's Massachusetts Militia brigade asleep in their camp. Despite having only about 250 men, less than half of Fellow's strength, Sutherland requested permission to attack. This could have been a follow-up to the 'Paoli Massacre', when Major General Charles Grey had attacked and routed rebel Brigadier General Anthony Wayne's sleeping Pennsylvania Division just over a fortnight earlier. Burgoyne decided that his forces was too weak to attack, and the opportunity was lost. Fellows, by now alerted, withdrew his brigade across the Hudson, and opened the way for Burgoyne to reach Fish Kill Creek.[70]

At 4:00 p.m. on the 10th, the British army set off again. Deteriorating weather meant that waggons and supplies were increasingly being abandoned. The Advance Corps and Germans reached and crossed the Fish Kill, but the high-water level and the weakness of the horses meant that the artillery could not cross. The following day the water level had abated and the remainder of the army with their guns crossed. Sutherland resumed the retirement. Gates now moved quickly with units closing in on Burgoyne from the south and west. Facing this situation, Burgoyne ordered his army to dig in hoping to entice Gates to attack again. Sutherland was recalled. According to Specht, Sutherland was just one hour from Fort Edward 'when he received orders to come back again in a hurry. [He] did not only express the greatest surprise but also the greatest annoyance that the army had not followed him but that instead he had to turn back.'[71] Corporal George Fox described the situation when 'we got as far as fort Edward 19 m[iles] and just crossing the river we saw the rebels had took possession of fort Edward hill and a large number of cannon planted to prevent'd our crossing over.'[72] Two days later, Captain Mackay, whom Sutherland had left guarding the bridge when he was recalled, obtained permission for as a many as one hundred loyalists and others who would most likely suffer at the hands of the rebels, to make good their escape. They reached Fort Ticonderoga on the 17th.[73] Sutherland's departure, but

---

70 Snow, *1777*, pp.298–299.
71 Specht, *Journal*, p.95, 11 October 1777.
72 Houlding and Yates, 'Corporal Fox', p.161.
73 Specht, *Journal*, p.94, n.121, 10 October 1777, p.96, n.122, 12 October 1777.

not his return, had been reported to Gates who interpreted this as another northward overnight movement by Burgoyne. Expecting to only find a rear guard in Burgoyne's camp, Gates ordered a dawn attack on the 11th across the Fish Kill.

Crossing in the early morning fog, they surprised and captured an entire 36-man piquet without a shot, and continued towards the British lines. Warned that they were approaching the main body, not just a rear guard, the rebels halted just in time, but when the fog lifted a little later, they found themselves exposed to the British guns, and beat a hasty retreat. The clearing fog also exposed the British to constant snipping from rifle armed marksmen beyond the range of their muskets. That evening, Burgoyne and his commanders met for the first time to consider surrender.

Burgoyne's force was now reduced to about 3,500 effectives, against which Gates commanded some 12,000 men. There were other formations in positions to interdict Burgoyne's line of retreat. The only glimmer of hope was that Clinton could breakthrough to them. By the 16th, Clinton had captured and burned Esopus, but a further advance to Livingston Manor encountered 6,000 rebel militia which halted any further progress. They were still 65 miles from Albany and Burgoyne was now moving in the opposite direction.[74]

Negotiations

Corporal George Fox describes the false bravado of a desperate situation where they knew full well what the outcome must be. When asked whether the 47th would fight again, 'they consented and gave three cheers, and we were drawn up in line of battle along the side of a wood (100 yds) from our first retreat.' Rations were becoming short. Hunger would have been worsened with the arrival of colder weather: 'from our first retreat), for ten day we liv'd on 4 buiscuits per man per day and then we had some flour serv'd out to us which we made dumplings of. we durst not go to our battooes for the little beef.' While in the last four days:

> They had three batterys playing upon us, which drive us out of our works and obliged us to retreat 100 yds back between two hills and all upon one another to screen us from their fire (here a six pound ball took the bottom of my knapsack of), our cannon play'd back with little effect. We continued in this situation four days wholy surrounded.[75]

On October 14, Burgoyne called a council of war with his senior commanders, which determined that surrender was the only option. Major Robert Kingston was sent to Gates under a flag of truce. He was surprised to be greeted with a prepared set of terms and conditions, demanding complete and immediate surrender, and including a truce until sunset, later extended until 10:00 a.m. on the 15th. A second letter

---

74 Cubbison, *Burgoyne*, p.329.
75 Houlding and Yates, 'Corporal Fox', pp.160–161.

from Gates demanded surrender by 3:00 p.m., and the laying down of arms by 5:00 p.m. The urgency and precise timings gave hope to Burgoyne that Clinton's expedition was closer than it actually was. Burgoyne played for time, including a request that his troops should return to Britain on condition that they served no further part in the war. Gates agreed. Lieutenant Colonel Sutherland and Captain Craig (both 47th) then met with Gates' representatives, Brigadier General Whipple and Lieutenant Colonel Wilkinson, to draft terms. That night the terms were presented to Burgoyne who agreed with a single, significant change: 'capitulation' should be replaced with 'convention'.[76] Captain Craig communicated Burgoyne's acceptance and terms to Whipple and Wilkinson. Gates had just heard of Clinton's successes in capturing the Highland forts. He was indeed very keen to agree to Burgoyne's surrender to avoid the very situation which Burgoyne's strategy had intended; to trap Gates' army within a multiple-pronged advance. Burgoyne heard of Clinton's success the following day and called a further council of war to determine whether he was, indeed, committed to the surrender. Fourteen of 22 officers thought he was indeed bound to the treaty, and in any case, Clinton was still too far away to be of assistance to them and their own troops were in no fit state to fight further. Burgoyne prevaricated and accused Gates of breaking the truce by sending troops away to fight Clinton, which of course Wilkinson denied. The latter departed, threatening to end the truce but he was caught up with and promised an answer within two hours. Burgoyne remained resolute, and sent Sutherland to inform Gates that the truce had ended. At this point Sutherland was shown Craig's letter communicating Burgoyne's acceptance of Gates' terms. Burgoyne finally accepted the reality of the situation and agreed to the inevitable.

At 10:00 a.m. on 17 October 1777 Burgoyne's men marched out with full honours to surrender between silent, disciplined ranks of the Northern Army; professional officers were complimentary of the bearing and discipline of the un-uniformed victors. A band stuck up *Yankee Doodle*, once a satire on the rustic appearance of the colonial militia which fought alongside the uniformed professionals, now the tables were turned.

Of the almost 7,000 soldiers who had set out from Canada, 5,895 soldiers laid down their arms. 1,300 remained at Fort Ticonderoga, but that figure included the survivors of St Leger's Expedition. Three officers were given permission to carry letters back to Canada, including the 47th's Captain James Craig.[77]

Of the 3,372 British troops who surrendered at Saratoga, the 47th accounted for 394: 15 officers, five staff, 18 sergeants, 14 drummers, 314 effective rank and file plus seven sick, nine musicians, and 12 batmen.

The regiment had suffered the following losses and casualties, killed, wounded, wounded and captured, and captured:

---

76 The text of the Saratoga Convention is reproduced in Appendix III.
77 For the letter, see Cubbin, *Burgoyne*, pp.321–332, n.223 says that Craig was seriously wounded at Hubbardton, and spent time while recuperating as Burgoyne's ADC; Specht, *Journal*, p.102 n.127, 18 October 1777.

Table 7.3

Officers				NCOs				Drummers				Soldiers				Servants				Regt Total				
K	W	W/C	C	K	W	W/C	C	K	W	W/C	C	K	W	W/C	C	K	W	W/C	C	K	W	W/C	C	Total
0	1	2	1	1	4	0	4	1	0	0	1	10	16	0	21	0	0	0	0	12	18	0	27	57[78]
																				12	21	2	27	62[79]

Specht also provided a list of wounded officers. He lists Captain Craig who was wounded at Hubbardton but evidently returned to duty as he was assisting Lieutenant Colonel Sutherland with the surrender negotiations, and subsequently carried despatches back to Canada. Lieutenant England is the only other officer named, he was wounded and taken prisoner during the Pawlet Raid.[80] On 8 November, Brigadier General Powell ordered the abandonment and destruction of Fort Ticonderoga. He then retired into Canada.

Conclusion

Why did the Saratoga Campaign fail? At the strategic level, there was nothing fundamentally wrong with the plan, indeed historian Steven Clay called it 'an excellent plan.'[81] Whether it would have succeeded in defeating the isolated New England extremists is a moot point, but in terms of defeating the rebel's Northern Army it was a fundamentally sound plan which played on three advantages held by the British to trap and destroy the rebels in a three pronged advance: control of significant bases (Quebec, New York City); control of water-based means of transport (River Hudson, Lake Champlain, Lake Ontario); good relations with Native Americans.

The plan would have survived the failure of St Leger's Expedition. The survivors of his force reached Fort Ticonderoga, and they could have joined Burgoyne for a triumphant advance into Albany. However, their strength was not sufficient to address the Northern Army's superior numbers. Where the plan failed was Howe's refusal to support Burgoyne until Clinton's belated advance with too few troops. Burgoyne was left to face the entirety of Gates' Northern Army on terrain of their choosing. He should have only had to face half that number with Gates keeping one eye over his shoulder. Under these circumstances, the only way to avoid disaster was to withdraw sooner, back to Fort Ticonderoga, and try again in 1778. By keeping his army 'in being', Burgoyne would have fixed Gates' Northern Army in upper New York and away from Howe. At the tactical level, Burgoyne's troops showed far greater aptitude than their rebel opponents in 1776 and 1777 with a steady series of victories from Quebec to the crossing of the Hudson. Burgoyne suffered the same problem as all British commanders during the war: a small

---

78   Specht, *Journal*, Chart J.
79   Recalculated by author.
80   For a similar list, see Lamb, *Journal*, pp.174–177 but he only mentions Captain Craig and does not mention Lieutenant England.
81   Clay, *Saratoga Campaign*, p.137.

army with uncertainty of casualty replacements. In this respect, Carleton's caution would have made him a more appropriate commander for 1777 than Burgoyne. Logistically, there were fundamental problems from the outset which were never satisfactorily addressed. In the following letter of 7 June 1777, Burgoyne's logistical difficulties are highlighted:

> Your Excellency will observe, that, in order to save the public expense as much as possible, I have reduced this requisition much below what would be adequate for the service, and I mean to trust to the resources of the expedition for the rest: 500 carts will barely carry fourteen days provisions at a time, and Major General Phillips means to demand as few horses as possible, subject to whatever future augmentations future services may require: the present number wanted will be about 400; these will then remain unprovided for (for expeditious movement) the transport of bateaux from lake George to Hudson's River, and the carriages of the tents of the army, and many other contingencies that I need not trouble your Excellency to point out to you.[82]

These supply difficulties were behind the decision to launch the Bennington Raid, which became a disaster for Burgoyne. The Pawlet Raid on Fort Ticonderoga which seized or destroyed labour, supplies, and means of transport only exasperated his supply problems and exposed the weakness of his lengthening logistics tail.

Ultimately, Burgoyne manoeuvred his army into a position, both geographically and logistically, from which he could not extract it. His vulnerabilities were exposed by his logistic difficulties and Howe's refusal to support him. Of greater concern, though, was that the three critical defeats of the war – Boston, Saratoga and Yorktown – all follow a similar pattern. On each occasion, British commanders had, for whatever reason, trapped themselves. All the rebels had to do was concentrate larger numbers to contain the British and wait. This undid all of the hard work and advantage gained on the battlefield.

---

82 Burgoyne to Carleton, 7 June 1777, quoted in Cubbin, *Burgoyne*, pp.248–249.

8

The Convention Army

When Burgoyne's men laid down their arms near Saratoga on 17 October 1777, they did not become prisoners of war. The purpose of the Saratoga Convention (see Appendix III) was to remove the troops from the American theatre with an agreement that they would not participate in the war again. The downside to this agreement, for the rebels, was that these men could relieve other troops in Britain, Ireland, or other garrisons, to participate in the war. Strictly speaking, the convention only applied to those who laid down their arms under it. Anyone taken captive before the convention was signed was not covered by it, for example during the Pawlet Raid or at Bennington. They were prisoners of war and were held under different conditions. In theory. The 'Convention Army', as Burgoyne's troops now became known, was intended to march to Boston where British ships would convey them out of the operational theatre.

The Strength of the 47th Foot in the Convention Army

A return of the 47th compiled on 1 April 1778 at Prospect Hill outside Boston, Massachusetts, gives the following strength:

Officers	Other Ranks	
17	255	Fit for Duty
	23	Sick
2	31	Prisoners
10	165	On Command
29	474	Total[1]

Those fit for duty and sick would have been part of the Convention Army, with the two officers (one was Lieutenant England) and 31 other ranks who were prisoners being captured under circumstances other than the Saratoga Convention. Those on command are those who avoided either capture or

---

1 Wylly, *Loyal North Lancashire*, vol.I, p.69.

being part of the Convention Army. They are the subject of the next chapter. We must also add to this figure the 24 authorised women, being the three per company permitted by Burgoyne.

On 13 December 1777, the Cambridge Parole was signed by the officers of the Convention Army. From the signatories, we can identify which of the regiment's officers were present. These were Lieutenant Colonel Sutherland, Major Irving, Captains England and Alcock, Captain Lieutenant Marr, Lieutenants Storey, Poe (adjutant), Baldwin, French, Ward, Rotton, and Bunbury, Ensigns Noble, Percy and Burroughs (formerly the surgeon's mate), Surgeon Dobbin and Quartermaster Paxon. This adds up to 17 of a potential 35 officers. We know that General Sir Guy Carleton and Chaplain Whitty did not join the regiment on the expedition and that Captain Craig was one of three captains permitted to leave with dispatches. Captain Sherriff was serving as deputy quarter master general to Howe, and Lieutenant Duport was serving as assistant quarter master general at Sorel, Canada. Three were on leave and one was recruiting. These last four were, of course, not amongst those that signed the Cambridge Parole. The surgeon's mate post may have been vacant. A further eight officers are named on the 1778 muster rolls. From this we can account for 32 of 35 officers. The one officer who stands out as being the most unfortunate is Lieutenant John Rotton. He was captured while on board a ship to America and even in the February 1777 muster roll is listed Captain Aubrey's company as a prisoner. Exchanged, he was clearly able to rejoin the regiment in time for the 1777 campaign but, if he was still in Aubrey's company, he should have been on Diamond Island and so would have escaped captivity with the Convention Army. Captain Poole England was captured during the Pawlet Raid on Fort Ticonderoga so was not part of the Convention Army but, as an officer and a gentleman, would have been expected to give his parole as a prisoner of war.[2]

Left: A three-piece copper alloy officer's button found in the grounds of Fort Ticonderoga during renovations in the early twentieth century. (Fort Ticonderoga)
Right: The button was secured by a cord or similar through holes in the 'core', rather than a metal shank; the white fibres are from the button being glued onto a board for an early display. (Fort Ticonderoga)

---

2 O'Callaghan (ed.), *Orderly Book*, Parole of Burgoyne's Officers, pp.176–179; Baule and Gilbert, *British Army Officers*, p.156; Wylly, *Loyal North Lancashire*, vol.I, p.69; Hadden, *Journal*, p.261, 22 August 1776.

THE CONVENTION ARMY

The March to Massachusetts Bay for Repatriation

Lieutenant William Digby (53rd Foot), described the emotionally charged atmosphere on the morning of 17 October 1777:

> About 10 o'clock we marched out, according to treaty, with drums beating and the honours of war, but the drums seemed to have lost their former inspiring sounds, and though we beat the Grenadiers' march, which not long before was so animating, yet then it seemed by its last feeble effort as if almost ashamed to be heard on such an occasion. Thus was Burgoyne's Army sacrificed to either the absurd opinions of blundering ministerial power, the stupid inaction of a general who, from his lethargic disposition, neglected every step he might have taken to assist their operations, or lastly, perhaps, his own misconduct in penetrating so far as to be unable to return.[3]

Desertion is a common theme throughout the existence of the Convention Army. *Oberst* Johann Specht first recorded the temptation on 23 October. Private Robert Young (33rd Foot attached to the artillery) deserted before reaching Cambridge. He was executed for the rape of a child on 11 November 1779 in Worcester, Massachusetts. His dying speech records how he reached Hadley, Massachusetts, about halfway to Cambridge 'where I became acquainted with a girl, who advised me to desert.'[4]

It took two days to ferry the Convention Army across the Hudson river. Thereafter the British and German contingents followed different routes. The former travelled via Williamstown, while the Germans took a more southerly route through Kinderhook. The rain which had commenced on 7 October continued. Writing from the relative comfort of Cambridge, Massachusetts; Lieutenant Thomas Anburey (29th Foot) described their journey in graphic terms:

> We were two days in crossing the Green Mountain, which are a part of the chain of mountains that run through the whole Continent of America, more commonly known by the name of the Allegany Mountains: the roads across them were almost impassable, and to add to the difficulty, when we had got half over, there came on a very heavy fall of snow. After this, it is impossible to describe the confusion that ensued; carts breaking down, others sticking fast, some oversetting, horses tumbling with their loads of baggage, men cursing, women shrieking, and children squalling! It should seem that I was to encounter every unpleasant duty that can fall to the lot of an officer, for this very day I had the baggage guard; exclusive of being covered in snow, and riding about after the bat-men, to keep them together, and to assist each other, my attention was directed to a scene, which I did not think it possible human nature could have supported, for in the midst of the heavy snow-storm, upon a baggage-cart, and nothing to shelter her from the inclemency of the weather but a bit of an old oil-cloth, a soldier's wife

---

3   Baxter, *British Invasion*, pp.319–320; See also Sampson, *Escape in America*, p.45 and Jones, *Captives of Liberty*, p.147.
4   Specht, *Journal*, p.104, 23 October 1777; Hagist, *British Soldiers, American War*, pp.133–143.

A VERY FINE REGIMENT

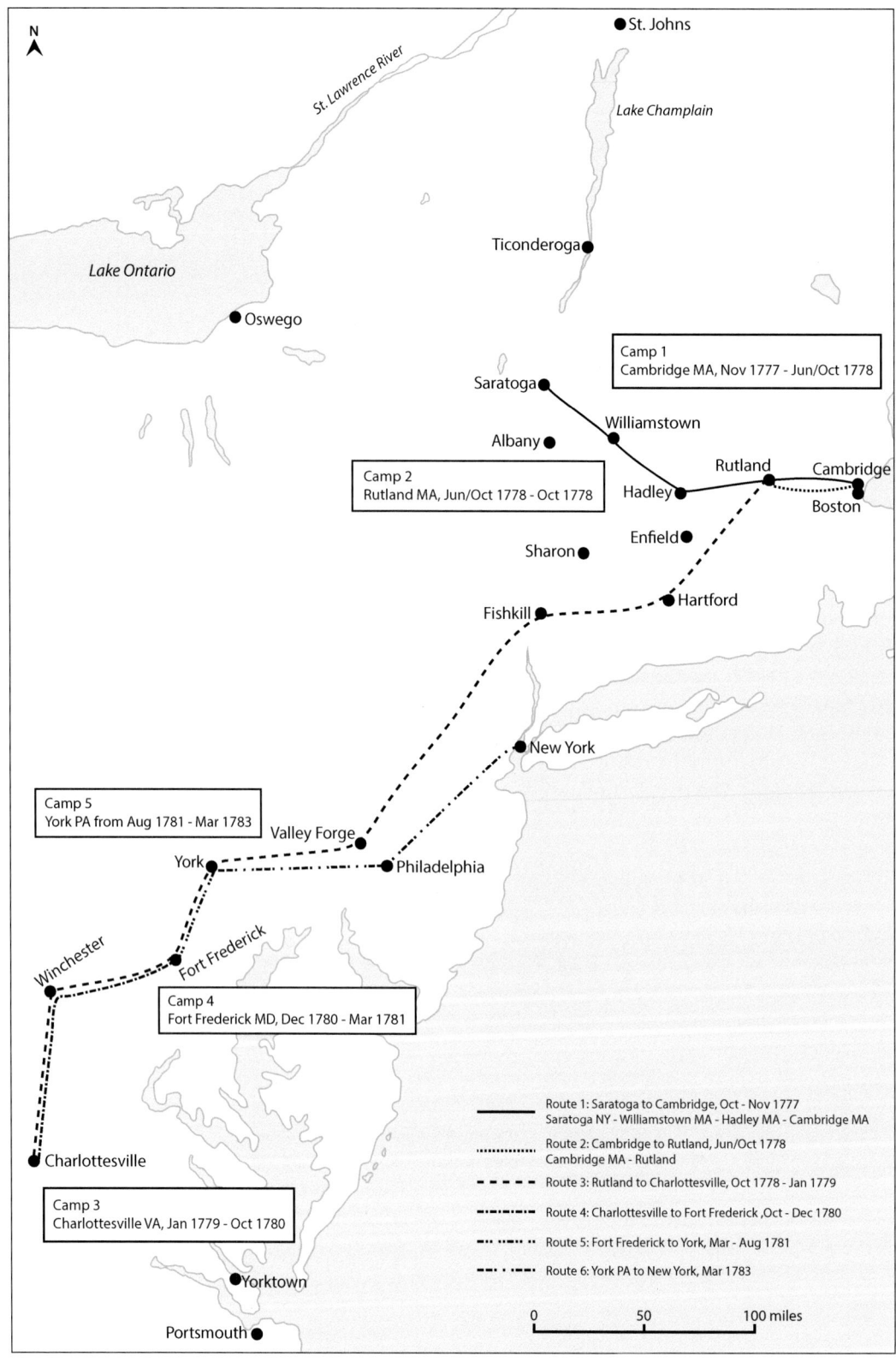

The marches of the Convention Army.

was delivered of a child, she and the infant are both well, and are now at this place. It may be said, that women who follow a camp are of such a masculine nature, they are able to bear all hardships; this woman was quiet the reverse, being small, and of a very delicate constitution.[5]

Corporal Roger Lamb found the journey no better than the previous campaigning, 'From the outset of our marching we experienced much hardship, sleeping in barns and having but bad clothing, and very scant provisions.'[6] The reference to 'bad clothing' is of course a reference to their 1776 clothing issue which they were still wearing.

Specht, with the German contingent, found the journey equally difficult:

Oct 28 The march today was the worst and most exhausting we ever had. The oldest soldiers admitted to never before having taken part in such a march. The air was piercingly cold and the wind cutting. Rain, snow, hail, and ice alternated. The roads were execrably set by nature and though the continuous bad weather, that had by now lasted 48 hours, they had gotten into such a state that you could scarcely walk on them any more. The poor soldiers left the remnants of their shoes and small boots stuck between the stones and in the mud. It was nearly impossible for the officers to hold their people together, who, afraid of freezing to death, ran into houses along the road to get a little warmth. In fact, one grenadier froze to death on this march.[7]

Baroness Fredericka von Riedesel, wife of *Generalmajor* von Riedesel, had accompanied him on campaign. Even she found the journey to Boston 'tedious and difficult', and she was riding in a calash. She also had all of her household goods stolen despite an American guard of 10 to 20 men in a land where 'nothing could be bought at any price'.[8]

Between the signing of the convention and 31 October 1777, an estimated 160 men were absent. Some of these may have deserted, or died, been left behind in a hospital, or fallen out en route. One of those in the latter category was the 47th's Private James Maguire. He was collected from the side of the road by local Americans and eventually reached the British lines at New York after a few years on the run. In the February 1777 muster rolls he was in Captain Thomas Gamble's company and should have been with him on Diamond Island, so exactly how Maguire came to be with the Convention Army is unclear.[9]

The Convention Army would quickly learn for the first time that they were economic as well as military and political pawns. The Continental Congress set the exchange rate at $4.50 to the Guinea (21 shillings, or £1 1s). However, Congress' paper dollars were largely worthless whereas the Convention

---

5   Anburey, *Travels*, vol.II, pp.38–40, Letter XLV, 20 Nov 1777.
6   Hagist, *British Soldier's Story*, p.55.
7   Specht, *Journal*, p.107, 28 October 1777.
8   M.L. Brown, (ed.), *Baroness von Reidesel and the American Revolution: journal and correspondence of a Tour of Duty, 1776–1783* (Chapel Hill: University of North Carolina Press, 1965), pp.65–66; Riedesel, *Memoirs*, vol.I, p.222.
9   Sampson, *Escape in America*, pp.49–50.

Army was a source of hard currency. The black-market exchange rate quickly rose from $9 to $20 as Americans realised the value of the gold being carried by the Convention Army and bid against one another to obtain it, raising the unofficial exchange rate in Convention Army's favour.[10] Lieutenant Anburey described the situation:

> Notwithstanding their displeasure with our Government, they are not so with our guineas, and although they are fighting for independency, they place very little dependence upon paper-money; for however material they are at present, still they have an eye to traffic and merchandize; what a weak state the Congress must be in, when those who are fighting for its support are depreciating its credit.[11]

Johann Specht recorded the same, although his calculations involved German currency and 'Halifax rate' which makes comparison of exchange rates difficult.[12]

It took three weeks for the Convention Army to march the 200 miles to Cambridge, Massachusetts. The prospect of rest followed by a long Atlantic crossing must has sustained many. Little did they know that this was the first of many such marches over the next five years.

Prospect Hill

Mrs Hanna Winthrop, an inhabitant of Cambridge, Massachusetts, described the Convention Army as it arrived in the town:

> Last Thursday, which was a very stormy day, a large number of British troops came softly through the town via Watertown to Prospect Hill. On Friday we heard the Hessians were to make a procession in the same route. We thought we should have nothing to do but view them as they passed. To be sure the sight was truly astonishing I never had the least idea that the creation produced such a sordid set of creatures in human form – poor, dirty, emaciated men. Great numbers of women, who seemed to be the beasts of burden, having bushel-baskets on their backs, by which they were bent double. The contents seem to be pots and kettles, various sorts of furniture, children peeping though gridirons and other utensils – some very young infants who were born on the road – the women barefoot, clothed in dirty rags. Such effluvia filled the air while they were passing, that had they not been smoking all the time, I should have been apprehensive of being contaminated by them. After a noble-looking advanced-guard, General Burgoyne headed this terrible group on horseback. The other generals also clothed in blue cloaks – Hessians, Waldeckers, Asnpackers, Brunswickers, etc., etc., followed on. The Hessian generals gave us a polite bow as they passed. Not so the British. Their baggage-wagons drawn by poor, half-starved horses.[13]

---

10   Sampson, *Escape in America*, p.51.
11   Anburey, *Travels*, vol.II, pp.54–55, Letter XLVI, 25 Nov 1777.
12   Specht, *Journal*, p.105, 23 October 1777.
13   Quoted in Sampson, *Escape in America*, p.55 and Cain, *Horrors of a Civil War*, p.135 n.194.

The followers of the army are the unsung heroes. Lieutenant Anburey comments on the wife of 'delicate constitution'[14] who gave birth at the side of the road as being and there is Mrs Middleton of the 47th, a 'modest, decent well looking woman'.[15] Corporal Roger Lamb also mentioned a woman giving birth during the campaign.[16] Sampson quotes a rebel observation of the German women, saying 'They were a good many woman accompanying the Germans, and a miserable looking set of oddly dressed, Gipsy featured females they were.'[17] These women had just endured a wilderness campaign so could hardly be expected to be in their finery, but there is a noticeable difference in the complimentary language in the British sources and the disparaging rebel comments.

Anburey recorded another occasion at Prospect Hill in which he praised the fortitude of a wife. The wives were allowed to pass the sentries to purchase food:

> ... but the other day a most ludicrous circumtance took place, by the obstinacy of an old man upon guard. He would not permit a woman, who was a true campaigner to go beyond him, great altercation ensued, in which the lady displayed much of the Billingsgate oratory, when the old man was so irritated as to present his firelock; the woman immediately ran up, snatched it from him, knocked him down, and striding over the prostate hero, in the exultation of triumph, profusely besprinkled him, not with Olympian dew, but that which is esteemed as emollient to the complexion – and 'faith, something more natural – nor did she quit her post, till a file of sturdy ragamuffins marched valiantly to his relief, dispossessed the Amazon, and enabled the knight of the grisly caxon to look fierce, and reshoulder his musquet.[18]

In other words, she urinated on the prone guard. The British contingent had good cause to fear the reaction of the inhabitants of the Boston and its environs. It was not just the 47th who knew Boston well. The flank companies of the 29th Foot knew the provocation behind the Boston Massacre.

The British contingent was allocated barracks on Prospect Hill, while the Germans were based on Winter Hill. Prospect Hill had originally been barracks for the rebel forces besieging Boston but in the intervening 18 months it had fallen into disrepair. All of the accounts describe the barracks as inadequate; there was also insufficient accomodation. The 47th's Corporal George Fox described them as 'good usage but very cold barracks.'[19]

The winter was particularly difficult:

> It was not infrequent for thirty, or forty persons, men, women and children, to be indiscriminately crowded together in one small, miserable, open hut; their

---

14   Anburey, *Travels*, vol.II, p.40, Letter XLV, 20 Nov 1777.
15   Quoted from British Soldiers, American Revolution: Robert and Mrs. Middleton, 47th Regiment of Foot, <https://redcoat76.blogspot.com/2009/12/robert-and-mrs-middleton-47th-regiment.html> accessed 20 September 2021.
16   Hagist, *British Soldier's Story*, p.44.
17   Quoted in Sampson, *Escape in America*, p.47.
18   Anburey, *Travels*, vol.II, pp.81–82, Letter XLVIII, 9 Dec 1777.
19   Houlding, and Yates, 'Corporal Fox', p.162. Also see Hagist, *British Soldiers, American War*, pp.182–215 for the conditions at Prospect Hill.

provisions and fire-wood on short allowance; and a scanty portion of straw their bed, their own blankets their only covering. In the night time, those that could lie down, and the many who sat up from the cold, were obliged frequently to rise and shake from them the snow which the wind drifted in at the openings; or, in the case of rain, to ensure the chill pelting of the merciless storm.[20]

Anburey agreed, despite the benefits he would have enjoyed as an officer:

> The method of quartering was dreadfully inconvenient, six officers in a room not twelve feet square, permission was denied us to accommodate ourselves with rooms in this town, till General Burgoyne arrived, and represented our situation to the Council at Boston, when it was reluctantly granted. We laboured under many distresses and difficulties; every species of previsions was very dear, and to add to our misfortune, could hardly be procured for money. You do not, I believe, in England, rank milk in the catalogue of luxuries, yet we were obliged, ourselves, to traverse a deep snow for a full mile, to get a small quantity for our breakfasts, as our servants were not permitted to pass the centinels.
>
> It was understood at the convention, that the troops were to be stationed on Prospect and Winter Hills, and the officers were to be quartered in Boston, and the neighbouring towns. On this supposition some of the officers had pushed forward and got into Boston but were immediately ordered out.[21]

The officers were allowed to obtain accommodation in Cambridge, Mystic and Watertown with a parole of 10 miles, although they were not permitted to enter Boston. However, officers' duties remained and in order to 'preserve order and regularity' three officers per regiment resided in the barracks. Anburey does not elaborate whether those three were permanently resident there or if this was a duty shared by all the officers.[22]

Such complaints were not limited to the British who were chaffing against their lot. Colonel Lee commanded the militia guards. He recorded the conditions and what he feared would be the outcome should the situation not be rectified: 'This morning rode round the lines and found the Field Officers and some others walking by their barracks to keep themselves from perishing with cold; not one stick of wood to put into the Fire, and if some other method cannot be found to supply them they must either perish or burn all the public buildings.'[23]

The arrival of some 6,000 of Convention Army, plus women and children, into the environs of Boston had a detrimental economic impact by increasing demand for food and accommodation which in turn raised prices for the civilians. Pre-war, the population of Boston had been around 15,000, but thousands had left the city and hinterland during the siege and evacuation. Even before the war, Boston had had to import wood from what is now Maine and the demands of the rebel army besieging Boston in 1775

---

20 Hagist, *British Soldier's Story*, p.55.
21 Anburey, *Travels*, vol.II, pp.59–60, Letter XLVII, 30 Nov 1777.
22 Anburey, *Travels*, vol.II, pp.59–60, Letter XLVII, 30 Nov 1777.
23 Quoted in Sampson, *Escape in America*, p.57.

and 1776 only exasperated the situation. Mrs Winthrop complained that the price a cord of wood had risen to £5 10s while Washington observed that the price was between $12 and $14, which the inhabitants could not afford.[24] If the inhabitants could not afford it, then how could the Convention Army be supplied? The same issues applied to all foodstuffs.

There was also a dispute about how Article V of the convention (concerning the supply of provisions and accommodation to the Convention Army) was to be interpreted. Gates had not consulted with the Massachusetts authorities whether it wanted to host the Convention Army, let alone whether they could feed and accommodate it. Clinton was permitted to provide supplies through Rhode Island, although these were not sufficient for all the Convention Army's needs. Massachusetts even refused to accept their own currency and demanded payment in gold. The British authorities did not object to this in principle, but in practice there were difficulties as hard currency had to be shipped from Britain. There were also complaints about what constituted legitimate expenses, for example charging for the costs of guards. There was also an issue with prisoners of war being accommodated in the Prospect Hill barracks but Major General William Phillips (RA) refused to take responsibility for them:

> I have nothing to do with prisoners of war – I received a number of them into my care at the request of the Commissary of Prisoners and with your consent. I did this as a relief to your provisions and prison ships and as an act of humanity to the prisoners of war, but I never stipulated for the delivery of payment of provisions for them.[25]

There was also a legitimate concern that bringing prisoners of war into the Convention Army would invalidate the convention. Prisoners of war had to wait to be exchanged for an equivalent rebel held by the British authorities, whereas the Convention Army was in Boston simply to await transport home. Finally, as a condition for Burgoyne leaving for Britain all of his debts had to be paid in hard currency.[26]

Despite these hardships, there were attempts to maintain a professional and disciplined body of men which included drill, much to the mystification of the militia. A more pressing issue was the state of Convention Army's clothing. As well as missing out on their new, 1777 clothing issue, the Convention Army had departed from Canada with summer clothing. Months later, these worn uniforms were in rags and it was not possible to obtain from Canada the warm winter clothing which they had worn the previous winter. Phillips described the men as 'quite naked.'[27] Lieutenant Anburey would write about their similarly poor state of clothing at the end of 1778. Large numbers of the Convention Army would desert, but Phillips accepted that

---

24 Sampson, *Escape in America*, p.57.
25 Quoted in Sampson, *Escape in America*, p.60.
26 Sampson, *Escape in America*, pp.58–61, 96.
27 Sampson, *Escape in America*, p.62.

many of these desertions were temporary, brought about by the hardships of their current environment.[28]

In the meantime, while the expectation of being returned to Great Britain still existed, the regimental officers were reluctant to endorse desertion. Corporal Roger Lamb (9th Foot) described how:

> … our officers (fearful of their regiments being, at their return to Europe, reduced to mere skeletons) had previously issued orders, that if any soldier should absent himself from his regiment only for one day or night, he should be returned as a deserter; and if brought back to his regiment by any of the inhabitants or American soldiers, he should be tried by a court marital, and punish accordingly.[29]

Desertions continued both for economic necessity, or to reach British Army lines and re-join the war. One of the problems encountered by any escapee in any war was how to traverse hostile terrain to the safety of friendly lines. Around Boston, the Convention Army hit upon a unique solution. Locals who were selected for the militia could avoid service by providing a substitute. British soldiers made themselves available as substitutes. Desertion into the rebel army was clearly not without its risks but it provided a legitimate means of travelling hostile territory to an operational zone where they could desert again and cross over to the British lines. Just how many attempted this and failed is unclear. Maybe their unit went into action before they could desert and they became a casualty, or a sharp-eyed sergeant apprehended them in the act, or a nervous British sentry fired before they could introduce themselves. However, it could be successful. Sampson identified multiple successful escapes using this method, including Private Robert Mansfield of the 47th's colonel's company. Mansfield joined Crane's artillery which was sent to West Point from which he was able to escape to the British lines at Stoney Point. Similarly, Privates John Sutherland (47th Foot) and George Molton (20th Foot) joined the 15th Massachusetts to reach the British lines at New York. Sutherland is probably the John Suther listed in Captain Robert L'Estrange's company. Not all attempts went according to plan. Private William Mason from Captain James Craig's company unsuccessfully attempted to enlist into a rebel artillery regiment and then worked on a farm for 12 months before leaving with another British soldier and finally joining the rebel artillery. However, rather than taking him towards British-held Rhode Island as he anticipated, the regiment was sent westwards for operations against the Native Americans. It was another 12 months before he could desert and he finally reached New York on 6 July 1780.

Others managed to escape by sea. A group of 13 from a range of regiments were serving on the rebel brig *Angelica* which was seized by the Royal Navy frigate *Andromeda* on 30 May 1778. In an ironic twist of fate, the *Andromeda* was carrying home General Sir William Howe to explain his role in the Saratoga Campaign. The four from the 47th were Thomas Jackson (Craig's company), Patrick Maloney (possibly Bryan Maloney of England's

---

28 Anburey, *Travels*, vol.II, p.251, Letter LVII, 6 Nov 1778.
29 Hagist, *British Soldier's Story*, p.61.

company), Thomas Fee (England's company) and George Lane (possibly Lowe from Craig's company). Were these genuine deserters or was this a convenient lie to avoid being executed for fighting for the rebels? Whichever it was, their explanation was accepted.[30]

Private John Deering is deserving of a special mention. We last met Deering when he and William Sheen were each sentenced to 1,000 lashes for robbing a loyalist during the Saratoga Campaign. In March 1778 he escaped from Cambridge but was recaptured and imprisoned in Easton, Massachusetts. After nine months imprisoned there, he was transferred to the Philadelphia prison where he spent another two years and four months. Eventually, he and 18 other British prisoners dug their way to freedom with nothing more than their knives, and escaped to New York.[31]

Reintegration into military life after so many years of insubordination to their rebel captors and time 'on the run' could be problematic. Five successful escapees who rejoined the ranks, including Patrick Shanley (Craig's company), were sentenced to 1,000 lashes each for mutiny. However, on account 'of the long and uncommon hardships the prisoners have undergone from want of their pay and every other necessary and from the good character given of some of them', the Court Martial recommended mercy which Clinton agreed to, and pardoned them.[32]

For those soldiers who did reach the safety of British lines, there was the question of which regiment they should join. Clinton offered a bounty of one and half guineas, later raising to two, for every soldier who reached British lines. Sergeants, corporals and drummers had the option of repatriation home where their additional companies were recruiting, or transferring to another regiment. Private soldiers were simply transferred. A bounty was paid to their former regiment for each man, as was the standard practice of the day. For most, their regiment was *hors de combat* and an alternative had to be found. Roger Lamb who joined the 23rd Fusiliers is the most famous example, but this was commonplace. A group of two sergeants, one corporal and 27 privates from eight regiments were collected together and transferred to the 52nd Foot. Some could re-join their regiments. Escapees from the flank companies of the 29th, 31st and 34th were sent back to Canada and their regiments, but this was not an option for the 47th because the headquarters and bulk of the regiment was part of the Convention Army. Sergeant Richard Nicolson became an NCO in a loyalist regiment due to lack suitable vacancies in regular regiments, William Warren also found himself in a provincial regiment, the King's American Provincial Regiment, and John Sudders (or Suthers) joined the 17th Light Dragoons.[33]

When Richard Sampson published *Escape from America* some 25 years ago, he was able to identify 51 escapees of the 47th who made home runs to British lines. Only one of these, Thomas Symester, was captured before the signing of the convention. He is recorded in Major Irving's company

---

30 Sampson, *Escape in America*, pp.66, 73,75–76.
31 Sampson, *Escape in America*, p.79.
32 Sampson, *Escape in America*, pp.11, 81.
33 Sampson, *Escape in America*, pp.65, 79, 80, 104, 133.

but having been drafted from the 27th Foot on 26 June 1776. More recently, Don Hagist has identified two more, Michael Tevin and Samuel Millington. Fifty-three represents more than a company's strength of the 47th Foot incarcerated since Saratoga, one in six or 16 percent, who made a successful home run. Some would have set out intending to reach British lines but were persuaded to abandon the attempt en route, like William Crawford (20th Foot) who was waylaid by the lady he subsequently married and made a new life with in Pennsylvania. Some died during their journey. Escape attempts were not without risk. When Joseph Alcock (24th Foot) reached New York, he explained how he and two colleagues had escaped from Guildford jail. One of the three was killed in the escape and Alcock himself was wounded. This 16 percent figure represents an absolute minimal figure of those who wished to soldier on for the crown with all of the risks that entailed. If this figure is compared with the desertion rates examined earlier in this work, we are left with loyalty that was a far greater force than the antipathy which is supposed to have arisen from the hardships and brutality of the soldier's lot in this period.[34]

How did these escapees survive in journeys over hundreds of miles taking weeks and months in hostile territory? This required an extensive network of loyalists who were prepared to assist. Roger Lamb relates how a woman in the first house he and two fellow escapees approached hid them during the day and then sent them on their way to another loyalist house. There the husband agreed to help, but the wife refused to let him help, saying:

> Do you mean to break my heart, by foolishly running into the jaws of death, depriving me of a husband, and my children of a father? You know that there are several camps and garrisons between this and New York, that you would not be able to go ten miles before you would be taken up, and they you would be hung up like a dog.[35]

A third house welcomed and fed them, but would not have them in the house and provided very unreliable guides. Abandoned, they eventually found a fourth couple who sheltered them, and then a fifth household just a mile from the British lines at Kingsbridge, who they successfully approached. Lamb reached New York and joined the 23rd Royal Welch Fusiliers where he was promoted to sergeant. Captured at Yorktown in 1781, he again escaped and successfully reached New York. In the interest of balance, it is worth noting that during his second escape, the lady of the first house he approached scolded him saying: 'How can you expect such a favour from me, or any of the Americans, seeing you came from England [Lamb was born in Dublin] with an intent to destroy our country?'[36] Her husband was more accommodating.

---

34   Sampson, *Escape in America*, pp.131, 194–199; Hagist, *British Soldiers, American War*, pp.64–72; see also Hagist *Noble Volunteers* p.100 for a similar story John Merrick.
35   Hagist, *British Soldier's Story*, p.64.
36   Hagist, *British Soldier's Story*, p.94.

Lamb was subsequently aided by a native of Dublin. Any one of these five families could have informed the rebel authorities on the escapees. They did not, but it is not difficult to see how desperate groups of escapees could have approached the wrong door, only to find themselves imprisoned or lynched. These five houses must have been replicated across all of the rebellious colonies to facilitate the escapees. Their willingness to help was checked by a realistic fear that if positively identified as loyalists, their fate could be execution, confiscation of goods and land, and being driven out of the locality to the uncertainty of becoming destitute refugees. Sampson in *Escape in America* devoted a chapter on 'Intelligence' which included the role of British intelligence officers (like Major John André) and loyalist agents. These loyalist agents were able to move behind rebel lines through a network of safehouses. If escapees stumbled on this loyalist network, or if it contacted potential escapees before they deserted, then there appears to have been an underground railroad to pass soldiers to British lines.[37]

Once soldiers were safely behind British lines, they were de-briefed on their journey and what they had seen by officers performing similar duties to modern intelligence officers.[38] In one case, an escaped soldier of the 47th became an agent. In September 1780, the commander of Fort Saint John wrote:

> Taylor a soldier of the 47th. I have got two men to go with him as guides. One of them he [k]new when in Vermont State that he is a good man I can depend upon him the other has been several times in the Colonies and brought in men. I have got fourteen dollars change for Talyor with great difficulty.[39]

This was probably Private Thomas Taylor from Captain England's grenadier company. The commander wrote the following month that another escaped prisoner of the 47th had been sent on to Quebec. Private Roger Clansey, or Clancy, (lieutenant colonel's company) escaped from Charlottesville in June 1779 and worked as a weaver which allowed him to reach Sussex County, New Jersey. There he became involved with the military activities of loyalist Lieutenant James 'Bonnell' Moody and before escaping into New York.[40] The existence of this underground railroad undermines the idea of a popular rebellion against a tyrannical monarch.

---

37 Sampson, *Escape in America*, pp.113–114; Hagist, *British Soldier's Story*, pp.62–69, 110–111. Donald Johnson in *Occupied America: British Military Rule and the Experience of Revolution* (Philadelphia, PA: University of Pennsylvania Press, 2020) examines the conflicting loyalties of Revolutionary America in great detail.
38 D. Hagist, 'Unpublished Writings of Roger Lamb, Soldier in the American War of Independence', Part 2, *Journal of the Society for Army Historical Research*, vol.90, No. 362 (Summer, 2012), p.83.
39 Quoted in Sampson, *Escape in America*, pp.152–153.
40 Quoted in Sampson, *Escape in America*, pp.155–160.

The Saratoga Convention Suspended

The Convention Army provided Congress with a major problem – what to do with their new charges? They were a logistical burden which neither Congress nor Massachusetts had the means to support. Burgoyne complained about the conditions which his men were being kept in. Congress in return accused him of not being honest in his dealings with regards to the convention. In response to Burgoyne's complaints, Congress established a committee to enquire into the background to the convention. Where was the public chest and the regimental colours? Why did the number of arms received, and other military stores, not tally with the size of the Convention Army?

Burgoyne had sent the public chest back to Canada before the convention was signed. The fate of the muskets and bayonets is less clear. Burgoyne's men had ceremonially stacked them all before becoming the Convention Army. It is highly unlikely that members of the Convention Army were allowed to march with their muskets. It was more likely that were appropriated by Congress' own poorly equipped troops. Congress' committee asked what had happened to the cartridge boxes? Gates had to admit that they had not been specified in the convention and so there was no need for them to have been surrendered. They had probably been sold or exchanged en route to Cambridge to buy supplies.

On the issue of the colours, Congress did have a point. The German troops had burned the flagpoles but smuggled their colours away in Baroness von Riedesel's mattress. The fate of the British colours is less clear. Those of the 9th Foot did make it back to Britain but the fate of the remainder is unknown. They certainly did not end up in the hands of Congress to be paraded as symbols of victory. On this point, Burgoyne had almost certainly been disingenuous. In the overall scheme of the fate of the Convention Army, this was a small, if symbolic, matter.[41]

The convention provided Congress with a far greater opportunity. They sent it to London to be ratified by the British government. That would mean recognising Congress as a legitimate body which of course the British government could not do. So, the Convention Army existed in a limbo state. This pretence of the convention was maintained even after the Convention Army left Massachusetts for Virginia, a clear violation of Article IV (that the Convention Army was to march to Boston to await transport ships) while Article V (feeding the Convention Army at the same rate as Major General Gates' Northern Army) was never met. It was not until April 1781 that Congress finally repudiated the convention. The officers were then separated from the men (Article VII).[42]

---

41 Frey, *British Soldier*, p.123.
42 Jones, *Captives of Liberty*, pp.154–157; Sampson, *Escape in America*, pp.82–88.

Rutland and Charlottesville

The proximity of Cambridge to the sea and to the British Army at Rhode Island made the Convention Army a tempting target for a rescue attempt. It was also, as we have seen, difficult to provide the Convention Army with the food, shelter and security it required. The arrival of a French fleet in need of maritime stores, medical assistance, food and accommodation, further escalated the shortages.

Relations between the Convention Army and their guards also deteriorated. Rebel camp commandant Colonel David Henley was a poor choice for managing the recalcitrant British. In December 1777, he became involved in a vocal and violent altercation with a Corporal Reeves. A larger disturbance occurred the following January when 100 Continental line troops passed a party of the Convention Army who swore in their presence. In the resulting disturbance, several British soldiers were stabbed or clubbed. Finally, in June 1778, Second Lieutenant Richard Brown (21st Fusiliers) was driving a cart at speed down Prospect Hill in the company of two young Bostonian women. Passing a rebel guard, he did not or could not halt and the guard fired, killing Brown. In the subsequent court martial, the 14-year-old guard was acquitted for following the correct procedures when someone failed to halt when ordered to do so. Behind these three headline events was a low-level tension between the British and their guards. *Generalmajor* von Riesdesel believed that the better discipline of his Germans prevented similar disturbances, but the reality was that they were not directly involved in this civil war and so could remain aloof.[43] A Major Brown was appointed as a supplier of provisions. He is reputed to have been a private in the 47th who deserted during Lexington and Concord. Two men are listed as missing from that day, neither called Brown; it has not been possible to positively identify him from the muster rolls. If he was a deserter, his appointment was hardly going to promote harmonious relationships on Prospect Hill.[44]

A return of the 47th dated 1 June 1778 reveals that 298 were with the Convention Army, 30 were prisoners of war, 153 were in Canada and 17 were dead or had deserted; making a total of 498.[45]

Rutland, Massachusetts was the next home of the Convention Army. Some 60 miles inland from Cambridge, Rutland already had a barracks consisting of huts surrounded by a high fence, although there was insufficient accommodation for all of the British contingent. The 9th Foot departed Cambridge in June 1778. The 21st and 47th departed in September following the appearance of a fleet of the Boston coast which was believed to be British but turned out to be French. The 24th and 62nd departed last, in October. Between April and October 1778, the strength of the British contingent had

---

43 Sampson, *Escape in America*, pp.89–100; Anburey, *Travels*, vol.II, pp.89–90, Letter XLIX, 19 Jan 1777; Riedesel, *Memoirs*, vol.II, p.8.
44 Anburey, *Travels*, vol.II, p.229, Letter LV, 20 May 1778; Riedesel, *Memoirs*, vol.I, p.225. This may be the same Brown referred to in Hagist, *Noble Volunteers*, p.14.
45 C.T. Atkinson, 'British Forces in North America, 1774–1781: Part II', *Journal of the Society for Army Historical Research*, vol.19, No. 75 (Autumn, 1940), pp.163–166.

fallen by 347. Successful escapes continued, including a group of five who escaped from Rutland on 17 September 1778 and reached Newport, Rhode Island on 9 October 1778, a distance of 90 miles in just over three weeks. Two of the five were from the 47th, James Robinson and William Heslop, both of Major Irving's company. The Convention Army's stay at Rutland was short-lived. In September 1778, Congress determined that unless the British agreed to provided passports for supply ships to enter Boston by 5 October 1778, then the Convention Army would be moved out of Massachusetts to a region where food was more plentiful. This was a clear violation of Article IV of the convention, which stated that the Convention Army should march to Boston, Massachusetts, be quartered nearby and should not be delayed when transports arrived to take them to Britain.[46]

John Harvie offered to Congress the use of some of his land near Charlottesville, western Virginia. This town was away from the sea and untouched by the war. Harvie was also a trustee of the estate of Thomas Jefferson's father at nearby Monticello. Harvie received $23,000 to build a camp to receive the Convention Army. To reach Charlottesville required a march of some 500 miles in winter, passing within striking distance of the British garrison at New York. Both national contingents would march in three divisions each, with Valley Forge being one of the staging camps. The 47th marched in the third British division with the 24th and 62nd Regiments under Brigadier General Hamilton. Corporal George Fox recorded the challenges of the winter journey:

> [We] march'd 27 m[iles] per day under a guard lay in the woods at night. when we were at towns we lay in goals or Churches, when in the woods we had a blanket over us and lay round fires. A deal of snow both night and day. one night upon the green Mountains there was snow upon us ½ yard deep.[47]

On arrival, the Convention Army was met by the result of Harvie's failure to fulfil his responsibilities, despite the huge outlay by Congress. Lieutenant Thomas Anburey (29th Foot) described the scene:

> As to the men, the situation was truly horrible, after the hard shifts they had experienced in their march from Potowmack, they were, instead of comfortable barracks, conducted into a wood, where a few log huts were just begun to be built, the most part not covered over, and all of them full of snow, these the men were obliged to clear out and cover over to secure themselves from the inclemency of the weather as quickly as they could, and in the course of two or three days rendered them habitable, but by no means a comfortable retirement; what added greatly to the distresses of the men, was the want of provisions, as none had as yet arrived for the troops, and for six days they subsisted on the meal of Indian corn made into cakes.[48]

Fox described how the men had to build their own camp:

---

46 Sampson, *Escape in America*, pp.102, 104–106.
47 Riedesel, *Memoirs*, vol.II, p.47; Houlding and Yates, 'Fox's Memoir', pp.162–163.
48 Anburey, *Travels*, vol.II, pp.317–318, Letter LXII, 20 January 1779.

> [T]hen they put us into the woods and put a [chain] of Centinals round us and we had to build huts in a regular form with regular streets between every range of huts after the form of C. town in England. six men to a hut and so many huts for a reg[t] according to their strength, the Germans after the same manner. the main street parted them and us. (we had no nails). after this we had to build our officers huts stables gardens &c. Then a general hospital a main guard house sink wells and necessary houses.[49]

There were also vegetable gardens, a church and a graveyard. It would take several weeks of hard work by the Convention Army to construct the facilities which were required at Charlottesville. The vegetable gardens that were planted proved to be most fortuitous as food remained inadequate in quality and quantity again. Anburey wrote home on 10 April 1779 that, 'the men received only twice or thrice a week, and for some weeks none, what they get is scarcely wholesome, this is at present what the poor fellows term a fast, they not having any meat served them since the twenty-fifth of last month.'[50] Although he lays the blame for this not on Congress but on Harvie: 'Congress certainly are to be acquitted of all this bad management, as they have been misguided and duped by one of their own members, a Colonel Harvey, who is a delegate for this Province.'[51] The situation did not improve as the year progressed:

> Although we have been now near a twelvemonth in this province, the soldiers fare little better than on their first arrival; for the greatest part of the summer they have been thirty and forty days, at different periods, without any other provision delivered to them than the meal of Indian corn. Great quantities of salt provisions have arrived at the barracks, but owing to some defect in airing, and the heat of the climate, are in a state of putrefacation; some person advised the American Commissary to bury the meat in the earth for a few days, and it would regain its purity, which, when dug up, and although swarming with vermin, he insisted was exceedingly good, only a little tainted with the weather, which the utmost care could not prevent, and served it out to the soldiers as so many days ratio [sic] of meat.[52]

Anburey went on to describe how, under these conditions, the men felt they had no option but to desert and make for New York, some 350 miles away. These men told their officers of their intentions and he described one group of 20 men under a sergeant to whom they swore a solemn oath to obey. One of the 47th's escapees was Corporal William Woodsides (L'Estrange's company). He was recaptured and imprisoned with a party of prisoners of war from the 17th Foot who had been captured at Princeton. This group was

---

49 Houlding and Yates, 'Fox's Memoir', p.163. See also Riedesel, *Journal*, vol.II, p.65.
50 Anburey, *Travels*, vol.II, pp.364, Letter LXV, 10 April 1779.
51 Anburey, *Travels*, vol.II, pp.364, Letter LXV, 10 April 1779.
52 Anburey, *Travels*, vol.II, Letter LXIX pp.436–437, 12 December 1779.

paroled and Woodsides was included in this exchange, eventually reaching New York.[53]

In the summer of 1779, Major Generals Phillips and Riedesel were exchanged. Before he departed, Phillips compiled a list of the Convention Army's remaining strength. With 1,484 soldiers at Charlottesville, the British contingent was now about half the strength it had been two years earlier.[54]

By 1780 the war had moved towards Virginia. On 12 May 1780, rebel Major General Benjamin Lincoln and some 5,000 troops were captured at Charleston, South Carolina. Charlottesville was no longer as safe and secure as it had been. Concerns increased about the prospect of a loyalist uprising in conjunction with the approaching British troops and the presence of the Convention Army. The prospect of an exchange of Major General Lincoln and his Charleston garrison for the remainder of the Convention Army was proposed, but Congress still held out for recognition of their legitimacy, as they had tried to secure in 1777. Both armies remained in captivity. Another British victory in August 1780 at Camden, North Carolina destroyed Major General Horatio Gates' Grand Army. Then in October the British landed near Portsmouth and Newport News, Virginia. The Convention Army was now too vulnerable to be held at Charlottesville. Plans were made for yet another winter move.[55]

Fort Frederick, Lancaster and York, and Windsor

The next home of the Convention Army was Fort Frederick, Maryland, about 180 miles north of Charlottesville. Again, the barracks were unfit to house them and the Governor of Maryland feared their presence would make them a target for British military actions. When they reached the Potomac River, they found the Maryland Militia on the far bank to prevent them crossing. The Convention Army returned to Winchester, Virginia while the situation was resolved. Initially there was opposition to the arrival of the prisoners, but attitudes changed once it was realised that the British paid for supplies whereas Congress impressed them. Escape attempts resumed with local assistance. When they finally reached Fort Frederick, they found the worst conditions waiting for them in all of their journeys. Once more, they had to start building their own accommodation with minimal assistance from the local authorities, and during winter.[56]

Maryland did not want the responsibility of the Convention Army, and petitioned Congress to remove them. Despite opposition from Pennsylvania, in March 1781 Congress directed that the British contingent would move to York, Pennsylvania while the German contingent, who had

---

53 Houlding and Yates, 'Fox's Memoir', p.164; see also Sampson, *Escape in America*, p.130; Hagist, *Noble Volunteer*, p.226.
54 Sampson, *Escape in America*, p.136.
55 Sampson, *Escape in America*, pp.143–145; Houlding and Yates, 'Fox's Memoir', p.164.
56 Sampson, *Escape in America*, p.161-163; Anburey, *Travels*, vol.II, pp.465–466 Letter LXXI, 20 November 1780.

by now followed the British and arrived at Winchester, Virginia, were to proceed to Lancaster, Pennsylvania. This was followed shortly afterwards by a congressional resolution which finally declared that the convention was void on the flimsy grounds that Burgoyne had violated it in 1777. As early as November 1777, a Congressional committee sat to investigate the disparity between military stores received from the Convention Army, and that anticipated. Most discrepancies were easily accounted for with evidence from Major General Horatio Gates, for example that drummers did not carry muskets so there were fewer muskets than men, or that he had not stipulated in the convention that accoutrements were to be surrendered. The only substantial grounds for nullifying the convention was that Burgoyne had not surrendered the colours.[57] By declaring the convention void, Congress was simply recognising the reality of the situation which had existed from shortly after the Convention Army had arrived in Cambridge. It also meant that the officers were now separated from the men and the ration level was reduced to two-thirds, although the actual supply to the Convention Army remained unaffected in reality. The officers departed from the men in Lancaster, en route to York; their new home was to be in Windsor, Connecticut.[58] Lieutenant Anburey (29th Foot) described the scene which, while not a little emotional, shows that the hardships and trials associated with military service created a bond between the officers and men, in contrast to the expected norms of eighteenth century society:

> Distressing and humiliating as the scene was, when we commanded our men to pile up their arms and abandon them on the plain of Saratoga, still much greater was the separation of the officers from the men at Lancaster. On the morning it took place the regiments were paraded near the barracks, which are picketed in, and converted into a prison. At a small distance was drawn up a regiment of continental troops, the Colonel of which behaved extremely polite, saying, he should not march the British troops to the barracks, till their officers informed him they were ready. When the Colonel was informed he might march the men, the American troops, forming a square around the British soldiers, conducted them to the prison.
>
> The sight was too deeply affecting, and we hastened from the spot. Could you have seen the faces of duty, respect, love and despair, you would carry the remembrance to the grave. It was the parting of child and parent, the separation of soul and body – it effected that which the united force of the inclement seasons, hunger and thirst, incessant barbarity, adverse fortune, and American insults heaped together, could never have effected – it drew tears from the eyes of veterans, who would rather have shed their blood. As far as sounds can convey, we heard a reiteration of 'God bless your honours'. It was such a scene as must leave an everlasting impression on the mind. To behold so many men, who had bravely fought by our side – who in all their sufferings looked up to us for protection, forced from us into a prison, where experiencing every severity, perhaps famishing

---

57   Quoted in Sampson, *Escape in America*, Ch. 5 esp p.84 on the colours.
58   Sampson, *Escape in America*, pp.165–166.

for want of food, and ready to perish with cold, they had no one to look up to for redress, and little to expect from the humanity of Americans.[59]

To ensure that the men were provided for without the protection of their officers, they were each given a sum of money. Corporal George Fox received half a Guinea, although Anburey believed that some received much more. Unfortunately, a portion of the money was immediately spent on alcohol resulting in some deaths. The officers, some 150 in number, did not go to Windsor, Connecticut unaccompanied. In total, nearly 400 were supplied and accommodated in Windsor, which suggests some 250 servants. This was not just a matter of social status but as the officers were more likely to be paroled and exchanged, it proved an opportunity to save men from imprisonment.[60]

The other ranks reached Lancaster, Pennsylvania in June and stayed there for nine weeks before moving to York in August. On 16 June, a list of the prisoners was taken. The 47th's contingent consisted of nine sergeants (seven of whom were accompanied by their wives), eight corporals (one with a wife), two drummers (one of whom was married) and 32 private soldiers (with another 10 wives); a total of 51 men and 19 women.[61] To this figure should be added an unknown number of children. Burgoyne had ordered three women per company to accompany the expedition. The eight companies of the 47th which entered the Convention Army would account for 24 women although this figure could be less because, as we will see in the next chapter, sufficient men avoided the Saratoga Convention to form a third, composite company and may have taken some of the women with them. This figure of 19 women accounts for most of the maximum of 24 women of the 47th, although it is impossible to know how many of the original women remained and how many were the result of marriages in the intervening years. The presence of a wife, and presumably children, also may have been a factor in dissuading those husbands attempting to desert.

A document in the Canadian archive's lists the 'clothing and necessaries' delivered to numerous regiments towards the end of their captivity.[62] Fifty-five NCOs and privates of the 47th are listed, including American-born Sergeant Francis Cook who would later petition to remain in North America, and the memorialist Corporal George Fox. Eleven men were held in Philadelphia Gaol in January 1783. The names on this list are distinct from those occurring in the two subsequent lists. The reason for this separation of personnel is unclear. The presence of one sergeant and 10 men indicates some form of organised party. There were 45 NCOs and privates at York in May 1782. This was reduced by eight private soldiers by April 1783, but the

---

59 Anburey, *Travels*, vol.II, pp.507–509, Letter LXXIV, 2 September 1781.
60 Anburey, *Travels*, vol.II, p.503, Letter LXXIII, 11 July 1781; Sampson, *Escape in America*, pp.167–168; Houlding and Yates, 'Fox's Memoir', p.165.
61 D. Hagist, 'Women on Burgoyne's Campaign', *The Brigade Dispatch*, vol.XXX, No. 4 (Winter, 2004), p.20.
62 Great Britain, War Office: In Letters and Papers, W.O. 1, vols.11-13, pp.103-5, <https://heritage.canadiana.ca/view/oocihm.lac_reel_c13064/667?r=0&s=4> accessed 20 September 2021; I am indebted to Paul Pace for bringing these documents to my attention.

net loss was reduced to seven by the appearance of Private Edward Larus. Corporal George Fox appears on both lists, which substantiates his own accounts of captivity there.

There was an attempt to provide one coat, waistcoat, pair of breeches and hat per person. There were also two shirts, pairs of stockings, pairs of shoes and pairs of soles (and heels for those in Philadelphia Gaol). Fourteen sets were provided to the 11 men in Philadelphia Gaol but for York in 1782 the provision equated to around three pairs for every two people. The deliveries to Philadelphia Gaol and to York in 1782 included a blanket, pair of mitts, pair of 'trowsers', and stock and buckle, again with Philadelphia Gaol being based on 14 personnel.

Of the 55 prisoners, 80 percent can be identified against the February 1777 muster rolls. Nine of the companies were represented. There was a solitary representative from Gamble's company; Private Robert Burton could represent an inter-company transfer or simple 'wrong place, wrong time.' There were 51 men listed in York in the summer of 1779, increasing slightly to 53 in May 1782 before reducing to 36 in April 1783. How the 11 prisoners in Philadelphia Gaol fits into this pattern is unclear, maybe a work party or possibly a party detained attempting a 'home run' to New York. This would suggest that there were still about two companies worth of the 47th in captivity awaiting exchange or the end of the war, as they were duty bound to do. One of the Lancaster escapees was Private Bryan Smith (England's company). His first attempt, in 1779, had led to his recapture at Morristown, but on his second attempt he was successful and reached New York. He joined the 2/84th Foot, the Royal Highland Emigrants, and served in the Carolinas.[63]

The British contingent of the Convention Army was by now just 600, although to this should be added the approximately 250 who had accompanied the officers to Windsor. Once in York, they were put to work building huts again. Corporal Fox described the work: 'We crossed the [Susquehanna River] and went with[in] four miles of L. York, and there they turn'd us into the woods and put a chian of Centinels round us. there we had to build huts. the ground was mark'd out for building regular streets… After the huts were builded we sunk wells and made a grave yard…'[64]

By now the men were almost without clothing and blankets again. More critically, Fox described for the first-time significant disease within the Convention Army, which he attributed to refugees from the Philadelphia prison who were there when the Convention Army arrived. Hundreds of soldiers, wives and children were struck down with 'Camp' or 'Jail' fever (which was usually Typhus); 'our men … died like rotten sheep.'[65]

Surgeon's Mate Benjamin Shield (21st Fusiliers) described the appalling conditions:

---

63 TNA: WO 30/55/82-324: Memorial of Private Bryan Smith.
64 Houlding and Yates, 'Fox's Memoir', pp.165–166.
65 Houlding and Yates, 'Fox's Memoir', p.165.

I assure you it is a distressing situation and I have often been at a loss to distinguish which most deserv'd to be lamented by their country in whose cause they have and are still hourly suffering, the sickening, the dying or the dead… (those) now here who have been at the very jaws of death, and yet live in hourly dread of falling a sacrafice to this infernal distemper, after having escaped perhaps three or four times, through a most escrusiating, and lingering sickness; there is now in camp a shocking instance of the distracted state of mind accompanying these poor men in their sickness of a man who in his delirium cut of the head of his own child with an axe. He belongs to the Canadian Companies [one of the flank companies of regiments whose centre companies did not join march with Burgoyne], is now recovered, and is thoroughly sensible of his own wretchedness there is much more distress these poor men apprehend from the severity of a long winter without your interposition in their favor for many of them have parted even from their shirts to support themselves in their sickness, and most of them are without blankets … need clothing, money & medicine.

PS There is now on the sick list 196 exclusive of those still at Lancaster.[66]

Escapes continued. Private Hawley (L'Estrange's company) got to New York with a party of 39 Yorktown prisoners. Others escaped in smaller parties while the old trick of enlisting into rebel militia regiments was revived.[67]

Sergeant Roger Lamb (23rd Fusiliers) was temporarily in the York camp during his attempts to escape following his second capture. He was critical of those of the 9th Foot who had apparently accepted their lot:

… I was astonished at the spirit of industry which prevailed among them. Men, women, and even the children were employed making lace, buckles, spoons, and exercising other mechanical trades which they had learned during their captivity. They had very great liberty from the Americans, and were allowed to go round the country and sell their goods.

I perceived that they had lost that animation which ought to possess the breast of the soldier, I strove, by every argument, to rouse them from their lethargy. I offered to head any number of them, and make a noble effort to escape not New York, and join our comrades in arms; but all my efforts proved ineffectual.[68]

It was probably men like Corporal Fox who had gained employment locally and appeared to be happy. He worked on the plantation of 'John Poke an Irish' for $2 a month and later for 'Mr John Ereman a Dutchman' for $3 a month.[69]

With Cornwallis' defeat at Yorktown in October 1781, fighting between the conventional armies largely ceased. The following May, General Sir Guy Carleton returned to North America. What he thought of the fate of the troops he had provided for before they left Canada five years earlier is not recorded. Carleton and Washington agreed that all prisoners would be

---

66 Quoted in Sampson, *Escape in America*, pp.170–171.
67 Sampson, *Escape in America*, p.172.
68 Hagist, *British Soldier's Story*, pp.100–101.
69 Houlding and Yates, 'Fox's Memoir', p.166; Berkovich, *Motivation in War*, p.169.

marched to Elizabeth Town, New Jersey from which they could be ferried to British-held Staten Island. Guards were provided for the various columns, but Corporal Fox considered that 'they were only a matter of form'. He still had to spend a night at the infamous Philadelphia prison – 'a nasty place.'[70] In the end, 511 men from the Convention Army marched into New York on 24 May 1783.[71]

Conclusion

The prisoner of war narrative has traditionally revolved around the fate of rebel prisoners in prison hulks at New York, like the *Jersey*. Those unfortunate souls who died there are now treated as martyrs and immortalised with a memorial. The story of the British and German prisoners has been far less well explored. It is clear from the recent research by Daniel Krebs into German prisoners and T. Cole Jones into the British that the Convention Army was a tool to be deliberately exploited to obtain political recognition by the British crown, and to support the war economy. The Convention Army endured the longest captivity of any British or German troops. We will never know how many of them died of disease, hardship, malnutrition, during escape attempts, and on multiple winter marches with inadequate accommodation to receive them. As Jones wrote 'Theirs is a painful story to tell.'[72]

We will also never know how many truly deserted into American society. We do know that a significant number of them endured the hardships of escape to rejoin the fight, while others remained loyal in captivity to be released at the end of the war. Their actions undermine the notion of the British Army as a cruel and hard master. Otherwise, they would not have voluntarily returned to risk their life in the war, or waited to return to this hostile environment when they could have deserted to take advantage of the opportunities which they were offered in Revolutionary America.

---

70   Houlding and Yates, 'Fox's Memoir', p.167; see also Hagist, *British Soldier's Story*, p.96–97.
71   Sampson, *Escape in America*, p.180.
72   Jones, *Captives of Liberty*, p.140.

9

With Aubrey and Gamble on the Great Lakes

The aftermath of the signing of the Saratoga Convention left those British forces not subject to the convention in a no man's land. Lieutenant General John Burgoyne was subject to the convention, General Sir William Howe was too far away and General Sir Guy Carleton's authority did not extend beyond the border of Canada. Article IX of the convention paroled Canadians to return home. They were to be escorted to Lake George. Lieutenant Colonel Peters of the Queen's Loyal Rangers in Canada recorded their experiences on the Lake:

> The 31st [October] in the Morning we proceeded to Fort George which was entirely reduced to Ashes; where in the Afternoon we fortunately met with a Boat which carried us to Diamond Island about five Miles up the Lake where lay a Detachment of British Troops. On our Arrival here it gave me unexpressible Pleasure to think myself at a happy Distance from those scenes of outrage, Tumult, and oppression, and to find myself secure from those petty Tyrants, who have involved my once happy Country in every species of Distress, & made it feel all the misery that cruelty gained with Power can cause.[1]

That 'unexpressible Pleasure' was provided by Captain Aubrey's and Gamble's companies of the 47th on Diamond Island.

The 47th Regiment of Foot Fights On

The muster rolls for early 1778 show that there were three, not two, companies of the 47th in Canada, under Captains Aubrey, Gamble and L'Estrange.[2] Captain L'Estrange's company was based on Belle Isle opposite Quebec

---

1 Cartwright, 'A Journey to Canada' <http://62ndregiment.org/A_Journey_to_Canada_by_Cartwright.pdf> accessed 20 September 2021, see also Cain, *Horrors of a Civil War*, p.134 n.192.
2 TNA: WO 12/5871: Muster Rolls, 47th Foot, 1778.

City on 26 March 1778. The company had a strength of three officers, four sergeants, two corporals and drummers, and 63 private soldiers. Of the private soldiers, eight are described as recruits received in late 1777. Of the remainder, only one officer, one sergeant, one drummer and eight private soldiers were in the same company in February 1777. L'Estrange's company in 1778 had very little in common with the company in 1777, and must be viewed as a composite company of all the remnants in Canada under a spare officer, including the 50 men per regiment left behind in Quebec when Burgoyne's army marched.

Of the three officers, Captain L'Estrange drowned on 5 April 1778. Lieutenant Digby thought that L'Estrange died when the cariole he was traveling in broke through the ice. Lieutenant Thomas Bunbury was commissioned on 18 June 1775 and was serving as the ensign in the colonel's company in February 1777, being promoted to lieutenant on 6 June 1777. He died on 9 March 1780. Ensign Gustavus Hamilton was a volunteer who had only been commissioned on 10 July 1776. He was serving in Captain Sherriff's company in February 1777 and was promoted lieutenant on 1 April 1780. Ensign Samuel Ford petitioned Carleton whether, as the oldest ensign in the regiment, he could be considered for a lieutenancy following L'Estrange's unfortunate death.[3]

Of the four sergeants in 1778 Robert Wardle was an original member of the company. William Loyd had belonged to Sherriff's company and John Boyd was formerly in Irving's company but the origin of William Smith is unclear. Similarly, Corporal John Connor had belonged to Irving's company but the origin of Thomas Shurly is unclear. Of the drummers, Jasper Dowdall was an existing member of L'Estrange's company, but the origin of Lewis Bright is not known. They may have belonged to other regiments now in the Convention Army and posted to the 47th to help create a deployable company. The role of William Lloyd is confused because Don Hagist has discovered him conducting a messaging service under a flag of truce between British New York and rebel Elizabeth, New Jersey, from 1779 into 1780. He was paid well for his troubles, 10 New York shillings per day, but it does raise the question of how a Canada-based sergeant found himself undertaking such duties in New York.[4]

In contrast, the muster rolls for Captain Thomas Aubrey's and Thomas Gamble's companies displayed all of the characteristics of an established company performing its routine administration. In February 1777, Aubrey's company mustered three officers, sergeants, and corporals, two drummers and 47 private soldiers. By March 1778, the company still mustered two of the officers, sergeants and corporals, both of the drummers and all but five of the private soldiers.

Of the three officers in February 1777, Thomas Aubrey remained as captain and William Eayne had been promoted to lieutenant. The third officer, Lieutenant John Rotton, was a prisoner of the rebels and was now

---

3 Baule and Gilbert, *British Army Officers*, pp.24, 60, 83; Baxter, *British Invasion*, pp.182, 221; TNA: WO 28/9-36: Ensign Ford's Memorial to General Carleton.
4 Hagist, *Noble Volunteers*, p.207.

listed on the Cambridge Parole, as part of Convention Army. This suggests that he fought the Saratoga Campaign in another company, because, as we will see below, several of the company were listed as 'Prisoner with the Rebels'.

All three sergeants from 1777 are recorded in 1778 although John Shaw is listed as a 'Prisoner of the Rebels'. This shows that, unlike the composite company of L'Estrange, Aubrey's was able to account for missing personnel. Of the three corporals, only one is unaccounted for. He was replaced by a promotion for Thomas Cross, and the acquisition of Peter Banford of unknown origins. Both drummers were still with the company. Of the private soldiers, one was promoted to corporal, four are described as 'Prisoners of the Rebels' and one as 'left at Ticonderoga 9 Nov 77'. Only five of the 1777 privates are unaccounted for in 1778.

The next surviving muster roll for Gamble's company was not completed until July 1778, but follows the same pattern of Aubrey's company of an established company fulfilling its administrative functions. Of the 1777 muster roll, all three officers, two of the three sergeants, all three corporals and both drummers were mustered in 1778. Of the private soldiers, 10 were recorded as 'Prisoners of the Rebels'.

So, two established companies and a composite company of the 47th escaped becoming part of the Convention Army. This provided the basis of the regiment's continued activities in Canada until the end of the war. Most histories note the survival of two companies, with occasional references to a third company. Thirteen members of Aubrey's and Gamble's companies were listed as 'Prisoners of the Rebels'. Their fate, as was explored in the previous chapter, was to endure the longest captivity of any soldiers during the war.

1778 Carleton Island and Fort Haldimand

1778 saw the arrival of the new Governor of Quebec, Major General Frederick Haldimand, on 27 June. He and Carleton undoubtedly had a great deal to discuss, not least of which was an aborted second invasion of Canada lead by the Marquis de Lafayette. Despite the losses sustained by both Burgoyne and St Leger the previous year, Quebec was in a stronger state of defence than it had been in early 1775. On 6 August, Carleton departed Canada. He could take pride in his defence of Quebec and the support he provided for 1777, but he would have been justifiably annoyed at the nature of his replacement. There was also another threatened invasion in 1781. Canada was not yet secure, but Canada's continued participation in the British, rather than American, world owes a lot to Carleton.[5]

Now serving in Quebec without their colonel, the senior officer of the 47th was Captain Aubrey. In July 1778, the 47th took up post at Longuiel, Montreal. There, private soldiers of the 24th and 33rd were drafted into the

---

5   G.K. Watt, *Fire and Desolation: the Revolutionary War's 1778 Campaign as waged from Quebec and Niagara against the American frontiers* (Toronto: Dundurn, 2017), pp.42–43, 49–50.

Coat and waistcoat buttons excavated on Carleton Island from the period when two companies of the 47th constructed Fort Haldimand. (St Lawrence River Historical Foundation)

47th.[6] In August 1778, Lieutenant William Twiss, Royal Engineers, Lieutenant John Schank, Royal Navy, and Captain Thomas Aubrey, 47th Foot, explored the region where the St Lawrence and Lake Ontario met. We last met Twiss examining Mount Defiance to place artillery which could dominate Fort Ticonderoga.[7]

The old French fort and shipyard at Cataraqui was the original choice, but as the force approached by river, they stopped at Deer Island and Lieutenant Schank decided this was a better site. He successfully persuaded Governor Haldimand of its merits. Under Captain Aubrey, three companies of the 47th,[8] two of the provincial King's Royal Regiment of New York (Royal Yorkers) and 28 artificers were on Deer Island to construct a fort and shipyard. The shipyard was being relocated from Oswegatchie to be closer to Lake Ontario.

The historian G.K. Watt believes that the 47th would have provided the garrison and worked on sawing planks, making shingles and mortar, while the Royal Yorkers would cut and draw timber, clear the landward side, and patrol the island and mainland with Native Americans. They would be directed by Twiss for the fort and Schank for the dockyard, with the artificers providing the craftsmen. The location of the island may have appeared defensible and, after the trials of the previous year, must have appeared safe and idyllic to the 47th Foot posted there. There was one problem with such an isolated location, as Captain Aubrey explained to Governor Haldimand:

---

6 G.K. Yates, 'His Majesty's 47th Regiment of Foot in Canada: 1777–1782', *Journal of the Society for Army Historical Research*, vol.74, No. 300, (Winter 1996), p.214, n.19 and n.20.
7 Pippin, *For Want of Provisions*, p.xxiii; Yates, '47th Foot', p.215.
8 Pippin, *For Want of Provisions*, p.151 quotes a letter from Governor Haldimand to Lord George Germain saying 'I sent Mr Twiss of the Engineers, with Captain Aubrey and three companies remaining of the 47th Regiment in Canada....'

> ... I beg leave to represent to your Excellency the situation of those solders, who are married, & obliged to maintain their families upon one ration, as they cannot buy any provisions on this island, if your Excellency would therefore allow a married man to draw two rations, it would be a great relief to several soldiers & their families, who are at present much distressed for want of sufficient quantity of provisions.[9]

Aubrey and Twiss also requested an extra ½ pound of bread per man per day on account of their strenuous work.

The isolation of the garrison, coupled with the long Canadian winter, appears to have generated conflict within the officers. A court of inquiry into returns of provisions was conducted in January 1779, and Lieutenants Thomas Bunbury (47th Foot) and James Glenie (RA) were arrested and charged. Bunbury drowned before the court martial and Gleine was found not guilty of making false returns but was found guilty of conduct unbecoming an officer.[10]

The 25-acre fort was located on a 60-foot-high bluff on the southwest end of the island overlooking the dockyards, in a double-harbour, and the storehouses. The location would prevent it being bombarded by small calibre naval guns. At some point, the fort was named Fort Haldimand and the island renamed Carleton Island. The island would become a refuge for loyalists and Native Americans although their role there was more transitory than that of the military.[11]

Carleton Island also served as a base for the Indian Department. On 18 September 1778 it was reported to Haldimand that Lieutenant Jacob Adams of the Indian Department was at Carleton Island and employed in scouting towards Fort Stanwix, which had been an objective of the St Leger Expedition the previous year. Adams returned to Carleton Island with two prisoners, although one was retained by his Native American warriors as evidence of their prowess. The second may have been in a group of eight prisoners received from Fort Niagara and mentioned in a report sent by Captain Aubrey.[12] After the war, these activities would transfer to Cataraqui, modern day Kingston, Ontario.

D.J. Pippin's master's dissertation on Fort Haldimand sees it as part of a series of defences to protect Canada from further rebel incursions. No further attacks materialised although this was not to be known. The war had moved away from New England and upper New York to New York City and southwards. Pippin writes:

> Despite the lack of military action, Carleton Island was an active port, shipyard and hub for a diverse range of activities, both military and civilian. It was a transfer point for lake ships and river bateaux, transporting materials and soldiers to and from the frontier posts at Niagara, Detroit and Michilimackinac and the cities of

---

9 Haldimand, quoted in Pippin, *For Want of Provisions*, pp.xxiii, p.244.
10 Yates, '47th Foot', p.215.
11 Watt, *Fire and Desolation*, p.263; Pippin, *For Want of Provisions*, pp.2, 125–126.
12 Watt, *Fire and Desolation*, pp.202, 272, 314.

Montréal, Trois-Rivières, and Québec, its primary military activity was to serve as a launching point from which British and Provincial troops made several raids on the Mohawk Valley in New York.[13]

Carleton Island and Fort Haldimand probably kept the 47th gainfully employed for the remainder of that campaigning season. Built on a bed of Trenton limestone, it was a substantial structure. A footpath was cut through the limestone from South Bay to the fort via a drawbridge. Pippin describes the fort:

> The most striking extant element of the fort is this [dry] moat, approximately twenty feet wide, six feet deep, and several hundred yards long. In the middle of each of the three sides, a bastion projects out from the wall. The purpose for the bastions was to provide placement for the fort's artillery. The three bastions face inland, to defend against an attack from across the island, but several cannon many have been placed near the bluff. The moat was only one element of the defensive works; additional parts include an interior wall, and a glacis outside of the moat made from stone dug out of the moat.[14]

Construction of the fort took time. By September 1778, Lieutenant William Twiss reported his achievements: '…a lime kiln made and 200 bushels of lime burnt, and the same quantity burning, charcoal burnt for present use, a saw pit, store house, carpenters and blacksmith's shops built and covered in together. With a general hospital in some forwardness, also 200 pine logs of 20 ft. long with 10,000 shingles now on the ground for building barracks.'[15] By the following month, the first barracks, 175 feet long, would be completed. In April 1779, the officers of the 47th petitioned Governor Haldimand for financial recompense for expenses incurred during the construction of their own cabins for the previous winter.

The wall of the fort consisted of an earthen mound. This was eight feet high, eight feet wide at the base tapering to five feet at the top and covered with a wooden palisade.[16] The combination of the dry moat, path down to the harbour, wall, and all of the work and accommodation buildings represented a massive investment in labour by the soldiers of the 47th and the other units assigned to the fort. This epitomised the other reality of soldiering in North America alongside the campaigning and fighting which receives far more attention.

Provisions for troops in garrisons in Canada, rather than on campaign, were laid down for Trois-Rivières as:

> The provisions for the army are to be delivered as follows. A complete ration for one man for one day in every species…
> Flour or Bread 1½ Pounds

---

13 Pippin, *For Want of Provisions*, p.xxiv.
14 Pippin, *For Want of Provisions*, p.15.
15 Pippin, *For Want of Provisions*, pp.65, 152–153.
16 Pippin, *For Want of Provisions*, pp.155–156.

Beef	1 Pound
or Pork	½ Pound
Pease	¼ Pint
Butter	1 Ounce
Rice	1 Ounce

Whenever the situation of the army prevents this distribution of provisions it will be delivered in the following manner, which is to be the compleat ration

Flour or Bread	1½ Pounds
Beef	1½ Pounds
or Pork	10 Ounces

Should it happen that no provisions except flour or bread or rice can be issued, a compleat ration is

Flour or Bread	8 Pounds
Or Rice	1½ Pounds

Whenever fresh provision can be procured for the army the rations to be the same allowance.

    Provisions will be delivered to the army by Commissary Genl Mr Day or his deputies & Receipts according to forms which the commissary general will settle to be given on the delivery. Garrison Orders, Three Rivers, 11th June 1776.[17]

Pippin's research for Carleton Island established that this ration was received with the exception of the salt beef. This is explained by the extra bulk of beef over pork which made transport difficult, but which was a permitted variation. The 'small specie' could include fresh beef and bread, raisins, barley, cheese, sugar, brandy, oil, beer, arrack and sauerkraut. Foraging parties were not permitted amongst a friendly population like Canada.[18] Soldiers could purchase additional foodstuffs and it would appear that there were traders on Carleton Island before the arrival of Captain Aubrey. Traders could supply the garrison with rations as well as items for private purchase, and use the island as a staging post between the Great Lakes and the St Lawrence River. There were occasional opportunities for additional paid employment on the island. In garrisons located in populous areas such opportunities were far more common, indeed routine, but less so in a frontier garrison like this. The strenuous work involved in building the fort earned additional pay for the soldiers. The only options for additional sustenance came from farming, hunting and fishing when off duty. Captain Aubrey received and planted 20 apple trees in November 1778, although it was too late in the year to sow winter wheat. There was also a King's Garden for vegetables, but in 1779 it was reported that these had failed due to insects and drought. Wheat and potatoes were also planted.[19]

---

17   Pippin, *For Want of Provisions*, pp.117–119.
18   Pippin, *For Want of Provisions*, pp.117–119, 125.
19   Pippin, *For Want of Provisions*, pp.117–119, 125, 141–144, 169, 239–240.

Throughout the war, most supplies had to be shipped from Britain and Ireland. From Quebec City, those supplies still had to be shipped through Trois-Rivières and Montreal to Carleton Island and then on to the other garrisons further west like Fort Detroit or Michilimackinac. Governor Haldimand wrote to Lord Germain on the matter:

> I have many years regretted that measures were not adopted such as to prevent the safety of those posts depending upon supplies from home, so very distant, the transport so extremely precarious & attended with so heavy an expense to government, all which might be obviated the troops infinitely better provided & the different poste be in perfect security, by raising grain & all kinds of stock…[20]

Reducing the demand on transatlantic logistics clearly made sense for cost and security. Fresh produce would also alleviate health problems arising from preserved foods. Archaeological studies suggest that freshwater fish remains made up to 50 percent of faunal deposits, with saltwater fish like cod, which would have been preserved, making up a small portion. A comparable study of Fort Machilimackinac shows 35 percent during the French occupation period, falling to 10 percent during the British occupation period. Game birds were present, but in smaller quantities. There is also evidence of animal waste and butchery, indicating that livestock was bred on the island to provide fresh meat. All of which would have contributed to improving food security, the health of the garrison and reducing the monotony of relying on rations.[21]

Despite the army's reputation for alcohol consumption, Pippin, and also Dunnigan in his work on the garrisons at Michilimackinac and Mackinac Island, argue that the half pint a day of rum ration was not a regular issue, but was reserved for special occasions. Transport difficulties over such distances were the explanation. Lieutenant William Twiss experienced such a shortage of rum during the fort's construction that he requested permission to pay 6d in Halifax currency per day extra to the workmen in lieu of rum. He did request about 1,700 gallons to be delivered! Returns show that the consumption of rum for June to December 1780 was 3,383 gallons, raising to 4,496 over the next six months so the supply situation was resolved. The size of the garrison could be 200 but by the end of 1782 rose to 700.[22]

Offensive Operations

There had been a successful raid into the Mohawk Valley in June 1778 under the command of Captain John Ross (34th Foot). Then, in late October, another raid was conducted under the command of Major Christopher Carleton. This raid was made up of 376 men from the 29th, 31st and 53rd Foot, the Royal Yorkers, and Native Americans, but none of the 47th. Carleton was the nephew of Sir Guy who had arrived in Canada as a captain in the 31st

---

20 Pippin, *For Want of Provisions*, p.210.
21 Pippin, *For Want of Provisions*, pp.211–222.
22 Pippin, *For Want of Provisions*, pp.129, 133–134.

Foot before being promoted major in the 29th Foot on 13 September 1777. He had, by all accounts, become fully integrated into the indigenous culture, living amongst them for several years, adopting their customs including getting tattooed and wearing a nose ring, and learning the dialects. So much so that the family experienced difficulties bringing him back to his previous, European, lifestyle. The aim of the Mohawk Valley raid was to maintain British control of Lake Champlain.[23]

Lieutenant John Enys, (29th Foot), wrote an account of the raid which seems very reminiscent of the 1777 campaign. They departed on 26 September 1778 and the following day, Carleton ordered them to 'practice… woodland fighting.' The awkwardness remained:

> During our Stay here our party went into the Woods a little way to practice tree[i]ng as they Call it, that is to Say the Manner of hiding ourselves Behind Trees S[t]umps &c. &c. &c. and at our return the Major was pleased to say the Men had exceeded his expectations tho I could See very plainly our Aukwardness diverted the Indians and Ro[y]alists who are by far better hands at this Work being bred in the Woods from the Infancy, and Accustomed to this Manner of hiding themselves in order to Shoot Deer, and other Wild Beasts.[24]

1779

The muster roll for the Carleton Island garrison of 14 May 1779, showed just 105 all ranks. These were five from the Royal Artillery and the remainder from the Royal Yorkers. Aubrey and the 47th had clearly moved on. For the final years of the war, the Royal Artillery and Royal Yorkers were still present, with the regular infantry component was provided by the 34th and 1/84th Foot.[25]

In the late summer of 1779, a rebel expedition was launched against the Six Nations of Native Americans allied to the British. Major General John Sullivan and Brigadier General James Clinton commanded the two-pronged attack. The two expeditions departed from Fort Stanwix, in modern-day Rome, New York, and consisted of some 6,400 regulars of the Continental line regiments. Clinton led 1,600 troops along the Mohawk Valley, south from Canajoharie to the attack communities around Tioga, while another 558 marched against the Onondagas. From Fort Pitt, modern-day Pittsburgh, Sullivan lead 3,500 troops into the Wyoming Valley, of modern Pennsylvania, into the centre of the Six Nations while a further 605 troops marched against southern Senaca, Mingo and Delaware country. Sullivan's and Clinton's expeditions then combined. On 29 August they met a combined British-Iroquois force of some 300 Iroquois, 300 Butler's Rangers militia from Canada and just 14 British Army regulars of the 8th Foot. The result was a forgone conclusion.

---

23   Watt, *Fire and Desolation*, pp.62–65; Baule and Gilbert, *British Army Officers*, p.33.
24   E. Cometti (ed.), *The American Journals of Lt John Enys* (Syracuse: Syracuse University Press, 1976), pp.24–26; See also Watt, *Fire and Desolation*, pp.66–67.
25   Pippin, *For Want of Provisions*, pp.298–304.

The longer-term impact was to break the Iroquois Confederacy and the Six Nations. The destruction of the villages and the winter stores of the Six Nations was devastating.

Governor Haldimand was initially concerned about rebel intentions towards Canada and was reluctant to weaken his defences further but as the year progressed it became evident that the Sullivan expedition's target was the Six Nations. Haldimand authorised an expedition of some 400 men under Lieutenant Colonel Sir John Johnson. Johnson had been inspector of Indian affairs until the outbreak of the war and now commanded the Royal Yorkers. He led four companies (151 men) from his regiment, Captain Robert Leake's independent company of 80 men, 140 of the 34th, 50 of the 47th and a Hanau jäger company of 80. As Butler's Rangers withdrew from the previous engagement, they were reinforced by the light companies of the 34th and 84th. Johnson's force was too late to offer any support to Butler and, even if they had arrived earlier, their combined force of less than 1,000 was inadequate to resist the combined forces of Sullivan and Clinton.[26]

1780

On 10 March 1780, William Johnson was promoted lieutenant in the 47th Foot. He had been commissioned as an ensign in the 29th four years earlier. He had been wounded and captured at Bennington in 1777 while serving with Captain Fraser's Marksmen. The 29th was one of those regiments which contributed their flank companies to Burgoyne's force, but as flank companies were established for a captain and two lieutenants, Johnson was not from one of those companies. Evidently, he was an officer in a centre company who volunteered for Fraser's Marksmen to gain operational experience. Being captured at Bennington meant he was not part of the Convention Army and so could be exchanged, which is evidently what did happen for him to return to Canada and obtain promotion in the 47th. In the February 1782 muster rolls, Lieutenant William Johnston is listed in Captain Henry Marr's company as being '[On] Command in Canada'.[27]

In October, Johnson joined an expedition at Split Rock Bay on Lake Champlain with 108 Canadian warriors. Johnson was seconded to the Quebec Indian Department. His military career in North America appears to have ended in 1780 when 'Wm. Johnston, Lt., 47 Regt' was part of the articles of capitulation for Fort George.[28]

Throughout the summer of 1780, the majority of the 47th arrived at Fort Detroit. Captain Gamble commanded the companies while Aubrey was preoccupied with the court martial.[29] The Bird Expedition was launched against

---

26 G.K. Watt, *The Burning of the Valleys: daring raids from Canada against the New York Frontier in the Fall of 1780* (Toronto: Dundurn, 1997), pp.61–62; Enys, *Journal*, p.37.
27 Baule and Gilbert, *British Army Officers*, p.97; Strach, 'Captain Alexander Fraser, Part II', p.171; TNA: WO 65/27: Army List 1777, 29th Foot, p.85.
28 Watt, *Burning of the Valleys*, pp.18, 96 n.29.
29 Yates, '47th Foot', pp.216–217.

rebel settlers in Kentucky in conjunction with Native Americans. Captain Henry Bird (8th Foot) was an experienced frontier officer. First commissioned in 1764, he was promoted to lieutenant in 1768, the same year that the regiment was posted to the far west of Canada, and then to captain in 1778. By the time he commanded the expedition, he had over a decade of experience on the frontier. He would command a force of some 800 Native Americans as well as Canadians, loyalists, and regulars from the 8th and 47th (one sergeant and 20 private soldiers). Kentucky was beyond the 1763 Proclamation Line which had been established to protect Native American tribes from western European colonial expansion and this commitment continued throughout the war, as with the unfortunately belated support the previous year.[30]

Archaeological finds of 47th buttons at Logan County, Ohio, alongside other items with connections to the British Army have been linked with Bird's Expedition. This is about 150 miles south of Detroit, from where the expedition departed.[31]

1781

This appears to have been a relatively quiet year for the 47th. In September, Captain Aubrey and two companies were at Fort Michilimackinac although detachments remained in Detroit. The 8th Foot's surgeon, Dr James Causeland, at Fort Niagara reported how he had, over the previous two years and more, treated members of various regiments, including those of the 47th.[32] Sergeant William Smith, who was last mentioned in 1778, received a commission and was posted to Butler's Rangers as their adjutant. He was recommended as: 'He is the son of an Officer who bears a very respectable character and is himself a decent, modest man. He has served in this country the last and present war, some part of the time in the light infantry.'[33] As well as loosing men like Smith, the 47th was regaining some men from the Convention Army. Lieutenant Matthew Howard of the King's Loyal Americans was leading a raid into what is now Vermont. He was able to find soldiers from the 9th, 47th and 53rd Foot.[34]

---

30 R. Mahan, *The Kentucky Kidnappings and Death March* (West Haven, UT: Historical Enterprises, 2020), pp.38-39; Baule and Gilbert, *British Army Officers*, p.15; WO 65/30 Army List 1780, p.74; Yates, '47th Foot', p.216; for Bird's earlier career around the rebel 1775 invasion of Quebec, see M.R. Anderson, *Down the Warpath to the Cedars: Indians' First Battles in the Revolution* (Norman: University of Oklahoma Press, 2021) especially pp.52–53, 86–87, 117, 157.
31 I would like to thank Greg Shipley for sharing this information with me.
32 G. Watt, *A Dirty, Trifling Piece of Business: the Revolutionary War as Waged from Canada in 1781* (Toronto: Dundurn, 2009), p.102; Yates, '47th Foot', p.217.
33 Watt, *A Dirty Trifling Piece of Business*, pp.280–281.
34 Watt, *A Dirty Trifling Piece of Business*, pp.244–245.

1782

On 25 June 1782, 128 private soldiers of the 47th were drafted into the 8th Foot. This rationalised the existing arrangement we saw with Bird's Expedition and Causeland's comment from the previous year where he had been treating members of the 47th.[35] The officers, NCOs and drummers made their way to Quebec City. There, on 26 October 1782, they boarded the *Amazon* for passage to England. It had been some 5½ years since the *Niger* had escorted the 47th from Halifax, Nova Scotia, to Quebec City and the relief of their besieged colonel. The only officers of the 47th remaining were Captain Gamble, in the Quartermaster Department, and Lieutenant William Johnson serving in the Indian Department.[36]

Peace

From New York, the surviving prisoners of war who were still on the 47th's strength sailed for Britain. In February 1782, the 47th was mustered in Lancaster, Lancashire. The state of the regiment is illustrated by the colonel's company; one sergeant, two corporals and five private soldiers had been struck off strength since 25 June 1781. One of those struck of strength from Captain Henry Marr's company at this time was Corporal George Fox. These men were the survivors of the Convention Army, who had endured the longest captivity of the war. Of 16 private soldiers, only one appears to have been with the company, Francis Atringbrough. Of the remainder, recruiting was a major activity to bring the regiment back up to strength. Ten were 'Command in Canada' and would shortly be drafted into the 8th Foot. Of the two sergeants, one corporal and two drummers, one of each was 'Command in Canada'. Sergeant John Fleming was 'On Furlow' and Drummer Nicholas Manley was newly enlisted.[37]

Not all of the soldiers were happy with the prospect of peace and all that it would entail. Sergeant Francis Cook petitioned to be sent to Canada or another American garrison. He had served in the regiment for 26 years, 23 of them as an NCO, having enlisted in 1757 when the regiment was in North America. During his captivity he appears to have married an American, and now had a wife and two young children but had 'no lawful means of providing for his family in Europe.' Presumably this meant that should he be discharged from the army, he had no alternative profession he could return to. While in captivity, he had been approached by his relatives to take advantage of the opportunities in the new country, 'but nothing would induce him to accept them.'[38]

The officers' posts were generally filled, although a large number of them were on leave, in Canada, or recruiting. The chaplain, Irvine Whitty, was

---

35 Yates, '47th Foot', p.217.
36 Yates, '47th Foot', p.217; Stanley, *For Want of a Horse*, p.69, 6 May 1776.
37 TNA: WO 12/5871: Muster Rolls, 47th Foot, February 1782.
38 TNA: PRO 30/55/71-35: Petition of Sergeant Francis Cook, 10 June 1783.

A VERY FINE REGIMENT

Grave of Lieutenant John Rotton. Any aspirations of martial glory in his uncle's regiment were severely curtailed by the misfortune of being captured twice in two years. He is buried at St Nicholas' church, Bathampton, near Bath. (David Babington-Smith)

on leave, as usual. Major Richard England was still a 'Prisoner on Parole in England' having been captured at Fort Ticonderoga during the Pawlet Raid of 1777, while Captain Robert Douglas was on an expedition with Colonel William Meadows (89th Foot) to Cape Town.[39] There were, however, familiar faces in the regiment, like Lieutenant John Rotton whose exchange from being a prisoner allowed him to return to the regiment in time to participate in the Saratoga Campaign and then return to captivity, and Lieutenant Medlicote Burrows, the former surgeon's mate.

One significant change occurred in October when the regiment received the title 'Lancashire':

> GEORGE R.
> Whereas We have been pleased to direct that Our 47th Regiment of Foot under your command shall take the County name of the Lancashire Regiment, and to be considered as attached to that County. These are to authorise you by beat of drum or to otherwise to raise so many men in the County of Lancashire in Our Kingdom of Great Britain as are or shall be wanting to recruit and fill up the respective members of Our said Regiment to the numbers allowed upon the

---

39   TNA: WO 65/30: Army List 1780, 89th Foot, p.162.

Establishment. And all Magistrates, Justices of the Peace, Constables and other of our Civil Officers whom it may concern, are hereby required to be assisting unto you in providing quarters, Impressing Carriages and otherwise as there shall be occasion. And for so doing this Our Order shall be and continue in force until the 25th day of March next.[40]

There was not much opportunity for the 47th (Lancashire) Regiment to capitalise on its new Lancashire connections. From Lancaster it marched to Warrington, and the following year to Preston, and finally Whitehaven, Cumberland, from where they sailed to Ireland. The remainder of the decade was passed, as with the years before 1773, in various dispersed garrisons. In 1790, the regiment once again crossed the Atlantic, for Halifax, Nova Scotia, and then to the Caribbean.[41]

It would take many years before the 47th Foot was fully recruited and restored to its former level of effectiveness. The destruction of the 47th, as well as other regiments, was the real outcome of the American War of Independence for the British Army. The following year, the Treaty of Paris would bring the American war to an end, but within six years, revolution would sweep France, plunging Europe into a generation of chaos. That did not leave a lot of time for the 47th to rebuild itself to become, once more, 'A Very Fine Regiment and Fit for Service'.

---

40   Quoted in Wylly, *Loyal North Lancashire*, vol.I, p.73.
41   Wylly, *Loyal North Lancashire*, vol.I, pp.73–74.

10

Conclusion

This work set out to establish the characteristics of an ordinary regiment of the British Army in the American War of Independence, who they were, how it fought, acted and behaved. The 47th Regiment of Foot was just such a regiment.

The 47th Foot was a product of the late-eighteenth century British world, be that in Britain, Ireland or North America; they were both part of society and the personification of the state with all of the flaws implicit in them both. In Ireland, the regiment was well recruited, with a low desertion rate and a high level of efficiency. That was as much as can be expected in the early 1770s. This was disrupted with news of their deployment to North America. Their last posting there had ended just 10 years before, and over the previous 13 years the regiment had fought in two bitter conflicts. Unsurprisingly, the posting to America again ushered in a disruptive period. Desertion rates increased, but so did recruitment with the opportunity to travel being a big incentive, including an opportunity to obtain a free passage to the new world.

Doctrinally, the British Army was not a moribund organisation. Significant changes had occurred since the previous war, including new uniforms, weapons, drill manuals and doctrine. The speed of these doctrinal and uniform changes would accelerate once peacetime transitioned to wartime.

In the interim, soldiers and officers had a difficult line to tread in the increasingly tense politics of New England. Their short time in New Jersey and New York passed amicably, but Massachusetts was different. From alcohol abuse, inducements to desert and attempts to acquire weapons, to open warfare, the regiment had to deal with a range of threats which are very modern in their range.

In 1773, maybe one in five had operational experience or would have been outside of the British Isles, men like Sergeant Francis Cook. The vast majority were young, new to the service and, in common with other studies by Frey, Hagist and Spring, likely to be economically active but fallen on hard times, or a youth in search of adventure. A typical soldier of the 47th was no war-hardened, veteran automaton.

Once hostilities broke out, the drills and tactics practiced in Ireland were put into effect. The results from Lexington and Concord were mixed, with

CONCLUSION

'A Winter View of the Falls of Montmorency', 12 April 1781 by James Peacey. British soldiers are going about their duties in winter attire while in the centre a habitant wears a white hooded coat. This area was the site of a failed 1759 attack which included the 47th. (Library and Archives Canada/James Peachey collection/2833903)

some effective deployment of flanking moves to disrupt ambushes during an operation which was physically demanding to the extreme. Bunker Hill was a frontal assault where time was critical and the opportunity for operational finesse limited, and the casualties were excessive.

The evacuation of Boston to Halifax and Quebec provided an opportunity for a doctrinal reassessment. The difficult transitional phase from peacetime to wartime soldiering was over. 1776 in Quebec saw faster manoeuvre, simplified drills, tactics, and clothing applicable for operational environment and, critically, a restoration of morale. Quebec was secured and would continue to be a safe base from which operations could be conducted. 1777 started as a successful campaign. Hubbardton was a costly victory but without achieving any real effect and Bennington was a disaster, but neither halted the army's advance deeper into hostile territory while the enemy failed to offer any meaningful opposition.

The fate of Burgoyne's men had significant repercussions for the progress of the war, primarily through France's official entry into the war. The failure of St Leger's expedition was not critical and the survivors reached Fort Ticonderoga. They were not lost to the campaign. But in the light of Howe's failure to participate, Burgoyne's 1777 campaign plan was no longer viable. Up to that point, Burgoyne had conducted a successful campaign in the same vein as 1776 and in marked contrast to 1775. Burgoyne's failure was in not abandoning the 1777 strategy once he was aware of Howe's intentions. He continued to risk his army in the vain hope of meeting another British force which was not advancing towards him. Withdrawing his army to a safe base for another campaign where its very existence threatened the rebellion was the correct military response. Unfortunately, the the fate of Generals Gage and Carleton was a warning for what happened to generals who kept their armies in being rather than risk their destruction unnecessarily.

The tactical innovations were successfully applied, especially the lighter, more dispersed approach with simplified drills, for example abandoning the loading drills in the *Manual of Arms*. For these to work effectively, the officers had to rely on the NCOs both for training and on operations. A company never had its full complement of officers. Even if it did have its full complement of officers, how were three men to control 50 operating in dispersed pairs in woodland? The recent work by Berkovich and Houlding show an army based on regimental or professional pride where the officers could rely on and trust the sergeants, corporals and even private soldiers to do their duty. These soldiers were not infallible, and did get into trouble with alcohol, desertion, and theft.

The unique circumstances of the Convention Army shows the attitude of soldiers towards the regiment, army and war. Some, like Sergeant Cook and Corporal Fox, remained loyal and awaited their release. Others, like Private Smith, made multiple escape attempts to re-join the war and risk his life again. There were many others who died in captivity, or on the run, or who succumbed to the temptations of civilian life in America, or who simply disappeared from the records. This is not the behaviour of men driven into the army through desperation, retained there through violence, and then forced into battle through fear of the NCOs.

Defeat at Saratoga did not destroy the 47th's purpose. The survivors fought on throughout the remainder of the war in the under-studied north-western and western frontiers. Many of their campaigns were to protect the Native Americans from western expansion.

When Major General the Earl of Drogheda reviewed the 47th at Charlesfort in June 1772, how little did he know how prophetic his words would be.

Appendix I

Townshend's 'Rules and Orders for the Discipline of the Light Infantry Companies in His Majesty's Army in Ireland'

The Light Infantry Companies are always to be drawn up two Deep with a space of Two Feet between the Files. Marching in a Wood upon any Service of a Secret Nature, they are to be taught to lower their arms in two motions and carry them in a diagonal Position, with their hands on the swell of the firelock; and they are to shoulder in three Motions. They are to perform all Evolutions by Files and never to wheel any part of the Circle by Platoons or subdivisions much less by a larger Body. When marching through a Wood or any Strong Country by Files and ordered to form a Front to the Left, the Right Hand File is to face to the Left and the others to run up briskly and dress by it, If to form a Front to the Right the Right Hand File is to face to the Right, the other Files are to form briskly to the Right of it; and then the Rear Rank of the Detatchment becomes the Front, when a few Files are formed the Commanding Officer is to order an Irregular Fire to begin, and to Continue until the sign shall be given for Ceasing. It is to be particularly observed that each file has an entirely dependence upon itself and that the Firelocks of the front and rear Men, are never to be unloaded at the same time, When the front Rank Man Fires, the Rear Rank Man is to make Ready and step up briskly before his Comrade, but is by no means to discharge his Firelock until the other has loaded, and then his is to step briskly before the Rear Rank Man, and this method to be followed until a signal shall be given for ceasing to Fire. The Mutual Defence and Confidence is one of the most Essential Principles of Light Infantry. The Men when in a Wood are to be taught to Cover themselves with Trees by placing the Right Foot about six inches behind the left, and presenting to the Right of the Tree, and after Firing to step back two paces, and give Room to the Rear Rank man to come up to the same Tree and to fire alternately, according to the directions before mentioned. All Officers Commanding Companies, and any body of Light Infantry, are to fix upon signals for extending their Front to the

Right or to the Left, or to both Flanks, or to Close to the Centre, to retire, or to advance, and these signals must be made by a loud whistle, a posting horn, or some other instrument capable of conveying a sufficient sound to be heard at a considerable Distance, and the stoutest of the Drummers is to be taught to sound these Instruments by directions from the Commanding Officer, who is to give the strictest Orders to the Men to be silent and attentive without which it is scarce possible that any action in a wood can be successful.

Tho' the posting of guards depends upon the ground yet in general, Officers who command Light Infantry, must never place their outposts at too great a distance from the Main Body. If it should be necessary to occupy an height, which Commands the Country, Care must be taken to post other guards near to the most advanced, which may Aid its retreat.

When a Corps of Light Infantry is composed of Companies from different Regiments they must do Duty by Companies with their own officers, and as double Centuries [sic] are always to be posted, the file must mount together to be relieved every hour Messes are to consist of a Non-Commissioned officer and three File and where it is necessary to detach a Corporal's Command the Men are to go together.

The Light Infantry mush also be taught to take Advantage of large stones, broken Inclosures [sic], old Houses, or any strong feature which presents itself upon the face of the Country. But they must take particular Care not to run in Crowds to these objectives.

When a Corps of Light Infantry shall be employed in this Kingdom a small Waggon loaded with Intrenching Tools will be Ordered to attend it, and the officers are therefore to make themselves acquainted with the usual Method of Constructing Redans, Square Redoubts, and other parts of Field Fortifications, likewise the Manner of felling and Freizing Trees for making abattis D'Arbres and to turn their Thoughts upon fortifying Church Yards and making Creneaus [crenelations] in Houses.

When there is appearance of service the Men must be instructed in the Use of the Intrenching Tools and to make Fascines and Gabeons of different sizes.

The Light Infantry must be Carefull not to fall into Ambuscades when they are marching through a Wood or any inclosed Country and Care must be taken to Advance a Guard, and to detach flanking parties. The flanking parties to March in front and the Files to move at the distance of ten yards from each other, when either of these parties shall discover an Enemy, they are not to run not the Main Body, but to take posts immediately and begin an attack according to the directions before mentioned, and the Commanding Officer is to form his Detachment to the flank that is Attacked and to support his party by sending a few Men under the Command of a subaltern Officer, and to repeat this reinforcement as frequently as the Exigency of the Case may require. He is also to be very Carefull that the Men do not Crowd, and that the Enemy do not turn his flank, when there is any likelihood of that being the Case he must Order a Signal to be Sounded for extending the Front. If he should Command a Considerable Corps he should keep a small Reserve disengaged as long as possible.

The success of any Engagement in a Wood or Strong Country depends upon the Coolness and presence of Mind of the Commanding Officer, and the Silence and Obedience of the men fully as much as upon their Bravery.

The Light Infantry are to be taught to fire at Marks, and each Soldier is to find out the proper Measure of Powder for his own Firelock and to make up his Cartridges accordingly.

The Arms of every Soldier should be always kept in good Order, But the Light Infantry Man, in particular, must not neglect his Arms, his Ammunition or throw away his Fire, as his Existence may depend upon a Single Shot's taking place. The Light Infantry must consider that the Service upon which they are likely to be Employed, is very different from that of heavy Troops. The former being always to Engage in open Order and the Attack may frequently become personal between Man and Man. It is therefore necessary to be particular in selecting Men for this Service not only of Activity and Bodyly Strength but also of some Experience and approved Spirit.

Each Man must have a sufficient Number of Cartridges made up. But as it may be necessary to have recourse to the Horn. The Men are to be taught to load from it. Every part of the Accoutrements must be kept in Constant repair, the Tomahawks Sharp, and fit for Use. The Hatchet Men of the Light Infantry Companies must be able Active Men and they should know how to Make Use of their Axes. When a considerable Corps of Light Infantry is to march through a Wood or inclosed Country that can admit of it, The Commanding Officer may Order it to move from the Right of Left of Companies by Files the Companies are then to March in parallel Lines, but the flanking Companies must march in Front and form flanking Parties.

An Officer Commanding a Corps of Light Infantry and marching thro' an open Country may shorten his line of March, or move them in whatever manner he may think best.

Should any of the Enemy's Cavalry appear near a Corps of Light Infantry they must endeavour to retire to a Wood or some strong Ground, in good Order and with a firm Countenance. But if that cannot be effected they must disperse by Files, at Considerable distances from one another, fix their Bayonets, take great Care not to throw away their Fire untill they are shure that a shot shall take place, still endeavouring to gain a Hedge, Broken House, Ravin, Wood or large Stone. Cavalry seldom attacks Infantry in this dispersed situation if men are resolute and determined not to throw away their Fire, and the files are attentive to the directions before given. The Light Infantry Companies are to practice Marching very frequently in quarters.

Besides what is before directed, the Light Companies are to be instructed in the manual and every other Evolution which the Battalion may be ordered to perform.

And Officers Commanding Regiments may employ the Light Infantry Company in the manner which shall appear to them most proper, for the safety and protection of the Battalion whether upon a March or in the Field. And We do hereby direct and require the Commander in Chief of

His Majesty's Forces in this Kingdom to cause these Rules and Orders to be duly observed and executed and he is to direct the Adjutant General to send Copies thereof to the General Officers upon the Staff and to the Commanding Officer of every Regiment of Foot upon this establishment.

Given &c the 15th Day of May 1772
   (Sd) George Macartney[1]

---

[1] Smythies, *40th Regiment*, Appendix IV, pp.549–552.

Appendix II

Light Infantry Movements before his Majesty at Richmond Park 3rd October 1774

Retreat in Columns to the Centre of Companies
Form and Change Front to the Right
Advance to the Right, in Columns by Companies
Form and Fire by Companies, from Flanks to Centre
Advance and Fire a Volley
Break off to the Rear, to regain the former situation
Form Line of March to the Centre of Battalion
March into a Wood and form to the Left in open order
March in Line into the Skirt of the Wood, and Fire by Files into the Plain
Advance across the Plain, and halt in the Wood in the Front of the Line.
March thro' the Wood in extended order, halt at the edge of it, Tree and Fire by Files
Advance across the opening and halt within the Skirt of the opposite Wood
March by the Right of Divisions and form again in extended order within the other side of the Wood.
Form the Line of March from the Centre of Companies, to the Centre of Battalion, with Flanking parties and Rear Guard
The Rear Guard Fires, and the Battalion forms to the Rear in open order, the Flanking parties are called in
Resume the Line of March with Flanking parties
The Left Flanking party Firing, the Battalions forms to the Left in open order. The flanking parties are called in
March thro' the Wood and extend
Advance into the Plain, and fire by Files gaining Ground.
March and advance into the Plain, in extended order
Form the line of March, from the Centre of Companies to the Centre of Battalion
Form to the Rear
Resume the Line of March
Form to the Right and to the Front

Form the Line of March to the Right from the Centre of the Comp[anys]

Form forward to the Right

Form Columns by Companies

March and form for the Discent, proceed. The files of each Company running up to form at order.

The Line extends to open Order and from thence to extended order. Firing by Files as it gains ground

The Corps advances into the Wood, and halts in the Skirt of it.

The Detachment of three Companies is made from the Left, to sieze [sic] a rising ground in Front of the Left, where the Enemy has taken post.

Another Detachment of three Companies is ordered from the Right for the Attack of a house in the Front of the Right.

One Company extends itself in the Wood to keep up the communications between the two Detachments, and advances under cover of the Trees near to the House and Fires from behind the at the Enemy posted there.

The Enemy upon the Plan in front of the Left receiving these disposition to attack him, and to force the house retreats to a Hill in his Rear, upon receiving a distant fire from the left Comp[anys]

The Body in the House being now exposed to be cut off, Retreats after the Main Body.

This being discovered by the Companies on the Right, and by the Centre Company, one of the Right Companies is sent forward to form on the Plain, the Centre Company moving round at the same time to the Left of the House and form to the Left of the Right Company.

The Left Detachment immediately advances and forms to the Left of the advanced Companies

The enemy being now discovered upon the opposite Hill and the advanced Parties skirmishing, the Light Companies advance rapidly to the attack. The Enemy fires upon them and retreats with all speed.

As soon as the Light Companies checked by the Fire, recover the summit of the Hill, they Fire upon the Flying Enemy, continuing to pursue from one strong Post to another until at length he surrenders.[1]

---

1 NAM: 6807-157-6: Howe, *Discipline*, pp.19–22.

Appendix III

Articles of Convention Between Lieutenant General Burgoyne and Major General Gates

1st

The Troops under Lieut. Genl. Burgoyne, to march out of their Camp with the Honours of War, and the Artillery of the Intrenchments, to the Verge of the River where the Old Fort stood ; where the Arms and Artillery are to be left. The Arms to be piled by Word of Command from their own Officers.

2d

A free Passage to be granted to the Army under [Burgoyne] to Great Britain, on Condition of not serving again in North America during the present Contest; and the Port of Boston is assigned for the Entry of Transports to receive the Troops, whenever General Howe shall so order.

3rd

Should any Cartel take place, by which the Army under [Burgoyne], or any part of it, may be exchanged, the foregoing Article to be void, as far as such exchange shall be made.

4th

The Army under [Burgoyne], to march to Massachusetts Bay by the easiest, most expeditious, and convenient Routes ; and to be quartered in, near, or as convenient as possible, to Boston, that the march of the Troops may not be delayed when Transports arrive to receive them.

5th

The Troops to be supplied on their March and during their being in Quarters, with Provisions, by [Gate's] Orders, at the same Rate of Rations as the Troops of his own Army; and if possible, the Officers' Horses and Cattle are to be supplied with forage at the usual Rates.

6th

All Officers to retain their Carriages, Bat Horses, and other Cattle, and no Baggage to be molested or searched, [Burgoyne] giving his Honour that there are no public Stores secreted therein. [Gates] will of course take the necessary Measures for the due performance of this Article. Should any Carriages be wanted during the March for the Transportation of Officers' Baggage, they are if possible to be supplied by the Country at the usual rates.

7th

Upon the March, and during the Time the Army shall remain in Quarters in Massachusetts Bay, the Officers are not, as far as Circumstances will admit, to be separated from their Men. The Officers are to be quartered according to Rank, and are not to be hindered from assembling their Men for Roll-Calling, and other necessary purposes of Regularity.

8th

All Corps whatever, of [Burgoyne's] Army, whether composed of Sailors, Batteau Men, Artificers, Drivers, Independent Companies, and Followers of the Army, of whatever Country, shall be included in the fullest Sense, and utmost Extent of the above Articles, and comprehended in every Respect as British Subjects.

9th

All Canadians and Persons belonging to the Canadian Establishment, consisting of Sailors, Batteau Men, Artificers, Drivers, Independent Companies, and many other Followers of the Army, who come under no particular Description, are to be permitted to return there; they are to be conducted immediately by the shortest Route to the first British Post on Lake George; are to be supplied with Provisions in the same Manner as other Troops, and are to be bound by the same condition of not serving during the present Contest in North America.

10th

Passport to be immediately granted for three Officers not exceeding the Rank of Captains, who shall be appointed by [Burgoyne], to carry Dispatches to Sir William Howe, Sir Guy Carleton, and to Great Britain, by the way of New York; and [Gates] engages the publick Faith, that the Despatches shall not be opened. These Officers are to set out immediately after receiving their Despatches, and are to travel the shortest Route, and in the most expeditious manner.

11th

During the stay of the Troops in Massachusetts Bay, the Officers are to be admitted on Parole, and are to be allowed to wear their Side Arms.

APPENDIX III

12th

Should the Army under [Burgoyne] find it necessary to send for their Cloathing and other Baggage to Canada, they are to be permitted to do it in the most convenient Manner, and the necessary Passports granted for that Purpose.

13th

These Articles are to be mutually signed and exchanged tomorrow Morning at 9 o'clock, and the Troops under [Burgoyne] are to march out of their Intrenchments at three o'clock in the Afternoon.

Camp at Saratoga, 16th Oct 1777.
    (Signed),   [Gates]

To prevent any Doubts that might arise from [Burgoyne's] name not being mentioned in the above Treaty, [Gates] hereby Declares, that he is understood to be comprehended in it, as fully as if his name had been specifically mentioned.
(Signed),   [Gates][1]

---

1   O'Callaghan (ed.), *Orderly Book*, pp.144–148.

Bibliography

Primary Sources

Archives Canada (AC)
    Great Britain. War Office: In Letters and Papers, W.O. 1, vols.11–13
Collection of the Fort Ticonderoga Museum (FTM)
    Orderly Book of the 47th Regiment of Foot
Huntingdon Library, California (HL)
    MSS HM 66, Journal of an Officer of the 47th Regiment of Foot
National Army Museum (NAM)
    6807-157-6: *Discipline established by Major General Howe for Light Infantry in Battalion* (Sarum, 1774)
The National Archives (TNA)
    PC 1/59/6/27 Petition of Lieutenant Richard Gold for land in Cape Breton, 2 July 1768
    PROB 30/55/194 Petition for Charles and Joyce Gold, minors, 18 March 1777
    PROB 30/55/194 Affidavit by Robert Munday, 10 March 1777
    PROB 31/651/771 Will of Lieutenant Richard Gold, 13 October 1777
    WO 1/11 Other Commanders, North America. Canada. Letter 17/18 Carleton to Barrington, 17 November 1776
    WO 4 War Office: Secretary-at-War: Out Letters, General Letters
    WO 12 General Muster Books and Pay Lists
    WO 27 Inspection Returns
    WO 28 Records of Military Headquarters
    WO 30 Miscellaneous Papers
    WO 32/3102 Petition of Widow of Lt Col Nesbitt.
    WO 36/1 War Office, Military Headquarters, North America, Entry Books, American Revolution, Orders.
    WO 65 Printed Annual Army Lists

Printed Primary Sources

Anburey, T., *Travels through the Interior Parts of America* (London: William Lane, 1789)
Anon., 'At a Meeting of the Delegates of every Town and District in the County of Suffolk …', MHS Collections Online, <http://www.masshist.org/database/viewer.php?item_id=696>, accessed 6 March 2021
Baxter, J.P. (ed.), *The British Invasion from the North – The Campaigns of Generals Carleton and Burgoyne, from Canada 1776–1777, with the Journal of Lieut. William Digby of the 53rd, or Shropshire Regiment of Foot* (Albany, NY: Joel Munsell's Sons, 1887)
Cometti, E. (ed.), *The American Journals of Lt John Enys* (Syracuse: Syracuse University Press, 1976)
Cartwright, R., *A Journey to Canada* <http://62ndregiment.org/A_Journey_to_Canada_by_Cartwright.pdf> accessed 20 September 2021
Cubbison, D.R. (ed.), *Burgoyne and the Saratoga Campaign: his papers* (Norman, OK: University of Oklahoma Press, 2012)

Cuthbertson, B., *A System for the Complete Interior Management and Œconomy of a Battalion of Infantry* (London: J. Millan, 1779)
Danna, E.E. (ed.), *John Barker diary – The British in Boston, 1774–1776* (Cambridge, MA: Harvard University Press, 1924)
Doblin, H. (trans.), *The Specht Journal: A Military Journal of the Burgoyne Campaign* (London: Greenwood, 1995)
Eelking, M. von, and Stone, W.L. (eds), *Memoirs, and Letters and Journals of Major General Riedesel during his Residence in America* (Albany, NY: J. Munsell, 1868)
French, A. (ed.), *A British Fusilier in Revolutionary Boston: Being the Diary of Lieutenant Frederick MacKenzie, Adjutant of the 23rd Royal Welch Fusiliers, January 5–April 30 1775* (Cambridge, MA: Harvard University Press, 1926)
Hadden, J.M., *Hadden's Journal and Orderly Books: A Journal Kept in Canada and Upon Burgoyne's Campaign in 1776 and 1777* (Albany, NY: Joel Munsell's Sons, 1884)
Hale, E.E., Stevens, B.F., Howe, W.H. (eds), *General Sir William Howe's Order Book 1775–1776* (London: Benjamin Franklin Stevens, 1890)
Hattendorf, J.B. (ed.), *A Redcoat in America: The Diaries of Lieutenant William Bamford, 1757–1765 and 1776* (Warwick: Helion, 2019)
Lamb, R., *Memoir of His Own Life* (Dublin: J. Jones, 1811)
Lamb, R., *An Original and Authentic Journal of Occurrences During the Late American War, from its Commencement to the Year 1783* (Dublin: Wilkinson & Courtney, 1809)
Nelson, W. (ed.), *Documents Relating to the Colonial History of the State of New Jersey,* First Series, Volume XXIX (Paterson, NJ: Call Printing and Publishing, 1917)
O'Callaghan, E.B. (ed.), *Orderly Book of Lieutenant General John Burgoyne from his entry into the State of New York until his Surrender at Saratoga, 16th October, 1777* (Albany, NY: J. Munsell, 1860)
Brown, M.L. (ed.), *Baroness von Reidesel and the American Revolution: Journal and Correspondence of a Tour of Duty, 1776–1783* (Chapel Hill, NC: University of North Carolina Press, 1965)
Rommel, E., *Infantry Attacks* (Barnsley: Pen & Sword, 2006)
Simes, T., *The Military Medley* (Dublin: S. Powell, 1767)
Simes, T., *The Military Guide for Young Officers,* (Philadelphia, PA: Humphreys, Bell and Aitken, 1776)
Stanley, G.F. G. (ed.), *For Want of a Horse* (Sackville, NB: Tribune Press, 1961)
Stone, W.L. (ed.), *Journal of Captain Pausch – Chief of the Hanau Artillery during the Burgoyne Campaign* (Albany, NY: Joel Munsell's Sons, 1886)

Dissertations and Thesis

Hubner, B.E., *The Formation of the British Light Infantry Companies and their Employment in the Saratoga Campaign of 1777* (MA, Saskatchewan 1986)
Pippin, D.J., *For Want of Provisions: an archaeological and historical investigation of the British soldier at Fort Haldimand (1778–1784)* (MA, Syracuse, 2010)
Saul, D., *No Contemptible Commander: Sir William Howe and the American War of Independence, 1775–1777* (PhD, Chester, 2013)

Secondary Sources

Anderson, M.R., *Down the Warpath to the Cedars: Indian's First Battles in the Revolution* (Norman: University of Oklahoma Press, 2021)
Archer, R., *As If An Enemy's Country: the British Occupation of Boston and the Origins of Revolution* (Oxford: Oxford University Press, 2010)
Atkinson, C.T., 'British Forces in North America, 1774-1781: Part II', *Journal of the Society for Army Historical Research,* Vol. 19, No. 75 (Autumn, 1940), pp.163–166
Atkinson, C.T., 'Some Evidence for Burgoyne's Expedition', *Journal of the Society for Army Historical Research,* Vol. 26, No. 108 (Winter, 1948), pp.132–142
Atkinson, R., *The British are Coming: The War for America 1775–1777* (London: HarperCollins, 2019)

Barbieri, M., 'Infamous Skulkers: the shooting of Brigadier General Patrick Gordon', *Journal of the American Revolution* (11 September, 2013), <https://allthingsliberty.com/2013/09/infamous-skulkers-shooting-brigadier-general-patrick-gordon/> accessed 20 September 2021.

Barbieri, M., 'Brown's Raid on Ticonderoga and Mount Independence', *Journal of the American Revolution*, 20 January 2022 <https://allthingsliberty.com/2022/01/browns-raid-on-ticonderoga-and-mount-independence/> accessed 20 January 2022

Baule, S.M. and Gilbert, M., *British Army Officers who Served in the American Revolution, 1775–1783* (Westminster, MD: Heritage Books, 2008)

Baule, S.M., *Protecting the Empire's Frontier: Officers of the 18th (Royal Irish) Regiment of Foot during its North American Service, 1767–1776* (Athens, OH: Ohio University Press, 2014)

Bell, J.L., *The Road to Concord: How Four Stolen Cannon Ignited the Revolutionary War* (Yardley, PA: Westholme Publishing, 2016)

Berkovich, I., *Motivation in War: The Experiences of Common Soldiers in Old-Regime Europe* (Cambridge: Cambridge University Press, 2017)

Blackmore, D., *Destructive and Formidable: British Infantry Firepower, 1642–1765* (Barnsley: Pen & Sword, 2014)

Bohstedt, J., *The Politics of Provisions: Food Riots, Moral Economy and Market Transition in England, c. 1550–1850* (Farnham: Routledge, 2010)

Bradford, S., 'Lord Francis Napier's Journal of the Burgoyne Campaign', *Maryland Historical Magazine*, Vol. 57, No. 4 (December 1962), pp.285–333

Brown, P., *The Army of George II, 1727–1760: The Soldiers who Forged an Empire* (Warwick: Helion, 2020)

Caine, A.R., *I See Nothing but the Horrors of a Civil War* (Independently published, 2nd edition, 2019)

Carmichael, E., *Like a Brazen Wall: the Battle of Minden, 1759, and its Place in the Seven Years War* (Warwick: Helion, 2021)

Carrington, H.B., *Battles of the American Revolution 1775–1781: Historical and Military Criticism, with Topographical Illustrations* (New York, 1876)

Cavendish, R., 'The Execution of Admiral Byng', *History Today*, Vol. 57, Issue 3, (March, 2007), pp.60–61

Chandler, D., *The Art of War in the Age of Marlborough* (London: Spellmount, 1990)

Chartrand, R., *Louisbourg 1758: Wolfe's First Siege* (Oxford: Osprey, 2000)

Chartrand, R., *Ticonderoga 1758: Montcalm's Victory Against All Odds* (Oxford: Osprey, 2000)

Chartrand, R., *Monongahela 1754–55: Washington's Defeat, Braddock's Disaster* (Oxford: Osprey, 2004)

Chartrand, R., *Gibraltar* 1779–83: the Great Siege (Oxford: Osprey, 2006)

Clay, S., *Staff Ride Handbook for the Saratoga Campaign, 13 June to 8 November 1777* (Fort Leavenworth: CSI Press, 2018)

Dalrymple, W., *The Anarchy: The Relentless Rise of the East India Company* (London: Bloomsbury, 2019)

Frey, S.R., *The British Soldier in America: A Social History of Military Life in the Revolutionary Period* (Austin: University of Texas Press, 1981)

Frothingham, R., 'Siege of Boston', *Proceedings of the Massachusetts Historical Society*, Vol. 14 (1876), pp.229–316

Goldstein, E., & Mowbray, S., *The Brown Bess: An Identification Guide and Illustrated Study of Britain's Most Famous Musket* (Woonsocket, WI: Mowbray, 2010)

Hagist, D., 'Women on Burgoyne's Campaign', *The Brigade Dispatch*, Vol. XXX, No. 4 (Winter, 2000), pp.18–20

Hagist, D., *A British Soldier's Story: Roger Lamb's Narrative of the American Revolution* (Baraboo, WI: Ballindalloch Press, 2004)

Hagist, D., British Soldiers, American Revolution: 'Robert and Mrs. Middleton, 47th Regiment of Foot', <https://redcoat76.blogspot.com/2009/12/robert-and-mrs-middleton-47th-regiment.html> accessed 20 September 2021

Hagist, D., 'Unpublished Writings of Roger Lamb, Soldier in the American War of Independence', Part I, *Journal of the Society for Army Historical Research*, Vol. 89, No. 360 (Winter, 2011) pp.280–290

Hagist, D., 'Unpublished Writings of Roger Lamb, Soldier in the American War of Independence', Part II, *Journal of the Society for Army Historical Research*, Vol. 90, No. 362 (Summer, 2012), pp.77–89

BIBLIOGRAPHY

Hagist, D., *British Soldiers American War: Voices of the American Revolution* (Yardley, PA: Westholme, 2012)

Hagist, D., *Noble Volunteers: The British Soldiers who fought the American Revolution* (Yardley, PA: Westholme Publishing, 2020)

Houlding, J.A., *Fit for Service: The Training of the British Army, 1715–1795* (Oxford: Oxford University Press, 2000)

Houlding, J.A., 'Commissioning of Non-Commissioned Officers, 1725–1792', *Journal of the Society for Army Historical Research,* Vol. 98., No. 395 (Winter, 2020), pp.348–361

Houlding, J.A., & Yates, G.K., 'Corporal Fox's Memoir of Service, 1766–1783: Quebec, Saratoga, and the Convention Army', *Journal of the Society for Army Historical Research*, Vol. 68, No. 275 (Autumn, 1990), pp. 146–169

Johnson, D.F., *Occupied America: British Military Rule and the Experience of Revolution* (Philadelphia, PA: University of Pennsylvania Press, 2020)

Jones, T.C., *Captives of Liberty: Prisoners of War and Politics of Vengeance in the American Revolution* (Philadelphia, PA: University of Pennsylvania Press, 2020)

Kelly, J., *Valcour: The 1776 Campaign that Saved the Cause of Liberty* (New York: St Martin's Press, 2021)

Krebs, D., *A Generous and Merciful Enemy: life for German Prisoners of War during the American Revolution* (Norman, OK: University of Oklahoma Press, 2013)

Luzader, J.F., *Saratoga: A Military History of the Decisive Campaign of the American Revolution* (New York: Savas Beatie, 2008)

Mahan, R., *The Kentucky Kidnappings and Death March: the Revolutionary War at Ruddell's Fort and Martin's Station* (West Haven, UT: Historical Enterprises, 2020)

McBurney, C.M., 'Why did a Boston Mob kill a French Officer?', *Journal of the American Revolution* (23 October, 2014), <https://allthingsliberty.com/2014/10/why-did-a-boston-mob-kill-a-french-officer/>, accessed 20 September 2021

McCoy, D., *General John Burgoyne: Soldier, Statesman, Playwright* (Massillon, OH: Spare Change Press, 2020)

McLynn, F., *1759: The Year Britain became Master of the World* (London: Jonathan Cape, 2004)

McNally, M., *Dettingen 1743: Miracle on the Main* (Oxford: Osprey, 2020)

Morrissey, B., *Boston 1775* (Oxford: Osprey, 1993)

Morrissey, B., *Saratoga 1777: Turning Point of a Revolution* (Oxford: Osprey, 2000)

MacNiven, R., *British Light Infantry in the American Revolution* (Oxford: Osprey, 2021)

O'Shaughnessy, A., *The Men Who Lost America: British Command during the Revolutionary War and the Preservation of the Empire* (London: One World, 2013)

Reid, S., *Culloden Moor 1746: The Death of the Jacobite Cause* (Oxford: Osprey, 2002)

Reid, S., *Quebec 1759: The battle that Won Canada* (Oxford: Osprey, 2003)

Reid, S., *North America 1755–63: British Redcoat versus French Fusilier* (Oxford: Osprey, 2016)

Reiter, J., *The Late Lord: the Life of John Pitt-2nd Earl of Chatham* (Barnsley: Pen & Sword, 2020)

Reynolds, R., *Guy Carleton: A Biography* (New York: William Morrow, 1980)

Rice, G.W., 'British Foreign Policy and the Falkland Islands Crisis of 1770–1771', *International History Review*, 32, No. 2 (June, 2010), pp.273–305

D.H. Robinson, 'Britain Between Continents', *History Today*, Vol. 71, Issue 3 (March 2021), pp.51–57

Rosenberg, C.M., 'James Henry Craig: The Pocket Hercules', *Journal of the American Revolution* (30 October, 2017), <https://allthingsliberty.com/2017/10/james-henry-craig-pocket-hercules/>, accessed 20 September 2021

Ruppert, B., 'Those Who Could Not Serve', *Journal of the American Revolution* (26 January, 2017), <https://allthingsliberty.com/2017/01/those-who-could-not-serve/> accessed 20 September 2021

Sampson, R., *Escape in America: The British Convention Prisoners, 1777–1783* (Chippenham: Picton, 1995)

Shattuck, G. 'Major Christopher French, Prisoner of War', *Journal of the American Revolution* (5 May, 2015), <https://allthingsliberty.com/2015/05/major-christopher-french-prisoner-of-war/#_ednref28>, accessed 19 October 2021

Shearwood, M.W., *The Perfection of Military Discipline: The Plug Bayonet and the English Army, 1660–1705* (Warwick: Helion, 2020)

Simms, B., *Three Victories and a Defeat: The Rise and Fall of the First British Empire, 1714–1783* (London: Penguin, 2007)

Smythies, R.H.R., *Historical Records of the 40th Regiment* (Devonport: A.W. Swiss, 1894)

Snow, D., *1777: Tipping Point at Saratoga* (Oxford: Oxford University Press, 2016)

Spring, M., *With Zeal and With Bayonets Only: The British Army on Campaign in North America, 1775-1783* (Norman, OK: University of Oklahoma Press, 2010)

Strach, S.G., 'A Memoir of the Exploits of Captain Alexander Fraser and His Company of British Marksmen, 1776-1777 Part I', *Journal of the Society for Army Historical Research*, Vol. 63, No. 254, (Summer 1985), pp.91–98

Strach, S.G., 'A Memoir of the Exploits of Captain Alexander Fraser and His Company of British Marksmen, 1776-1777 Part II', *Journal of the Society for Army Historical Research*, Vol. 63, No. 255, (Autumn, 1985), pp.164–179

Strohn M. (ed.), *How Armies Grow: The Expansion of Military Forces in the Age of Total War, 1789-1945* (Casement: Oxford, 2019)

Tanner, J., *Instruments of Battle: The Fighting Drummers and Buglers of the British Army from the Late 17th Century to the Present Day* (Oxford: Casement, 2017)

Urban, M., *Fusiliers: How the British Army Lost America but Learned to Fight* (London: Faber and Faber, 2007)

Usherwood, S., 'The Black Must Be Discharged', *History Today*, vol.31, Issue.3, (March, 1981), pp.40–45

Watt., G.K., *The Burning of the Valleys: Daring Raids from Canada against the New York Frontier in the Fall of 1780* (Toronto: Dundurn, 1997)

Watt., G.K., *Dirty, Trifling Piece of Business: Revolutionary War as Waged from Canada in 1781* (Toronto: Dundurn, 2009)

Watt., G.K., *Fire and Desolation: The Revolutionary War's 1778 Campaign a Waged from Quebec and Niagara against the American Frontiers* (Toronto: Dundurn, 2017)

Weddle, K.J., *The Compleat Victory: Saratoga and the American Revolution*, (Oxford: Oxford University Press, 2021)

Wrong, G.M., *Canada and the American Revolution* (New York: Cooper Square, 1935)

Wylly, H.C., *The Loyal North Lancashire Regiment,* (London: Royal United Services Institution, 1933)

Yates, G.K., 'His Majesty's 47th Regiment of Foot in Canada: 1777–1782', *Journal of the Society for Army Historical Research*, Vol. 74, No. 300, (Winter 1996), pp.212–217

Zembo, M., 'The Training and Tactics of the British Army in Preparation for the Burgoyne Campaign and the Invasion of New York in 1777: The Case for the Battle of Fort Anne', presented at 85th Annual Meeting of the Society for Military History (April 2018)

Zembo, M., 'Counter insurgency: Ireland and America', *The Lion and the Dragon* (forthcoming, spring, 2022)